BBC
RADIO 5 LIVE

BBC
SPORTS
REPORT

This book is dedicated to Angus Mackay. Hardest of taskmasters, most inspirational of producers – the most important figure in Sports Report's history.

BBC RADIO 5 LIVE

BBC
SPORTS
REPORT

A celebration of the world's longest-running sports radio programme

PAT MURPHY

BLOOMSBURY SPORT
LONDON · OXFORD · NEW YORK · NEW DELHI · SYDNEY

Bloomsbury Sport
Bloomsbury Publishing Plc
50 Bedford Square, London, WC1B 3DP, UK
29 Earlsfort Terrace, Dublin 2, Ireland

BLOOMSBURY, BLOOMSBURY SPORT and the Diana logo are trademarks
of Bloomsbury Publishing Plc

First published in Great Britain in 2022

A catalogue record for this book is available from the British Library

Library of Congress Cataloguing-in-Publication data has been applied for

ISBN: HB: 978-1-4729-9422-6; eBook: 978-1-4729-9420-2

Typeset in Adobe Garamond Pro by Deanta Global Publishing Services, Chennai, India
Printed and bound in Great Britain by CPI (Group) UK Ltd, Croydon CR0 4YY

To find out more about our authors and books, visit www.bloomsbury.com
and sign up for our newsletters

CONTENTS

PREFACE

It's December 1981. I've just got home after reporting on Leicester City v Watford for BBC Radio 2, with my final despatch appearing on *Sports Report*. My debut on the programme. Not quite graduation *summa cum laude*, but I hadn't made a nincompoop of myself.

My mother phones. In her beguiling Wexford tones, she says, 'Well, you've done it, son.'

'Done what, mother?' in a tone adopted by countless sons trying desperately hard not to patronise their indulgent mothers.

'You've finally made it on to *Sports Report*.'

She then proceeds to regale me with an anecdote from down the decades. It seems that our sports-mad family of five was sat around the kitchen table one Saturday night, troughing heartily while listening to the radio.

Catching up on the football results, the reports and then the sports conversations via the Light Programme on the BBC was a rite of passage for our family, along with millions of others, starved as we were of entertainment options early on a Saturday evening. *Sports Report* was the only show in town, especially as it was presented by an Irishman with a mellifluous accent, showing just how to talk sport with a light, breezy touch. An Irish family loving the success of one of our own.

Biased? Of course!

As Eamonn Andrews glided effortlessly through *Sports Report*, my mother told me that I had declared with irritating finality, 'I'm going to work on that programme one day.'

I was seven years old.

Young enough to be indulged, not old enough to be rewarded by derision from my two elder brothers.

I remembered nothing of that moment, but I was pleased for my mother. And given that I knew I'd been a precocious, cocksure young sniveller, I was even prouder for myself.

There have been four other *Sports Report* books – featuring contributions from the great and the good, in 1954, 1955, 1988 and 1998 – but there was no overall structure to them, no guiding hand telling a comprehensive story about the programme. Rather than yet another pot-pourri with a different sport per chapter, I felt there needed to be a seamless narrative of the 75 years of *Sports Report*. It deserved a structure, rather than various walk-on parts, but I've tried not to make the book too chronological, apart from the early chapters that set out the context in which *Sports Report* was first established, then flourished.

So this is no historical tract with successive chapters devoted to the forties, fifties, sixties etc. Once the foundations of *Sports Report* were firmly in place, I've opted for themes: memorable programmes, fascinating interviews, the pride exuded by the results readers, the turf wars fought over the programme in Broadcasting House, the increasing competition from other radio and television outlets.

Fundamentally, this book is a history of post-war sport – especially seen through a British perspective. From Billy Wright to Harry Kane, Denis Compton to Joe Root, Randolph Turpin to Anthony Joshua, Fred Perry wondering if a Briton would ever emulate his Wimbledon triumphs to Andy Murray doing just that, more than 60 years later.

It's also an account of how a revered broadcasting institution has covered the triumphs, such as Bob Champion's Grand national win after beating cancer Matthew Hoggard's hat-trick live on air from the Barbados Test Match and Frankie Dettori's 7 wins from 7 rides at Ascot and the tragedies, such as Ibrox, Bradford and Hillsborough. It traces the increasing influence of women on the programme, after decades of male dominance. After the first woman football reporter's debut in 1969, it took another 20 years before her baton was picked up – unthinkable today.

My research for this book has thrown up so many fascinating anecdotes and memories, and I now know the answers to these intriguing questions:

- Who was the regular *Sports Report* broadcaster who taught English to a future prime minister?
- How much did James Alexander Gordon win on the pools, after the much-loved announcer read the relevant results, live on air?
- What were the accumulated odds against Frankie Dettori winning all seven races on the Ascot card in 1996?
- Which great cricket commentator was the first to give a football report on the initial *Sports Report* in 1948?

Apart from such enjoyable diversions, I've tried to give a flavour of the fun involved in working on *Sports Report*; the narrow squeaks when we somehow pulled off a scoop; the tensions in the studio when all seemed to be falling apart; the camaraderie that underpinned so much of our work.

And there have been sadnesses, too. Some valued and cherished contributors died too early, including Peter Jones, our greatest all-round commentator. Peter's life ended at just 60, when he suffered a massive stroke while commentating on the 1990 Boat Race. The testimonies of those colleagues with him on that desperate day still hit hard, but I owed it to him and his matchless contribution to *Sports Report* over 25 years to give those harrowing eyewitness accounts.

Sports Report has kept pace with the sporting landscape. It's had a valued perch from which it could observe so many vicissitudes. From Clement Attlee to Boris Johnson at Number Ten, and from the young Princess Elizabeth all the way through her long reign as queen, it has presided over vast social changes in the UK, and not just in sport. It remains adaptable, relevant and cherished by many.

Those of us who have sailed so long before its mast have never forgotten our own voyages, and I hope that affection and respect are the main messages of this book.

1

'THE WEEKLY MIRACLE'

The description was coined by Patrick Collins, distinguished newspaper sports columnist and multiple award-winner. If anyone's qualified to assess a semblance of order amid the mayhem of the media world, it's someone of Collins' stature – 45 years in his trade, while retaining respect for any outlet that managed a coherent end product.

Collins made many contributions – masterpieces of erudite concision, covering the issues of the week – to *Sports Report* and he remains in wonder that the apparent disarray in the studio, with one presenter linking to reports from around the world, could conjure up what appeared to be a seamless robe for an hour every Saturday at 5.00 p.m.

'We in Fleet Street regarded the radio sports people as charming, but slightly showbiz – but when you watched how they got on air in the studio, all split-second timing, you soon grasped the professionalism needed. I never knew how the presenter or reporters out in the field managed to deliver gems off the cuff, to the required duration.'

And the major players would take note as well. Long before Gary Lineker became a BBC stalwart of presenting, he was a rather handy footballer, much in demand for post-match interviews. He never turned down *Sports Report*. 'It was part and parcel of growing up as a sports obsessive. I listened to it from the age of seven in the car with my dad. I was shy and monosyllabic when I started out at Leicester City, but I never minded doing *Sports Report* interviews, because it meant I'd done all right. It was a comfort blanket, a pat on the back.'

Lord Coe, Olympic gold medallist, athletics administrator, commentator and always a Chelsea supporter feels the same way. 'For me, it's everything about British sport in my lifetime. It's still a source of reliable reportage and comment. The reports are well-crafted and knowledgeable.'

Sir Geoffrey Boycott has always been discriminating in his praise, happy to play the curmudgeonly Yorkshireman. 'I loved it because it was fair, honest, cared about sport. It was the sort of programme that made you love the BBC. No agendas, honey rather than vinegar in the way they did the interviews. None of this irritating aggression you often get nowadays.'

Another great Yorkshire and England batsman, of a more contemporary vintage than Sir Geoffrey, has warm memories of *Sports Report*. Joe Root and three members of his family associate the programme with a Saturday watching their beloved Sheffield United. 'On a Saturday afternoon in the autumn and winter where we'd just seen The Blades win a gritty league match at Bramall Lane, I remember as a kid with my dad, grandad and brother we'd head back to the car for the trip home. Of course, the first thing we'd do was stick on the radio and tune into *Sports Report*. It was the opening theme tune that sucked you in – it's synonymous with British sport and a staple diet of listening and watching sport on a Saturday afternoon.

'For us, it was listening to the headlines of the afternoon – it could be Manchester United or Arsenal cementing their place at the top of the table after another Premier League win, an England Six Nations victory at Twickenham or news of an outsider winning the big horse race of the afternoon, whatever it was it created debate and chatter.

'Once we got the headlines, we would move on to BBC Sheffield's coverage, It was our family ritual and part of our Sheffield United routine. Even now, I look back on those times with fondness and familiarity – we loved it.'

So what is still so special about a radio programme, launched in January 1948, with a signature tune written in 1931, hemmed in today on all sides by competing radio and TV challengers, some more strident than others?

When *Sports Report* first impinged itself on the national consciousness, the country may not have known it, but it was thirsting for diversions amid the post-war austerity of rationing and rebuilding from so much rubble. Life in peace time was still hard as millions readjusted.

Sport was to play an essential role in that recovery. In the football season that saw the launch of *Sports Report*, more than 40 million packed into English grounds and the following season saw a record 41,271,414.

The year 1948 was an historic one for sport in Britain. The FA Cup Final between Manchester United and Blackpool is still regarded as one of the great encounters (listened to on the radio by a third of the population), Stanley Matthews became the first Footballer of the Year, Don Bradman brought his outstanding Australian team over on his last tour, Freddie Mills became a world boxing champion and Gordon Richards was champion jockey for the 21st time.

Above all, there was the London Olympics. While prime minister, Clement Attlee called for 'sacrifice akin to war', saying he had 'no easy words for the people' amid the debris of blitzed streets and grim unemployment figures, the public opted out of reality for a few blissful weeks.

Tickets flew out of the various box offices. It mattered little that Britain won no gold medals in track and field – the deeds of a Dutch housewife, Fanny Blankers-Koen, who won four gold medals, were enough to engage the country.

So *Sports Report* was leaning against an open door when the fruity tones of Raymond Glendenning introduced the first programme. Its presiding genius, the producer, Angus Mackay, knew he was on to something when approached to launch the new show the previous autumn. He was aware that sport could divert, entrance and entertain the country at such a grim time. The glorious narrative of the 2012 London Olympics would suggest the old boy read the race card expertly in the year the NHS entered our lives. Sport remains the opium of the masses.

Longevity has been one of *Sports Report*'s greatest achievements. It has been a chronicle of sport, from Joe Louis (a guest on the first programme) to Anthony Joshua, from Dorothy Manley to Katarina Johnson-Thompson, Don Bradman to Ben Stokes, Tom Finney to Raheem Sterling.

The sheer breadth of sports featured on the programme is striking. Down the years, some sports have become voguish. Snooker and darts were very fashionable in the seventies and eighties, as was Formula One in the days of Stirling Moss and Jim Clark, later James Hunt, Nigel Mansell and Damon Hill, and now Sir Lewis Hamilton. Boxing was massively popular in the early years of *Sports Report*, before dissent from abolitionists and fatalities began to chip away at its popularity. Then the charisma and talent of Muhammad Ali transcended the narrow confines of one particular sport. Ali's worldwide appeal simply had to be handsomely accommodated by *Sports Report*.

It's the role of the editorial team to keep abreast of changing attitudes in public opinion towards specific sports. In the 1970s and 1980s the dark shadow of football hooliganism reduced the sport's popular appeal and *Sports Report* adjusted accordingly. It was common for a rugby international to lead the programme in those days. That is still the case if justified journalistically. You can't marginalise an international sporting occasion in the UK that afternoon in favour of the juggernaut of football. 'Change is the only constant' as the philosopher Heraclitus put it, before turning out for the Ancient Greece Football X1.

The production demands have altered regularly. Initially, a leisurely discourse over a couple of minutes on a football match was deemed acceptable by the dictatorial producer, Angus Mackay, but he soon realised that the programme needed to be faster, more 'on point.' Any reporters who couldn't meet Mackay's exacting demands for shorter, snappier contributions were ruthlessly jettisoned. Do it in a minute or you're out.

Later on, accepted staples such as the second reading of the classified football results, the county cricket scoreboard, the racing, rugby union and league results were all dropped. At times the programme resembled an all-you-can-eat buffet, with so many dishes having to be tasted, so, gradually, the wheat had to be separated from the chaff. The fact that all these results could be absorbed via the BBC Sport website was attractive to the modern breed of producer and editor. If it meant extra, live interviews could be squeezed in before 6.00 p.m., then the loss of the result from Rosslyn Park or the 5.20 from Sandown Park was deemed acceptable. Now, anyone listening to *Sports Report* from even as recently as a decade ago will notice a change in tempo and tone. And it seems like a Neolithic Age if you manage to turn up *Sports Report*s from the archives of 40 years ago. Neither era is preferable – just different. And all the better for that.

Demands for greater technical excellence have become infinitely more insistent since I started on the programme. If the quality of sound from the ground isn't up to an acceptable level, then you simply don't get on air.

The restless quest for high journalistic and sound quality, and the peripatetic approach to stories breaking on the other side of the world, delineate *Sports Report*'s unceasing search for the distinctive. In the fifties and sixties a live interview from outside the UK was considered daring and risky. When Randolph Turpin lost a world middleweight title fight in New York to Sugar Ray Robinson in 1951, public interest in Britain was so high that Angus Mackay took a chance on setting up a live interview with Turpin on his way home. He was on the *Queen Mary*, licking his wounds, when the programme's resourceful engineers somehow fixed up a phone link with the presenter, Eamonn Andrews. It was deemed a ground-breaking triumph, acknowledged by Fleet Street and indicative of the regard the boxing industry had for *Sports Report*.

Today, the *Sports Report* producer thinks little of getting a report or interview on to the programme from thousands of miles away, provided the technology is working up to snuff. In September 2021, Cristiano Ronaldo's return to Manchester United was clearly the top story of the day, especially as he scored twice against Newcastle United, but the production team was equally intent on doing justice to Emma Raducanu's achievement in reaching that night's US Womens' singles final, the first qualifier to do so, at the age of just 18. So first, a preview from our tennis correspondent Russell Fuller in New York, then a live interview with Pat Cash, no stranger to Grand Slam triumphs against the odds. All in pristine quality.

Sports Report's readiness to adapt has been one of its hallmarks. In 1948, it was redolent of the British Empire, evoking a conformist, socially constipated attitude. Raymond Glendenning, the foremost and most versatile sports commentator of the day, may have been a great coup by Mackay to front the first programme, but his style smacked of the lord of the manor having to deal with his tenant farmers at the Christmas gathering in the Great Hall. Topped off by a luxuriant handlebar moustache and a staccato, brisk style of commentating.

Today's successor to Glendenning is irreverent, warm, breezy, yet brimming with research and ready to switch into hard-nosed journalistic mode when the occasion desires. Mark Chapman makes no attempt to hide his flat Mancunian vowels and his presenting style is all the better for it. He is classless, yet classy.

Chapman's flexibility, and that of the programme, was brilliantly encapsulated by a gripping interview in the autumn of 2019, when Haringey's manager took his players off the field in an FA Cup qualifier against Yeovil Town, after his goalkeeper had been subjected to racial abuse and spitting from the Yeovil end. A few days earlier England players had been racially abused in Bulgaria and this was a hot topic. The interview lasted 12 minutes, at a time when other reporters and interviewees were queuing up to make their customary contributions, after 5.30 p.m. This was almost unprecedented in the programme's history, but it was the right call, given it was one of football's burning issues – and, sadly, still is.

That adaptability is hard-wired into *Sports Report*. When Joe Biden was judged to have succeeded Donald Trump as the next President of the United States, a 10-minute section was built into the programme. The same in 2003, when the Space Shuttle Columbia disintegrated as it re-entered the earth's atmosphere, killing all seven of the crew. Room was also found for the announcement of the death of the Queen Mother in 2002. And the Hillsborough disaster of 1989 meant the decks were immediately cleared for the next hour.

Many have said that programme was *Sports Report* at its finest, with the commentator Peter Jones at his most sensitive and incisive. However, working as that day's outside broadcast producer inside the ground, I know that we all wished that Peter hadn't needed to be so superlative, but the story had to be told, with graphic interviews and Peter's peerless stewardship of the unfolding tragedy. The support and understanding from the production team at Broadcasting House remain one of my abiding memories of that gruesome, sunlit day. They stayed with us as the tally of deaths mounted. They knew what needed to be done from Hillsborough.

Longevity, then. Adaptability – tick. Relevance – tick. How about the view of us from inside the football industry? This is where the waters muddy. In terms of getting live interviews, things are nowhere near as simple for *Sports Report* as they once were. We had a clear run before *Grandstand* began on TV on Saturday afternoons in 1958 – unashamedly trying to emulate the programme's style – but it wasn't until *Match of the Day* was launched in 1964 that television muscled into the post-match interview scene. So radio had the pick of the low-hanging fruit in the first 20 years of *Sports Report*. Many veteran reporters of that era have regaled me with tales of dragging illustrious players out of the team bath to get them live on *Sports Report*, wearing just a towel, water gathering around their feet. Without demur.

Now, it's akin to hand-to-hand combat in the dressing-room environs, populated as they are by earnest TV floor managers, whispering into walkie-talkies, as if the President had just landed. The clubs have entered a Faustian pact with TV companies, hoovering up the ridiculous sums of money and leaving it to their press officers to manage the chaotic situations, with so many of us clamouring for precious minutes with managers who rarely seem to have been briefed about their post-match obligations. Every spare yard seems to be taken up by some TV station and any objections are met with the realpolitik of 'We pay a lot of money for this.'

It's the Tower of Babble.

So the humble radio reporter or producer, flying solo amid the testosterone-fuelled frenzy, has to rely on low cunning, sharp wits and remembering where there's a quiet area. This is where good contacts are invaluable.

Down the years, *Sports Report* has enjoyed an excellent working relationship with many managers who respect and understand what we're trying to do amid the post-match tumult, where every minute counts and you knew that, after 5.30 p.m., the chances of getting an interview on air were rapidly diminishing.

Harry Redknapp always co-operated. He used to whistle the programme's signature tune as he hoved to, while Tony Pulis would insist on doing a one-to-one with 5 Live, reflecting his days as a listener while a youngster growing up in Newport, then playing in Hong Kong, rushing back to his apartment to catch up on sports news from home, and culminating in his time as a manager, on a scouting mission or simply out of work. Martin O'Neill once asked my colleague Ian Dennis to halt a post-match interview which was being recorded for transmission a few minutes later, because he had been distracted, feeling that he wasn't doing himself or the programme justice. That stemmed from his respect for *Sports Report*.

Such sympathetic managers were gold dust and they also would find you a relevant player. The likes of Roy Hodgson, Steve Bruce, Gareth Southgate, Graeme Souness and Mick McCarthy have been very helpful down the years – but it's getting tougher. The influx of foreign managers with no awareness of the programme's history leads to a sense of ennui, of crop rotation when doing the interviews. Churn them out. By the time they come to radio, they're talked out.

It remains gratifying, though, when a notable football figure recognises the stature of *Sports Report*. Brian Clough was of that stamp. In the 1950s and 1960s he was a splendidly iconoclastic presence on the programme and, as his managerial brilliance flourished, in the 1970s his appearances were relished. But he then began to ration his availability, enjoying the chase and the attention we lavished on him.

Ron Jones still dines out on the day he knocked on the Nottingham Forest dressing-room door at the Dell, after an impressive performance by Clough's side. The quarry was Clough, for *Sports Report*. The door was opened by the man himself. 'Mr Jones, so nice to see you,' he drawled. 'I'd rather not, but stay there and I'll get you someone not quite as big a catch as me – but good enough for you.' Five minutes later Clough reappeared, alongside a morose Stuart Pearce, looking as if he was about to undergo root canal surgery. 'Mr Jones, this is Mr Pearce – he's my captain and also of England, in case you didn't know. He will do your interview for *Sports Report*. Now off you go, Mr Pearce – and make sure you do a good one, because it's for an absolutely superb programme.'

Graham Taylor was always delighted to be on the show and in 1988, to mark the 40th anniversary of *Sports Report*, I asked the Aston Villa manager if he would come on, to be interviewed from the studio by Peter Jones. 'Give me five minutes, Pat, and I'll be back. I've just got to phone my dad – he'll be chuffed to listen out.'

When Graham returned to Watford in 1996 after his bruising experience with England, our reporter Peter Drury landed a notable scoop. After Drury had finished his post-match interview with Taylor, he discovered his reporter's job wasn't over for the day. En route to the car park, he spotted a familiar figure. Elton John – the owner who had persuaded Taylor to come back to Vicarage Road. Drury chanced his arm, asked for an interview, only to be knocked back. 'Sorry, not today – it's been a disappointing result.' Peter persisted, said 'It's for *Sports Report*.' Elton John stopped, looked at him, and said, 'Oh, I'll do it for *Sports Report*.' Drury couldn't believe his luck. 'Twenty seconds either way, I'd have missed him. He was obviously a fan of ours. He gave me a brilliant six minutes interview, full of support for Graham. That was a good day at the office.'

The programme also had a special relationship with Liverpool Football Club in its halcyon years, beginning with the voluble, charismatic Bill Shankly, and one of Shankly's Anfield successors, Kenny Dalglish, has long been a fan of the programme, too. After an away match, he and Mark Lawrenson would sit at the front of the team coach and ask for the radio to be switched on. 'Me and Lawro always wanted to know about the other games and in those days *Sports Report* was the first port of call. Your research for the next game started on the team coach. Had anyone been sent off or injured? It was always about the next game. And I could find out how Celtic, my old club, had got on, along with the other Scottish results.'

Lawrenson remembers those days clearly. 'Kenny and I weren't interested in card games, we wanted football news. It was a great thrill to be part of *Sports Report* when I became a pundit. Grown-up radio – TV is like SnapChat. I've always been a big radio man...'

But it wasn't just football where *Sports Report* relied on favours, buttressed by goodwill. When England won the Rugby Union World Cup in Sydney in 2003, the programme needed to sound fresh on such a historic day, with the match ending just after 11 in the morning.

Ed Marriage, the rugby producer, sent Alastair Hignell off to do the triumphant interviews and all proceeded well. It was a physical problem for Hignell, who had been diagnosed with multiple sclerosis four years earlier, but – typically of this former England full-back – he never expected any concessions because of the crippling disease. Marriage, operating on his own, dealing with innumerable programme requests, had to leave Hignell to his own devices, conducting his interviews at the furthest part of the stadium, away from the England dressing room.

Hignell swept up all the relevant interviews and was just about to leave the area on his mobility scooter when Marriage said to him on the talkback, 'Higgy, what about Clive Woodward? We need him – where is he?' Commendably, Ed battered his way into the packed England dressing room, apologised to the head coach and said, 'We need you Clive.' Woodward put down his glass of champagne and said, 'No problem – anything for Higgy.' Marriage had to return to the production area, leaving Woodward to walk alone over to the far side of the ground, where he gave Higgy a great interview. 'By then it was quiet so it sounded great for *Sports Report*, five hours later. But that showed the respect Clive had for BBC Radio and Higgy in particular, when he could easily have stayed, enjoying all the dressing-room craic.'

John Inverdale, who presented the programme with such élan and authority in the 1980s, was part of the rugby team that day in Sydney and he commended Marriage and Hignell for going the extra mile. Inverdale says the leitmotif was always, 'Don't miss out on anything that will make the Sunday papers. We had to be sure we had all bases covered. So much depended on our reporters out there.'

For Henry Winter, *The Times* Chief Football Writer, the variety of voices attract. 'I've sung as a boy in Westminster Abbey and St Paul's Cathedral, and I've always been fascinated by the texture and tone of voices. That's why I loved Bryon Butler when he was the BBC football correspondent. Bryon had that Fleet Street journalistic edge from working a few years at the *Daily Telegraph* and he grafted on that lovely Somerset burr to his rich voice. He was a wordsmith, as well as a consummate broadcaster.

'People don't realise what an amazing operation *Sports Report* is, with the machinery moving like clockwork when so many people are running around, making it happen. Every carriage is joined seamlessly together, like the Orient

Express. The presenter Mark Chapman is an absolute genius, making you feel as if you're eavesdropping on a friendly conversation, that also tells you fresh things.

'I trust their top reporters implicitly. They capture the essence, against the clock. I can always press "delete" if I'm not happy with my efforts, but the *Sports Report* lot are against the gun all the time. Week after week, *Sports Report* is a triumph. Given my obsession with voices and fondness for choirs, I give it the ultimate compliment. It's the Treorchy Male Voice Choir of sports broadcasting.'

Amid the smorgasbord of facts necessary for an acceptable report into the programme, there is the opportunity to include an element of romanticism, fantasy or daring to lift your contribution that day out of the ordinary.

The master of the lyrical prose at the microphone was Bryon Butler, the BBC's football correspondent for more than two decades. Bryon was no lover of exacting deadlines, cleaving to the Latin adage *festina lente* (make haste slowly), but he invariably found *le mot juste*. The man who once described the star-studded Inter Milan side as 'an international sweet trolley of a team' also captured the fundamental appeal of *Sports Report* beautifully, 'The format endures. Measured voices up front, sweet disorder behind the scenes: headlines, results, interviews, reflection, controversy, instant solutions, humour, news and more news. All sports, all countries. Evergreen and everywhere.'

I can confirm that a phone call of appreciation on a Monday from Bryon was treasured. He knew that golden sentences didn't just appear at precisely the desired moment, they had to be squirrelled away for relevant use – but you had to make sure you delivered them boldly. Bryon was so revered by novitiates in the sports room that he was often pumped for the secrets to his wonderful scripts. Jonathan Legard recalls some kindly advice, 'He told me, "Grab them straight away with a good line, don't worry too much about the bit in the middle – a few facts will do – but always end with something special at the end. That will linger."'

He was right. Bryon would have something ready and, in the words of the doyenne of radio critics, Gillian Reynolds, that helped make *Sports Report* the 'academy of sports broadcasting.' Gillian has been a singular voice on radio issues since 1967, first in the *Guardian*, then the *Telegraph*, *The Times* and the *Independent*, and she appreciates how the landscape has changed amid stern competition from other sources in recent years. 'But talkSPORT, the commercial rival, will never match what the BBC can do with serious issues; talkSPORT doesn't aim for that, they go for banter, with an urge to be laddish. The vocabulary of the broadcasters isn't good enough and they tend to drop their voices at the end of sentences. I'm glad that more women are now on air in *Sports Report*, bringing more variety. In its heyday it was a programme of real substance, with a concern for the English language.'

The roll call of distinguished broadcasters who have graced the programme is matchless. John Arlott, the great cricket commentator, was also an authority on football in his early days and his was the first report to grace the inaugural edition. He continued his superb opinion pieces and reports on both sports for a couple of decades. Christopher Martin-Jenkins, an outstanding cricket correspondent and commentator, put in many appearances on early editions of *Sports Report*, rounding up the football news from the lower divisions, and Brian Johnston and Peter West were always popping up, while developing enviable broadcasting portfolios across radio and television. The ubiquitous Eamonn Andrews, who presented *Sports Report* for 14 years, became a household name on television in the sixties and seventies. Peter Jones commentated on state funerals, royal weddings, state openings of Parliament and Maundy services. Des Lynam became the first person regularly to introduce both *Sports Report* and *Grandstand*, as well as standing in for John Dunn on Radio 2, while Jones, Lynam and Liam Nolan also presented *Today*, Radio 4's flagship morning current affairs programme.

The first radio football correspondent, Brian Moore, graduated to an outstanding lead ITV commentator and presenter role, while David Coleman – an early contributor to *Sports Report* from the Midlands – proved to be one of the most versatile sports broadcasters in TV history. Jim Rosenthal, a great all-rounder with a very sharp news sense, was another who honed his trade presenting *Sports Report*, before going on to a long and admirable career with ITV Sport. John Motson and Barry Davies graced televised football coverage for many years after cutting their respective teeth on *Sports Report*, and Mike Ingham, presenter for four years, was the BBC's distinguished football correspondent for more than 20.

Cliff Morgan, wonderful rugby player, captivating wordsmith, passionate reporter and commentator, presented *Sport on Four* with undiminished care and subtlety for many years. John Inverdale moved effortlessly from the Saturday show to presenting a daily afternoon programme, mixing sport, current affairs and entertainment, before yielding to the siren song of television. These days, Mark Chapman presents *Match of the Day 2* on Sunday nights with the same aplomb he shows on *Sports Report*. He has also been a witty, informed presenter of BBC TV's NFL and rugby league coverage.

Versatile, authoritative broadcasters such as Alan Parry, Ian Darke, Jon Champion, Eddie Hemmings, Garry Richardson, John Helm and Peter Brackley, having grasped the gospel according to Angus Mackay, moved on to eminence in television, but never forgot the invaluable early education picked up from *Sports Report*. Clare Balding, Sonja McLaughlan and Jacqui Oatley followed similar paths, once attitudes towards women broadcasters mercifully changed. All-rounders, every one of them.

And for half the programme's life, the football results were read in masterly, calm fashion by James Alexander Gordon, with his unique way of signposting one of the three possible results by a deliberate emphasis of intonation on the home team's score. All done in the warmest and friendliest of Scots burrs. JAG, as he was affectionately known by us, was your favoured squishy armchair in the front parlour, the one you always made a beeline for. The sporting world was in good order when JAG had cleared his tubes, ready for football fans to run the gamut of emotions.

Yet somehow the programme has felt undervalued in the august portals of Broadcasting House. After all, it's in the top 10 of long-running BBC programmes, ahead of *Today* and *The Archers*, but it doesn't garner much press coverage and seems to lack the cachet of those two.

Roger Mosey is ideally placed to assess this conundrum. He's now out of broadcasting – he's Master of Selwyn College, Cambridge – but he was editor of *PM*, then *Today*, before becoming controller of Radio 5 Live in 1997. As an avid sports fan, Mosey never needed convincing of *Sports Report*'s merits, but even he was amazed at the assurance with which the production team handled that delicate Ming vase across the tape-strewn floor, getting on air with the minimum of angst.

'The technical achievement of turning all those tapes around to get on air at short notice was remarkable. I'd been a hands-on producer on Radio 4 and *Sports Report* was definitely a notch above the programmes I'd worked on. On *PM*, starting at 5 p.m., we'd often have all the tapes and scripts in by 4.30. On *Sports Report*, it didn't evolve until as late as 4.45 and they'd go on air at 5 p.m. with the sketchiest of running orders. It was a bit like getting out a mini general election programme every Saturday, handling really difficult stories at speed and with great authority. I'd sit and watch the miracle unfolding in front of me and felt so proud.

'On my watch, *Sports Report* and 5 Live Sport in the afternoon on a Saturday were always the most important ones of the week. *Sports Report* had a clear mission and it still carries that out with distinction.'

And in Mosey's day, the 5 Live audience on a Saturday afternoon was between 2.5 and 3 million. Two decades on, it's around 1.8 million, the highest in the fourth quarter for five years, in 2021. Given the increased scale of competition – talkSPORT 894,000, all BBC local radio stations in England 1.46 million – and the multiple platforms that now ping out the latest sports news, that's a healthy figure. In fact, the Saturday show from midday to 6pm on 5 Live had the highest audience figures of any radio sports programme in the country, during the 2021–22 football season.

Sports Report has always prided itself on being the sports newspaper of the airwaves – immediate, informed, accessible, putting flesh on the bone. As a reporter, you never hesitate to go that extra yard, even if there are only a few minutes of the programme left. While other electronic media competitors are content to pack up their equipment or take the easy option of the fans' phone-in, if there's a chance of gaining extra news or insight on a developing story at your game, then you keep hacking away at the coalface until you've run out of time or cracked it. You owe that to the programme's heritage and reputation, while respecting that a production team of just seven back in the studio manage to get *Sports Report* on the air.

There's the producer, editor, two studio managers, a broadcast assistant and two back-up producers – a remarkable team effort covering all the requirements, such as evaluating the top stories, liaising with the reporters and presenter, and judging the quality of the sound, all while keeping live contributions on air. Simon Foat, for years one of the sterling septet, laughs about the paucity of staff in the studio. 'Sometimes it feels as if a hundred are working on it, but we get there. You certainly have to concentrate. That first pint after the programme doesn't last very long!'

While admitting bias, I'd submit that, as it tucks a comforting blanket around its septuagenarian knees, the mewling child of January 1948 has exceeded the expectations of Angus Mackay. Over eight decades, it has survived. For once, I believe the word 'iconic' is justified. In the modern media it rarely is, but it fits here, although now, like Bobby Moore's No. 6 West Ham jersey, it will be retired and for the rest of this book other laudatory words will be used to celebrate *Sports Report*.

2

IN THE BEGINNING

'You'll never get it on air so early – there's just not enough time.' That crushing verdict was repeated endlessly as Angus Mackay toured the BBC's regions in the autumn of 1947. Mackay had joined the BBC in 1936, working on sport in the newsroom at Broadcasting House, and he had been charged with the responsibility of setting up a new half-hour show on a Saturday evening, highlighting the nation's growing fascination with sport, after the privations and tragedies of wartime.

Mackay was given just three months to set up *Sports Report*. This cussed Scot wouldn't acknowledge the pitfalls as he met BBC engineers and outside broadcast producers up and down the land. They were all happy to help, but kept stressing the practicalities – getting reporters from grounds to studios in time for a 5.30 p.m. live programme, establishing circuits, hooking up with the studio in London. Producers at the BBC in those days were conditioned to have enough time for a leisurely run-up to a programme, while the reporters were used to writing mini-essays, with nothing as common as a fierce deadline to distract them from their gilded prose.

Mackay would be having none of that and brooked no negativity. He was enthralled by this challenge. He knew that the country would be changing socially, that so many institutions would be challenged and that sport would play a vital part in the rehabilitation of morale.

Mackay was deeply frustrated that there had been just a single five-minute sports bulletin per day on BBC Radio before the war, and that was only expanded in peacetime to three a day in the summer and two in the winter. The county cricket scores and racing results took up most of that time, with the summer bulletins a particular challenge in getting a quart into a pint pot. Sport was considered 'below stairs' at the BBC.

The prospect of a half-hour live sports programme every Saturday, incorporating all the day's action, invigorated Mackay. 'We have just 30 minutes to tell our story,' he wrote. He wouldn't be indulging any technical or production staff who wavered in their commitment. They would all be doing it his way. There simply wasn't time for interminable meetings, as Mackay travelled far and wide, getting the BBC sceptics onside.

This innate conservatism among BBC foot soldiers reflected the attitude of the country. Britain was tired out. Pinched, gaunt faces stared out of newsreel images of the time, reflecting the growing awareness that the 'brave new world' of post-1945 would take some time to seep through. Ration books, blitzed streets, ubiquitous rubble, restrictions on petrol impacting on freedom of travel – all these were part of adapting to peacetime. A quarter of homes had no electricity. Only the fireplace generated precious heat, with central heating a decade away for the wealthy. A weekly wage was around £3.90 in today's currency. Most adults worked in manufacturing industries – coal, steel, iron and shipbuilding – with long hours and unhealthy working conditions. The majority of women stayed at home, as the 'baby boomers' reflected the soaring birth rate after the end of the war.

An exhausted, disillusioned nation needed diversion, temporary excitement to sideline the nagging sense of anti-climax, austerity and social stagnation that seeped in soon after Winston Churchill acknowledged the rapturous cheers from the balcony at Buckingham Palace in May 1945. Angus Mackay believed passionately that sport could help lift the collective spirit. It would only be one Saturday sports programme, but he was adamant that it would not only get on air in January 1948, but within a few weeks many would be wondering why no one had thought about it earlier.

He certainly had fertile field at his disposal. There were only 14,500 television sets in the UK at the time and just one channel. Radio remained the undoubted big beast in the broadcasting jungle. The war had made stars out of reporters such as Richard Dimbleby, Wynford Vaughan-Thomas, Ed Murrow and Chester Wilmot. Mackay knew that radio was still deeply respected and trusted, and he'd be tapping into that deep reservoir of goodwill. Later, he would gladly employ the gifted Vaughan-Thomas on *Sports Report*, reporting and commentating on rugby union.

Britain craved entertainment in the winter of 1947–48. One third of the population went to the cinema at least once a week. Radio programmes such as *Dick Barton: Special Agent*, *Children's Hour*, *Housewives' Choice* and *Much-Binding-in-the-Marsh* were appointments to listen, as families gathered around large wooden radios in their millions.

Football was also proving a massive consolation to millions who clocked off from their factory labours at lunchtime on Saturdays, then walked to the ground. It was a ritual keenly anticipated all week, topped off later by sitting in front of the fire at home, checking the pools coupon, as they dared to dream of a lucrative escape from all the drudgery. And *Sports Report* would provide the vehicle for this escape as the results were read out twice. That vignette would be lodged in the memories of so many children from 1948 onwards, recalling the near misses and occasional triumphs as they sat alongside their anxious parents.

A fortnight after *Sports Report* was first aired, a crowd of 83,260 watched Manchester United draw with Arsenal. It was the perfect time for Angus Mackay to usher in a ground-breaking sports programme. The demand was there, even if the listeners didn't know it at the time.

However, the BBC hardly welcomed the new programme with a skirl of the pipes or banging of timpani. There was a small plug for it on the front cover of *Radio Times* (bottom right-hand corner), highlighting the inaugural programme, but that reflected the Corporation's priorities in relation to the content of the Light Programme, home of this brash newcomer.

Formed just after the war ended, the Light Programme was a mix of light entertainment, undemanding classical music, drama serials and worthy discussions on the latest books or famous authors. After just one year, 61 out of every 100 listeners tuned into the Light Programme, while in 1948 and 1949, an average of nine and a half hours a week was spent listening to that network, compared to seven hours for the Home Service and three for the Third Programme. So at least *Sports Report* would be featured on the BBC's most popular network. On the Saturday of *Sports Report*'s debut, *Dick Barton: Special Agent* and *Paul Temple* – two hugely popular crime serials – were broadcast, followed by a concert by the Midland Light Orchestra, an excerpt from a pantomime featuring Max Wall, then *Jazz Club*, a variety show, and a live broadcast between 7.30 p.m. and 10 p.m. from the Henry Wood Promenade Concert, featuring works by Delius, Schubert, Rossini and Grieg. After Big Ben chimed 11 p.m., the Light Programme closed down.

The 'warm-up' programme for the first edition of *Sports Report* was *Band Call*, featuring the BBC Variety Orchestra and Chorus – at 45 minutes, hardly the ideal hors d'oeuvre to whet the appetite of sports fans who might have been intrigued by this promising newcomer to BBC Radio's sparse coverage of sport.

There was nothing in the national press to herald *Sports Report*, partly due to a shortage of newsprint curtailing the quantity of pages and also because Fleet Street had no intention of trumpeting a new competitor in the market. Every Saturday by 6.15 p.m., special editions of local newspapers would be on the streets of every city, giving results and match reports. They would be eagerly snapped up by those sports fans desperate for news and to check their pools coupons. *Sports Report* would be ahead of this flow of vital information by almost an hour, broadcasting the first reading of the football results just after 5.30 p.m.. This new kid on the block would be getting no plugs from an envious and worried newspaper industry, intent on marking out its territory.

So *Sports Report* crept on to the air, aware that any serious impact on the listeners' habits would be the responsibility of the production team, reporters, studio guests and presenter. No one in the media – least of all the BBC hierarchy – would be doing *Sports Report* any publicity favours. Angus Mackay knew all that, but he was adamant that with radio still the only substantial broadcasting voice in Britain, there was a demand for *Sports Report*. Mackay willingly imbued his charges with a zealous pioneering spirit. He would make sports fans take notice. Mackay vowed that one day, the Light Programme would be chockful of sport on a Saturday afternoon.

At just after 5.30 p.m. on Saturday 3 January 1948, even the legendary broadcaster Raymond Glendenning was a tad nervous as he prepared to introduce the first edition of *Sports Report*. At the age of 40, a BBC veteran since 1932, he had become a fixture in the sporting firmament since the war ended. He was versatile – boxing, football and horse racing his favourites – and distinctive in appearance as well as style of broadcasting. He was once timed at 320 words a minute, while commentating on the Greyhound Derby!

Glendenning was established as the country's most distinguished and ubiquitous sports broadcaster. He could pick and choose where and what sport he would grace with his presence. No scraps from the table for a hungry freelance for Raymond Glendenning. But he was intrigued by the potential appeal of *Sports Report* at a time when the BBC would allow no sports programmes or results on air until at least 6.15 p.m. The stately, self-confident Glendenning liked the cut of this eager chappie Mackay's jib. He'd give *Sports Report* a go for a few weeks.

As the strains of the new signature tune 'Out of the Blue' ebbed away for the first time, Glendenning cleared his throat and attacked his script with his customary alacrity and brio... 'Hello there, sports fans and welcome to *Sports Report* – a weekly programme on air at this time every Saturday, with a roving microphone, to bring you not only the football results but up-to-the-minute accounts of the major sporting fixtures from all parts of the country, and an 'open' microphone over which we shall be airing the personal views of experts on sport on topics of the moment.'

Next the headlines – always a vital selling point for Mackay. Arsenal beat Sheffield United to go six points clear in Division One... Don Bradman scores another Test century... In rugby union, Australia beat England 11–0 at Twickenham.

Then the football results were read by Philip Slessor, a staff announcer who was making a name for himself as the host of *Variety Bandbox*, a highly popular Sunday night variety show on the Light Programme that launched the careers of, among others, Frankie Howerd, Arthur English, Tony Hancock and Peter Sellers.

Due to the immense technical difficulties of broadcasting from the grounds, the live reports came from studios, so there were only four of them – from Scotland, the Rangers v Dundee match, then the rugby union international and before that just two football reports. Alan Clarke, who became a fixture on the show for the next 20 years, gave his views on Manchester City v Aston Villa, but the honour of the first report on the new programme went to a broadcaster who would become one of the immortals in another sport. John Arlott was becoming known in cricket circles (later that year he commentated on Bradman's last Test innings, bowled for nought at the Oval), but for many years he covered football for the *Guardian* and for BBC Radio, before giving up in disgust at encroaching hooliganism in and out of grounds.

John began his report in simple, unadorned terms. 'The game between Portsmouth and Huddersfield was a magnificent one to watch, because both forward lines kept up the attack and the wing-halves of each side gave them all the support they could possibly want, bringing the ball to them along the ground.' Of its time, yes; anachronistic, yes; but Arlott always had the priceless gift of painting a sporting picture.

Time simply flew past for Angus Mackay in that first programme. He made a mental note that the durations of the live reports would have to be cut from two and a half minutes by about a half. They were too florid, too self-indulgent. 'It wasn't long before we realised that a good radio reporter could give us an accurate, informative picture of a game in something like a minute and a quarter.'

And the producer's dictate was non-negotiable, as many reporters would find out the hard way.

Mackay managed to squeeze in two more items before that first programme was over. Alan Hoby, a household name on Fleet Street, talked about paying part-time money to top athletes, a distinctly unfashionable line to take in those days when the status of amateurs was lauded by so many idealistic dinosaurs. Later the *Sunday Express* football correspondent, Hoby contributed many entertaining and thoughtful opinion pieces to *Sports Report*.

Then the show was closed by Peter Wilson, the most eminent and provocative columnist in national newspapers. Wilson, billed as 'The Man They Can't Gag' on newspaper placards, specialised in trenchant, angry polemics, out of kilter with his private persona as a roistering, genial drinking and dining companion to his many friends in the business. Mackay loved Wilson's recklessness, his explosive willingness to slay perceived sacred cows in the docile corridors of sports administration. He relished the notion of such a major journalistic figure breezing into the sports room on a Saturday afternoon, bellowing his latest professional frustration at him, then hammering it out on a typewriter. The two combustibles got on famously and Wilson later admitted he would have gone on the programme for nothing.

On the first *Sports Report*, Wilson, a noted boxing expert, gave his first-hand impressions of the recent Joe Louis v Jersey Joe Walcott world heavyweight title fight, looked forward to the prospect of a rematch and, for good measure, threw in his opinions on the current American sporting scene. It was light years ahead of the familiar, constipated BBC reporting on sport and Mackay was captivated. Over the next decade, Wilson, J. L. Manning, Bill Hicks, Geoffrey Green and other luminaries from Fleet Street would provide supreme entertainment, insight and courageous opinions on the programme – much to Mackay's delight. He loved the Talking Sport section, 'This is a feature which calls for broadcasters who have a first-class working knowledge of most sports; flexible minds which can adapt themselves quickly to the ebb and flow of radio discussions; and, above all, absolute reliability, trustworthiness at the microphone.'

Those contributions from distinguished columnists became a cherished feature of *Sports Report* until the early 1990s, when the relentless presence of live football reports and interviews meant there was no room anymore for considered, layered opinion pieces. Many bemoaned the loss.

Just three months after being offered a shot at producing a new, challenging live sports programme, Mackay was convinced that after just one show, he was on to a winner. 'New fields to explore and profit by; risks to be met and taken; above all, something new – something with the taste of adventure to it.' He was immediately justified in such enthusiasm. That first *Sports Report* was listened to by 15 per cent of the adult civilian population of Great Britain – about 5.4 million out of around 36 million. In the North, 22 per cent tuned in and 16 per cent from the Midlands. These figures didn't include about 150,000 on national service, many of those young adults in uniform being part of the key demographic target of the programme. That 15 per cent was the best of the day's listening figures, surpassing hugely popular programmes such as *Dick Barton* (5 per cent), *Paul Temple* (7 per cent) and the morning's regular request show, *Housewives' Choice* (14 per cent). It was a spectacular introduction to the Saturday scheduling and proof there was a vast audience out there, thirsting for greater coverage of sport.

There was little reaction to the new programme within the portals of the BBC. The major, popular programmes occupied executive attention. With sport being barely acknowledged amid the star names and shows on the Light Programme, Mackay just kept his head down and beavered away at improving *Sports Report*, trying out various presenters, refining the duration and quality of the live reports, exploring new studios in remote parts of the country. As a proud Scot, he had no intention of producing a programme deemed to be London-centric. In his eyes, *Sports Report* was for every fan throughout the UK.

For years, the executive attitude towards *Sports Report* was at best tolerance and at worst benign neglect. Even the official history of the BBC's first 50 years, by Asa Briggs, continues that theme. Published in 1972, it runs to 439 pages. This magisterial tome contains just one mention of *Sports Report*, and one of Raymond Glendenning and Angus Mackay, neither pertaining to their stints on the programme. There are no references to John Arlott or John Webster, who read the football results for the best part of 22 years.

From pages 363 to 401, Briggs lists BBC milestones, for example the first time *Desert Island Discs*, *Woman's Hour*, *The Archers*, *Today*, *World at One*, *Just a Minute* and *Any Questions?* were broadcast. *Mrs Dale's Diary*, a drama about the daily concerns of a doctor's wife that ran five days a week for 21 years, is catalogued – highlighting its first airing on 5 January 1948. *Sports Report*, on air for the first time two days earlier, doesn't get a mention. Yet in 1972, it was already 24 years old, going from strength to strength, adapting cleverly to changing broadcasting styles, acknowledged as a vital pillar of sports broadcasting in the industry. But not in *The BBC: The First Fifty Years*. The emphasis on news and its connection with politics, at the expense of sport, is emblematic of the way Angus Mackay and many talented members of the sports department were viewed for decades among the elite of Broadcasting House.

But Mackay would not have been fussed by a lack of support from his BBC bosses. After more than a decade in newspapers, then broadcasting, he knew instinctively what would work and he was never one of those clubbable producers who knew how to flatter the hierarchy. He would continue to tinker editorially, cajole the technical wizards into conquering new frontiers and usher in a new way of bringing sport into homes. Angus Mackay knew best – don't you forget it.

3

ANGUS AND EAMONN – THE ODD COUPLE

Angus Mackay was content with the public's reaction to the success that was *Sports Report* in its early months, while oblivious to the indifference from the upper echelons in Broadcasting House. He instinctively knew he was on to a winner and nothing would distract him from his aim of planting *Sports Report* squarely into the centre of the nation's weekly sporting conversation. Fleet Street was having to take notice, because Mackay kept employing the most famous columnists for weekly diatribes that illuminated the programme. The papers could hardly ignore *Sports Report* when their big names kept extolling the programme.

Just one particular issue gnawed away at Mackay. He was still looking for the ideal presenter, someone to epitomise the new, dynamic feel he demanded for radio sport. He tried out 17 presenters in those first couple of years. Rex Alston, a fluent rugby, athletics, tennis and cricket commentator was too redolent of another, more deferential age, while John Webster lacked the necessary knowledge of football and was more suited to reading the results, albeit impeccably. Cliff Michelmore, later a highly successful TV presenter, was more comfortable in the news division and the hugely successful *Family Favourites* programme. Max Robertson, later a mainstay of BBC Radio's tennis coverage, had a rapid style that didn't offer enough light and shade in the presenter's chair, and Stephen Grenfell eventually settled in South Africa, where he became a gifted writer and versatile broadcaster. Alex McCrindle, a Scots actor who later appeared in the *Star Wars* film and the original *All Creatures Great and Small* TV series had a few stints as presenter, but his acting career soon blossomed and he was lost to Hollywood for a long spell.

Mackay wasn't convinced that the original custodian, Raymond Glendenning, was ideal temperamentally. Listening to an interviewee was never Glendenning's forte. Mackay also insisted that the presenter listened to him, at all times, in that crucial 30 minutes of *Sports Report*. For the first couple of years with the fledgling programme the irascible producer searched tirelessly for the ideal front man and he was never afraid to gamble on a hunch, but one backfired spectacularly in October 1949.

Glendenning was away that Saturday and Mackay decided to take a bold punt on the stand-in presenter. George Allison had commentated for the BBC on big footballing occasions from 1927 to 1938, as well as managing Arsenal. He was a great supporter of the programme and Mackay relished his deep, fruity voice. Allison was cajoled by the great persuader to come out of retirement and see how he'd cope with presenting *Sports Report*.

It didn't go well. Too many outside sources to studios outside London went down, Allison would cue to reporters who just weren't there and precious time was lost as Mackay kept rushing in with rewritten scripts. As he later wrote, 'Here was chaos on a grand scale, even for *Sports Report*.' After this disastrous programme drew mercifully to a close, Mackay escorted his perspiring, portly friend to a taxi outside Broadcasting House. Allison, clearly regretting yielding to Mackay's earlier entreaties, simply gasped, 'Never again, Angus, never again.'

So Mackay kept looking for his ideal presenter and in May 1950 he happened to be listening at home to a programme called *Ignorance is Bliss*. He was struck by the affable personality and warm voice of the young Irishman presenting this nondescript quiz show and made a note to listen to the programme again. Too late – the show was taken off the air and Mackay thought no more of it. A chance meeting in the BBC Club (now part of the Langham Hotel, just across the road from Broadcasting House) that September, courtesy of a colleague, Brian George, impressed Mackay and after pondering the possibilities that afternoon, he phoned Brian to arrange a meeting with the genial Irishman. After a discussion that convinced Mackay the young man knew enough about sport, he told him, 'Come along this Saturday and see how we do it. If you think you can manage it, I'll give you a programme to compere.'

On 9 December 1950 Eamonn Andrews duly presented *Sports Report* for the first time. Within a couple of minutes, Mackay knew his long search was over. He had found the perfect presenter, awash with charm, who blended informality with up-to-the-minute facts.

Andrews and Mackay eventually became inseparable professionally. They were like the old dears who've been married for over 70 years and finish each

23

other's sentences, knowing what the other is thinking, with no secrets or grudges. A cranky, exacting Scot with a Presbyterian work ethic and a relaxed Irishman, who did as he was told, but made it appear as if he was plucking whimsy and imparting facts off the top of his head.

From the end of 1950, they were at the helm of *Sports Report* for almost 14 years – in broadcasting terms an aeon. When Andrews left in 1964, unable to resist television's entreaties any longer, many wondered if *Sports Report* could continue without the presenter who made the job look so easy, who seemed to broadcast with a permanent smile, one whose approachable style persuaded some of sport's biggest names to walk through the august portals of Broadcasting House.

They reckoned without the enduring legacy and rigorous standards set by Angus Mackay. After Andrews' departure, he remained in charge for another eight years, successfully winkling a couple of years out of BBC management to carry on after his official retirement age; precious time to inculcate his imperishable broadcasting principles into a new generation of great talent that needed direction, as the programme faced new, stern challenges from television.

The fact that *Sports Report* consolidated its reputation while tweaking its approach to sports stories throughout the seventies and eighties is the ultimate tribute to Angus Mackay. He was always looking for greater flexibility, testing his reporters, looking for technical breakthroughs. The huge advances subsequently made in covering radio sport pleased him greatly as he listened in after retiring.

He is the most important, influential figure in the programme's history. Normally it's the presenters who stamp their authority on a show known for its longevity and public affection. Devotees of *Sports Report* can reel off the names of those who steered it for years every Saturday night, but I wonder how many will conjure up the dapper, dour workaholic with the Captain Mainwaring moustache and an intimidating brevity with words?

It was entirely typical of Mackay that when he finally retired in 1972, he resisted all pleas to give an interview to mark his final programme. Peter Jones and Cliff Morgan, brilliant broadcasters with a winning Welsh penchant for dramatic accounts of sporting derring-do, were both highly regarded by Mackay. In effect, he discovered them, then nurtured, cajoled and ushered them into the broadcasting pantheon. Peter and Cliff vowed to get their revered producer on air for once, correctly reasoning that Mackay had a few tales to offer from his tenure of 24 years. They took him out to lunch, flattered him, poured him some handsome wee drams and tried every ruse at their considerable disposal.

Not a chance. 'I'm a producer, not a broadcaster. I will not be heard.' End of discussion. Angus Mackay invariably had the last word.

Eamonn Andrews was certainly a broadcaster and a great one. Some presenters of huge status are basically all hat and no cattle. There's nothing there, fundamentally, but Eamonn was remarkably versatile, with the priceless gift of making it sound as if he was randomly plucking the right words out of the air. He appeared to be talking to just you, the only listener.

Somehow, he steered the programme with Mackay sat right alongside him, often scribbling down the next link in pencil, his left arm linked into Eamonn's right, pointing vigorously. Miraculously, Eamonn somehow sounded natural, prepared, up to the mark. Whenever he conducted live interviews – either in a studio discussion or with someone elsewhere, at an outside broadcast – he would engage in a natural, relaxed manner, all the while fielding terse instructions from his producer, who'd then moved to the studio next door, all the better to bark at him.

Mackay knew he was pushing his presenter hard and at the end of the programme, Eamonn's blue suit was usually black with perspiration on the back. But he just seemed to sail serenely through the shoals, chuckling at any obstacle, never stuck for a winning comment that would defuse any tension on air.

His producer would make no apologies for putting him through the wringer, but he remained hugely fond of the tall Dubliner, with the dark crinkly hair and long face that seemed forever creased in a ready smile. 'Eamonn,' he once said, with a hint of a twinkle,' I just wish I had the courage of your lack of convictions.'

Colleagues were amazed at their intuition. Vincent Duggleby, later a *Sports Report* presenter, started out in the sports room doing various admin jobs, like dealing with Eamonn's enormous fan mail, and he was struck by the telepathy on air between producer and presenter. 'Angus would tell him anything and in a heartbeat it would be coming out of Eamonn's mouth. Some looked down on Eamonn because Angus wrote all his scripts, but they didn't understand what a gift it is to be able to repeat those words, without hesitation and still sound natural. I thought Eamonn was brilliant.'

Mackay's daughter, Sheena Harold, still remembers those endearing qualities that made Eamonn Andrews so popular with the public. 'I adored Eamonn. He was so kind to me as a little girl. He stayed at our house for a time when his wife was in hospital, being treated for tuberculosis, and I think he really loved being part of our home life. When he went to television and became an even bigger name, he used to send me autographs of the stars he'd interviewed.

'He and Dad were joined at the hip. It was a real partnership. They leaned on each other, trusted each other totally. When Eamonn was abroad, commentating on boxing, the phone would be ringing at all hours of the night, as he took instructions from Dad about the Saturday show.'

It was boxing that brought Andrews into broadcasting in England. He never pretended to be a sports anorak, but he was a good enough boxer to be a schoolboy champion back in Ireland. After trying a few radio commentaries, he kept knocking on the door of the state broadcaster, RTE, with varying degrees of success – and frustration.

He then tried his hand at the BBC in London, refusing nothing and chasing everything. Eventually he came to Mackay's notice, who saw something different in him. It was probably the voice. One of the early *Sports Report* presenters was a Canadian called Stewart MacPherson, who had a speedy, excited style best suited to ice hockey commentaries.

MacPherson eventually went to work in the United States, but he made an impression on Andrews, who was desperate to find a niche somewhere. He listened intently to MacPherson's commentaries and trained himself to introduce a hint of mid-Atlantic into his own style. Finessing his Dublin accent, slowing down his delivery and grafting on a scintilla of North American tones meant that Eamonn became a highly distinctive broadcaster, instantly recognisable.

His boxing commentaries throughout the fifties were masterpieces of vivid description, controlled excitement and the instinctive awareness of when to let the ringside atmosphere guide the narrative, rather than crashing all over the drama. He didn't need the baleful control of Mackay at ringside. In boxing, Eamonn was master of all he surveyed.

To do justice to a broadcaster who last presented *Sports Report* almost 60 years ago, it's instructive to grasp the scale and peaks of Andrews in his pomp. While anchoring *Sports Report* and many other programmes on radio, he presented the massively popular TV panel show *What's My Line* and the compulsive *This Is Your Life* (with yer man himself the subject of the first programme), while entrancing a generation of children in the *Crackerjack!* series. He was also presenter of the annual Miss World competition.

As a versatile household name, in terms of ubiquity he was a combination of Terry Wogan, Clare Balding, Phillip Schofield, and Ant and Dec, and he was greatly loved for his genial good nature and unflappable professionalism. He didn't frighten the horses, radiating decency. On his premature death from heart failure in 1987, a memorial mass at Westminster Cathedral underlined the affection several generations of Britons felt for this particular Irishman.

So Eamonn Andrews brought stardust and cachet to *Sports Report* as he cemented his hold on the public consciousness. At a time of social conformity, Eamonn was the quintessential safe pair of hands. Nothing edgy about him, no discernible ego, no showbiz tantrums.

Jill Reeves worked with Eamonn on *Sports Report* for six years during the fifties, an invaluable presence as Angus Mackay's production secretary, knitting all the disparate elements together, guiding the contributors on air, giving them Mackay's last-minute instructions. 'Eamonn was a lovely man,' she says, 'not at all starry. He mixed easily with all of us, asking about our families regularly. Such an easy-going chap.'

Angus Mackay must be commended on spotting Andrews' innate talent, but the stars aligned when he decided to take a chance on the novice. Eamonn was 28 and hungry, desperate to get a toe in somewhere after numerous rebuffs. He later wrote in the 1955 *Sports Report* anthology, 'At the time, I was busy giving displays of nonchalance, hints of hidden wealth and conversations on the I-don't-know-if-I-can-fit-it-in principle that are the surest signs of the out-of-work actor, or the show-business character who hasn't a single engagement between him and his Maker. I was ready for it. With all my pauper's pride I was ready for it.'

So was Mackay. He was still looking for his ideal presenter, mostly using Stuart MacPherson and Raymond Glendenning. MacPherson's departure to the USA created a vacancy, while Glendenning was an issue for Mackay. The most versatile sports broadcaster of his age, but although acknowledged throughout the land, he spread his butter over a wide expanse of loaf.

Mackay wanted a presenter who was an enabler, someone who would willingly defer to others on air who had strong views to impart. Mackay valued that trait in Andrews, 'He is one of the few people in the entertainment business who, when necessary, voluntarily reduce their own contributions in order to bring out the best in others.'

Not something that could ever be levelled against Raymond Glendenning. He had an air of 'de haut en bas' about him, a patrician Sir Bufton Tufton instructing his gardener to cut back the azaleas more ruthlessly. He wasn't suited to a sports news programme such as this new one, under Mackay's despotic rule.

It would take almost three years of *Sports Report*'s growing influence before Mackay could be satisfied he'd found the ideal presenter.

Angus and Eamonn, in their vastly contrasting ways, were made for each other. Mackay's achievement in getting the programme up and running inside just three months had been remarkable. He had harangued the sports producers in the regions into buying into his vision, while enlisting the support of the technicians, a rapport that never wavered in his time as producer and Angus always ensured they were plied with drinks in the BBC Club after the programme ended.

It was the perfect bar for Angus Mackay to wind down in after *Sports Report*. He'd start off with a couple of halves of bitter, with a shot or two of Scotch for company, then from his designated seat at the bar, he'd flatter the technicians with praise that astonished the on-air broadcasters, who were used to caustic broadsides from the martinet. He did introduce a young Dick Scales to the joys of alcohol after his first broadcast on *Sports Report*. Dick was feeling fairly pleased with his two-minute appearance, giving the Division Three and Four round-up, and when the great man asked what he'd like to drink, he demurely asked for a tomato juice. 'Make that a double scotch,' Mackay rasped at the barman. Dick did as he was told and swallowed hard. 'It was the first time I had touched alcohol, but I quickly caught on to the benefits – one of them was staying on the right side of Angus.'

The most cursory perusal of Mackay's career up to then would have confirmed he was a graduate of the School of Hard Knocks. He'd served his time on the sports desk at *The Scotsman* in Edinburgh, before securing an interview with the BBC at Broadcasting House. Assuming he'd failed to pass muster, he was no sooner back in Edinburgh than a telegram arrived, summoning him back to London for another interview. He had to borrow money from his grandmother to afford the train journey.

Angus got the job – specialising in sport in the radio newsroom – and a new nickname. He'd been christened Harry Murdoch Mackay and some wag in the BBC newsroom said, 'That's not Scottish enough – we'll call you Angus,' and it stuck.

He'd always enjoyed the company of journalists in Edinburgh and continued that rapport in London. The hard-living combination of punishing hours, smoking and alcohol suited Angus, and that fondness for newspapermen was obvious when he launched *Sports Report*. At the time newspaper columnists were massively influential and popular, and Angus enlisted the services of the biggest names, who were fearless, opinionated and irreverent and knew their worth.

Newspaper placards outside football matches would announce 'J. L. Manning is here today for the *Daily Mail*' and, if one of Fleet Street's sporting grandees later took his seat in the press box, it was announced on the public address system.

Mackay relished the unguarded anti-Establishment riffs on air by his Fleet Street cronies, laughing afterwards in the bar about how close they had sailed to the wind. He knew that his BBC staff contributors would not offer such non-conformity and Peter Wilson *et al* commanded a massive following. All he needed was more time on air for their iconoclastic asides, which were so unusual in such po-faced times. The newspaper cadre gave *Sports Report* heft and authority, and Eamonn christened them 'The Old Firm.'

So Mackay had assembled his experienced band of fearless newspaper columnists, but he was determined to sharpen up the contributions of his match reporters. In later years he was horrified to recall that the football reports in the first year would run to over two minutes in a programme that only lasted 29 minutes and 59 seconds. 'They were flowery, well-padded stories, which contained a good deal of wholly unnecessary information,' he wrote. The word came down from on high – from now on, a minute and a quarter, and not one second longer. Later, that became a minute, with the same dire warning.

His method of sanction was ruthless and effective. Reporters who strayed beyond their allotted timespan were cut off in mid-flow, with Eamonn Andrews saying that the studio had somehow lost contact, and then they didn't work for *Sports Report* for some time – or, indeed, ever again. Every reporter or commentator from Angus Mackay's time that I have interviewed brought up this fishbone that stuck in the producer's throat. He simply would not tolerate anyone going over time.

David Coleman, who quickly made a name for himself in the mid-fifties on *Sports Report* and the lunchtime preview programme, *Sports Parade*, used to joke that he carried Angus Mackay's stopwatch around in his mind when he became the foremost sports presenter on TV for a generation. Alan Parry, superb all-rounder for television, had the benefit of Mackay's unbending strictures about time constraints in the early seventies and says, 'To this day, I could do a one-minute report on anything, because of Angus Mackay's discipline.' Brian Moore often used to talk about that particular aspect of Mackay's production if we ever bumped into each other at a football match, telling me, 'Years later, long after I'd gone to ITV, I'd suddenly remember what Angus told me about certain disciplines, when I was about to go on air. The need for accuracy, good words and above all, talking to time, listen to what your guest is saying. No half measures. Everything he instilled in me stayed with me.'

Angus Mackay and 'getting the last word' became synonymous terms. Even the most prestigious broadcasters on the programme were cowed by him. Peter Bromley, for decades BBC Radio's outstanding racing correspondent, was not a man who opted for the diplomatic approach, no matter who was in his crosshairs. Vesuvius and Bromley were often used in the same sentence. Yet he couldn't outwit Mackay, a man of few words, but every one of them telling.

Peter was scheduled to do a preview of the Cheltenham Gold Cup for *Sports Report*, but got sidetracked by a one-eyed horse winning the Champion Hurdle, ridden by the first winning amateur jockey since before the Second World War. He gave what he felt was a first-rate news story 20 seconds before starting his Gold Cup preview. Big mistake in the eyes of Mackay.

After being bollocked for departing from his brief, Bromley went into print – always a sign that it's a serious matter when you're a BBC wallah, because it normally goes on your personal file. Peter wrote, 'I would like to point out that: 1) I was convinced that there was a news story in the Champion Hurdle. 2) I suggested the 20 seconds on the Champion Hurdle to the producer before the programme, who accepted it. 3) I did not over-run. 4.) I did tip the winner of the Gold Cup.'

That memo led to the following withering backhand volley down the tramlines from Angus Mackay, '1) We weren't. 2) He didn't. 3) You're not expected to. 4) You are expected to.'

Bromley, a tough-as-teak taskmaster, was grudgingly impressed. It was one of his proudest BBC possessions until the day he died and he once wrote, 'For all his fire and brimstone I regard Angus Mackay as the true architect of this fast-moving programme that has become the envy of the world.' Coming from Peter Bromley, that is the most worthy of tributes. The two men were not known for yielding an inch, yet this time Bromley blinked first.

I can only find one occasion when Mackay backed down and it came from an unlikely source. Christopher Martin-Jenkins, later the BBC's estimable cricket correspondent, was a sports assistant for a few years in the late sixties before ascending his own personal Mount Olympus. Once, he was limbering up for the Third and Fourth Division round-ups in *Sports Report* (not one of CMJ's fortes, it has to be said) when Angus checked on how he'd be introduced. 'So we'll call you Chris Jenkins, right?' he confirmed, only to be told by the seemingly diffident tyro,' Actually my name is Christopher Martin-Jenkins, if you don't mind.' Presumably Mackay hadn't come up against many youngsters from Marlborough College and Cambridge University in his time as a hard-nosed sports producer. CMJ prevailed, to the astonishment of his colleagues, who had expected a volley of derision from Mackay.

Others weren't cut any slack. Godfrey Dixey, a gentle Old Harrovian with a distinguished war record that he flatly refused to discuss, was tolerated by Mackay – but no more than that. Once, with the 5 p.m. deadline remorselessly approaching and Mackay scribbling out his presenter's script for the headlines, Godfrey was unlucky enough to catch the flak…

> Mackay: 'Godfrey, stop talking, I'm trying to concentrate.'
> Dixey: 'I'm not talking, Angus – I'm just breathing.'
> Mackay: 'Well, stop breathing then.'

Mackay was a bonny fighter for his department's interests. Internecine feuds with the outside broadcasts department were long and legendary, and he kept the details to himself, draining though they were. The top executives disapproved of him favouring newspaper reporters and columnists at the expense of BBC staffers, but Mackay stood his ground. Jill Reeves, his indispensable production assistant, knew when the waters were choppy. 'He'd come into the office, brooding, ill-tempered and not say a word for most of the day. I didn't take it personally. I knew there were problems. I just got on with my job, which I loved. He was very loyal to his staff and defended them against anyone.'

But Mackay could never feel comfortable among those executives more attuned to office politics. When *Sports Report* was at last extended by an hour in 1955 – long overdue in the implacable producer's opinion – he faced an early shot across the bows before the first programme. The Light Programme's controller, H. Rooney Pelletier, sent a memo to Mackay, making it clear the extended duration was merely an experiment, exhorting Mackay to, 'Keep an eye on costs, please. A relatively expensive undertaking has a chance of a long life – an expensive one must, perforce, be brief. If by some unfortunate chance, it does not prove a success we must withdraw. That is why I place a "review point" in three months' time.'

Pelletier was soon mollified, with 16 per cent of the adult civilian population (around 6.1 million), tuning into the revamped *Sports Report* in late April 1955. Yet again, Mackay had seen off the doubters.

His daughter Sheena saw how those battles affected Angus. 'There were four in our family – me, my Mum, Dad and *Sports Report*. He'd put the programme first every time. I had to get married on a Sunday, because Dad imposed this strict rule that no one in the sports department could have Saturdays off in the football season, so he couldn't give me away unless it was on a Sunday. He worked very long hours. He'd write ideas down on bar mats, napkins, old envelopes, train tickets – all in pencil. Our house was full of newspapers and he'd read everything. Dad had a wonderful way with words and was a stickler for grammar – telling me off if ever I split an infinitive. He had a sign in the sports room "Do it now and do it right."

'I know many thought he was a tyrant, rude and cantankerous, but I think he was shy and put up a barrier to hide that. He was a creature of habit. Same seat in the same corner of the BBC bar and in our local pub. He'd take Mum and I to the Odeon at Twickenham every Wednesday afternoon after school, for the matinee. It didn't matter what film was on, we'd always be there, in the same seats.'

Sir Paul Fox, grandee of TV sport in later years, chuckles at the thought there was a softer side to his old adversary, 'Angus Mackay was the rudest person I ever met at the BBC.' Quite a comment from a former editor of *Panorama*, BBC1 controller, Managing Director of the BBC and the executive who launched the *Two Ronnies*, *Dad's Army*, *The Generation Game* and the *Parkinson* chat show. Presumably, Sir Paul's met a few martinets along the way since first joining the BBC just after the war?

'Yes – but no one like Angus. He was so bloody-minded, everyone deferred to him in his department. His fiefdom was absolute, you just didn't argue back. He hated everything that TV stood for. I tried to get him to come over to us once sport started to develop on the telly, but he'd have none of it. He regarded us as the enemy. Angus knew that he'd be accountable in a larger BBC department if he came over and I don't really blame him.

'I do take my hat off to him, though. We unashamedly borrowed the *Sports Report* format when I launched *Sportsview* in 1954, a weekly round-up that also featured that day's sports news. I had huge admiration for him and his vision, but he was a difficult, self-centred bastard.'

No one dared sit in Mackay's seat in his office, even when he was on holiday. His writ ran far and wide. His standards were recognised and he would brook no interference. When Vincent Duggleby presented *Sports Report*,

Mackay would let him know what was expected. 'He'd put a stopwatch in front of me and that was the signal that I had a minute to go. No ifs or buts. Do what you're told.'

The Monday morning review of Saturday's *Sports Report* would go into granular detail. A grief encounter. Phil King produced the programme several times, with Mackay valuing him for his sharp journalistic antennae and ability to work calmly under pressure, but he recalls those Mondays with a shudder. 'They became inquests. We'd pore over the programme in minute detail. All the big hitters on air would attend and Angus would spare no one. God knows how often he'd listen back on a Sunday before coming in next day to dissect everything. He'd look at the next Saturday's football fixtures and say, "Right – where's the story there for the 5 o'clock show?" Des Lynam would joke, "If I knew that, Angus, I'd have won the pools and be lying on a beach in Barbados!" Angus didn't often see the funny side.'

But, unwittingly, Mackay was responsible for a classic anecdote that still does the rounds when veterans of *Sports Report* gather, and it speaks volumes for the producer's dedication and occasional myopia. Des Lynam was there. 'We were sat around in the office one Saturday morning, chewing over the options, throwing some ideas around. One of the secretaries came over and said there was an urgent call for Angus. He didn't want to take it. Too busy. But the caller insisted.

'Angus, by now irritated, took the call and his face and tone changed. It was J. L. Manning's wife. The legendary columnist and long-time friend of the programme had been booked to come in later on, to do one of his special three-minute pieces that we always enjoyed. But this time, he couldn't make it, for the best of reasons.

'The conversation went something like this, in Angus' words ... "Oh, no ... a coronary in the middle of the night? Intensive care, you say? ... The next 24 hours are crucial? Oh, I'm so sorry, Amy ... Well, we're thinking of you and Jim, of course."

'Angus put the phone down and shouted at us, 'Bloody hell, we've got a problem. Manning's let us down for tonight!'

It's not that Mackay didn't care for Manning. Far from it. He enjoyed his irascibility and fearlessness of opinions, and greatly respected what he'd brought to the programme's palette over the past two decades. But *Sports Report* came first, especially on a Saturday.

Mackay spared no one, including himself. He would do the heavy lifting, if necessary. He had an excellent personal and professional relationship with Joe Davis, the greatest snooker player of the 1950s. Davis was a regular, popular guest on the programme, even after he retired from competitive snooker and did the lucrative rounds of exhibitions. One Saturday, news filtered through that Davis had become the first to reach 500 breaks of a century. It was a big story in an era when snooker – a cheap sport to play in post-war austerity Britain – was of major interest to the public.

Mackay swiftly knew he had to get Davis on the show and set out in a taxi to find him. By the time he had got to the location of his history-making round, Davis had left. Into a foggy London afternoon. Mackay, bit between clenched teeth, steeled himself to land his quarry, his taxi careering around Davis' regular haunts. These days, a simple mobile call or two would have sufficed.

With three hours before transmission, Mackay kept drawing blanks. Where was the maestro? By chance, Mackay bumped into a friend who told him that he thought Davis was at that time giving a private lesson in the Kensington area. Mackay put a call through, fixed up the interview time and repaired back to Broadcasting House to organise the rest of *Sports Report*. He would be entitled to a glow of satisfaction and a quiet promise to himself that an extra whisky chaser would be in order later on at the BBC Club. With Joe Davis in his company.

But the dense fog that bedevilled London so often in the fifties nearly stymied the live interview. Davis's taxi got lost and with Mackay steeling himself for plans B and C, the star guest finally rushed into the studio, with 30 seconds to spare. The stoical Eamonn Andrews handled the interview with his usual reliability, after Davis sat down in front of the microphone, still wearing his overcoat and hat. No time for any of those niceties.

Getting the story was always paramount to Mackay, as you'd expect from a former newspaper man, steeped in deadlines and sailing close to the wind. He knew the importance of contacts, and expected his reporters and correspondents to do the foot-slogging, bar-propping and schmoozing that led the stars of sport to trust them. He was excellent at discerning star quality in talented people making their way in sport. He spotted the charisma of Cassius Clay earlier than most. Seeing past the bombast, the doggerel masquerading as poetry, he focused on the articulacy and undeniable boxing talent. This lad would beguile and infuriate the sporting world in equal measure.

After Clay had won his Olympic gold medal in 1960, then fought a memorable contest with Henry Cooper in London in 1963, Mackay kept in touch with the blossoming heavyweight, chasing him on the phone all around the United States at various times. He became a regular turn on the programme, warming to Eamonn Andrews' genial readiness to afford him top billing and enough time to show off. For Mackay, the dazzling young man provided light relief on *Sports Report*, initially predicting he would end the long career of Archie Moore, the former light-heavyweight champion of the world. This was an early glimpse of the precocious Clay's penchant for irreverent verse – 'Archie Moore, if you don't fall in four, I won't fight no more.' Mackay was vindicated in championing him when he won the world title sensationally in 1964. Clay – soon to be Muhammad Ali – never forgot that support and in later years he would often oblige *Sports Report* with his time. By then, of course, such an interview would be a genuine scoop – all due to Angus Mackay's vision and persistence.

Yet if it hadn't been for Mackay's inner steel and a huge dollop of fortune, he would have died years before Ali entranced and amused him. If he hadn't been a heavy smoker, he would have been one of the fatalities in a tragic rail disaster, at the age of 44.

The rail crash at Barnes in South London late in 1955 led to 13 deaths and 41 injuries, after a passenger train collided at 35 mph with the rear of a freight train. At the time it was one of the most serious train crashes in British history. Mackay was on that train, in a smoking compartment. He had the window down, letting some fresh air in, amid the fug, at the moment of impact. He was the only one in the compartment to survive because of that open window. He managed to squeeze out, as the carriage lay on its side, clambered up a muddy slope, hailed down a passing car and shouted, 'This is my home telephone number. Call my wife and tell her I'm OK.' He then returned to help the casualties.

Sheena Harold was just 13 at the time and horrified at her father's burns. 'He looked like something out of a horror movie. All bandaged up. He spent months in the Middlesex Hospital. Dad couldn't eat on his own or get dressed. It was awful for such a proud, self-reliant man, who'd served at the front in the war. It didn't stop him working, though. As he convalesced, he'd be firing off dictated letters to BBC people, trying to run the programme from his hospital bed. So many of sport's big names tried to get into see him, but they were kept away because of worries about tuberculosis infections – a little like coronavirus. For the rest of his life, he had a florid colour on his face, due to the burns. The skin layers were burned off. He suffered a lot from chapped lips and he was forever applying balm to them.

'It was a horrible time for him. Ironically, smoking eventually killed him, he had emphysema. Apparently, he always had a weak chest when he was younger. Fred Perry, the great tennis player, used to bring him loads of packets over duty-free from the United States and that didn't help. But his smoking habit saved him for us that night in Barnes.'

Such was the respect for Mackay in the sports department that no one needed to say that 'the show must go on.' It was ingrained in their psyche. They knew their demanding producer would expect nothing less. Jill Reeves, his irreplaceable production assistant, was told to cut short her holiday and help steer the ship. 'It was just a natural thing. Angus had created the show out of nothing and we simply had to keep it going. Eamonn also stepped up to the plate, taking on producer's duties, rallying everyone. With his charm and popularity, he was perfect at raising morale. He'd put himself in the boss's shoes and work out what Angus would have done.'

Typically, Mackay never referred to that rail tragedy when he finally returned to work. To all intents and purposes he was the same individual and professional. But how would *Sports Report*'s status and legacy have been affected if the great producer's fondness for a fag not saved his life, just seven years into his tenure? He would enjoy a further 17 years at the helm, before reluctantly calling it a day. I wonder if *Sports Report* would have still been on air, decade after decade, without his influence and demanding standards?

Barry Davies joined the sports department in 1963, just after coming out of the Army. Mackay gave him the job of checking some of the scripts then handing them to the esteemed presenter. 'I was just a glorified errand boy, paid five guineas a week for each Saturday. I just hung around, hoping to pick up work. Angus was always on the brink of sacking me. Everyone was scared of him, a definite rod of iron. Years later, when I made something of a name for myself in television, Angus would refer to me as one of his boys. I don't think so.

'But Eamonn was very kind to me. No ego. He did exactly what he was told by Angus. I was in awe of Eamonn then. He was the premier all-round broadcaster in the country. I was so much in awe of him that for the only time I smoked, it was with a cigarette holder because Eamonn did. I hoped some of his stardust would rub off on me!'

Eammon's early death in 1987 at the age of 65 hit Mackay hard. 'He barely spoke a word that day,' his daughter, Sheena, recalls. 'So many memories must have swirled around him. They kept in touch right until Eamonn's death. He'd come and sit with Dad, and they'd knock ideas around. They still wanted to work together, but it was not to be. I used to love taking Eamonn's phone calls in the middle of the night, from halfway round the world. He'd chuckle and say, 'Can I speak to the Lord Mayor of London, please,' and I'd go off and wake Dad up. They were so close. Never a cross word.'

Sports Report was blessed that the Mackay/Andrews partnership lasted as long as 14 years, when you consider how big a media personality Eamonn became. Reluctant guests would come on the show because it was Eamonn doing the interview and Angus fixing it. Not many turned down Angus Mackay in those days, despite his fearsome reputation among his charges in the sports department.

Des Lynam, another brilliant all-rounder of sports broadcasting, believes Mackay was the biggest influence on his long, award-laden career. 'Angus changed my life in taking a chance on me, soon after pitching up from Radio Brighton. I felt humbled and privileged to present *Sports Report* so early. He taught me so much about broadcasting – a stickler for details, he was so pedantic. Angus always had that pencil ready. He was very fond of interesting words, encouraged us to show off our vocabulary. I only ever got one commendation from him, after doing the Grand National programme in 1970. That didn't matter. I knew he cared about his staff, even if I was terrified of him in those early days! In my opinion, Angus Mackay is the most important person in *Sports Report*'s history and yet who's heard of him today?'

That's always the case with producers – the hewers of wood and drawers of water compared to the galacticos in front of the microphone. They do the unsung and unseen work, and battle with the suits at umpteen frustrating meetings, while the presenters garner the glittering prizes. But Angus Mackay remains the only one to get name-checked as producer of *Sports Report* in every *Radio Times* edition. He certainly earned that accolade. That instinctive grasp of what constitutes great radio was never illustrated better than his decision, after a two-minute conversation with Eamonn Andrews, that he was the man to present his cherished programme. Eamonn never looked back after 9 December 1950. Nor did *Sports Report*.

4

THAT SIGNATURE TUNE

November 1987. The London Hilton. Around 600 of the great and the good from the British sporting world are gathered for a black tie bash for an early celebration of the 40th anniversary of *Sports Report*. Terry Wogan's the compere, Rory Bremner will treat us to his pin-sharp impersonations. Comedic sketches involving sports-room stalwarts such as Peter Jones, Bryon Butler, Gerald Williams, Peter Bromley, David Mercer, Garry Richardson and Peter Brackley will be endured – and in some cases enjoyed. As the guests get seated, someone has a smart idea to get the gathering in a jolly mood. The PA system blasts out a highly familiar tune…

Dee-dum, dee-dum, dee-dum, dee-dum, dee diddledy dum dee-dah…

Everyone smiles, hums along or bangs the table with spoons. The *Sports Report* signature tune, called 'Out of the Blue'. On the radio for almost 40 years, instantly recognised and much-loved. Played by every military band you can shake a baton at and the likes of the Grimethorpe Colliery Band, and still an integral part of *Sports Report*. The calling card down the generations for sports fans to move a little closer to the radio or, in these sophisticated times, the smartphone or iPad or snuggle up to Alexa.

Almost everyone I have spoken to for this project has mentioned 'Out of the Blue' in the first five minutes. A communal feeling of affection, comfort and familiarity. 'They're not going to drop it, are they?' they ask. As if I was privy to such rarefied discussions. Beyond my pay grade.

That signature tune has seen off those of so many sports programmes. *Ski Sunday*, *Pot Black*, *Grandstand*, *World of Sport*. Only *Match of the Day* resonates as much as *Sports Report*'s greetings card and, starting in 1970, that's a young shaver by comparison. I'd suggest only *Desert Island Discs* (first broadcast 1942) and *The Archers* (1955) are blessed with theme tunes that are equally evocative. Who said nostalgia isn't what it used to be?

'Out of the Blue' is a military march, performed with pace and brio. 'Music with hairs on its chest,' as Sir Michael Parkinson once dubbed it. It's gloriously anachronistic for a fast-moving, 21st-century programme that prides itself on adaptability, swift responses to developing news stories and high-tech, cutting-edge brilliance in getting the story on air.

It's a whimsical dichotomy that the swift pace of today's *Sports Report* is heralded by music from such a different age, a deferential time, epitomised by that classic TV interview with Clement Attlee ('Prime Minister, do you have anything to say to the British public?' 'No'). A world of knowing your place – *Woman's Hour, Children's Hour* and *Workers' Playtime* – including on the radio. Television was known to just a couple of thousand when *Sports Report* first came on air, relegated to just two pages at the back of *Radio Times*.

Somehow there would always be *Dick Barton: Special Agent* solving devilish murders in swish parts of London and Miss Marple tending lovingly to her wisteria in St Mary Mead. And yet, and yet. 'Out of the Blue' still introduces our flexible friend, locked in a time warp for 30 seconds or so, before the presenter moves urgently through the gears: the headlines, the classified football results, then the match reports.

Why did this signature tune survive, when the programme continued to evolve, always adaptable, confident in exploring new ways to develop an hour of live sporting news? Sir Tim Rice, Oscar-winning lyricist, also knows a thing or two about a winning tune. A Sunderland supporter since he was a boy, he appreciates the need to be cheered up when results aren't going his way. 'It perks you up. It's a martial tune, a call to arms, telling you to listen closer. It's not a tune that calls for a lyric, it's stirring, cheerful. Perfect to start a programme which guarantees you an hour of quality sports news and comment.

'I've been listening to *Sports Report* for decades and I can't imagine it not starting with 'Out of the Blue'. It's like a West End production without its best songs. It would be like taking 'Don't Cry For Me Argentina' out of *Evita*.'

Mark Steel is a waspishly non-conformist comedian, hardly the sort to push a nostalgic theme when there's a citadel to topple. Yet he values the continuity of the programme's traditional opening. 'It transports me back to my bedroom at the age of 11 or 12, listening all day to the radio sport. It's comforting. Hearing the signature tune, then the classified results, makes it all official for me...'

Patrick Barclay, vastly experienced broadsheet football writer, was born in Dundee the year before *Sports Report* started and he cherishes 'Out of the Blue'. 'The end of the war was a celebratory time and marching bands were everywhere, playing military music. When I went to a football game, it was the same sort of musical entertainment. So 'Out of the Blue' was the perfect choice.

'It speaks well of the BBC that this quasi-militaristic symbol of the Empire hasn't been torn down like the Towers of Wembley. It's part of the fabric of the programme. I like ritual, habit and tradition, and I think most sports fans are as naturally conservative as me – with a small 'c' mind you! I celebrate they've kept 'Out of the Blue'. They won't admit it, but young people aren't worth chasing for their core audience. They have butterfly minds and won't appreciate that signature tune. But millions of us older types do.'

The former England cricketer Graeme Swann has always marched to a different drum in his life and career, yet he happily conforms to an appreciation of 'Out of the Blue'. 'I'm an old-fashioned Englishman, fiercely patriotic, and when I hear that signature tune, I feel warm, tingly and emotional. Happy childhood memories come flooding back and I love to see my kids dancing to that music.'

I can confirm Swann's affection for the signature tune. One August Saturday, I was reporting on a Test match at Edgbaston, with Swann as my expert summariser. The football season had just started in earnest and as we crept towards 5 p.m., I tentatively suggested to the studio that my confrere would absolutely love to cue up the signature tune. My producer liked the idea and Swann was allowed to say 'It's now 5 o'clock – time for *Sports Report*.' He was ecstatic. 'With England I took five wickets in a Test innings 17 times, but I would gladly trade any of them for that moment. I couldn't have said anything more on air after that first sentence, because I was overcome.'

Jonathan Pearce, the *Match of the Day* commentator, spent a year in a kibbutz on the Israeli/Lebanese border in the early eighties and that signature tune always sparked off pangs of nostalgia and homesickness. 'It was like a lasso from war-torn Israel to the UK for me and my new friends were entranced by the signature tune, then the programme. A Kenyan friend called Mike thought it was magical and he couldn't believe how much *Sports Report* brought to listeners all around the world. We'd huddle round the radio in a bomb shelter that improvised as a disco and bar, and my new pals would enjoy me bigging up my team, Bristol City, who were then in the old Fourth Division. When we lost 7–1 to Northampton in September 1982, they had a great time at my expense that night. I still remember the hangover!'

Those lucky enough to present *Sports Report* recognised what was involved when they cued up 'Out of the Blue'. John Inverdale, doing it for the first time, recalls thinking, 'Bloody hell, this is for real,' while Jonathan Legard still remembers New Year's Day 1991. 'My first time and I was conscious I was walking in the footsteps of giants. I felt everything had to be word perfect, that it was an honour. An extraordinary feeling, accentuated by that signature tune, picking up the baton that had been passed along by so many greats.'

Tony Adamson had been listening to the BBC's radio sports coverage before *Sports Report* was ever broadcast. Growing up in Northern Ireland, with his mother instrumental in fostering his love for sport, the Adamson family was very proud that an Irishman, Eamonn Andrews, was presenting the programme with such style and authority. So when Tony first presented *Sports Report* in 1980, the signature tune resonated with his psyche. 'I was crapping myself when they played it, and then I had to read the headlines over the music. I was just happy that I hadn't cocked up at the start, because 'Out of the Blue' was so important in setting the tone for the rest of that hour. You had to get the opening spot on. It was nerve-racking, I was shaking.'

And yet 'Out of the Blue' came literally out of the blue to *Sports Report*. As the deadline for the first programme loomed in January 1948, Angus Mackay had a major problem: the signature tune. In those days, that was a very important consideration, to give the new programme an identity. Potential listeners needed to know what lay ahead when the opening bars were heard. Mackay knew this and wrestled with the dilemma for days, as he continued to reject suggestions from the BBC's gramophone library. He had enough logistical challenges to grapple with as the hours ticked by to 5.30 p.m. that Saturday, but getting the right signature tune was proving to be like eating consommé with a fork.

Two hours to go and Mackay was still not happy with the musical options. A call from the gramophone library suggested a final trawl through a few more discs before a decision had to be made. A stirring march was placed on the turntable and Mackay had his lightbulb moment. 'That's it! Perfect!' Mackay declared, ushering in millions of hours when the nation checked pools coupons while ensuring the crumpets were toasting nicely by the fire.

It was pure happenstance. Mackay needed some luck at that juncture, as he battled against general scepticism that he'd get a live sports show on the air, with scant resources, multifarious technical challenges and time constraints. But at least he now had the perfect signature tune.

The irony was that the composer had died three years earlier and had no knowledge or affection of sport. Hubert Bath had written 'Out of the Blue' to feature in the Hendon Air Show in 1931. Bath wrote a lot of brass band music in the 1920s and 1930s, and thought no more about this particular march, which would supplement the crowd's enjoyment of the air display in North London.

Bath was a musical all-rounder, turning his hand to anything if the fee was satisfactory. After singing in the church choir in Barnstaple, he attended the Royal Academy of Music. He was a composer, musical director and conductor, contributing to some of Alfred Hitchcock's early films made in Hollywood and the seminal movie, *Blackmail* (1929), the first British talkie. Films proved lucrative for Bath and he composed for the Oscar-winning documentary *Wings Over Everest* (1934), and *A Yank at Oxford* (1938). One of his most famous compositions, 'Cornish Rhapsody', featured in the 1944 romantic weepie *Love Story*, starring Margaret Lockwood and Stewart Granger, an unashamedly sentimental film, tapping into wartime's necessity for sweeping melodrama to distract a nation needing some emotional respite from the war. Bath's lush score provided perfect musical escapism. The movie was also a box-office success, so Bath was doubly content.

A year later, he passed away. He was only 61, yet he had lived a full life. Respected in his profession for his creativity and productivity, Hubert didn't keep his nose totally to the grindstone. He had a colourful private life, featuring in a messy divorce involving an actress and a war hero, Jean Aylwin and Colonel Alfred Rawlinson. Hubert was named as the co-respondent in the 1924 divorce, which garnered unsympathetic headlines for him, due to the Colonel's unimpeachable war record. The scandal didn't appear to affect Hubert's marriage to Dorothy, who ran a touring operatic company. They stayed together and Dorothy outlived her husband by a couple of decades, grateful for the royalty payments from the BBC for using 'Out of the Blue'.

My invaluable source for all this is Hubert's grandson, Michael, who was born a year after his death. He is amused at the notoriety attached to Hubert. 'He was quite a character from what I've gleaned. Although the newspapers picked up the divorce case in 1924, it just wasn't talked about in our family when I was growing up. My brother unearthed it and we were fascinated. I suppose it's a reflection on the mores of those times that much was made of it. I understand my grandfather liked a beer as well. During the day, he'd write music for the

Gainsborough Films company at their Lime Grove studios in London, then adjourn to the pub soon after 5 o'clock. Thirsty work being a musician!'

Michael, an Accrington Stanley supporter, was the only one of his family interested in sport when a teenager and always listened to *Sports Report*. One day, he was stunned to discover the family's connection to the programme. 'My father walked in one day and said, "You know that music? Your grandfather wrote that." I said "What? Why not tell me before?" I was amazed, and after that I puffed out my chest and dropped it into the conversation with football fans whenever I could.'

Music still runs in the Bath family. Michael's son is an accomplished conductor and composer, as well as running a musical charity and providing tuition. 'To me, music is more than just a vocation, it's a calling,' says Michael. 'And "Out of the Blue" makes me immensely proud. It's the theme tune for our country, inextricably bound up with who you are. It precedes the sacred recitation of those place names that have football clubs, you're transported to where you were born. I love the fact that the signature tune sounds so dated. It's place, not race, that makes us British. I do hope "Out of the Blue" is never replaced.'

Well, it was for a time in the early seventies. The executives responsible waited until Angus Mackay retired in 1972, before thinking the unthinkable, then acting on it. Broadcasters, programmes and signature tunes don't die, they just decompose and some influential new brooms thought it was time to clear away the musical deadwood. A nondescript piece of up-tempo music replaced 'Out of the Blue' for the 1972–73 football season. Two of the programme's production team – John Taylor and Bryan Tremble – were asked by Mackay's successor, Bob Burrows, to come up with a replacement tune that reflected the current age, rather than the world of rationing, conscription and marching bands. They insist they were simply following instructions. Above their pay grade.

Fair enough. Desmond Lynam and Alan Parry were more voluble about the issue. Parry, a relative newcomer to the sports department, was aghast. 'I fell in love with "Out of the Blue" when I was at school, coming back from Anfield on a Saturday. The buses would line up outside the Kop, and everybody would race back in time for the start of *Sports Report*. Someone would have a transistor radio and we'd all stamp our feet on the floor in time. And then we'd keep quiet for the results and reports. It was part of the fabric of the programme and our childhoods, so I was horrified when they dropped the tune.'

Not as much as Des Lynam. After just a couple of years presenting the programme, Lynam was established as a brilliant performer, who brought added kudos to *Sports Report*'s 25-year history. But even his voice didn't prevail, initially. He broke ranks on the programme in April 1973, when he mentioned the absence of 'Out of the Blue' – 'Our old signature tune, which for some reason better known to others than to me, has gone out of the window.' He had used an interview with the ailing Raymond Glendenning as the peg for his strictures, as Glendenning – near the end of his life – reminisced fondly about presenting the very first *Sports Report* and cueing up that evocative signature tune. In his last interview, Glendenning mused, 'I still listened after I left the show. When I got into the car on a Saturday, I'd switch on *Sports Report* straight away – and there was the old familiar Dee-dum, dee-dum, dee-dum, dee-dum, dee diddely dum dee-dah. Oh yes…' And on those final words, Bryan Tremble faded up the strains of 'Out of the Blue'. It was a poignant moment, a fitting tribute to a major sports broadcaster, who was just 66 when he died of a heart attack. Glendenning's valedictory tribute hit home, accelerating the re-think about the signature tune. Lynam's gentle coaxing of his illustrious predecessor was masterful and he knew that he could get away with his barbed comment at the end of the interview, because it was live on air.

He didn't let the matter rest. He and Parry, backed up by the bulk of the sports department, mobilised support for reinstatement. Lynam's plea to management – 'You wouldn't knock down Tower Bridge and replace it with some monstrous reinforced concrete edifice simply because it's old-fashioned, would you? Well, don't tamper with this. It's part of the fabric of sports broadcasting. A tradition'– struck a chord with the suits, possibly because it came from such an invaluable, accomplished representative of the department. The *Guardian*'s Frank Keating, always a generous supporter of *Sports Report*, weighed in with several columns that lamented the absence of 'Out of the Blue'.

At that time, in the early seventies, there was enormous public affection for that signature tune. Barry Hines, author, playwright, screenwriter – notably of that wonderful 1969 film, *Kes*, with football featuring largely – captured the appeal of 'Out of the Blue' in his 1971 novel, *The Blinder*…

'They turned down Sloame Street… and the same tune muffled through the walls as they passed from house to house, fading then swelling between the space of each lighted window. "Hey up, Dad, that's *Sports Report*, I'll race you."'

Alan Parry, may not have read *The Blinder*, but he was a doughty debater on all issues in the department, as befitting a voluble Scouser, and had no qualms about taking on the management. 'We didn't need any focus groups to tell us it was a daft decision. So after we presented our case, Bob Burrows asked a meeting of the department for their views and all were in agreement we should bring back 'Out of the Blue'. Why lose something that was perfect?'

It was then just a case of the relevant management hoping the issue would simply fade away and reinstating 'Out of the Blue' for the new season. But make sure it hits the airwaves perfectly at the first time of asking. That responsibility lay with Dave Gordon. Later the programme's producer, he eventually became the editor of BBC TV's *Grandstand*, so he has enough memorable moments to savour, but the day he pressed the appropriate button to restore 'Out of the Blue' stands out.

'I was the studio manager that day, responsible for playing it. There had to be a two seconds' delay to allow BBC local radio stations to join us for the start of *Sports Report*, including the music. I'd better get this right, I thought, and I could feel Bob Burrow's eyes boring into my back. I felt quite nervous, knowing that the tune had been absent for so long – Lord knows why. It was now restored to its rightful place. Having been associated with two sports programmes with a great history – *Sports Report*, then *Grandstand*, I look back on that day in the radio studio with pride.'

Yet two decades later, the barbarians were at the gate again, although they were seen off with due despatch. Larry Hodgson, a veteran of the news division, had come in as the new head of sport and outside broadcasts and, as usual with new management, wished to make an early impression with a raft of seemingly far-sighted decisions. He floated the notion of dropping 'Out of the Blue' to modernise the programme's sound, but soon withdrew.

Gill Pulsford, who began on *Sports Report* as a production assistant in 1979, had risen deservedly through the ranks to become producer. 'My reaction was "over my dead body" – not a hope. "Out of the Blue" would be one of my desert island discs.' Mike Lewis, Editor, Sport, counselled Hodgson against such an extreme decision. 'I told him how many of us had grown up with the signature tune, that it really was an important part of *Sports Report*. Larry thought it a bit old-fashioned. I said, "True – it's not Kylie Minogue," but to fair to him, he could've said, "I'm the head of the department, we're doing it" – but he listened to us.'

Bob Shennan, then the programme's editor, says of the tune, 'It signifies a moment, it's a shared reference point right across the country, a common bond between a radio programme and its listeners. Yes, it sounds out of time, but it gives *Sports Report* status and longevity. Anyone meddling with it would be crazy.' Hopefully future mandarins in charge of *Sports Report* will eschew any temptation to indulge in virility tests of their managerial mettle.

There was just one more day when millions of listeners thought the charmed life enjoyed for decades by 'Out of the Blue' had come to an end and an illustrious page really had been turned. It was 5 January 2013, the programme's 65th birthday, and the third round of the FA Cup, usually *Sports Report's* busiest Saturday and the one most insiders look forward to above all others. Drama, human interest stories, late winners, heartbreak – a genuine test of the production team's fast footwork and experience.

It's a day the producer Graham McMillan will never forget. 'It'll be on my gravestone,' he ruefully admits, 'and in the first paragraph of any BBC obit about me.' It was the day when the wrong music was played at the top of *Sports Report*, prompting a blizzard of social media messages that 'Out of the Blue' had been sensationally dropped, without the listeners' knowledge. In the words of that day's presenter, Mark Pougatch, 'The public thought the ravens had finally left the Tower.' Nick Robinson, one of the *Today* programme's presenters and a massive fan of *Sports Report*, even tweeted 'I can't believe they've axed the *Sports Report* signature tune.'

The truth is more prosaic. It was a cock-up. And the two senior members of the production team, with 25 years combined on the programme, put their hands up and admitted as much. When you consider the build-up to the 5 p.m. start, it's amazing that such a human error hadn't happened before in 65 years. Pougatch had been whizzing around that afternoon, starting at Brighton then off to Crawley, in search of a classic FA Cup giant-killing. He would present the show from there – always a fraught scenario, with his producer in the Salford studio and the lines of communication stretched, the hastily scribbled links to the headlines and reports coming through on his tablet. With 29 Cup games being played that day, the scope for mishaps was tangible.

At 4.55 p.m., McMillan justifiably zipped the show around the big stories of the day for final scores. Underneath a bed of mundane, fast tempo music, he went to Macclesfield v Cardiff (featuring two late goals for Macclesfield, to win it), then to Luton, where Jonathan Overend did a burst of live commentary as non-League Luton closed out the win over Wolves, 59 league places above the victors. Two big stories. With Pougatch frantically rewriting his headlines at 4.59 p.m., Overend wrapped up his piece just in time for a seamless handover to his presenter. 'So

Mark – two big shocks today, then.' Just in time for a quick promotional trail then, bang on 5 p.m., Pougatch announced it was time for *Sports Report*.

Cue the famous signature tune. Except something else came on air. It was the dance band music that had been the bed for the quick whizz around a few grounds at 4.55 p.m., covering the shocks of the day. It had been so frantic in the studio that the producer and studio manager had neglected to check that the tape console had been updated. It hadn't. 'Out of the Blue' wasn't in its customary position and the relevant button hadn't been pre-set.

Pougatch, presenting from Crawley, just ploughed on with the headlines, over a bed of music totally unfamiliar to him. McMillan, aware that the buck stopped with him, had to take instant decisions. 'It's amazing how many conversations you can have in about eight seconds. We all looked at each other, wondering what had happened. I decided against playing in "Out of the Blue" over the new, unfamiliar music and just opted for getting it done and moving on. It would've sounded awful doing that. As McMillan tried to unscramble his brains, the editor of the sports department texted, 'I only need to know one thing – that it wasn't deliberate.' After reassuring the boss there hadn't been a palace coup, one of McMillan's production team, who was a brilliant techy, got on to social media and tweeted, "We haven't forgotten it – here's a reminder of the *Sports Report* theme tune," and played a clip of "Out of the Blue".

'We decided not to refer to the mistake after James Alexander Gordan had finished reading the results and waited until Mike Ingham handed back to us at six o'clock at half-time in the West Ham game. Then Mark Pougatch said from Crawley "The time is now 6 o'clock and I promise you... this really is *Sports Report*." My heart was in my mouth at the gap between those words and the music coming through my headphones. I just couldn't make the same mistake twice. I let out an enormous sigh of relief.

'The news spread like wildfire among the Twitterati. I even got a text from a former producer of the programme, who was on holiday in Spain, wondering what was going on. So many were aghast that we'd supposedly dropped the signature tune without telling anyone. The truth is that it was simply a glitch.'

When McMillan turned up at the Monday meeting, he was greeted with a ribald round of applause, tinged with sympathy. Those on the production team knew it could easily have been one of them. 'Let's hope no one ever makes that mistake ever again. You tamper at your peril with "Out of the Blue". But the public reaction showed how many are emotionally attached to it and the programme.'

Steve Rosenberg will vouch for that. As the BBC's Moscow editor, he loves getting his weekly fix of sport on a Saturday evening, three hours ahead of the 5.00 p.m. headlines. During the pandemic, unable to visit the UK, he felt the stabs of homesickness keenly and decided to pay tribute in a musical manner. Steve's an accomplished pianist and on social media he put out a clip of his rendition of 'Out of the Blue'. It was particularly moving, because he didn't go at a lick, like the usual marching bands, he took it slowly, accompanied by photos of James Alexander Gordon at his desk, ready to read the classified results.

'I hoped that worked because I wanted people to see their childhood in front of them as "Out of the Blue" slowly enveloped the senses. In my case, I was thinking of my grandfather and Dad, who shared my love of sport. I wanted that tweet to be a musical connection between the generations. Without "Out of the Blue", the programme would be like a Russian winter without snow.' Steve has had more than enough on his professional plate, covering the Ukraine war from Russia with such bravery and resolution, but for him *Sports Report* and its signature tune remain a vital connection to a happier world.

Lee Child, fabulously successful author of the Reacher novels, still an Aston Villa fan, thinks fondly of the signature tune from his home in Colorado. 'I love the BBC for sticking to the familiarity of "Out of the Blue". It takes courage not to follow a trend towards modernising. If you hear that signature tune, anywhere in the world, you think of going home or your loved ones.'

Hubert Bath, happily ignorant of sport, should nevertheless be content with his contribution, 17 years before the first edition of *Sports Report*. Of all the key components in the programme's history, a musician who died before it was even a mote in the producer's eye remains unheralded. I hope the royalty payments kept Dorothy Bath in a degree of comfort.

5

MEMORABLE PROGRAMMES
1948–1988

Over its 75 years, there have been around 3000 editions of *Sports Report*. Until August 1955, it ran for just half an hour, which seems staggering given the nationwide interest in sport and lack of many other social distractions. That time constraint over the first seven years of the programme would bring much aggravation to its producer, Angus Mackay, and grief to those hapless reporters and contributors who exceeded their allotted quota.

Countless editions were memorable for ground-breaking technical achievements, exclusive stories or captivating live studio discussions, the latter one of Mackay's favourite parts of any show. Others stay in the memory for sadder reasons.

One of the most salient areas of progress was that listeners could at last hear sports performers actually talk. Before *Sports Report*, those making the headlines were rarely heard. Deeds, definitely not words.

There would be the occasional stilted contribution on Pathé News, so that cinema patrons could hear a few hackneyed sentences delivered uncomfortably, without any warmth or insight. Len Hutton's shy, monosyllabic reaction to making a world record 364 against Australia in the 1938 Oval Test, reading a few sentences composed by a scriptwriter with no feel for sport, was a classic example. Usually, the Pathé News people made do with the footballer, jockey or tennis player grinning inanely at the camera, desperately willing the director to bark 'cut.'

Sports Report changed that outmoded notion. Angus Mackay wanted to sell sport to a receptive nation, who wanted to know more about the major sports stars – their accents, their sense of humour, their thoughts on their profession. He sought out those who had shone in their chosen sport and who would now be able to bring light and shade to a greater understanding of the pressures involved. People like Charles Buchan (football), Freddie Mills (boxing), Fred

Perry (tennis) and Harold Abrahams (athletics) brought a new dimension, shaped by their past experiences, to appreciating and relishing sport.

As a result, more and more current sporting luminaries came to trust the newcomer to the airwaves. They realised that, backed up by his coterie of former stars, Angus Mackay simply wanted increased passion in sports coverage, to shine a more penetrating light on a facet of post-war life that was becoming more and more important to the nation's wellbeing. The sympathetic, kind stewardship of Eamonn Andrews ensured the guests would be treated respectfully, with humour and time to state their opinions, without feeling they were on trial for their lives.

Mackay's obsession with getting to the warp and woof of sport was integral in establishing *Sports Report*'s reputation in the early 1950s. Within a few years it became a byword for broadcasting excellence. Memorable editions of the show tumbled over each other.

Boxing Day 1953: A special gabfest

The year 1953 was an historic one for sport, for both young and old. Nineteen-year-old Maureen Connolly became the first woman to win all four Grand Slam tennis tournaments in a calendar year, while 38-year-old Stanley Matthews finally picked up an FA Cup winner's medal, inspiring Blackpool to a famous 4–3 victory over Bolton Wanderers. England's cricketers retained the Ashes at the Oval, after a gap of 16 years.

Conversely, the national football team was humiliated at Wembley by Hungary, their 6–3 thrashing prompting an orgy of navel-contemplation and soul-searching that seemed to last for years. The citadel of certainty among England's football players, managers and fans was crumbling and a 7–1 hammering the following year, again by Hungary, prompted even more inquests – with *Sports Report*'s regular pundits weighing in forcefully.

In golf, Sam Snead inspired the United States to a one-point victory over Great Britain in the Ryder Cup, while in athletics, the Londoner, Jim Peters, became the first runner to complete a marathon in under two hours 20 minutes. He improved on his world record the following year.

More than enough, then, for Angus Mackay to get his teeth into as he planned a special *Sports Report* to mark an illustrious sporting year. He managed to coax an extra half-hour out of the BBC schedulers and the programme went out on Boxing Day.

Mackay was determined to give all the major sports equal exposure. Boxing, highly popular in Britain at the time, was represented by Freddie Mills, a former world champion and natural radio performer, for whom the term 'colourful' was hardly adequate. Freddie had just retired, but his amusing, outspoken take on the boxing scene made him a valued, regular guest on *Sports Report*. Cricket was represented by the England captain, Len Hutton, and his great bowler, Alec Bedser, who had taken 39 wickets in the historic Ashes series. Stanley Matthews, of course, represented football.

The roll call of 22 to be interviewed by Eamonn Andrews was an autograph hunter's delight, but how would Mackay manage to do them all justice in an hour? By the rigorous attention to detail that had already become the Mackay trademark. He prepared seven (!) foolscap pages, outlining questions that could be put to everyone inside the allotted time – but only given to the chosen 22 just before they went on air.

The last guest was to be Gordon Richards, the great jockey, who had finally ridden his first Derby winner at the age of 39, in the week he learned he would be knighted for his services to horse racing. The son of a Shropshire miner, who had won his first race in 1921, champion jockey 26 times and the first jockey to be knighted, Sir Gordon was the ideal choice to round off this star-laden celebratory programme.

There was just one problem – and a rare one for the enemy of time to confront. Mackay's timings were awry for once. The previous 21 luminaries had been scrupulous in observing the need for brevity – Mackay's writ ran far and wide in those days! Sir Gordon had around five minutes to play with and, although he was always a superb ambassador for horse racing, invariably happy to oblige reporters, Mackay reasoned it would sound odd that he had more time than the others, irrespective of his *annus mirabilis*. Mackay took a punt. Was Lady Richards on hand? She was, listening to *Sports Report* next door at their home in Marlborough. Could she oblige with a few thoughts on this momentous year for her husband? No problem. She came to the microphone and rounded off the programme perfectly. Mackay later wrote, 'It was for me, personally, one of the most enjoyable broadcasts it has been my duty to produce.'

One quibble about that Boxing Day show: Lady Richards was the first woman to be heard on it. So, in the year our new monarch just happened to be female, no British sportswomen had achieved anything of note? That particular nettle would take decades to grasp.

1958: The Munich Air Disaster

Just two days after the dreadful plane crash that claimed 23 lives, Angus Mackay and Eamonn Andrews had to attempt to do justice to such an enormous news story, as well as handle their own personal grief.

Eight Manchester United players and eight football journalists were among those who died that snowy afternoon in Munich, as the plane vainly tried to take off. The United manager Matt Busby remained critically ill – happily recovering later – while Duncan Edwards, surely destined to be one of the great England players, eventually succumbed at the age of just 21.

It was, of course, a tragedy for all those grieving, but *Sports Report* had to deal with it compassionately, yet with some semblance of insight, and come to terms with the death of three distinguished journalists in particular. Frank Swift, the former Manchester City and England goalkeeper – by now a columnist with the *News of the World* – the *Guardian*'s Donny Davies and Henry Rose of the *Daily Express* were regulars on *Sports Report*.

Swift's newspaper was read by up to eight million people on a Sunday and, a genial approachable man, he was always a welcome guest on *Sports Report*, modestly deflecting the acclaim due to one of England's greatest goalkeepers. Rose, a flamboyant figure accustomed to doling out provocative opinions in his columns without bothering with a contrary view, deliberately courted controversy. In his pomp, he had the widest-read sports column in British journalism and his funeral attracted one of the largest number of mourners seen in Manchester.

But the loss of Donny Davies was felt most keenly. He had been almost a constant presence on *Sports Report* since its inception. Mackay respected his scholarship, witty command of the English language and evident love of football and cricket, his two favourite sports. Michael Parkinson, growing up in Barnsley in the 1950s, wondering if he would ever manage to break through into journalism, revered Donny Davies.

'He inspired a generation of young journalists by proving it was possible to create literature out of reporting a sporting event. No matter how good he was on the page – and you could smell Old Trafford when he described it – the addition of his voice brought the prose to life. Then you could touch the crowd, hear the jokes, taste the hot pot.'

Donny's death was a shattering blow to Mackay and Andrews, but they simply had to honour him and the others who had perished at Munich just two days earlier. On the Saturday show Mackay turned to a journalist who could normally be guaranteed to lift the most lugubrious of spirits, but Geoffrey Green was struggling with grief and guilt. The *Times'* football correspondent was due to accompany his friends on that flight, but he had been over-ruled by his sports editor. He told Andrews, 'I had the tickets for the Manchester United game and was all set to go, but I was told it was too expensive and they sent me to Cardiff instead, to cover Wales v Israel. I feel I should be among those missing.'

No wonder Angus Mackay warmed to him. And after his own brush with the Grim Reaper in the Barnes train crash just over two years earlier, he could relate to the grieving over Munich. That Saturday programme on 8 February 1958 was one that had to be tackled with as much respect and affection as possible.

1964: Cassius Clay helps break new ground

In February of that year, the brash upstart that was Cassius Clay was preparing to fight the brooding ogre Sonny Liston for the world heavyweight title in Miami. Angus Mackay was determined that *Sports Report* would mark the fight in historic fashion.

Mackay had been fascinated by Clay, ever since he won the Olympic title and then came over to London in the summer of '63, stopping Henry Cooper after he'd been ingloriously dumped on the canvas. He loved Clay's chutzpah and his remarkable public relations antennae, and he also sensed that the Louisville Lip could become one of the all-time greats of the fight game – a sentiment with which Clay could only agree.

Mackay decided that, for the first time, *Sports Report* would be broadcast in its entirety from abroad. He knew he had to get the engineers and technical maestros on board for such a daunting challenge. Luckily, those worthies had developed an excellent working relationship with Mackay, admiring his questing imagination, confidence in the face of daunting challenges and his readiness to buy them drinks in the BBC Club.

In Eamonn Andrews he had a presenter steeped in boxing, his favourite sport. He also approached Harry Carpenter, late of the *Sports Report* parish, then building an impressive career in televised boxing, but respectful enough of the programme to get fully involved for over a week in the United States.

They were despatched, seven days before the fight, gathering interviews and taking the temperature of a sporting encounter that had gripped the nation. In the aftermath of President Kennedy's assassination the previous November, the States needed some collective distractions. The remarkable impact of the Beatles over there and the Clay/Liston fight would help.

Lillian Lang, the BBC's producer at the New York bureau, helped set up the circuits at her end, willingly traversing new territory for such a programme. She established a studio in Miami, connected to her in New York, which in turn went straight through to Broadcasting House. 'Angus had masterminded a deaf aid instrument, whereby he could pass on information, live, to Eamonn from London. At the time it was a remarkable innovation. Soon it became part of our broadcasting lives, but it was a thrill to be there at the beginning.'

Harry Carpenter loved the pioneering nature of that programme. 'We got to the Miami studio in a taxi, dodging the fallen trees from a recent storm, wondering if the whole thing would work. The local radio people were astounded at our optimism, but, against all the odds, it worked. Angus would give me instructions into my deaf aid and I'd pass notes over to Eamonn – including all the links to football and rugby matches just finished in the UK. Eamonn handled it all brilliantly, with great command, but plaudits to Angus. He was a technical genius who pioneered so much in radio sports broadcasting.'

Frank Butler, sports editor of the *News of the World*, an old friend of the programme, was also in the studio to preview the fight and, years later, he would give due credit to Eamonn's faith in Clay and belief that he would cause a sensation. 'Eamonn was the only one who though Liston could be beaten. The rest of us just wouldn't have it.' Harry Carpenter agreed. 'Clay was perceived as a bizarrcly talented whippersnapper, who could move nicely, but whose mouth was considerably larger than his ability.'

And the 7-1 outsider vindicated the Andrews hunch, stopping Liston after six rounds, as he sat on his stool and refused to come out for the next round. Eamonn's biggest challenge at ringside wasn't commentating on the fight, it was getting into the ring amid all the pandemonium, trying to get a live interview with the new champion. 'I was the first reporter to get into the ring, dodging so many cops. I had a bigger fight there than Liston put up!'

1964: Eamonn's farewell

It had to happen eventually. Angus Mackay had done a herculean job keeping the most popular broadcaster of his generation in the seat for so long. It certainly wasn't the money that kept Eamonn there for so many years – he was well aware of the Mackay parsimony – but finally, in April 1964, Eamonn could resist the call of television no more.

His farewell programme was handled with Eamonn's usual grace and charm. The great and the good chipped in with fond anecdotes and Mackay played in a few telling contributions from the archives. The late Donny Davies on the genesis of football's appeal struck a chord with this listener at the time and his lament seems even more prescient today, in a period where Mammon bestrides the football landscape, 'Association football was largely the creation of the industrial working class – in grim places, you need football. We used to play for hours on end in side streets and passages, often with a tennis ball. The industrial working class brought the game out of dark streets and cinders wastes and sent it triumphantly all over the world.'

Eamonn was just about holding it together near the end, hailing *Sports Report* as, 'Still the most under-rehearsed programme in existence. How I'll miss it.' He said his biggest wrench would be parting company with the production team, 'who did most of the work while I received all the praise.' After handing over to John Webster, 'who'll read the classified football results in his own inimitable fashion,' Eamonn steeled himself for his pay-off line, aware that the gimlet-eyed Mackay would still be judging his words acutely. Eamonn didn't disappoint...

'Now the dustsheets are off, hands are on the switches – just time for a final goodbye. My first engagement with the 5 o'clock show was made over a glass of beer in 1950 with Angus Mackay, one of the greats in radio broadcasting – the only difference today is that every man jack of the outfit is set to join us. It's going to end the same way. We'll toast your good health and hope the sun shines for you always. Goodbye.'

And the strains of 'Out of the Blue' were faded up to close the show.

1971: The Ibrox Disaster

The biggest crowd disaster in British football at the time happened with very few of the 80,000 crammed into Ibrox knowing about it. And *Sports Report* was understandably slow to gather live reports on the unfolding tragedy, unlike Heysel and Hillsborough in the next decade, when technical communications had improved markedly. But eventually the programme managed to flesh out the bare details of the horrific events unfolding at 4.45 p.m. on a freezing, misty January afternoon in Glasgow.

The Rangers v Celtic match had ended in an inconsequential 1–1 draw, the late Rangers equaliser ensuring a share of the bragging rights with their rivals. But it was that goal which sparked off the nightmare, as thousands of fans on their way out of the packed stadium turned and crammed forward down stairway 13 to find out more and celebrate. Some pushed down the stairs, others resisted, trying to get back up and out of the crush. Some fans stumbled down the steps while others fell down on to them. Seven lanes divided by tubular steels rails buckled, then collapsed. White handkerchiefs were fluttered, desperately seeking assistance. Some died fully upright. Coins fell from victims' pockets as they were eventually carried away. In a space hardly larger than the 18-yard box, 66 died and more than 200 were injured. Half the victims were under the age of 20, the youngest only nine.

And yet most of the spectators at the ground were oblivious to the crush and fatalities. So many were just trying to get out of Ibrox. Roddy Forsyth, *Sports Report*'s Scotland reporter for more than 30 years, was at the match, aged 16, with his father. 'He had told me never to use stairway 13, because it was rundown and a hazard, with broken steps. There'd been a crush there in 1961, when two died. I used stairway 19, because it was closer to the underground station and the supporters' coaches. We knew nothing about what was happening on stairway 13.'

Jack Pirrie, who was covering the match for *Sports Report*, filed three despatches for the programme. He was cognisant of Angus Mackay's advice when he started reporting for *Sports Report* – 'Speak slower, Jack, they might struggle to understand you down here in England' – so he was careful to weigh his words judiciously and avoid sensationalism. One of his live reports began.

'From where I'm sitting high up in the press box, I can see through the darkness and the fog ambulances alongside the goalposts. There are sirens wailing outside. Everything is turmoil. Now they're bringing them across the field on stretchers and the kiss of life's being given by ambulance people. Stretcher bearers are running into the tunnel. The latest fatalities I'm hearing is 16, but there's just no saying how many there have been.' Sadly, Jack's estimate of the dead proved conservative and as *Sports Report* went off air at 6.00 p.m. the scale of the tragedy began to take shape.

That night, television began to react. On BBC 1, the newsreader Kenneth Kendall appeared between editions of *Dr Who* and *The Generation Game*, bringing the sombre news. No footage of the disaster exists, because the TV outside broadcast unit packed up on the final whistle and decamped swiftly. It was, after all, the festive period in Scotland and initially there was no suggestion anything untoward had happened. Newspaper stills remain the only evidence of the horror on stairway 13.

1972: Angus Mackay's farewell

He didn't really want to go, but Angus had already winkled two extra years out of the top brass, to help a reorganisation and streamlining of the sports department. He had fought hard for the interests of Bob Burrows and Cliff Morgan, two lieutenants he could totally trust, and he was reassured that they would be at the helm when he left. The programme would be in safe, sensitive and dynamic hands. And it was.

Eamonn Andrews was brought back to present the last hurrah, as was John Webster, retired two years, to read the classified football results. Des Lynam, by now the established and worthy successor to Eamonn, was content to report on Division One and Two matches, while Alan Parry did the honours for Divisions Three and Four, singling out at an attendance of 37,000 at Villa Park – for a Third Division match!

For the first and only time, *Sports Report* exceeded its duration of an hour, as so many celebrities trooped in and out of the studio over 90 minutes or joined the programme from an outside broadcast. Brian Moore recalled Angus not speaking to him for a couple of weeks, because he was seven minutes late for the Monday meeting. Henry Cooper called *Sports Report*, 'My lucky programme – whenever I was asked to go in to plug my next fight in a few days I would win.' They linked Henry up with his most illustrious opponent and Muhammad Ali didn't disappoint with his banter. 'I was just starting to do my road work and I said cancel it for the next two hours when I heard Angus and Eamonn wanted me.'

Harold Abrahams, Olympic sprint gold medallist in 1924, BBC reporter at the 1936 Olympics and an athletics journalist for 48 years paid rueful tribute to the Mackay discipline. 'I believe I have been on *Sports Report* around 200 times and, because of Angus, I always have a stopwatch in my pocket. I learned never to use two words when one would do.' David Coleman bemoaned Angus' retirement, 'I'm astonished, it just shouldn't be allowed.'

The leading football administrators queued up to laud the programme and its producer – Sir Stanley Rous from FIFA, Denis Follows from the FA and the

Football League's Alan Hardaker. Normally one to out-curmudgeon Angus Mackay, Hardaker was surprisingly benign about *Sports Report*. 'It has been an example of the right way to report on football. I've never known it to set a trap for players in interviews.'

One name was missing from the roll call of illustrious contributors – Angus Mackay. He steadfastly refused to talk, determined there'd be no publicity. He even tore a strip off his trusted consigliere, Bob Burrows, because the backroom staff were given two bottles of champagne in the sports room to toast the old boy. 'I protested that they'd been working their socks off for the programme, but Angus wouldn't have it. He didn't like drink around the place or any of the fuss and nonsense. Extraordinary man. He had a lasting effect on everybody who ever worked for him. You always knew people who had worked for Angus, because they remembered his rules. He could reduce you to tears, then be amazed to find you crying.'

Angus lived for another 20 years after he retired and his daughter, Sheena, struggled to glean any of his thoughts on later eras of *Sports Report*. 'He'd sit there listening intently, but he never gave his opinions. I couldn't tell what he was thinking. His hearing deteriorated badly after he retired. One eardrum collapsed – must have been all those years with a phone clamped to it! So it was sometimes difficult to talk to him.'

He was a proud old so-and-so, never craving the limelight, always striving for perfection. But even he, with his 36 years' service at the BBC, must have realised how special it was to have a 90-minute programme dedicated to its producer and guiding light. Not that Angus Mackay would ever acknowledge that.

1973: Bobby Charlton's final game

English football's greatest ambassador played his 604th and final League game at Stamford Bridge in front of 44,000 people, with the gates locked an hour before kick-off. The programme selected Geoffrey Green, a huge admirer of Charlton and the Manchester United heritage, to sign off a wonderful career.

In a sign of the times, Charlton was presented with a silver cigarette box by the Chelsea chairman – hardly an expensive outlay, especially as, in an age when so many players smoked, Charlton's living room was probably awash with them.

Green called the match 'lazy and dozy' and seemed unwilling to pay due homage to such a great player. 'He did a lap of honour by himself, followed by a crowd of around a thousand kids, like the pied piper of Hamlyn.' And that was it. No interview with Charlton. Just time for a couple of waspish asides from the unpredictable Green. He made it clear what he thought of United's voluble, media-friendly United manager, Tommy Docherty. 'I can see him down there on the pitch, waffling away like a mini-Napoleon,' while he dismissed the United side as, 'almost as unpredictable as a woman,' an aside that told you more about Geoffrey Green's antediluvian social views than the growing support for feminism in 1973, just two years before Margaret Thatcher became leader of the Conservative party.

Bobby Charlton shared the *Sports Report* headlines with Liverpool, as they sealed another title win. The programme started with an atmospheric mix – Desmond Lynam cueing up the voice of Peter Jones saying 'Bill Shankly is still in the Kop,' then fading up the strains of 'You'll Never Walk Alone', with Jones returning to say, 'Bill Shankly has stayed with the supporters and he's waving to his team,' followed by more of 'You'll Never Walk Alone'. It was an arresting, moving opener, typical of the imagination of the brilliant producer, Bryan Tremble.

In the next decade, Tremble would finesse *Sports Report* with many clever packages that grabbed attention. By common consent, he had a great 'ear', knowing what would work on radio, with judicious use of relevant music and sharp editing. Later in this edition, he produced a masterly review of the 1972–73 sporting season, narrated by Lynam, covering everything from a Shankly interview – 'My players give it to the nearest red jersey and go from there – we don't believe in fancy tricks, we believe in simplicity' – to the doyenne of newspaper columnists Jean Rook fulminating at 'the thoroughly aggravating George Best, with his white Rolls-Royce and girls at his feet' to Eric Morecambe describing his sorrow at a defeat for Luton Town – 'It affects me more than money affects Ernie.' The prime minister, Edward Heath, talked about his passion for sailing – 'It's not enough to lie around in the sun, I have to be stretched in a different direction.' Tony Lewis, England's cricket captain on their recent tour to India gave a fascinating insight into the pressure on umpires over there, while Muhammad Ali, never slow to appear on *Sports Report*, sent a message to the new heavyweight hope of British boxing, Joe Bugner, 'I want to come over and wipe him out because this is my world. I want to prove I'm still the greatest.'

It was a tight review, with barely a superfluous word from Lynam and a subtle mix of music. It ended with a poignant clip from Raymond Glendenning. Within a few months of his death, sounding frail but still alert, he told Des

Lynam he still listened to the show and hummed the famous signature tune. It was the perfect 'out' to the package and as 'Out of the Blue' played, Lynam made his subversive comment about it being dropped at the start of the football season. It was brave of him and it worked. New brooms were set to sweep elsewhere and the old order was restored.

But nostalgia didn't dominate that particular programme. Peter Jones tracked down Kevin Keegan as Liverpool's players celebrated (Jones was rewarded with the unusual view that 'Everyone's over the moon'), Jon Hughes reported from Elland Road that Jack Charlton was out of next week's FA Cup Final with a hamstring strain and Leeds' opponents Sunderland had a serious doubt over their goalkeeper, Jim Montgomery. Their manager Bob Stokoe came on air live to reveal Montgomery's ankle injury and forecast, 'I feel we can give them something to talk about next week.' He was as good as his word, as Sunderland secured a famous triumph, with the recovered Montgomery making an historic double save to deny Trevor Cherry and Peter Lorimer.

Jimmy Sirrell, basking in Notts County's promotion from Division Three, let slip 'Christ' in his interview with Des Lynam, prompting a stifled splutter from the urbane presenter, Jack Pirrie reported on Celtic's eighth successive title win, with a youngster called Kenny Dalglish scoring, and Brian Johnston filed from Worcester, describing Glenn Turner's 143 against the touring New Zealanders, an opening salvo from Turner that saw him eventually reach the rare feat of a thousand runs in May.

Ten minutes of the programme were swallowed up by the results from five meetings, the latest cricket scoreboard and the second reading of the classified football results. I cannot imagine how Bryan Tremble and his production team managed to cram so much into one hour. It was a tour de force, with news, comment, a season's review and important interviews all shoehorned in, without any sign of panic, all expertly helmed by Des Lynam. Listening at home, a year into his retirement, Angus Mackay would surely have conceded that his beloved programme was in good hands.

1981: Bob Champion wins the Grand National

Normally, the winning horse in the world's most famous horse race would garner most of the headlines, but the 1981 National was truly special for Bob Champion.

The National invariably throws up an emotional story, but this time, it was a case of 'Who writes your scripts, Bob?' Never has it been won by a jockey who had beaten cancer, when a year earlier, at Aintree, he looked as if his time would soon be up. Aldaniti, the winning horse, was a down-page story compared to Champion.

In July 1979, aged 31 and at the peak of his career, Bob had been diagnosed with testicular cancer. He also developed cancer in his lymph nodes and the omens were not propitious. He was invited to Aintree for the 1980 Grand National coverage by BBC Radio, to give insights into the big race. It also helped to take his mind off his painful treatment. Des Lynam remembered how shocked he was when he first saw Bob. 'He looked like death. You'd never believe that he'd be the hero next year. What a story that was. It was fantastic to interview him as the winning jockey.'

Des' producer Bryan Tremble, while totally sympathetic to Bob's condition, correctly reasoned that he wouldn't want to be treated with kid gloves. So he deputed his racing reporter, Derek Thompson, to take Bob out the day before to look at the fences and describe the challenges faced by the jockeys in the National. It worked a treat. Thompson, a naturally jolly, ebullient character, got the best out of Bob and the revealing interview was an essential part of the next day's coverage, with Bob on hand in the makeshift studio before and after the race. Bob had been a terrific guest, even though the circumstances were so challenging for him. But no one would bet against him being there next year, never mind wearing the laurel wreath of victory.

Astonishingly, Aldaniti and Champion won it and afterwards Bob sat in the studio, reminiscing with Des about his morale a year earlier and just how far he had come on this remarkable journey. Peter Bromley, as ever the race's main commentator, presented Bob with his race card – a thing of beauty, with its assorted jockey's colours and notes on each horse, in his immaculate hand. It was always Peter's gift to the winning jockey, but never was it appreciated more than by Bob Champion.

And Peter Bromley never missed a beat as he called the horses home in the 1981 National. He was too experienced a hand to miss the significance of the finish. 'Aldaniti wins it for Bob Champion!' he roared out in his familiar controlled excitement. Peter knew that, for once, it was a jockey's day not the horse's.

1988: The 40th anniversary show

This was the first time *Sports Report* was presented by a dapper gentleman in a dinner jacket (Peter Jones), ditto for the classified football results (James Alexander Gordon), with the producer (Rob Hastie) similarly clad in the studio. And, for good measure, the key moment in the programme was introduced on BBC TV's *Grandstand* by a *Sports Report* alumnus (Des Lynam).

As Lynam and Jones reminisced genially, the television presenter remembered his training at the feet of Angus Mackay and cued up Peter perfectly...

'How many seconds now, Peter, before that famous old music?'

'Twelve seconds, Des.' And with typical panache, Peter cued up an historic *Sports Report*, bang on the second. And sports fans, both on television and radio, joined for a vintage moment, serenaded by 'Out of the Blue'.

It was generous of television to acknowledge the 40th birthday, something that's sometimes honoured more in the breach than the observance in the guerrilla warfare that is sports broadcasting. Considering that *Sports Report* graduates teemed through TV Centre in those days, a nod in the direction of a famous landmark was the least it deserved.

Nostalgia isn't what it used to be, the old saw has it, but that 40th anniversary edition had a fair old stab at it. Illustrious names popped in and out of the programme. Fred Perry, then still the last British male Wimbledon singles champion called from Beverly Hills, California, Cliff Morgan was his usual lyrical self ('*Sports Report* reached out and touched a nation, made you think and wonder and smile'), Roy Hattersley, deputy leader of the Labour Party, recalled dashing home from Hillsborough to hear how Nottingham Forest, his dad's team, had fared.

Distinguished newspaper columnists Patrick Collins, Michael Parkinson and Geoffrey Green sprinkled their distinctive stardust; Denis Law confided 'I played at the nicest time'; and Stuart Hall recalled the days when 'all centre-forwards had Brylcreemed hair and a centre parting' while his match report from Maine Road suggested that Manchester City's home defeat by Shrewsbury Town in front of just 21,455 was 'bread and margarine rather than stuffed swan and Gevrey-Chambertin'. One of Shrewsbury's goalscorers, a young centre-half called David Moyes, was as 'alone as Greta Garbo on 42nd Street' when he scored.

Harry Carpenter, joining the programme from TV Centre, paid graceful tribute to Eamonn Andrews, who had died just two months earlier. 'One of the greatest pros of our time' was Harry's opinion, in contrast to a letter Eamonn received after his first stab at football commentary on BBC Radio, 'Our great national game should not be brought to the nation by an Irishman with a North American accent.' As Harry pointed out, it was fortunate that wasn't a view shared by Angus Mackay. 'He laid the foundations for all of us in sport with his insistence on crisp reporting. He taught us so much.' Typically, Angus had resisted the entreaties of Peter Jones and refused to give an interview for this celebratory programme. He had the great virtue of consistency...

Angus would have approved of the final contribution to that special programme – 'the 5 o'clock show' as he always called it. Mackay liked grit in the oyster, rather than too much showbiz schmaltz, and he would have surely purred at the opinion piece from Ian Wooldridge, a guest on the programme many times and a dedicated pourer of cold water on any grandiose notions in sport.

Wooldridge looked ahead to how sport would be reported in 2028, 40 years on, and he was characteristically acerbic, 'The football authorities say they're pleased that only 83 players were sent off today... There was a small riot in the Karachi Test. Not many dead.' He was 'grimly pessimistic' about the impact on TV and regretted the decline of the genuine amateur, while pleading for 'some more worthy administrators, because sport has fallen into some dubious hands.'

It was a bleak, dystopian piece, typical of the individualism that made Wooldridge such a valued contributor to *Sports Report*. And it was fitting to inject a hard-nosed note into the celebratory proceedings. Geoffrey Green said near the end, 'It was all fun and laughter – let's go on with the play.' But don't ignore the realities of sport.

* * *

Amid this panegyric to *Sports Report*, it's instructive to post a jarring note. It would be remiss to ignore the coverage of the Bradford Fire in May 1985. On 13 May, the Monday morning meeting to discuss the weekend's sporting output was dominated by one question. Why didn't *Sports Report* cover the Bradford tragedy properly? It was a serious fault by the sports department that Saturday, when 56 spectators died and over 250 were injured as fire swept through the Valley Parade stadium. It started just after half-time and within minutes the main stand was engulfed by fire and smoke. It proved to be the worst sporting tragedy in England at that time, only surpassed in Britain by the Ibrox disaster in January 1971. From a journalistic point of view, *Sports Report* caught up with the developing Ibrox horror before the programme went off air at 6.00 p.m. Not so with Bradford. ITV's *World of Sport* and BBC TV's *Grandstand* carried horrific footage after 4.00 p.m. on the day, while Yorkshire TV covered the match for its Sunday afternoon *The Big Match* show. *Sports Report* proved to be lamentably slow, just delivering agency reports from the Broadcasting House studio.

Ian Darke, the presenter that day, calls it 'the worst day editorially in the programme's history. I felt responsible to an extent. We weren't the only ones to be slow, but at its best *Sports Report* would have got up to speed quickly. We alluded to a fire in the stand and referenced several casualties, but it took too long for news to filter through to us.'

The Monday morning meeting considered the extenuating circumstances. The programme had no reporter at the game – Bradford City had already won the Division Three title, opponents Lincoln City were mid-table and it was the final game of the season. BBC local radio was simply too busy to help and there were few journalists present to offer eyewitness accounts. Today, the prevalence of social media would mean a similar tragedy would be comprehensively covered, but in 1985 urgent communication with a Third Division club was scant. It seemed a routine, final-day scenario, with attention firmly on other issues higher up the football chain.

Yet Bradford 1985 marks a stain on *Sports Report*'s reputation. We didn't get to the story before the Sunday papers. We got off lightly in the eyes of Fleet Street, whose denizens were too busy reporting on the tragedy to spray vitriol in our direction. Homer nodded just this once, in my experience, but it was once too many and has to be acknowledged.

6

THE FRONT OF HOUSE

Presenters can sometimes just not fit the programme's ethos, simply not getting it. I am sure everyone in the back of the store has a jaundiced memory of a presenter in the shop window who just read the autocue as bidden or conducted desultory interviews. That has not been the case with *Sports Report*. All the presenters I have interviewed have used words such as 'privilege' and 'highlight of my career', and I see no reason to doubt their sincerity. The bar was raised exceedingly high by Eamonn Andrews in the fifties and sixties, and his successors were gratifyingly aware of that.

With such a programme, reacting smoothly and capably to fast-moving events inside an hour slot demands flexibility and an unhurried natural authority. Every presenter of *Sports Report* has experienced moments like that depicted by *The Scream*, Edvard Munch's masterly depiction of the anxiety of the human condition. Hands over ears, emitting a piercing scream that epitomises angst, every presenter had their Munch moments – if only for a few seconds at a time.

In the 75 years of *Sports Report*, there have been 11 presenters who could be deemed full-time and not on probation, with the producer keeping a sceptical eye on their progress. Eamonn Andrews, 'primus inter pares', a beacon of national popularity, did the job for 14 years, a remarkable tribute to Angus Mackay's persuasiveness and his close relationship with the most famous media figure in the land at the time.

The first to experience Louis XV's *après moi le deluge* moment after Eamonn departed for even more fame on TV was Robin Marlar, in August 1964. Whoever stepped up to the plate then was going to need a huge dollop of luck and immense natural ability. David Moyes, succeeding Sir Alex Ferguson at Manchester United, might relate to that.

Marlar just wasn't the answer. Not his fault – his talents lay elsewhere on the programme. For a decade, he had been a truculent contributor to Fleet Street's view of the sporting world – fearless, always appearing to be in a dreadful bate about something, cleaving to his producer's demand to ruffle the dovecotes. Mackay, admiring Marlar's wide vocabulary and abrasive contributions to studio debates, thought Robin would give the programme a new, more dynamic feel. A former captain of Sussex County Cricket Club and a regular on the cricket and rugby pages of the *Sunday Times*, in 1964 Robin had public traction, in print and radio.

But he lacked luck. The first programme, at the start of the football season, was a technical nightmare. The lines to and from the various outside broadcasts kept going down and the new presenter floundered in a situation that would have tested even his urbane and vastly experienced predecessor. The programme sounded flaky and ill-prepared, not at all like the Mackay/Andrews model, honed over the previous 14 years.

'It was a shambles. Angus was livid, sitting right alongside me. He took it as a personal insult and was furious at the technical people. I had no idea what was going on, linking to various reporters who no one could hear. I was bobbing along like a cork.'

Mackay persevered with his new charge, but after six more programmes conceded defeat. A new presenter was needed. 'Angus did me a favour, there wasn't a lingering death. I went back to my spiritual home at the *Sunday Times*, where I eventually clocked up 50 years.'

Robin continued to be a regular on the programme for the next decade, slotting back effortlessly into his role of gleefully tilting at Establishment windmills. His value was in the post-5.30 p.m. slots, not at the top of the hour, when mental clarity and swift verbal reactions were vital. Different skills, that's all.

So Mackay grappled with his succession plan. He now knew that a gifted polemicist, a Yorick who was 'wont to set the table on a roar' would be a gamble not worth taking. He needed a presenter with a slow heartbeat, verbal fluency and natural authority, who could talk coherently without any alarms, while various crises were dealt with on the other side of the glass. Over the next eight years before he retired, Mackay got those big calls right. His hunches were invariably on the money. Using the qualification of two years in the presenter's chair, the 10 regulars who succeeded Andrews have clocked up almost 56 years in the job. They all state categorically that the experience illuminated their careers.

Liam Nolan eased himself into the role with the minimum of fuss and the maximum of impact. He may have been just 32, but without realising it, he'd had an appointment with the task for a few years. Angus Mackay had observed him from a distance as Nolan filed rugby reports for the old Home Service. He was aware Nolan was a hungry fighter, who had steeled himself for a career in journalism after leaving home in County Cork at the age of 21. National Service, ending up as an Army lieutenant, then a dead-end job in an accounts department, had sharpened his ambitions even more, as he sensed that the clock was ticking inexorably. He landed a researcher's job on the hugely popular TV programme *This Is Your Life*, fronted by... Eamonn Andrews. The two had never met, but Liam sent a telegram to the great man, who suggested he contacted a colleague on the programme. After graduating to a senior writer's role, Liam enlisted Eamonn's advice about getting into sports broadcasting. 'Write to Angus Mackay,' he was told.

He did, and Mackay was impressed by his soft, lilting brogue and calmness at the microphone. This was not a fluke. 'I had grown up listening to the great broadcasting voices on the BBC. I'd done a fair amount of amateur dramatics, so I had the gift of the gab. I was also a voracious reader, so I think I had a good enough vocabulary to impress Mr Mackay.' And, in 1964, with so many broadcasters on BBC Radio still sounding as if they had taken courses in received pronunciation, filling in as courtiers to the monarchy, Liam's distinctive brogue was very attractive to Mackay, never an Establishment man.

As a freelance at Broadcasting House, Nolan took every job that came his way, with some more attractive than others. He was the first journalist to present the *Today* programme, impressing with his strong news sense, a salutary contrast to the bumbling of the entrenched presenter, Jack de Manio, whose speciality seemed to be misreading the studio clock and getting the names of his interviewees wrong.

Mackay had noted Liam's maturity in one so young and was aware that, specialising in athletics, boxing and rugby union, there was more to him than just football knowledge. And he always had a soft spot for wordsmiths. Liam had no thought at all about presenting *Sports Report*.

Given his natural modesty and charm, Liam made many friends in the sports room. He'd happily decamp to the BBC Club after 6.00 p.m. on a Saturday, enjoying the debriefing in a bibulous atmosphere, even though Liam didn't drink alcohol. John Arlott and Brian Johnston, regulars on *Sports Report*, would seek him out, regaling him with priceless anecdotes. Hugh McIlvanney, a brilliant sportswriter and resonant contributor of opinion pieces on the programme, was a particular favourite of Liam's. 'I loved their voices and opinions, so beautifully expressed. For me, every Saturday was a challenge as I strived to be the best I could.'

Liam's career in England seemed set fair by the end of the sixties. He had been offered the main presenter's job on the *Today* programme and even Angus Mackay was content with his second Irish presenter, but home beckoned and after a year of prevarication, he took a job with the state broadcaster, RTE, fronting their mid-morning show. Ratings soared, predictably.

'My time at RTE was wonderful, but as a sports broadcaster, I would say that presenting *Sports Report* was the very peak. Nerve, timing and accuracy were vital – every time I hear that signature tune, I get that tingle between my belly button and chest, and sometimes even further down!'

Given his talents, BBC Radio Sport was lucky to hold him for just four years. If you accept that the best *Sports Report* presenters have been gifted all-rounders, there's a case for saying that Liam Nolan was in the pantheon. Not that he would ever entertain such a grandiose notion.

Peter Jones was 35 before he broke into broadcasting and 38 when he presented *Sports Report* for the first time. That maturity helped invest his work with an authority that was unsurpassed in a brilliantly versatile broadcasting career. Peter's natural lucidity was burnished by a degree in modern languages from Cambridge University, then several years teaching at Kimbolton School and Bradfield College. He never appeared to suffer from nerves, either while broadcasting in front of a live audience or to millions with a microphone.

Peter Jones was, above all, the man for the big occasion. Away from sport, he was a veteran of royal weddings and state funerals, the Festival of Remembrance, royal tours and the State Opening of Parliament. In his 25 years in the sports department, no major sporting event seemed to take place without Peter in the commentary box.

Nobody from the sports room could match the depth of his body of work. And yet, as so often, it was a complete fluke that brought him into broadcasting. Peter was a highly talented teacher, but his heart was always in sport. He won a Cambridge soccer Blue and played for Swansea reserves, his hometown club, but it needed a chance encounter with Maurice Edelston to change his life.

Maurice was one of BBC Radio's regular football commentators in the sixties and after befriending him, Jones asked if he could put in a word for him at Broadcasting House. He had no formal training, just a deep love of the game and a winning personal manner that never left him.

Angus Mackay, that supreme talent spotter, appreciated Peter's obvious intelligence, desire to learn and willingness to keep his mouth shut when given invaluable advice. He took a chance on Peter and he joined the BBC as a sports assistant, doing the usual dogsbody tasks for a few months. It would be the last time Peter Jones was not in the fast lane.

Mackay soon realised that Jones needed practical experience at such a comparatively advanced age for a novitiate broadcaster. So, while fast-tracking him to the major commentating roles across a wide range of sports, from 1968 onwards he also developed him as a sports presenter. Mackay was impressed by Peter's style at the microphone in the studio – a light tone, the odd chuckle in his interviews, a breadth of descriptive skills, all delivered in the standard, clear English of an educated man.

His producer didn't want him to spend all his time on the road, covering the major events. He felt his developing authority would give a lustre to *Sports Report*, a feeling that, in Peter Jones' hands, the programme would sound special, an 'appointment to listen'. That was the USP of Peter Jones. We all admired Peter's knack of making any broadcast or programme sound as if it was the greatest yet. Miss it at your peril, you'll be sorry you didn't hear this if you turn off.

Peter was an old ham actor at times, but none of his colleagues minded that. He'd simply blossom in front of a microphone. He was a Barnum and Bailey figure, unashamedly milking the occasion, entreating you to, 'Roll up, roll up – come a little closer.' His style was Panglossian, romantic, boosterish. In Peter's eyes, he echoed Molière's Candide: all was for the best 'in the best of all possible worlds'.

He would never try to pin down an interviewee on *Sports Report*, partly due to a romanticised view of sport and his innate good manners, partly due to arriving lateish to the sports broadcasting party. Phil King, an, important senior member of the production team at the time, knows why Peter kept his sword in the scabbard. 'He had no journalistic training, unlike the rest of us, who were brasher and earthier, but not in the same class as Peter in front of a mic. That was fine, we had others who could do the hard interviews, while Peter laid on the waffly charm. And what charm!'

Jim Rosenthal, who later presented *Sports Report* with such distinction, admired Peter's chutzpah and style. 'He was a great showman, always full of energy, rubbing his hands with pleasure when we were about to go live at a football match together. "Make it sing, Rosey," he'd say to me. Peter wasn't a reporter and made no pretence about that, but he left me for dead as a wordsmith.

Top class. Today, with his good looks and unflappability, he'd be on TV in a heartbeat – and at the very top of the tree.'

Peter always appeared unenamoured by the lure of television. 'We paint better pictures on radio,' he'd say and certainly no one did that better, in studio or commentary box. Sadly, those priceless descriptive skills were deployed in the most harrowing fashion towards the end of his life, first at the Heysel Stadium in 1985 and then at Hillsborough in 1989, when the lives of so many football supporters were lost. There was no need on each occasion for a journalistic eye, because Peter Jones' vast experience and emotional hinterland were priceless assets. It took two tragedies unfolding before his eyes to chip away at the joie de vivre that had always been one of his hallmarks.

Peter's massive commentating talents and personable qualities would have served the sports department nobly through his sixties, and with a touch of class and a playful awareness that it was only sport, after all. What a dreadful irony it was that this most enthusiastic of personalities met his premature end at a sporting event, as he collapsed while commentating on the 1990 Boat Race. He was just 60 when he died the following day.

Desmond Lynam is, in the opinion of many of his sports room contemporaries, the best presenter in *Sports Report*'s history. He made it look so easy, with a flexible yet composed voice that could cover all the emotions of a dramatic day's sport at 5.00 p.m. on a Saturday. Humour, authority, courteous persistence in interviews, brevity when necessary – Des Lynam had it all. And there was always a hint of a sardonic raise of the eyebrow, as he viewed sport's capacity for daftness with deft irony. Later on, that archness would be one of his hallmarks in his superb television career, but Des perfected that air of detachment on the radio in the seventies.

Dave Gordon, who produced him on *Sports Report* and later on *Grandstand*, says he had an intuition that was invaluable. 'He had a feel for the audience. Radio developed that in Des and just knew where to pitch it. He was a phenomenal presenter, the best in my time.'

Bob Burrows, Angus Mackay's successor as the sports department's driving force, admired Lynam's imperturbable style. 'I can't ever remember him ever being ruffled by anything. He just had this knack of shrugging off difficulties during the programme. Des could handle any crisis.'

Des would never miss the chance of a whimsical comment, when it was justified. When Dick Scales, reporting from Luton Town, found his equipment malfunctioning, he sounded as if he was broadcasting under the sea, with horrendous echoes. Des, a friend of Scales, aware that he'd be pulling his leg that night, remarked, 'Dick Scales, there – on top of things as usual!'

The professional tributes to Des Lynam pile up. It would seem an effortless, meteoric rise – from selling insurance to a stint at Radio Brighton for a year, then off to Radio London, and then to the Sports Unit in Broadcasting House. Two months later, he was presenting *Sports Report*, aged 27. Yet there were early doubts. Des needed to get Angus Mackay on board in his interview. 'I knew I had to work on Angus on that interview panel, so I focused on him. I even made him laugh once, which was a feat!'

Vincent Duggleby was also on that panel, and he and Mackay were enormously impressed by this self-assured, tall young man, with the fashionably long hair of the late sixties. 'We thought, "Is there nothing he doesn't know about sport?", so we sent him outside to kick his heels for a while so that we could set him a test. We drafted 20 sporting questions – he got 19 of them straight away. Desmond's interview was the best I've known.'

Yet Des didn't know that and he was unsure just what the fearsome Mackay thought of him. His first stint as presenter of *Sports Report* didn't go well. He fluffed the opening headlines – always the key litmus paper test – spoke on air unwittingly to someone next door on the control panel and came out of the show early, leaving a pronounced silence before the reassuring sounds of 'Out of the Blue'. The rest of that weekend seemed interminable to him, before he could regain some confidence and build for his second attempt.

Unknown to him, members of senior management on Radio 2 were monitoring the progress of Angus Mackay's protégé. They weren't impressed. One of those executives wrote, 'We have nothing against him, but think he lacks background, experience and personality.' Almost on a par with the dismissive screen test verdict on the young Fred Astaire, 'Can't sing. Can't act. Can dance a little.'

Luckily for Des, Angus Mackay was usually dismissive of senior management's opinions and this was no exception. He persevered, impressed by Des's deep knowledge of sport. Des found him frightening in those early days and a short exchange after six weeks in the job shook him. 'He said, "Come into my office" and then asked me, "What's the most important part of *Sports Report*?" I said, "The sport" and he replied, "Correct – but you're making it sound as if it's you. Stop doing that." As always with Angus, it was a quick word and all one way – but I never forgot that.'

He was also conscious of Peter Jones' maturity and effortless self-confidence. Peter had already made a great impression as presenter, but his producer also wanted him out on the road, developing contacts at football matches and spreading the gospel of *Sports Report*. So Des was bloodied early. 'I was in awe of Peter – such an erudite, classy guy, who spoke fluent French and Spanish, and made it look so easy. We became friends, he called me 'Liners', but he never gave me any help. He saw me as competition.'

But Des was a quick learner and, crucially, quick-witted. He mixed well socially, bonding with James Hunt one afternoon when he came into the studio for an early interview and ended up staying until the programme ended. The boxing fraternity warmed to Des and he learned a great deal from the likes of Henry Cooper, Jim Wicks and Harry Levene, which paid off when he later became an outstanding boxing commentator, as his career broadened out.

Dick Scales is interesting on the contrast as presenters between Jones and Lynam. He shared a flat with Des for a year and, travelling the world with Peter on major events, was very fond of them both. 'They had the great gift of being the same off air as they were on it; they were absolute naturals. With his cut-glass accent, Peter could pick out five words and make them sound so effective. Des had a strong voice, with a soft edge to it. You never saw either of them panic in the studio; they could be trusted in any circumstances. Des and Peter were the best two broadcasters I ever worked with.

'When things got rough and you were losing lines to live sport all over the studio, you could be sure that Des would hold it together on air effortlessly. Just one word from the producer and he'd riff along, waiting for further guidance. The listener would have no idea all hell was breaking loose in our studio. He was the best I knew on talkback, when only the producer can talk to the presenter. He picked up things amazingly quickly.'

There's no doubt that Des blossomed after Angus Mackay retired in 1972. He could never get used to his producer sitting right beside him as he broadcast live and knew that Mackay would never change his ways. His trusted lieutenant, Bob Burrows, the ideas man, another workaholic and excellent talent spotter, joined forces with the brilliant technician Bryan Tremble to usher in a dynamic period for *Sports Report* – fizzing with daring, technically advanced, supremely self-confident, with a 30-year-old presenter approaching the top of his versatile game.

Inevitably, television came sniffing around the slim, urbane Lynam. He wondered about making the leap, but one of his mentors in the Sports Unit had other ideas. Cliff Morgan was greatly admired by Des, not only for his brilliance as a rugby player, but for his inspirational man-management of the young charges in the sports room. When Des answered an advert for a TV job at Southern TV, he sought Morgan's advice. 'You what, boyo? Are you mad? You'll be reporting on Bournemouth and Boscombe, and living on the Isle of Wight. You'll go to telly when I say so.' Des did as he was told and had to ring up and withdraw his application.

But, by the end of the seventies, time was up for him on *Sports Report*. He kept wondering how he would fare on television. Stints on the *Today* programme and *The John Dunn Show* may have briefly diverted him, but Des had too much respect for *Sports Report* to allow a Groundhog Day feeling to settle on him. Off then to TV Centre, with Des becoming the first person to regularly present both *Sports Report* and *Grandstand*. He found the first year tough. 'I wanted to come back to radio. I felt I wasn't natural enough, like a rabbit trapped in the headlights. There was a lot of backbiting and I found it edgy. I talked to Bob Burrows and Cliff Morgan, and they advised, "Give it a year," and eventually I got the hang of telly.' So it wasn't a bed of roses throughout for Des Lynam, even though he made it appear so. That marked him out and he has always credited *Sports Report* for whatever distinction people may want to attach to his long career.

Jim Rosenthal brought an extra sharpness to *Sports Report* in his three and a half years at the helm. The old dictum of never missing a news story during the programme wasn't threatened when he was presenting. Jim's background was news, and it showed. Four years on the *Oxford Mail*, the same again at BBC Radio Oxford and another four at Radio Birmingham, where he worked throughout the night on the Birmingham pub bombings tragedy, all gave him the background and experience to spot a story, and pursue it with enviable zeal.

Just before Jim joined the sports department in 1976, he gave a hint of what he would be offering. He was covering the Montreal Olympics for the BBC local radio services and sniffed out a genuine scoop. He knew the sprinter Sonia Lannaman from the Birmingham athletics scene and, as she was a genuine medal hope in both the 100 and 200 metres, he determined to keep close to her in the build-up. Sue Reeve, one of her club-mates, was also competing in Montreal and, when Jim conducted what he thought was a routine interview with Reeve, he hit pay dirt. 'It's such a shame about Sonia being ruled out with that sore hamstring,' she said. Jim didn't feign surprise, letting Sue Reeve believe he was in on the story and picked up all the necessary quotes from her, correctly reasoning that Sonia Lannaman would be off-limits from now on.

Jim instantly knew the strength of that story and, after persuading Bob Burrows and Dick Scales about its worth, they allowed the local radio man to break it on the national sports news. Despite the inevitable official denials, the story stood up and Lannaman didn't race in that Olympic Games. Jim had handsomely demonstrated qualities that underpinned his work for Radio 2 Sport – listen carefully to what someone is saying in an interview, no interview is ever just routine, maintain and develop your contacts, and stand by your story when someone tries to denigrate it.

Bob Burrows, who mentored Jim when he came to Broadcasting House, was impressed by his new, 30-year-old recruit. 'Jim was knowledgeable, proficient, likeable and versatile. He could turn his hand to anything.' For his part, Jim was never fazed by Burrows' habit of ringing him five minutes after he presented a sports desk – early morning or late at night – asking him why he chose a certain story to lead his bulletin. 'He drove us hard, but Bob would always listen and encourage me.'

The Rosenthal work ethic was soon noticed when he started in the sports room. He would sweat the details, interview fearlessly, showing he had prepped prodigiously in advance. With Des Lynam beginning to look elsewhere, the search was quietly underway for the next presenter of *Sports Report*. Jim had presented an equivalent to *Sports Report* every Saturday afternoon on Radio Birmingham and after a few trials when Lynam was away, it was clear that the national stage held no terrors for him. He quickly developed a fruitful understanding with the programme's producer, Bryan Tremble. 'We'd gather early on a Saturday morning in the canteen and over breakfast Jim and I would toss ideas around. He had a great attitude and work ethic, and a wonderful voice.'

By 1977, Jim Rosenthal was clearly the anointed one for *Sports Report*. He had won his spurs as a football commentator alongside Peter Jones and/or Bryan Butler, on top of his subject, and he regularly brought in sports news stories that stemmed from his wide range of contacts, developed in the regions. Unlike previous *Sports Report* presenters, he insisted on writing the 5.00 p.m. headlines himself, showing brevity and humour when necessary. The programme just felt slicker, irrespective of the many qualities Lynam and Jones had shown over the previous decade. When Jim and his producer held their five-minute meeting midway through the second-half football commentary, 45 minutes before the start of *Sports Report*, Jim would be fizzing with ideas for interviews and treatment of breaking stories. Bryan Tremble would then attempt to make it happen. He invariably succeeded.

Jim says, 'I just knew how to identify a story and I'd rip the guts out of it. I was just a sharper newshound than Des or Jonesy, not a better presenter. If I brought anything to the programme it was a certain fleetness of foot. *Sports Report* was part of the day's narrative, where you tried to put everything in context. The essentials remain the same – tell the story concisely and then get to the essential characters involved. At that time, the quality of broadcast journalists was very high on *Sports Report*.'

Although Des Lynam was eyeing up pastures new when Rosenthal arrived, he was aware of comparisons that were being made by some of the old guard. Jim's voice was slightly lower than Des's, but it was authoritative and distinctive – and similar to Lynam's. One day Lynam confided in his old friend, Dick Scales,

'Bloody Rosenthal's trying to copy me, you know.'

'Do you know why?'

'No.'

'Because I told him to sit in the studio and listen to tapes of you presenting. That way, I told him, he'll learn. It was meant as a compliment to you.'

Scales recalls, 'Des never moaned about that again. Jim did his homework on Des, slowed down his delivery, put even more bass into his tone and in the end, sounded different from Des. Voices were very important to our output in those days and Jim and Des were very distinctive.'

Jim's versatility and unflappability were amply demonstrated on Boat Race afternoon in 1980. He and Bryan Tremble started *Sport on 2* in a portable studio at Mortlake, anchored the show until the race started, then dashed back to Broadcasting House to get *Sports Report* under way. All in a day's work, except the studio guest was John Snagge, the doyen of newsreaders on the radio and, at the age of 75, still indelibly associated with the BBC's coverage of the Boat Race. Jim interviewed John with proper respect and affection, and, charmed by the old boy's responses, wrapped up the live interview with, 'John, the Boat Race wouldn't be the same without you – we look forward to seeing you there again next year.' A voice on Jim's talkback chipped in. 'Didn't you know? We're not using him next year!' Jim calmly moved on. 'I just hoped no one would remember what I said when the news leaked out that he'd been dropped. I decided not to draw attention to it. Typical…everyone else seemed to know, apart from the interviewer.'

Within a few months of that interview, Jim Rosenthal had left the BBC. He joined London Weekend Television, taking advantage of ITV grabbing the rights for Saturday night football to become the number two to Brian Moore. After more than 30 years with ITV Sport, he clocked up presenting and reporting on over 150 Grand Prix, eight football World Cups and six Rugby Union World Cups, and had a contacts book the envy of his many friends and colleagues.

Television's gain was undoubtedly radio's loss. Some of the heavy hitters who presented *Sports Report* reached their natural end of the road, but not Jim Rosenthal. He was gone too soon, without establishing himself in the pantheon. I have no doubt that a few more years with *Sports Report* would have done that. He had the authority, the respect for the role, a compelling versatility and a restless desire to nail the story of the day.

Mike Ingham was the BBC's chief football correspondent for nearly a quarter of a century. He commentated on 28 FA Cup Finals, covered eight World Cup Finals and worked with 10 full-time England managers. More than enough to qualify for an outstanding career. Before any of all that, he also presented *Sports Report* for four years. 'That was even bigger than commentating on a World Cup Final. I still have to pinch myself that I presented *Sports Report*, when I was so young, just 30. Others develop their careers out in the field, gaining vital contacts, then graduate to the role in the studio, but mine was the other way round.'

To understand what *Sports Report* meant to Mike, it's important to establish that he was, and remains, a genuine radio romantic. At no stage in his career was he ever tempted to dabble in television. Mike values words and heritage too much. Walking home from school as a scruffy urchin, he'd imagine himself presenting the programme, handing over to the likes of Geoffrey Green, Robin Marlar, J. L. Manning and Simon Smith, luxuriating in the signature tune. Mike's team – Derby County – had always won that day, while their bitter rivals – Nottingham Forest – lost.

Yet when he began his invaluable apprenticeship at BBC Radio Derby, it was as a sports reporter, specialising in football and cricket. The presenter's role fell into his lap on national radio in 1980, just a year after joining the Radio 2 sports department. As so often, luck played the key role. Jim Rosenthal was about to leave for television, leaving a gaping hole. The bosses simply took a chance on Mike Ingham. There weren't many other candidates.

He didn't sleep the night before his debut, but thought he eventually acquitted himself well enough. On the Monday, he had a visitor in the sports room. Cliff Morgan, one of the great characters of the department, a revered figure of supreme sporting and broadcasting gifts. When Cliff sought you out, you clicked your heels and pinned back your ears.

Cliff told Mike, 'Time for you to understand what broadcasting's really all about. Stand up against the wall.' He told the tyro presenter to fill his lungs and breathe. 'It's like being an opera singer. You can't perform unless you know how to breathe properly.' All this in front of the rest of the sports room. 'I felt humiliated at the time but it was in retrospect a calculated yet caring reminder of the privilege I should be feeling to be allowed to set foot in Broadcasting House, never mind presenting *Sports Report*.'

Mike learned quickly and well, not least of all because Morgan would be giving a practical demonstration of the art every Saturday morning, as he presented *Sport on Four* so expertly on Radio 4, an agreeable entrée to the afternoon's sporting coverage over on Radio 2.

Mike knew he had to move up another gear at 5.00 p.m., as at least another 25 local radio stations would join the programme on his cue. His calm, measured style was agreeably mature; he was introducing a sports programme, not a frenetic news and current affairs show. When the relevant action was sufficiently dramatic, he would pitch his delivery accordingly. No presenter of my experience surpassed his exemplary ability to close the programme in such an unhurried style. The producer would give him four sports news items, tell him he had 75 seconds left and Mike would get the show off-air with consummate ease. The 5.00 p.m. headlines, written by him, gave a teaser to the ensuing main stories, 'I would aim for about 30 seconds for the headlines. I didn't want to give it all away, in case they switched off because they'd heard all they needed.'

He always valued the contributions from the reporters – something I can happily confirm, as the recipient of a few kind, handwritten notes from him. 'We had a great mix of voices – the regional football reporters like George Bayley, Stuart Hall, Larry Canning and Bill Bothwell; the newspaper columnists such as Frank Keating, Hugh McIlvanney, Geoffrey Green, Patrick Collins and Ian Wooldridge, stirring the pot with their opinion pieces. Freelance newspaper reporters such as Simon Taylor, Renton Laidlaw, Colin Hart and John Parsons – experts in their sports – were very valuable. Bryon Butler was the personification of quality, every word he wrote was considered and classy. It's very hard to sustain that standard when your game might have finished just 10 minutes before you're live on air. Bryan always managed it.'

Mike presided over it all with a dignified, considered air that belied his youth. Even his equanimity was tested in one programme when Ken Bates, the owner of Chelsea, barrelled on to *Sports Report* with his distinctive views on the recurring nightmare of football hooliganism. Bates had tried to solve the problem at Stamford Bridge by erecting an electric perimeter fence around the pitch to prevent crowd invasions. It was predictably controversial and Bates revelled in the notoriety. Appearing live on *Sports Report*, the bellicose Bates reacted boorishly to Mike's courteous yet relevant probing and his posturing was laid bare to the national audience. Eventually the local council refused Bates permission to turn the electricity on and the idea was scrapped, but not before Ingham had given a masterclass in dealing with a difficult interviewee.

Mike's self-discipline was equally tested on another occasion, albeit in more amusing circumstances. One afternoon in late 1982, the designated reporter was preparing his round-up of Divisions Three and Four, to appear in *Sports Report* soon after 5.30 p.m. It's only fair to gloss over his identity, as he was on an attachment from a local radio station, hoping to kick on to a permanent role in the Broadcasting House set-up. He had been given his designated time of two minutes for the round-up and, diligently, was determined to stick to that, in the best traditions of Angus Mackay's exacting production dictates.

One scoreline stood out – Doncaster Rovers 7, Reading 5. The Rovers manager was Billy Bremner, always a willing interviewee as player and now manager. By the time the reporter was on air, Bremner had not been tracked down. Mike was in studio B9, the basement studio, from where *Sports Report* was always broadcast and the reporter was three floors up, in studio 3H. Fortunately, as he started his two-minute round-up, Bremner was contacted and prepared to be interviewed about this remarkable game of 12 goals.

The reporter, with one eye on the second hand, started with, 'Thanks for joining us, Billy – what an amazing scoreline.'

'Well, it was just one of those days.'

'Billy Bremner there', said the hapless reporter and closed his round-up, bang on the allotted time.

He was unlucky to be three floors away from the producer, who would undoubtedly have given him more time to develop the Bremner live interview. But Mike almost corpsed on air at the words, 'Billy Bremner there'.

'How did I keep a straight face? It was astonishing. I felt for the guy, who was so obviously desperate to finish on two minutes, but that became a cliché saying in the sports room for a few weeks. If someone came out with a comment, you'd hear "Garry Richardson there" or "Mike Ingham there". I didn't know what to say when poor Billy Bremner got just one sentence. It had to be the shortest interview in *Sports Report*'s history – and the funniest!'

Mike didn't know it then, but within a few couple of months his career was to take a considerable shift of emphasis. Patricia Ewing, the new head of sport, was very keen on older, more experienced broadcasters, those who had served their time on the road, and who had wide and valuable contacts. She decided that Peter Jones would return to the studio for the 1984–85 football season, while Mike would be repositioned as one of the football commentators. He would also miss out on the imminent Los Angeles Olympics.

It was a blow to his *amour-propre* and professional pride, but he appreciated his good fortune in getting the *Sports Report* role without any proper audition or earning his stripes out in the field. 'I hadn't even been a football commentator at Radio Derby, so how could I be expected to swap roles with Peter Jones, one of my heroes?

'This was a management decision presumably taken for the future. I eventually realised that Pat Ewing was right, that I got *Sports Report* too early and needed to know more people in sport, so that they could put a face to my voice. Did I peak too soon? Ten years later, I might have been better suited, establishing a chemistry in my live interviews into the programme, because I had spent valuable time with so many.'

He shouldn't dwell too long on imponderables. He didn't lose sight of the programme's heritage and his dignified calmness, and respect for sport and colleagues in that industry, never deserted him until his retirement in 2013.

Renton Laidlaw suffered from the wrong management decision to catapult him into the presenter's chair. Pat Ewing, persisting in her conviction that an older hand was needed, decided to return Peter Jones to football commentaries on Saturdays and, to general surprise, brought in Renton. That was no reflection on him. With a warm, beautifully modulated Scots accent, he was an adornment to our golf coverage, a superb commentator and presenter on that sole sport. As golf correspondent for the London *Evening Standard*, he had travelled the golf world for decades, a reliable, informative figure, hugely respected by both golfers and its media.

All that would butter no parsnips when it came to Renton conducting live interviews with leading football managers or reporters at matches. It's true that football at the time was in danger of becoming a pariah of a sport, with hooliganism and under-achievement at tournament level a factor in national disillusionment, but it was still the main driving force behind the *Sports Report* engine and Renton just couldn't switch on to it instinctively.

One of the reasons was because each week he was rarely in the country until Friday afternoons and he found it hard to catch up on the week's other sporting news and stories, that would germinate over the next 24 hours. Rob Hastie, his Saturday producer, sympathised; he had worked with Renton on radio in Scotland and, like everyone else in the department, had great respect and affection for him. 'Renton was so reliable as a reporter for us – if you wanted 40 seconds on a tournament from the Gobi desert, he'd do it, spot on, for you. He was brilliant at golf, but he was never on top of the football. It wasn't ever in depth, it was just headline stuff.'

Renton accepts he wasn't doing the *Sports Report* job as well as he'd have liked. 'But it was Pat Ewing's idea. She wanted to reduce the emphasis on football, which didn't have a great image then. I was delighted to be chosen, aware of the history and legacy, and I'd have regretted turning it down. But I never felt comfortable or that I did it in my own style. I knew there were a few people in the sports room wondering what the hell was going on. But I had great support from Peter Jones, who'd have dinner with me every Friday evening in the BBC canteen, and Cliff Morgan. Nobody said anything to me about my performances. There was just a feeling about the sports room that I wasn't suited. I don't think I did all that badly, or that I missed out anything vital in my football interviews, I just didn't feel *Sports Report* saw the real me.'

Eventually Pat Ewing was persuaded that the experiment had failed. Renton's two-year contract in the role was up, so a civilised parting of the ways ensued. It was the end of an error. He continued commentating on golf for BBC Radio for a number of years, a cherished and popular presence with his colleagues.

One singular notch on his escutcheon – he was the first to commentate, then present, a whole afternoon's coverage, climaxing with *Sports Report*. It was the Saturday of the Ryder Cup in September 1985. 'I found that really exhilarating and I was very proud of that.' Understandably so. And for his 25 years' service with the department as a kindly, shrewd chronicler of his beloved sport. When he passed away in October 2021, aged 82, the tributes from his former colleagues in the radio sports room were warm and affectionate. Renton Laidlaw will be remembered for much more than the occasional verbal infelicity over a footballer's name.

John Inverdale had only one person in mind when he presented *Sports Report* with such skill for six years – his mum.

He and his dad were sports-mad and, inevitably, the programme was on the car radio. Mum was a good enough tennis player to represent her county, but she baulked at wall-to-wall sport on a Saturday afternoon. 'We'd have so many arguments in the car. Mum would say, "Do we have to keep listening to this?" and we'd say, "Yes!" When I got the *Sports Report* job, I always thought I was talking to only her, trying to get her interest, even though she had already passed away. She wouldn't be interested intrinsically in a report on Blackburn v Bolton, so I wanted to imagine her being engaged in what I was saying to set up the report.

'I regarded the programme in the context of the Radio 2 entertainment package, not just for the sporting anorak. I felt we needed to change the tone to reflect we weren't an all-sport channel. Just go with the flow, reflect that there's an element of showbiz involved and escape the rigidity.'

John's period as *Sports Report* straddled Radio 2, then, in August 1990, Radio 5 for another four years, before Radio 5 Live hoovered up live sport to become the news and sport channel. He was sharp enough to adapt to the change of tone necessary in those years. By common consent, he was one of the most quick-witted presenters of the show – adaptable, humorous, with an antennae that switched to serious when necessary. That was never more salient when he anchored our coverage of the Hillsborough disaster in 1989. His wide range of sporting knowledge was a huge asset, bringing authority to our rugby union, horse racing, golf and athletics coverage, as well as the staple Saturday afternoon fare of football.

On air he was as smooth as George Clooney and it was rare to hear John stumble over any link or interview in *Sports Report*. When briefed by producers, it was common knowledge that he only needed to hear the information once. In the modern parlance, he got it – straight away.

Pat Thornton produced him for four years and she relished every *Sports Report*. 'John was so quick on his feet, such a fast thinker. He could get out of an interview very smartly, without the listener realising the urgency involved. He had great sporting knowledge. I could trust him totally. I used to tell him, "You run it on air, I'll run it off air" and it worked.'

John respected the reporters out in the field. 'I liked the disparate nature of the contributors, their varied humour and views. I'd grown up listening to strong opinions on *Sports Report* and I encouraged the newer ones to sound off, if necessary. I liked slipping in a follow-up question, knowing I could light the blue touch paper and stand back.'

Peter Drury, new to the 5.00 p.m. parish, appreciated this. 'John wasn't a greedy presenter, he encouraged individualism. I felt he was captain of the team and I was proud to be in it. If he reacted well to something I'd said on air, that was praise indeed.'

John's period in the *Sports Report* chair coincided with an overhaul in the way sport was covered. 'There was a seismic shift, especially in the way football was treated. In my early days, football wasn't cool, with half-empty grounds and hooliganism.

'After 1992, when Sky altered the football landscape, we had to adapt and reflect that football was becoming trendy again, and the public wanted to hear from more managers and players. So we lost those valuable opinion pieces from our senior reporters to an extent and took the risk that we were alienating listeners who wanted to hear about other sports.'

John helped shape the tone of Saturday afternoon by lobbying for it to go out on the road, climaxing with *Sports Report* to be hosted from that day's location. 'It was a very studio-based programme when I started, apart from the Grand National. I thought we needed to create an atmosphere, to make people wish they were there, at the main sporting event of the day.' He met some resistance, but got lucky at the first attempt.

In August 1989, the businessman Michael Knighton lodged a £20 million bid to buy Manchester United. It was a record bid for a British club and all week it was a major, developing story. United were at home to Arsenal on the opening day of the league season and Inverdale pushed hard for the programme to come from Old Trafford. 'Let's take the story to the audience,' he said. He was fortunate that Knighton was hardly a shrinking violet and he rarely spurned a proffered microphone.

The afternoon programme started with a montage of Manchester United clips and goals, and as Inverdale was setting the scene for the latest on the bid, Knighton was walking towards him. Showing impressive flexibility, John jettisoned his script and said, 'Well the afternoon here at Old Trafford is all about one man – Michael Knighton. And here he is, Michael Knighton. Good afternoon...'

It got better. Knighton, fulfilling a childhood ambition, went out to the Stretford End with a ball and performed some handy keepie-uppies in front of a receptive crowd. For good measure, he still had the United kit on when he fronted up for another interview at the top of *Sports Report*. Vindication for its presenter and a trifling concern that Knighton's bid foundered a few weeks later. 'On the train back, I said to the production team, "We should do this more often" and, being purely selfish, I found it exhilarating to be at events like that, instead of being in the studio.'

That flexibility of location should stand as one of John Inverdale's legacies to *Sports Report*. The programme became more dynamic and ambitious under his sure-footed stewardship, laced with an enjoyable sense of irreverence from the presenter and a welcome sense of detachment. John never lost sight of the imperatives from 5.00 to 6.00 p.m., but it was always only sport. After his glittering stint on *Sports Report*, he became one of the great sporting all-rounders, both on radio and television. Occasional gaffes on air later on brought him unwanted and (in my opinion) unwarranted brickbats, failing to grasp that brain and tongue sometimes get disengaged in the crucible of live presentation. He should be remembered as one of the most distinguished presenters in *Sports Report*'s history.

For his part, John remains in debt to the programme, 'When I went back to playing club rugby after I came off *Sports Report* in 1994, I'd listen in the car with my team-mates and think, "Bloody hell, I used to do that." You'd realise *Sports Report*'s importance in bringing you the right atmosphere and disseminating the necessary information. I'll forever be proud to have been involved in it for six years, when it was a must-listen programme.'

Ian Payne was the most idiosyncratic of the main *Sports Report* presenters. He was highly talented – twice a Sony Radio Award-winner, the equivalent to the Oscars in radio – and he stood out from the norm because of his knack of saying what was on his mind. Not always the acme of supreme radio presenting, but it was never dull when Ian was presenting *Sports Report*.

When Stan Collymore was going through a tough period with his own team-mates at Nottingham Forest, admitting to issues over his mental health, he came on to *Sports Report* to chat to Ian in the London studio from the City Ground. One of Ian's first questions was, 'Why do so many hate you, Stan?' Mike Lewis, editing the programme in the studio recalls, 'It was a breathtaking moment. We all looked at each other, wondering where this was going. Remember, it was live.' Fortunately,

Collymore took the question well. Ian's response? 'I took Stan seriously about mental health matters and he appreciated that, so he didn't drop the mic and storm off.'

Unlike Gerard Houllier, managing Liverpool in 1999. His player, Robbie Fowler, was at the centre of a major story, having simulated snorting cocaine along the white line of the penalty area, after scoring against Everton. Fowler had been heavily fined by Liverpool and Houllier was very jumpy about making any public comment. At the next game, he agreed to come on *Sports Report* for a live interview, but only after stipulating that he would not want a barrage of questions about his errant striker. Ian was told that in no uncertain terms by his producer, Claire McDonnell. 'We told him to get to Fowler later on, but just ease Houllier in with a few other questions. So what happens? The first question is about Fowler. So Houllier puts the mic down and leaves abruptly. We asked Ian afterwards why he did that and he just said, "It was the only question I could think of." That was rather irritating.'

Such rifts did cause problem for Ian's producers, as they tried to keep a tally of managers who weren't currently speaking to *Sports Report*, because they felt the presenter had been guilty of *lèse-majesté* by persisting in asking awkward questions. That's understandably tougher for the production team, but I had sympathy and respect for Ian's modus operandi. In the brave new world of the Premier League, modern football was taking itself too seriously, with too many deferential questions being lobbed at managers and players. Ian Payne had a different take on that. 'I didn't set out to upset people deliberately, I was like a fan who got lucky and got to ask what it was like. Sometimes it worked and sometimes it didn't.'

Ian was basically cheekier than other presenters. He upset David Ginola when he was at Newcastle, pulling his leg about his shampoo adverts, featuring his luxuriant hair, but that told me more about the Frenchman, rather than the presenter. Jonathan Wall, one of his producers, describes him a 'an empathetic broadcaster, who tried to be different,' while another, Gill Pulsford, recalls, 'Sometimes you'd tell him something three times before he'd grasp it. He was a gifted maverick. A slight naiveté was his schtick as a presenter.'

Gill remembers Ian's skill at compiling features – going off for a day, and coming back with a few whacky interviews and an amusing slant on a subject. It didn't work out one day at Manchester United's training ground, when he interviewed Ryan Giggs. His manager, Alex Ferguson, gave permission for the interview, under the impression that it was simply a preview for the next match. Instead, Ian wanted to focus on Giggs' public persona as a male pin-up, the poster boy for the new breed of female football fan. Ferguson heard about it and went Full Gammon about what he saw as sharp practice by Ian. Fergie's familiar foam-flecked fury saw 5 Live Sport consigned to his personal gulag for another spell, with our management trying peace initiatives in vain. There was usually something we did or said that angered Fergie.

At the 1997 Grand National, Ian showed there was more to him than just having the chops to ask left-field questions from the presenter's chair. On that April Saturday afternoon, the Aintree course was evacuated, due to a threatened IRA bomb blast. Ian and the rest of the *Sport on 5* team were ushered out peremptorily to adjoining roads and Ian, as presenter, was left to hold the coverage on his own for an hour, interviewing punters and locals who lived nearby. He held the fort manfully until the batteries on his equipment ran out and a stand-by production team in Broadcasting House took over.

Ian grew in stature that day, subsequently recognised by a Sony Award, as he demonstrated a presenter's true value. 'I loved it, I wasn't scared for a second. I was conscious of being the eyes and ears for so many, loved being the centre of attention.'

By 2000, Ian felt he needed another challenge and moved to 5 Live's afternoon show, where his flair for the quirky was appreciated. '*Sports Report* presenting meant everything, in terms of radio. All those people you admired in sport being brought to a microphone to talk to you? It was a dream job, that I just fell into.' Payne was different from the other regular *Sports Report* presenters. Not inferior. Just different. And he stood out by being just that. There are worse professional epitaphs.

Mark Pougatch holds the record for the longest stint as *Sports Report* presenter – 16 years, from August 2000 to May 2016. And if you had told him that when he sat as a boy, watching his father clean his shoes, he would have been incredulous. Mark's dad fostered his son's love of the programme while preparing for his job in the City of London as a merchant banker. 'He would always clean five pairs of shoes, ready for the week ahead. A stickler for spick and span at work, he'd polish and shine them, somehow managing to spin it out for the whole programme. I cherished that hour with my dad. He died in 1991, of heart failure, and it's a great regret that he never heard me present *Sports Report*.'

The call came after an apprenticeship at Radio London, then Radio Essex and a few commentary stints on *Match of the Day*. He took a nano-second to accept the offer. He clocked up four football World Cups, six Olympic Games, three Euros and a couple of Ashes series in Australia before joining commercial television. In the process he built up a deserved reputation for reliability, integrity and love of sport. He also remained deservedly popular among his colleagues, not always a given with a high-profile presenter. Mark's impeccable manners on air were matched by his relationship with his work colleagues, his willingness to laugh at himself an endearing factor.

Mark won't mind me saying this, but he was the poshest of the regular *Sports Report* presenters. Captain of the 1st X1 cricket team at Malvern College, a degree in politics from Durham University and a wedding photo in the society magazine *Harpers and Queen* in 2000, when he married Lady Victoria Scott, the youngest daughter of the 5th Earl of Eldon. He must have winced when the proles in the sports room got wind of that personal CV, but he never showed it. He would take all the ribbing with immense grace, refusing to dumb down in either accent or his shabby chic country garb.

Mark Pougatch was simply one of the classiest acts in the programme's history and we bemoaned his eventual departure after 20 years in the department. His success anchoring ITV's coverage of the Euros in 2021, disarming even Roy Keane with his gentle leg-pulling, surprised none of his former colleagues.

His excellent manners were graphically displayed one Saturday in 2001, when England was preparing for a vital World Cup qualifier the following week against Greece. Their priceless striker Michael Owen had been injured playing for Liverpool and would not be fit. Brilliant work by the production team managed to line up four former England managers for *Sports Report* to discuss who should replace Owen. Graham Taylor, Bobby Robson and Glenn Hoddle were perfectly amenable and interesting in their thoughts, but Kevin Keegan, then Manchester City's manager, took umbrage. 'Why are you asking me about England? I don't talk about England.' Pougatch was taken aback and offered the reasonable line, 'Well, people would be interested in what you have to say as a recent England manager.' But Keegan continued to bridle and the interview fizzled out.

Mark was upset afterwards, wondering what he had done wrong, aware that it was only a year since Keegan resigned from the job, reasoning that he was still raw about it. After the programme, Manchester City's press officer rang up Mark and tore a strip off him. I'm not sure why he thought Mark would know that Keegan didn't want to talk about England, and I can think of a few *Sports Report* presenters who would have given him a stern response, but Mark was too polite even then to rasp a dusty rejoinder. I can't think of any other occasion in 16 years at the helm when Mark upset an interviewee.

One occasion he did show some steel. Glenn Hoddle, then Southampton's manager, was hotly tipped to return to Tottenham and he was booked for a *Sports Report* interview after what proved to be his last game in charge of the Saints. Word came back that under no circumstances should he be asked about going back to White Hart Lane. Mark told his producer 'In that case, we're not going to talk to him.' He believed it would have been ridiculous to ignore the elephant in the room. A case of, 'Apart from that, Mrs Lincoln, did you enjoy the play?'

Like John Inverdale, Pougatch enjoyed getting out on a Saturday afternoon, presenting the programme from anywhere suitable. 'My mantra was to travel light on these Saturday trips. A pencil, notepad and a phone – that was all. I needed to know exactly what was going on – I'd tell my producer I was a bear with a small brain, so don't tell me too much in advance – and then I just kept my eyes open, looking around. My job was to talk for 30 seconds or so, look up to see if my next interview was about to happen and if it wasn't, then talk some more. Or ask my producer to remind me what I was doing next.

'If anything went wrong, I would always remember John Inverdale's sage advice – nobody died, it's not the end of the world, find some humour in a cock-up.' As he did when his producer failed to play 'Out of the Blue' at the start of the programme in 2013 and Mark pulled it back brilliantly half an hour later.

Eventually, as Mark developed his TV portfolio, something had to give and it was *Sports Report*. 'I'm extremely proud to have the longest stint on the programme and I owe everything in my career to it. But you should always leave a party when you're enjoying it. I had to stop riding two horses at once.

'What I remember most about it was the need to concentrate hard for that hour. The closer you get to six o'clock the easier it is to lose your place. I would be very tired on a Saturday night. It was a matter of personal pride not to stuff up.'

Mark Chapman had a close personal connection with *Sports Report* more than 20 years before he took over as its presenter. Aged 21, studying for his postgraduate degree in broadcast journalism, he wrote a treatise on *Sports Report*. To put flesh on the bone, he emailed Ian Payne, then the programme's presenter. Commendably, Ian responded and gave him some invaluable insights. Chapman was on his way.

His first full-time job with the BBC was in local radio in Newcastle, where he became the North East's cricket correspondent. He was given the job by Ian

Dennis, now 5 Live's senior football reporter and a regular verbal jouster on air with Chapman every Saturday afternoon. Later they shared a flat in Ealing, as they learned their respective trades in BBC TV Centre and Dennis remembers Chapman's voracious hunger for sports news. 'He'd read everything. He developed an outstanding ability to turn his hands to all sports, consuming all the research. He was a worthy successor to all the previous great presenters of *Sports Report*.'

The zeitgeist suited Mark when the bosses were casting around for a successor to Mark Pougatch in 2016. A few years earlier, BBC Sport had decamped to Salford from TV Centre in London and the new presenter captured perfectly the breezy, non-conformist atmosphere of MediaCity. The 5 Live network and its flagship Saturday afternoon programme would sound different. More accessible, extra emphasis on showcasing listeners' views via social media. And flat vowels were embraced. The ideal presenter to fit that template would hail from the Manchester area, epitomising the gulf between it and London, for too long the epicentre of the national media.

Mark Williams has edited the programme in both the Pougatch and the Chapman era, and finds the contrast in tone and presenter fascinating. 'Mark P was more formal, more representative of the BBC's enduring qualities. Cool and unflappable. A tremendous presenter, but just different from Mark C, [who] uses a different technique in interviews. He's very good at not getting involved, he just waits for the answer to determine where he goes next in the interview. He brings a lot of humour into his interviews, doesn't ever sound overawed.' That brings the risk of too much 'bants' in live exchanges, where occasionally those involved talk over each other and the listener's in danger of feeling excluded as the laughter drowns the comments. Overwhelmingly, though, Chapman gets the tone right.

Mark has the priceless ability to see the funny side of a situation, when it all seems up in the air. The fourth round of the FA Cup in 2017 saw him standing on the Sincil Bank touchline, conducting live interviews at the end of the Lincoln v Brighton match, manfully trying to reflect on non-League Lincoln's tremendous victory over Championship leaders, Brighton. He had to interview, live, players he had never seen before, winging it as best he could. 'The Cowley brothers, Lincoln's joint managers, were superb, but I needed more than those two as we got into *Sports Report* and the spectators crowded on to the pitch where I was standing, microphone in hand. Lincoln players were being led towards me and I was desperately looking for the numbers on their shorts so that I could match them up on the matchday programme. It does help in such situations if you know who you're talking to! It was chaotic, a challenge professionally, but a joy. And it was a great laugh, which I tried to convey.'

He did – triumphantly. Mark is a committed football fan, but also of both rugby codes. One of his favourite Saturdays each year is rugby league's Grand Final, in October. 'Nights that like those stay with me, they reflect the passion in the North West for a particular sport. Rugby league's a proper community sport, and working with and interviewing great men like Kevin Sinfield, Jamie Peacock, and Rob Burrow has been an absolute privilege.'

One of Mark's particular skills is handling tricky interviews down the line. This is where an interviewee is handed a set of headphones at a match by the reporter or producer and has to field questions from the presenter, stuck in a studio in Salford. Some are more than happy to oblige, because they are familiar with Chapman and his genial style from watching him on Sunday night's *Match of the Day Two* on BBC Two, or listening to him on 5 Live. 'Occasionally, when someone's had a bad day, they'll still happily talk to us because of familiarity. People like Rafa Benítez, Sean Dyche, Sam Allardyce, Steve Bruce, Tony Pulis, Harry Redknapp and Nigel Pearson know what we're about. Some, like Jürgen Klopp, don't really get the significance of *Sports Report*, because they haven't grown up with it. But Klopp is very enjoyable and cute – sometimes I've done a live interview with him and I realise he's given us nothing. But he does it in such a smiling, jovial way that you can't take offence. The thrill of live interviews can't be underestimated.'

Sports Report hasn't just been a career milestone for Mark Chapman, it has been a safe haven psychologically, at a desperately sad time. In 2018, his wife Sara was diagnosed with cancer. After two awful years for the Chapman family, she eventually succumbed in the summer of 2020, leaving Mark and his three children utterly bereft. For Mark, *Sports Report* helped him deal with the ongoing challenge of keeping his family together.

'We decided that I'd work on the programme for as long as possible, to bring a semblance of normality to every Saturday. The kids were fully on board. We reasoned that it was vital to keep going, for them at school and me at work. We felt it was important for them to hear me on the radio, having a laugh in the studio, knowing that for a few hours at least, I could be in a supportive, caring environment with a team that meant so much to me.

'I'd be driving home after the programme, energised, hoping that Sara would be feeling better, but at least ready to deal with anything. As it never felt [like] a proper job, I was always in a better place. It was horrific, but *Sports Report* each Saturday helped make me a better carer, a better husband and a better father. Since Sara passed away, the affection and compassion we received have at times been overwhelming. I still grumble and moan about comparative trivia, but that experience made me appreciate those 20 years of marriage. Without being able to work on *Sports Report*, I don't know [if] I could have dealt with it all.'

Thankfully, he did. It's a measure of Mark Chapman's professionalism that his cheerful demeanour never darkened on air during those desperate times. *Sports Report* helped bring him perspective, as well as solace.

So many other superb broadcasters have sat in as presenters down the decades, destined to demonstrate their abilities in other areas as reporters or commentators. This is not an exhaustive list, by any means, but huzzahs to, among others:

- Vincent Duggleby: mainstay of the Sports Unit in the late 1960s, presented *Sports Report* for 18 months before forging a splendid career on Radio 4 as a financial expert.
- Tony Adamson: quirky reporter who injected a great deal of humour into the programme. Later tennis and golf correspondent. Presented *Sports Report* with a whimsical, light touch. To his great embarrassment, once voted country and western DJ of the year, while at Radio Oxford, and has never been allowed to forget it!
- Alan Parry: outstanding athletics and football reporter/commentator. Alternated as a presenter with Peter Jones for one season, but always happier commentating.
- George Hamilton: immensely talented rugby, football and athletics commentator, with a keen eye for the absurd. Stood in for Mike Ingham in the early 1980s. 'I was just a boy from the provinces in Northern Ireland, but it's still something I treasured.'
- Ian Darke: versatile, assured, with a sharp news judgement and an impressive grasp of all sporting nuances, particularly boxing and football. Still a fine football commentator for television.
- Eleanor Oldroyd: the first female presenter, in 1995. Branched out into presenting across the Radio 5 Live spectrum, later reporting regularly on England's cricket fortunes. Broadcast across the radio networks on the funeral of the Duke of Edinburgh in 2021, and the Platinum Jubilee celebrations in 2022.

- Jon Champion: only 24 when he first presented *Sports Report* 'which was ridiculously young after just three months in the department.' Later specialised in football commentary for both Radio 5 Live and television.
- Mark Saggers: two spells in the sports department, sandwiched by a stint at Sky News. 'I was the perennial filler-in, when Mark Pougatch was away, but it was always a privilege.'

And two more who have a special place on the subs' bench...

- John Helm: the only one to present, produce and (occasionally) read the classified football results. 'They can't take that away from me!' A long and rewarding career in television followed his decade with Radio Sport, 'but I'm proud to have been part of a special time on *Sports Report*.'
- Jonathan Overend: 25 years in the department, almost 20 of them as understudy to Ian Payne and the two Marks, Pougatch and Chapman. Presented the programme more times than anyone else, bar the 11 main presenters, from Eamonn Andrews onwards. Tennis correspondent when Andy Murray won Wimbledon for the first time 'and only that means more to me than presenting *Sports Report*.' Always prepared to front the programme on Friday afternoons and Saturday mornings – just in case the regular presenter pulled out. 'To me it was as vital as the understudy in the theatre, ready to take the leading role at a few minutes' notice. There was an understanding that I would stand in, so I didn't just prepare for my Saturday afternoon football game, I was across all the other action.' His Marti Webb/Elaine Paige/*Evita* moment came when he was once diverted from his home in Newbury, while en route to cover Arsenal at home. Mark Pougatch was ill and Jonathan was sent to Molineux to present the programme. 'I loved it. I was prepared for centre stage when I got to Wolves.'

Now that's what I call dedication. Methinks even Angus Mackay would have approved.

7

IN THE STUDIO

It's 4.59 on a Saturday afternoon in a Broadcasting House studio and *Sports Report* is about to burst on air. A technician is ready to play 'Out of the Blue', the presenter's throat has been cleared, the second hand is ticking remorselessly and an eerie calm descends after sustained mayhem. The brace position is assumed by the personnel in the studio. Quick nods exchanged, with just enough eye contact.

At that moment, the editor, Bob Shennan, passes a slip of paper to his producer, Graeme Reid-Davies. A simple instruction from him, 'Just sign that.' Graeme looks at the paper. Only two words on it, 'I RESIGN.' It became a ritual for them every Saturday. Black humour was often vital to get through the most testing hour of the week for all those stretched to the limit getting *Sports Report* on air.

Sometimes the stress of it all induced the most incongruous of instructions to the presenter, alone next door in another studio, reliant on the production team guiding him to the next location. Outside sources, in technical parlance. Sometimes that outside source would go down for no real reason; another option was needed, and quickly. The producer, on talkback to the presenter, had to sound calm, assured, with plan B ready.

On rare occasions. Eleanor Oldroyd experienced one particular day when the fates dogged her every presenting step. She'd cue to a particular ground and no reporter appeared on air. Next, the line went down after two sentences. Glancing through the glass, Eleanor could sense the chaos, so she styled it out as best she could, relying on reading out sports news from various corners of the earth, awaiting cogent instructions. When they arrived, they weren't particularly helpful, 'Prepare to go anywhere!'

That particular producer was soon gainfully employed in other parts of the Radio Sport empire. Eleanor remained admirably calm on air, but twisting slowly in the wind shouldn't be on the *Sports Report* presenter's agenda. That vignette mercifully remained an exception to the rule.

Without the tightest of teamwork and scrupulous attention to detail in the studio, the programme would not have survived and prospered down the decades. It's remarkable that a group of fewer than 10 people gets *Sports Report* on the air. A producer is in charge of running the programme, the editor listens to the live output throughout the afternoon, assessing the relevant news stories to be developed later, keeping an eye on the news wires, deciding on the skeleton running order and writing the 5.00 p.m. headlines as near as possible to the deadline. Back-up producers are recording interviews and monitoring other live action elsewhere, courtesy of a bank of television screens, while studio managers and assistants are supervising the actual sounds coming from the outside broadcasts, and also editing clips and interviews in an adjoining studio.

The trust between the producer and back-ups is essential. 'Is that interview ready? How long is it? What are the in words – and the out? How does the presenter pick up from it?'

The key questions are regularly – and urgently – framed, 'Is that interview good enough? No? Drop it then. Get on with the next one. We can give it a couple of minutes. Right, are we ready with the Scottish football round-up? What's happening with the racing package? Any news of Pep Guardiola? We want him live, not recorded. Have telly got him yet? Stand by to record that and run him if we can't get him live in the next five minutes.'

Things are smoother in these digital days, when editing is so much swifter, but conversely competition for those pressurised post-match interviews is a lot more intense. Matches finish later now – thank you VAR and you players who feign injury – so by 5.30 p.m., if the key football interviews weren't in the can, you'd be chasing your tail as the clock ticked towards 6.00 p.m. and other sports were jostling with football for attention on the programme.

The return of Cristiano Ronaldo to Manchester United in September 2021 brought editor Mark Williams a thorny problem. Due to a vigilant supervision of score flashes from other reporters around the grounds, the afternoon programme was away from the action between Manchester United and Newcastle for no more than a few seconds at a time. 'We were desperate to get a good commentary clip from Ian Dennis, if Ronaldo scored – ideal for the *Sports Report* headlines,' recalls Williams. 'He scored twice, so that was the first hurdle cleared. The icing on the cake for *Sports Report* would be hearing from Ronaldo before we went off air.'

That proved the biggest problem. Countless TV and radio stations were after the same thing. In the end, as the clock neared 5.45 p.m., Ronaldo came out of the tunnel to do just one interview – with television. It would have to be pooled with other media outlets, including *Sports Report*. Yet the sound quality was poor and Williams had to make a hasty ruling. 'There were thousands of fans still milling around at Old Trafford, trying to get a glimpse of Ronaldo, nearly an hour after the final whistle. Because of Covid regulations, we couldn't get into the interview areas inside, so anything agreed would have to be done on the perimeter of the pitch. When the fans saw Ronaldo, they just kept up a constant barrage of chanting. Because our microphone couldn't extend all that far, it was inevitably picking up the chanting as the interviewer tried to get as close as he could to Ronaldo. But it really wasn't broadcastable, by our usual standards.'

Williams had to compromise. He reasoned that just a few seconds of Ronaldo talking, backed up by all the fans' chants, was preferable to nothing at all. So that went on air for about 20 seconds, followed by presenter Mark Chapman summarising the gist of the player's comments – including the nugget that he had been very nervous before the game. 'That was quite an admission from someone as self-confident as Ronaldo,' says Williams. 'I decided that, for once, we had to lower our standards – just to get Ronaldo on!'

At least Williams doesn't have to worry these days about blood being spilt in the studio. In the pre-digital days, small reels of tape had to be played in, the proposed edit areas had to be marked with chinagraph pencils and then the exact spots cut with razor blades.

Ian Darke, early in his career one of the back-up producers, shudders at the memory of working with those razor blades. 'Editing at speed, with the producer asking for the interview quickly, could be a risky business with a razor blade. Often, there was blood from cut fingers as you battled a tight deadline. Health and safety today would have had fits. You'd have the producer saying the edited piece was too long by 30 seconds and you'd try to cut it again. Then it would be dropped because a bigger story had broken while you were battling with the chinagraph and razor blade. The scene was one of organised chaos and if you stood in the studio as a spectator, you'd wonder how the programme ever got on air. But it did. And usually very smoothly.'

But it could get very hairy when editing tape. Graham McMillan, producer or editor of *Sports Report* on around 250 occasions, hasn't forgotten some of the horrors with tapes when he started in the late nineties. 'Woe betide you if you put the edit in the wrong place and had to start again. You'd be getting the glare from the producer. It's so much easier now, editing digitally, you just press Undo on a button and start again.'

Sonja McLaughlan spent five years as back-up producer on *Sports Report* before becoming a rugby union and athletics reporter/presenter, and she considers it invaluable training. 'When I joined *Sports Report*, I suddenly realised I'd hit the Premier League, part of an elite squad. You had to bring your A game in every Saturday – and don't have a hangover! It all happened so quickly after 5 o'clock and you were terrified of being the weakest link. I remember editing a rugby interview and forgetting to edit out some swearing, and it went out, live on air. I was mortified. You concentrate for so long and when you walk out the studio door just after six o'clock the adrenalin suddenly dissipates, and you could sleep for a week.'

Claire Ackling, one of the most skilled, resourceful and speedy back-up producers for over a decade, relished the adrenalin surge. 'I loved editing at speed with razor blades, although you always worried that the best bit of the interview remained on the floor and it would get in the Sunday papers, rather than *Sports Report*! It was great to be relied on by your producer to get it right. For a sports nut like me, getting paid on a Saturday afternoon, close to all the action, it was nerve-racking, but so exciting.'

Claire, Graham, Sonja and Ian all brought massive respect to the programme in their unsung capacities. They had grown up listening to *Sports Report* and they knew all the stories about the early years under Angus Mackay. We were all amazed at the ferocious deadlines that football reporters or newspaper columnists had to surmount to get to the studio in time to broadcast live, sometimes unscripted, so there was always the sense among my contemporaries on the programme that it was far tougher in those formative years.

Mackay was well aware he was asking a lot of a radio reporter to leave White Hart Lane or Highbury at full-time and pitch up at Broadcasting House, to be ready to go on air, as early as 5.35 p.m., with *Sports Report* starting at 5.30 p.m. in those days. The same applies in the regions, where the reporter had to get to a BBC studio at speed, on full-time, where the production team would be anxiously waiting.

'I can say without fear of contradiction,' Mackay wrote, 'that the radio reporter has a very much more difficult and exacting task than his counterpart on the newspaper. The greatest bugbear in the life of a radio reporter is the clock and the hands which seem to move faster on Saturdays than they do in mid-week.'

Mike Ingham, presenter of the programme over four years in the 1980s, agrees. 'I'd present from studio B9, in the basement of Broadcasting House, and you could hear and feel the Bakerloo Tube trains coming through the floorboards. It was a bizarre set-up then. The presentation studio was the size of a ballroom, with one little table in the middle. You'd be on your own as the presenter whereas, on the other side of the glass, the engine room was about the size of a telephone box! It was amazing how it held up to 10 people, with colleagues falling over each other, coffee cups piling up, newspapers strewn all over the place. Yet no matter how much chaos and confusion was going on, I'd get calm, measured communication through my talkback from the producer. It was as measured as Mission Control, Houston.'

During most of Ingham's tenure, the producer was the outstanding Bryan Tremble, by common consent the most influential in *Sports Report*'s history, apart from Angus Mackay. Bryan did not fit the identikit sports producer's image. Immaculately dressed, crisp white shirt, tie knotted neatly, he was a man of few words, but made every one count. Unfailingly polite, softly spoken, he radiated calm assurance.

Ian Darke was in awe of Tremble. 'He had this instinctive feel of what made great radio. I'd come back with a 20-minute interview, wondering how it could be edited down, and Bryan would say quietly, 'I'll have a listen.' He'd dissect it, put a bit of music behind some of the words, pop in a relevant commentary clip and he'd turned in about three minutes of gold dust, beautifully crafted. He made us reporters actually look quite talented!'

Producers on *Sports Report* still use Tremble's ideas when they have time. Those funky pieces with just the right amount of music and atmospheric commentary clips illuminating the relevant bits from the interview take time to construct – but Tremble always seemed to have time. He was cherished by all the *Sports Report* presenters, for his originality, work ethic, attention to detail and brevity on talkback. 'Bryan always said just enough,' recalls Ingham. 'He'd say "Go to Tottenham" when you were about to cue to Old Trafford. Bryan didn't want to bother you with the glitches he was sorting out. He was the master.'

If Mackay was the restless taskmaster and driving force among producers of *Sports Report*, Tremble was the creative pioneer, turning base metal into gold every Saturday. He must be among the five most important figures in *Sports*

Report's history. All the programme's household names from his decade in charge would agree.

By his own personal example, Tremble also established a calm studio discipline that still exists on *Sports Report*. He never raised his voice, and always treated colleagues with the utmost courtesy and respect, both in the studio and on talkback – and that has remained the prevailing custom. The atmosphere is chaotic at times, exasperation is not unusual, tough decisions are made every few seconds by one of the team, but trust and mutual respect bind it all together on the most exacting of Saturdays. Testosterone is commendably absent.

Gill Pulsford worked alongside Tremble as production assistant, talking to all the reporters and commentators out in the field, relaying Tremble's instructions, and after she became the first to graduate from PA to programme producer 15 years later, she put Tremble's behavioural standards into practice. 'Bryan was so quiet and unassuming, but clear about what he wanted. We'd stick to a decision he made. When I became producer, I wouldn't have any shouting in the studio. Too much noise creates tension. There was a pride among our team; you knew you were doing something important.'

Bob Nettles worked on the programme as studio manager, in charge of technical matters, from 1987 to 2001. He has been senior studio manager for BBC Radio's coverage of every royal occasion from Charles and Diana's wedding in 1981 through to the Duke of Edinburgh's funeral in 2021 and working on *Sports Report* ranks equally high in his impressive career. 'If you're at the eye of the storm, and you're dealing with 30 outside sources, that keeps you on your toes. It's something I'm still proud of. People from other departments at the BBC – like news and current affairs– are astounded at how the production team on *Sports Report* manages without a script when it starts. I still get a frisson when it's 5 o'clock on a Saturday, even though I've been gone from the programme for 20 years now.

Successors to Gill Pulsford are all adamant that the Tremble dictate about studio calmness is necessary. Unprompted, both Claire McDonnell and Simon Foat use the same analogy – that of an air traffic controller. Claire, producer from 1998 to 2006, remarks, 'I've always liked that analogy. You have to be calm and in control and hope all the planes land on the tarmac eventually. I always used to get nervous just before the 5 o'clock headlines, thinking, "This is where we sink or swim." The adrenalin was so intense that I almost never went out on a Saturday night, I was drained. Falling asleep in front of *Match of the Day* was about my lot.'

Simon Foat, another long-serving producer, offers another interesting analogy. 'As *Sports Report* unfolds, it's like peeling away the Fabergé egg, wearing the white gloves, revealing all sorts of goodies. I feel like I'm directing the air traffic as we get to 5 o'clock. Am I good to go? Yes! Bring it on! I don't know how the editor has the calmness to write the headlines when I'm so keyed up. I'm busy checking with the studio manager for the umpteenth time that we've got 'Out of the Blue' ready. The football results give you a buffer of about 2 minutes 45 seconds these days and then you plunge into it. The vital thing for me is to nail your top story as soon as you can, once the second half commentary is finished. That gives you time to work out some sort of sequence from 5.10 p.m. onwards, but you have to rely on your experienced reporters out in the field for guidance about the status of a story. There was no golden rule after 5.30 p.m. – if there was an important goal, try or wicket, then we'd take it live.'

Simon's point about adaptability is an important one. If something relevant is happening somewhere in the sporting world, it must feature on the programme. Alistair Bruce-Ball, one of our most gifted all-round broadcasters, has two examples of that. In December 2012, he was covering England's T20 match against India, under the Mumbai floodlights, and it looked like an exciting finish. He told the production team that Eoin Morgan, the England captain, was batting superbly, with 15 needed off seven balls, then nine off six. They crossed to Alistair for the final ball, with three needed. Morgan smashed a six straight back over the bowler's head, for a brilliant finish, live on the radio. 'It sounded superb, with the bowler running in as they came to me. It only took up around 40 seconds, near the end of *Sports Report*, but it was great work to get to me in time.'

Four years later, Jason Kenny was competing in the individual sprint in the World Cycling Championships at the London Velodrome, an important event with the Olympics in Rio just a few months ahead and Kenny one of Great Britain's major gold medal hopes. The handover to Alistair was perfectly judged. 'I told them not to come too early, as it would be cat-and-mouse for a time, so they came just before the bell. Then it was all-out sprinting. It was all done and dusted inside 30 seconds, with Kenny winning – a good story, but atmospherically covered. All down to the production team.'

But it doesn't always pan out so satisfactorily, as Tony Adamson can confirm. One of the sports department's most versatile broadcasters over three decades, Tony was often sent on slightly unusual assignments, because he had the wit and nous to make them entertaining.

In April 1981, the London Marathon was staged for the first time and the organisers were keen to drum up some publicity. BBC Radio Sport had decided to cover it and *Sports Report* sent Tony to do a preview piece for the event the following day. It was basically a puff piece on the merits of pasta for marathon competitors and Tony dutifully went along, talked to a few people and rang into *Sports Report*. Anything offered by Tony Adamson came with guarantees of humour and excellence, so Bryan Tremble agreed to have him on near the end of the programme. It could only be by phone, though, outside a Central London restaurant. Tony duly dialled in, was told to stand by, then pushed back for a few minutes. He was horrified to observe the phone box drinking up his available coins and became concerned he might be cut off in his prime. He was – just after clearing his throat and starting his piece about pasta and the historic introduction of the London Marathon. As the 'pip, pip, pip' rang out on air, presenter George Hamilton quipped, 'Typical Tony Adamson – he never has any money on him!' Even a cheery cove like Tony failed to see the funny side for a few minutes.

There are times, though, when *Sports Report* is assailed by the behemoth of news, especially since 1994 and the establishment of Radio 5 Live, the news and sport network. Tanks from both departments have been parked on the other's lawns at times and the relationship hasn't always been harmonious.

In 2002, the Queen Mother's death was announced in *Sports Report*. The news came through to the studio just after John Murray had started commentary on the 5.30 p.m. match at Middlesbrough – not perfect timing, but, of course, this was one occasion where news exigencies would hold sway. But not immediately. The producer, Claire McDonnell, was not going to be bounced into a premature exit from Middlesbrough v Tottenham to a half-cock item on the Queen Mother's death. The relevant news producer had burst into the *Sports Report* studio, telling Claire, 'You need to hand back to us now – we've got a piece from Nicholas Witchell.' That would be a filed obituary from the BBC's royal correspondent, ready to run whenever the Queen Mother died. Claire, unfazed, knew that and asked, 'Have you got permission to break the story?', aware of the protocol involved. 'Not yet', she was told. 'Then we'll wait,' was the firm rejoinder. Eventually, convinced at last that all the necessary ducks were in order, Claire went on talkback and instructed John Murray, 'Hand back to Mark, NOW.' Presenter Mark Pougatch read the bare bones out and Radio 4 took over from Radio 5 Live.

Claire was right to stick to her guns. A few more minutes made little difference, and it was vital that the story was triple-checked for veracity and the coverage ready to go. 'I wanted to get it right and as promptly as possible, but needed to be sure when we ought to come out of the commentary. John Murray knew it was important when I talked down the line to him. "NOW" was always a key word for me!'

Another challenge involving the two empires of news and sport came when President Donald Trump's health became a major story in October 2020. He had been taken to hospital suffering from coronavirus, at the height of the pandemic in the USA and the news agencies were ramping up the coverage late on Saturday afternoon. Graham McMillan, producing *Sport on 5* then *Sports Report*, knew that, at any time, he might need to pull out of the Everton v Brighton second-half commentary and forget any thoughts he might have for *Sports Report*. If the medical prognosis was serious, then news would take precedence over sport.

'It would be massive if President Trump slipped into a coma or even died – it was a reminder that the world keeps turning on a Saturday afternoon.' Eventually, McMillan told commentator Ian Dennis to hand back from Goodison Park and, in the studio, presenter Mark Chapman gave the guts of the Trump story before cueing over to a live press conference at the medical centre, near Washington. A few minutes of that presser established that the President was not in immediate danger, so McMillan took the decision to return to the football commentary. 'But we had to reflect on it an hour later, in *Sports Report*, so we did a 15-minute round-up just after 5.30 p.m., after getting the main sports news of the day done and dusted. That left us enough time to wrap up the sport after the Trump segment.'

That Trump story illustrates the changing landscape of *Sports Report*. It's more newsy, with shorter interviews and more flexibility. The introduction in the early nineties of Integrated Services Digital Network – ISDN, for short – meant the programme could zip all round the world without a great deal of administrative hassle. In the past, a piece of wire from the back of a reporter's microphone would go through a copper wire in the studio sound desk. The lines had to be booked via the Post Office every Saturday. Now, with permanent ISDN lines installed at many sporting arenas, engineers don't have to be sent out every week to establish the connection. All you do is plug your equipment into a socket on the wall, dial up a number and you're through to the studio. It was a tremendous innovation, designed to capitalise on the formation of the Premier League in 1992 and the explosion of interest in football, giving the *Sports Report* studio vital access to the heart of the post-match atmosphere. And if you were reporting from overseas, it would be a great thrill to provide a 10-second flash report into the 5.00 p.m. headlines, with the strains of 'Out of the Blue' just underneath your voice.

Computers have also drastically changed how the results are included in the programme. In days of yore, someone had to type up the racing, rugby and football results, update the county cricket scores, then send them via a rudimentary closed-circuit TV system from the third floor down to the basement studio. On the final day of the football season it was someone's task to work out who'd been promoted or relegated in all the divisions, even down to goal difference if necessary – and get it done quickly. Then type it out and get it to the presenter, producer and editor. It was a major responsibility. Now computers do the hard yards, much to the relief of the production team. Imagine getting the wrong team relegated through basic human error!

The brains behind the statistical back-up in those innocent, pre-computer days was one Bill Ross. Bill may have retired in 1984, but when veterans of the programme gather for a noggin and natter, everyone has a story about him. He was a marvel at his job, the keeper of sports statistics in his precious blue books. If anyone dared to venture into Bill's domain in the sports room, trying to glean some information from his blue books, his Vesuvian eruptions would be a wonder to behold. But his reliability was a byword. Bill would never send a scoreline or result to the *Sports Report* studio unless corroborated by the Press Association. He gave one key piece of advice to Chris Rhys, who used to stand in for him when away on holiday, 'Keep everything simple. The listener wants to know what the score is and then where does it place his team in the table. That's why people tune in – the rest is flannel.'

Bill Ross struggled with social niceties and only he could remain impervious to Muhammad Ali, as he made his way through the sports room one afternoon in 1981, to be interviewed by Mike Ingham. As Ali enjoyed the affectionate and loud applause from a packed room, Bill carried on checking the racing results were accurate for *Sports Report*.

Bill never acknowledged fashion changes, flicked ash happily over his blue jumper and at times talked to himself as he hammered away on his battered Remington typewriter, 'Now then, what do you think we should start with?' 'Yes, I think that's a good idea.' A plume of cigarette smoke hung over Bill's working area by late morning, but no one would ever dare suggest opening a window. By 12.30 p.m. he was in the BBC Club, just across the road from Broadcasting House, a copy of *The Times* under his arm. He would always polish off the crossword within 20 minutes, en route to a prodigious consumption of beer. Mike Ingham remembers Bill's legendary capacity, 'He'd put away four pints to your half and, while swigging away, finish the crossword. Within an hour, he'd be back at his desk, ready to check the early racing results.'

For all his idiosyncrasies, Bill was vital to the operation – in the words of Bryon Butler, 'the belt and braces of the sports room', while Emily McMahon, a senior longstanding producer, thought he was indispensable. 'Very, very underestimated. Gruff, bad-tempered, yes – but it took three people to do Bill's job on a Saturday afternoon when he wasn't around. I was one of them.'

Bill's successor was that rarity – a woman that he respected. That accolade probably amuses Audrey Adams more than anything she's experienced in her 40 years in the sports department. Between them, Bill and Audrey clocked up more than 60 years on *Sports Report*. They were contrasting individuals. Where Bill was brilliant yet bellicose, Audrey is just as impressive professionally, while universally popular.

Audrey's utter reliability was soon apparent and even Bill Ross mellowed towards this particular woman before he retired. She was the obvious candidate to succeed him and soon began a fruitful working partnership with James Alexander Gordon and then Charlotte Green, producing the football results. 'From 3.00 p.m. onwards on Saturday, I'm across all the scores, ready to check on any delays to kick-offs or any incidents at obscure grounds. Then it's utter concentration – using as many sources as I can find to get it absolutely right. I've got online and a teleprinter and the television in my workshop, so that if one source of results goes down, then I'm not isolated. Charlotte sits alongside me and when I finish one page, I pass it to her. Total concentration from us both. Sometimes I have to write a result in over her shoulder, because it came through late.'

Countless producers and editors over the years have been grateful that Audrey slotted seamlessly into the operation. No one can remember her making a mistake in all her time on *Sports Report*, but she modestly bats that one away. 'I love doing live programmes, with that adrenalin surge, so *Sports Report* looms large for me. Even before I worked for the BBC, I'd tune in on a Saturday afternoon.'

Any newcomer to the production team with a modicum of common sense would stand in the studio for at least one Saturday to gauge just what was expected in such a small space, with so few involved. Graham McMillan likens the atmosphere to a beehive, with so many vital contributions. 'The decibel level is never high, but there's always dialogue between four or five people, often speaking in shorthand.'

Claire McDonnell remembers one sound from her time as *Sports Report*'s producer. 'That beep! beep! beep! of all the ISDNs checking in from two o'clock from all around the country. That's when you knew the challenge was on. Phones would be ringing in the studio and you'd be well aware that some of those calls would be bringing technical problems. And we were still four hours away from the end of *Sports Report* and that large gin and tonic!'

Even the well-oiled machine that is *Sports Report* can be derailed by technical issues. It was for an hour in December 1996, when I managed a career highlight – presenting *Sport on 5*. I was in Bulawayo, reporting on the Zimbabwe v England Test match, when I was woken from my reverie by an urgent call from producer, Gill Pulsford. All the microphones from the studio had packed up at the same time and the production team needed precious time to solve the problem, so I anchored the programme for a blissful period, providing the Test details, handing over to Ascot for a race commentary, then to Sale for some rugby union, while whizzing around the various football grounds. It certainly shifted me from my routine Saturday afternoon on tour and I started to fantasise that I might even be able to present *Sports Report* – from Bulawayo. That, I realise, would have been plan X or Y. Peter Drury, commentating on Nottingham Forest v Arsenal, had been alerted that he might have to step into the breach at full-time. Alas, perchance to dream...

In the end, the brilliant, resourceful engineers had decamped to a tiny studio and ensured the mics were indeed working, so Ian Payne could resume presenting from London. Hopefully, no one noticed why I was wittering on from Bulawayo for over an hour. It's moments like that when you realise just what a team effort *Sports Report* is, steered by dedicated professionals who are unknown to the vast majority of the public.

The illustrious presenters of *Sports Report* have been vital in shaping the tone and tenor of the programme, adjusting to changes of pace in broadcasting, and the altering content and its style. They are the ones who get their names in *Radio Times* and are eventually coveted by media giants with larger chequebooks than BBC Radio, but without those who make it happen in the studio, their lustre would be seriously dimmed. And they'd be the first to admit it.

8

STANDOUT MOMENTS

Over a period of 75 years, any programme is bound to have its fustian editions, routine efforts that served their purpose, but provided little to linger in the memory bank. *Sports Report* has always had the saving grace of providing a news service as a consolation for those days when the flame of inspiration just guttered, never bursting into life. No point in suggesting every edition was a belter, but when the foot soldiers of *Sports Report* gather for reunions, funerals or retirements, attention inevitably turns to memorable moments in the programme. Hunches that worked triumphantly, huge dollops of luck, as well as cock-ups. 'How did we get away with that?' is the general consensus. It all added to the fun…

1951: Stanley Matthews to the rescue

In the early years of *Sports Report*, Stanley Matthews was the most famous and revered English footballer. He was dubbed 'The Wizard of Dribble', a wonderfully talented right-winger whose speciality was landing opposing full-backs on their backsides, laying on stacks of goals for Blackpool and England. Long before the term 'assists' became part of football's lexicon Matthews was the supreme provider in the game.

Matthews was also modest, but, coming from a humble background in the Potteries, he was no orator and it was a challenge trying to prise many worthwhile quotes from him. However, he knew his worth and appreciated the nationwide respect that grew every year, courtesy of an admiring press, so Stanley would help out those reporters he felt deserved a hand 'in extremis'. One of those was Donny Davies, of the *Manchester Guardian*, a journalist who clearly loved the game, writing about it with immense flair, wit and integrity. When *Sports Report* asked Matthews to contribute to a studio discussion after an FA Cup tie against Fulham, he was only too willing to oblige, once he ascertained that it would be Donny Davies escorting him to the studio in Blackpool.

The initial problem was the studio location. In those pioneering times, a live discussion involving a football ground and the Broadcasting House studio was fraught with various technical traps, and the usual recourse was to get the interviewee to a local BBC studio, then rely on the engineers to work the oracle. Blackpool's studio just happened to be in the Blackpool Tower, near the top floor of the famous building. With Matthews not ready to leave Bloomfield Road until soon after 5.00 p.m. it was a challenge to get him to the studio on time for an interview just after 5.30 p.m. The mind boggles at the most famous footballer in the land being prepared to submit himself to this, after running up and down the right wing at the age of 36, but Stanley Matthews would do it for *Sports Report* and Donny Davies. Comparisons with the modern era would be odious.

Davies later described the scene as 'a narrow, confined space rather like the inside of a submarine... the congestion may be imagined.' But, with the minutes ticking away remorselessly, it was vital to establish contact with Broadcasting House. Matthews surveyed the chaos phlegmatically, grateful that his station in life appeared less complicated than that of a BBC Radio reporter or engineer. All he knew was that Davies would report live on Blackpool's 1–0 win and that he'd be interviewed by the master, Eamonn Andrews.

All seemed in order until, around 45 seconds before the Blackpool contribution, the lights fused in the studio. Davies was not used to such a late drama and having to broadcast in the dark, his script now superfluous. As the engineers clambered over each other, trying to disentangle pieces of wire, someone said quietly, 'Stay put, chaps. Take your matches out and empty them on the table.' It was Stanley Matthews.

Davies was suitably impressed. 'Picking the matches up a dozen at a time, Stan lit them in relays and I had the novel experience of reading to the world a glowing tribute to a master winger from a script illuminated by the glow of matches lit by the master himself. The circle of faces leaning over that pocket of light in the velvety blackness was a subject fit for a Rembrandt.'

Matthews had faced sterner tests than this one. At times he must have felt the burden of expectation hugely. This 1951 FA Cup run ended with another defeat at a Wembley final, to add to Matthews' disappointment in 1948, and it seemed he would never pick up a winner's medal. But, like Sir Gordon Richards in the same summer of 1953, Matthews got there. His virtuoso performance in that legendary 4–3 defeat of Bolton sealed his immortality, at the age of 38, and his countless admirers could savour football history. Just as a prolonged encore, he was still playing top-flight football in his 50th year! And, a mere stripling at 41, he was to become the first European Footballer of the Year.

A sportsman who deserves the 'legendary' description and, as he demonstrated in the Blackpool Tower, a good man to have around in a crisis. Just as well every adult seemed to smoke in those days. In modern times, you'd be relying on mobile phones to shed the necessary light.

1952: Cliff Morgan's *Sports Report* debut

He was just 21, but Cliff Morgan's first appearance on *Sports Report* marked him out as a natural broadcaster. He was also a wonderful rugby player, a quicksilver, beautifully balanced fly-half, but that's for another book, another day.

Cliff could pinpoint exactly the moment his life changed – 5.35 p.m. on Saturday 8 March 1952. His precocious skills had helped Wales win the Triple Crown in Dublin. In the aftermath of victory, Morgan lay in the bath, luxuriating in a special day for his country. He couldn't quite understand why his leg hurt so painfully. During the match, the physio rubbed some oil into his leg, it felt better so he kept going. Adrenalin had helped, but he had broken a fibula. He couldn't walk. What a time to pick up a serious injury, he thought. All this and the BBC wanted to interview him about Wales' great achievement. The emissary to the dressing room was Sammy Walker, who had captained the British Lions and was now working occasionally for *Sports Report*. Cliff, as befitted a chapel boy from a loving, dutiful family, was properly respectful towards Walker, but apologised. He just couldn't walk. Cliff recalled, 'He went back and reported to Angus Mackay, who simply never took "no" for an answer, so Sammy was told to get some help and carry me up the stairs to the commentary box.'

Already, Cliff was a massive fan of *Sports Report*. The English master at his grammar school insisted that his pupils listened to the radio over the weekend and then, every Monday afternoon, discussed the various programmes in class. One of those was *Sports Report*. 'I would have given my Welsh jersey to talk to Eamonn Andrews, despite all the pain. When he asked me on air what I would remember most about that afternoon, I said: "My father losing his teeth and he wasn't even playing!"' Morgan Senior was so excited at Ken Jones' dynamic run, which led to the crucial Welsh try, that he leapt to his feet. 'He shouted with joy, but he spat his top set 12 rows in front of him. He never got them back!'

That anecdote from one so young, live on air, beguiled not only Eamonn and the huge radio audience, but kept Cliff going in his masterful after-dinner speeches. although he was trumped one day when telling the story on Irish television. Tony O'Reilly, that brilliant Irish wing and superb raconteur responded, 'Morgan, I know a fella in Cork who is still wearing them!'

Instinctively, Morgan knew on his broadcasting debut that he was on to something as a communicator. Throughout the rest of his glittering playing days, he kept his door open to the media. He was 28 when he retired, ushering in a new career as an outstanding broadcaster and mentor to so many novitiates. But it all began with a broken leg in Dublin and an elusive pair of false teeth.

1961: Bing Crosby and Bob Hope talk golf

When *Sports Report*'s producer heard that the final 'Road' movie was being filmed at Shepperton Studios, the hunt was on to get the two stars on the show, talking about their sporting passion – golf. *The Road to Hong Kong* was the last of the series of seven that began in 1940, a mixture of corny gags, flimsy plotlines and forgettable songs, but they were hugely popular worldwide, not least in the UK. By 1961, Hope and Crosby, both nudging 60, were weary of the genre and they didn't take much persuading to talk golf with Eamonn Andrews, who was always at his best when charming American stars.

Crosby happily name-dropped American presidents past and present. 'I've played with both Eisenhower and Kennedy. Ike is methodical, studies every shot and plays straight. JFK could potentially be a fine golfer. He's got the distance, hits a very long shot off the tee. He's a better golfer than Ike.'

Hope confessed to being a golf addict. 'I live a couple of minutes from a very good course, but I've got three holes also in my back garden. I play now and again with Ben Hogan and Arnold Palmer, and with Bing – but it's tough with him. If you beat Bing, you have to hire an attorney to get your money!'

But, aside from the obligatory jibes about Crosby's alleged meanness, Hope gave a prophetic assessment of a powerfully built American, just 21 years of age. 'This fellow Jack Nicklaus, who's just won the Amateur Championship at Pebble Beach, is one of the great young golfers. He went round 136 holes 19 under par. He's husky and strong – he'll go on to be a top golfer.'

Hope lived long enough to enjoy Nicklaus' glorious career after turning professional in October 1961. He won 117 pro tournaments, including 18

Majors, suggesting Hope was a handy talent spotter. Crosby, at one time playing off a handicap of two, competed in both the American and British Amateur Championships. He died in a manner that surely seems appropriate – of a massive heart attack just after completing 18 holes, near Madrid, in 1977. What a way to go, loving golf as much as he did. And he always knew he was a better player than his old movie partner.

1973: Red Rum wins one of the great Grand Nationals

Red Rum and the Aintree course are inextricably linked. Locally trained by Ginger McCain at his Southport stables, Red Rum became one of the greatest horses to win the Grand National, with a phenomenal record. First in 1973, again the following year, then in 1977, second in both 1975 and 1976 – no other horse approaches that.

But the horse eclipsed at the last gasp by Red Rum in 1973 could fairly be described as the greatest never to win the National. Crisp carried 23 pounds more than Red Rum and had to race more than twice the distance he usually tackled, yet he charged on valiantly over the 30 massive fences. He was 15 lengths clear after the final fence and the crowd sensed a famous victory as the jockey Richard Pitman steeled himself for the challenge from Brian Fletcher on Red Rum. By now, Crisp was visibly tiring: could he hang on for National glory?

Peter Bromley, as usual, called the two horses home in his inimitable fashion… 'As they come to the Elbow now, Crisp is under pressure – he doesn't know where he's going – Richard Pitman is trying to keep him going. Red Rum is closing the gap – defeat is facing him as Crisp has 200 yards to run and the National isn't over yet. Crisp is keeping going – it's going to be a desperately near thing, but Crisp is walking… 25 yards to go, Red Rum goes sailing past to snatch the National. Crisp is second and the rest don't matter, for we will never see another race like that in a hundred years!'

At one stage Crisp was 30 lengths clear, the biggest lead ever in a National, but the disparity in weight proved crucial. He was a massive horse, seven inches taller than Red Rum, and in the end he lost out by just two strides.

Bromley's definitive commentary illuminated the *Sports Report* headlines and Pitman then gave him the classiest of interviews. He admitted he'd been deflated for a few seconds after the finish, but by the time he had pulled up Crisp, he was delighted with his performance. 'I'm a happy chappy who loves riding, but I had the ride of my life, something money can't buy. It's hardly disastrous, we're all healthy – we're just about £25,000 short!'

Pitman's philosophical attitude imbued his commentaries for BBC TV in later years, an enjoyable contrast to some of those operating with tighter tunnel vision. He never won the National, but succeeded in the Whitbread Gold Cup, the King George VI Chase and the Champion Hurdle. He rode Crisp to victory over Red Rum the following year, at Doncaster – on equal weights – but Crisp suffered a serious leg injury and never rode again in the National. By all means, cherish Red Rum, but let's not forget the horse that contributed to one of the great finishes in the Grand National.

1975: FA Cup draw live goes belly-up

It seemed a good idea at the time. Broadcast the draw for the third round of the FA Cup live on *Sports Report*. After all, *Grandstand* was set to stage it, so why not follow suit? You can't beat a bit of live drama in sport and the third-round draw always throws up some great, unlikely stories.

Usually, the third-round draw would go out live on Radio 2 on Monday lunchtime. The stilton and port wine tones of our football correspondent, Bryon Butler, would introduce proceedings from Lancaster Gate, the FA's headquarters, and his link to the draw would always be 'and the first voice you will hear will be that of the FA's secretary, Ted Croker.'

All very smooth, with nary a hitch, year after year. But the key BBC Sport executives wanted to shake up the presentation, so *Grandstand* set up on the FA's manicured lawn and Saturday at 5.00 p.m. it was to be. *Sports Report* would do the same. Can't let these TV wallahs steal a march on us with their razzamatazz, can we?

Alan Parry was presenting *Sports Report* that day and the ensuing shambles is burnished in his memory, with accompanying winces. His designated assistant, Godfrey Dixey, was a veteran of the sports department, a charming gentleman, beloved by everyone, but not the swiftest at taking crucial decisions at speed.

Throughout the afternoon, on *Sport on 2*, the live draw would be trailed: a break with the Monday afternoon tradition, so don't miss it on *Sports Report*. After the draw, live on TV and radio, it would be repeated on *Sports Report* and then the programme would take its usual chaotic course, adapting to the eddies and whirlpools of the day's action.

Godfrey Dixey's job was to write down legibly who was playing whom, so that Parry could repeat them once the draw had taken place. Godfrey decided to write each team on sticky jam jar labels and place them in order. Parry and the producer felt that was foolproof.

The draw started sedately enough and Godfrey's system appeared ideal. Parry was content. But then… 'The officials at FA headquarters got a little carried away by the thought of appearing on television and took far too long to make the early part of the draw. They were instructed to move at a faster pace. As the draw speeded up, dear old Goddo got more and more agitated. Soon his sticky labels began to tear in half and his neat white paper looked as though it had been out in the rain. I could read "Arsenal v Coventry" but the rest became a chaotic mess. Goddo's fingers got shakier and his breathing heavier. I started scribbling down the names myself, but I must have missed at least four of the ties!'

Through the glass, the production team could bear witness to the shambles, with Parry in a fit of giggles while poor Godfrey struggled manfully. Somehow Parry scrambled together the complete draw, 'but it bore no similarity to the whole thing. Leeds fans must have been cursing their luck at being drawn away to Everton when in fact they were at home to Darlington!'

The following year, BBC Radio reverted to Bryon Butler, Ted Croker and, live from Lancaster Gate, Monday lunchtime. The old order was restored, thankfully, and footballers and managers again gathered around their trannies to hear their fate. There's something to be said for tradition, especially if it prevents the *Sports Report* presenter from lying down in a darkened room, gibbering about jam jar labels.

1975: Muhammad Ali turns presenter

There have been many illustrious presenters of *Sports Report*, but they would all happily yield the palm to Muhammad Ali. He and the spotlight were irresistibly drawn to each other, but he was invariably up for a laugh with *Sports Report*. When Des Lynam turned up in Kuala Lumpur, to preview and commentate on Ali's world title fight against Joe Bugner, he only had to suggest that Ali might care to introduce the Saturday show and he jumped at the chance…

'Welcome to *Sports Report*. This is Muhammad Ali in Malaysia. I like your class and I like your style – but your pay is so cheap I won't be back for a while. Now the classified football results.'

James Alexander Gordon never had a better warm-up man. It was typical Ali. Anything out of the ordinary that would reflect well on him was never batted away and no hanger-on would determine what he would say or do. A couple of years after that Kuala Lumpur cameo, with a defence of his world title coming up, Ali decided he wasn't going to talk to the media anymore. It was akin to the ravens leaving the Tower of London. Des Lynam, out in Las Vegas to cover the fight, had to plead with Ali to start talking again. The UK wanted to hear from him. It worked – and for the umpteenth time in a decade and a half, the *Sports Report* producer was grateful.

Des Lyman recalls getting a herogram for that Kuala Lumpur stunt. 'They all thought I was a genius back at Broadcasting House for that, but he'd have done it for anyone. He loved the limelight. I wasn't that close to him, but he did once say to me 'You're not as dumb as you look.' I was grateful to him a few times for going along with the hype. It made for great radio.'

Des would agree that he and *Sports Report* were the beneficiaries of the hard work put into developing a working relationship with Ali by Angus Mackay and Eamonn Andrews, followed up by Harry Carpenter. The BBC branding helped also; Ali knew that he wasn't being pilloried in the UK for his religious or anti-Vietnam War convictions. His usual dip into the brantub of hyperbole and some rhyming couplets would be enough to satisfy the most demanding of producers.

For so long, Muhammad Ali was the most famous sporting celebrity in the world and he knew it. *Sports Report* was more than happy to go to the well with him for many years.

1977: Call the Doc and lead *Sports Report*

In September 1977, the two biggest names in English football were inextricably linked with Derby County. Brian Clough, late of that parish, was being wooed to return after four years away. He was flirting with Derby, enjoying the attention and the media speculation. No one knew his intentions.

The same applied to Tommy Docherty. Two months earlier, Docherty was the central figure in a massive news story. Two months later, after his exciting young Manchester United side had beaten a superb Liverpool team in the FA Cup Final, Docherty was sacked after admitting he was involved in a relationship with Mary Brown, the wife of United's physio. That story encapsulated most of the dramatis personae that would satisfy the most taxing of news editors and

Docherty, predictably, was in the public eye for months afterwards. Where would he fetch up next?

There was no doubt that Docherty would stay in football. Like Clough, he loved being the cynosure of all. The scandal, his success at Wembley and his certain return to football management was peak Docherty. It was just a case of him riding out the storm. In 1977, with his experience and penchant for attacking football, he was still attractive to club chairmen – as a breed, hardly justified in being too morally censorious.

By the time Leeds came to the Baseball Ground on Saturday 17 September, it looked as if Docherty was heading to Norway, to manage Lillestrøm. Before the match, the Derby board had given a vote of confidence to their manager, Colin Murphy, who had been in charge for a year. The pursuit of the elusive Clough was over. Murphy would continue in the job.

Straight after the 2–2 draw, the tectonic plates had shifted. The Derby chairman, George Hardy, issued a statement, live on *Sports Report*, saying that Murphy had been sacked. He hoped, though, that Murphy would stay at Derby, working with the new manager: Tommy Docherty.

From the chairman's statement, *Sports Report* went straight to the commentary box, to interview Docherty. It was a sleight of hand that clearly delighted Derby's power brokers to unveil Docherty in such a spectacular manner, live on national radio. Docherty made it clear that he had been wooed ardently by Derby.

'I phoned Norway only an hour ago and they very kindly agreed to release me from the contract. I went up to Sunderland this morning on the 9 o'clock train to see my lad, Michael, play against Bolton. I was watching television when a flash came on with my picture reporting that Tommy Docherty could be the next manager of Derby County. Then I got a phone call from them and they very kindly sent a car to bring me here.

'It's the first time in my career that I never began a season and I missed it very much. I'm told Colin Murphy would like to stay. I'm absolutely delighted with that as he's a nice fella. I'm sure Colin can learn a tremendous amount from me and I'm sure I can learn something from him.'

In retrospect, you could drive a coach and horses through those comments from Docherty, a manager who never expressed a modest view of himself. If you asked Tommy Docherty for the time of day, you'd be advised quickly to seek a second opinion. In fact, Lillestrøm were furious at him reneging on his new contract and had to be mollified by Derby County after protracted negotiations. Murphy was booted out of Derby soon afterwards, with Docherty's long-time associate, Frank Blunstone, coming in. And Derby hadn't just homed in on Docherty out of the blue, he had been holding out against their desperate overtures for several days, once it was clear that Clough wasn't leaving Nottingham Forest.

None of that mattered to *Sports Report* at 5.05 p.m. that Saturday afternoon. The programme's close relationship with Docherty, built up over the years at Old Trafford, proved mutually beneficial in announcing his arrival at Derby in style, live on *Sports Report* – even if some of the shenanigans were rather murky. Mike Ingham, then a Radio Derby reporter, covering the daily activities of a club rarely in the shadows, was impressed by the exclusive, 'Fair play. We were chasing the story about who would be the new manager and we never got a whiff about Docherty. We had a great relationship with Tommy when he was there, but that day, *Sports Report* cleaned up, and every other media outlet had to follow their exclusive.'

Docherty's air of innocence in that live interview was risible and many were unsurprised that he failed to pull up too many trees in his two years at Derby. But he was big news in 1977 and no self-respecting *Sports Report* producer or reporter could afford to hold their noses at such an exclusive, concerned about the morality of the situation. Certainly, nobody working for a newspaper would. Cleansing the Augean stables of football was above any sports executive's pay grade in those days.

1982: An exclusive, out of Africa

In 1982, when Ireland won rugby union's Triple Crown for the first time in over 30 years, they were inspired by their talismanic fly-half, Ollie Campbell. Tactically smart and a wonderful goalkicker, Campbell was the heartbeat of that side. He scored 46 points in that Five Nations championship, including all of Ireland's 21 that clinched the Triple Crown in Dublin against Scotland. Good judges hailed Campbell as Ireland's most complete fly-half since Jackie Kyle, the orchestrator of Ireland's Triple Crowns in 1948 and 1949 and the Championship in 1952.

The story of the day for *Sports Report* in February 1982 was obviously their win over Scotland, with the spotlight on Ollie Campbell. But producer Bryan Tremble wanted more. What had happened to Jackie Kyle in the previous 30 years? Could he be tracked down to give his slant on Ireland's latest Triple Crown? One fly-half talking about the latest star Irish fly-half?

That was the task given to Emily McMahon around 8.00 a.m. that Saturday morning. Find Jackie Kyle, wherever he is in the world, and tee him up for *Sports Report* in nine hours' time if Ireland win the Triple Crown. 'Last time we heard, he was somewhere in Africa' was the only clue she had.

Emily was the ideal producer for such a challenge. Many Saturday mornings, she'd be greeted with 'Here's one for you, Emily,' and she'd relish it. Starting at the age of 17 as a production secretary, she'd come through the ranks, eventually becoming producer of *Sunday Sport* and also the boxing producer. For Emily, there was never a lost cause. An indefatigable basher of the phone, she had developed some great contacts and she called in a few favours in her pursuit of Jackie Kyle.

Kyle is widely acknowledged as one of Ireland's greatest-ever rugby players, but there was far more to him than that. He studied medicine at Queen's University Belfast, while starring at rugby, and after his retirement spent some years on humanitarian work in Sumatra and Indonesia. Then he became a consultant surgeon in the mining town of Chingola, Zambia, before returning to Ireland at the age of 74. Until he was 60, he was the only surgeon working in a hospital containing 500 beds. In all, he spent 34 years in Africa. He admitted to being inspired by Albert Schweitzer, the German philosopher, theologian and medical missionary in Africa.

Emily tapped into her contacts at the World Service to establish a trail to Kyle. She finally tracked him down in Zambia, only to find he was on the golf course. 'It felt like I'd phoned the whole of Africa! But the calls led me closer and closer to him. His housekeeper promised me she'd pass the message on to Mr Kyle and she did so. He came through for us and we got the interview.

'That was like manna from heaven for me. I loved chasing that sort of story. Getting Jackie Kyle that day was an absolute thrill.' And I'm sure that Kyle, a man known for his tremendous work ethic, would have been impressed by Emily's dedication in tracking him down.

1982: Kevin Keegan breezes into Newcastle

At the start of the 1982–83 English football season one news story dominated. Kevin Keegan, once European Footballer of the Year, a serial winner with

Liverpool and the current England captain, had signed for Newcastle United, a Second Division club.

It was a triumph for Arthur Cox, Newcastle's homespun and understated manager, profiting from Keegan's disillusionment at Southampton and his restless ambition to keep proving himself as a footballer. Cox may not have enjoyed a glamorous managerial career – his only previous role as the number one had been at Chesterfield – but he wasn't short of psychological insight and knew what Keegan could offer on Tyneside.

Luckily, Arthur Cox was a huge fan of *Sports Report*, something I swiftly picked up when he joined Derby County and proved very helpful to me on my Midlands patch. Arthur always found time for the programme and never baulked when big-name players were chosen ahead of him for live interviews. He made it clear he had grown up with *Sports Report*. That was to prove crucial when Keegan was top of every football media agenda as the 1982–83 season loomed.

Ian Darke was our designated reporter for Newcastle's first game, home to QPR. He wasn't at all surprised when his producer, Bryan Tremble, said to him in midweek, 'I'd like you with Kevin Keegan, live, straight after the football results, at five past five. So get up there and see what you can do.'

Ian, not a broadcaster easily cowed by a challenge, yet aware that many bosses were saying the same to their designated reporters, hightailed up to Newcastle on Friday morning. At the training ground, he immediately spied Kevin Keegan, obligingly signing countless autographs, sitting on a wall, enjoying the craic with the excited fans. Ian broached the subject of *Sports Report* and Keegan responded, 'No problem with me, but you'll have to check it out with the manager.'

Arthur Cox welcomed Darke into his office as if he was the club's new owner. 'I love *Sports Report*, it's the greatest sports programme in the world. I want Kevin on the show, but I can't make it work for you, technically. If you can do that, and make sure you're in my office at 5 o'clock tomorrow, Kevin Keegan will be here.'

Darke was too steeped in his trade to think he'd cracked it, especially as so many would be after Keegan for quotes after the game. His producer would organise the technical issues, so that Keegan would be patched straight through from St James' Park to London, but would Keegan pitch up at the appointed time? So many imponderables – the demands of sponsors, autograph hunters in the tunnel, competing television outlets, hangers-on looking for a photograph. And he was needed by *Sports Report* just 20 minutes after coming off the pitch. It wasn't the most relaxing Friday night on Tyneside for our intrepid reporter.

The match itself would satisfy the most ardent newsgatherer. Newcastle won 1–0 and the goal was scored by… Kevin Keegan. He celebrated by diving into the crowd, delighting them and a host of newspaper photographers. A love affair was consummated on the first date and that relationship survived eight years of drama, as Keegan inspired as player, then as manager in two spells, before ending in 2008.

As the delirious Newcastle fans celebrated outside, Ian Darke was anxiously awaiting the source of all their euphoria. Darke knew enough about football and its contrary ways to think the odds were against getting Keegan at the appointed time.

'We were into the Division Two results in Scotland, and Bryan Tremble in London and I were getting desperate. Bryan was all set to go elsewhere and hope Keegan eventually turned up. Then the door opened and this small figure, soaking wet, with just a towel around his waist, walked in. "Are you Ian?" he said. "Arthur Cox sent me." I had to say as politely as possible, "Please come over here quickly, Kevin." It was a wonderful moment and Kevin said all the right things. He was a real pro.

'That was real seat-of-the-pants stuff, classic *Sports Report*. We led the field that day and I was immensely proud. But I can't thank Arthur Cox enough for making it happen.'

1983: Dundee United make history

The ideal scenario for *Sports Report* when sporting history is made would be telling the story of the day, fitting it into context, and then hoping to get a live reaction from the key figure responsible. The latter is usually the imponderable, especially when you're dealing with a combustible character like Dundee United's manager Jim McLean.

Winning the Scottish title ahead of Aberdeen, Celtic and Rangers was a monumental feat by McLean. Sealing it against their rivals, Dundee, at Dens Park, 350 yards from United's ground, made it even more satisfying. The problem for *Sports Report* was getting co-operation from McLean in the post-match chaos.

McLean's attitude to the media was invariably wary, spilling over to hostility at times. He once punched a BBC Scotland reporter who had displeased him, live, on camera. McLean's outbursts could eclipse even the volcanic eruptions from Alex Ferguson, then changing Aberdeen's fortunes, 65 miles north of Dundee.

Roddy Forsyth, working his passage then as BBC Radio's occasional football reporter, was well aware that he would be expected by his bosses in London to deliver Mclean to *Sports Report* if Dundee United won the title for the first time.

Roddy made a very wise decision on the Friday to prepare the ground by pitching up at Tannadice for a chat with the manager, paving the way for a big favour from him on the morrow. It had already been a busy week for Roddy. He'd been in Gothenburg on the Wednesday night, working alongside Peter Jones for Radio 2, as Ferguson's Aberdeen won the European Cup Winners' Cup, then covering their triumphal reception from supporters the following day in Aberdeen.

When he got to Tannadice, he found the manager alone and even more morose than usual. 'Where were you?' he barked at Forsyth. 'In an age long before emails, mobile phones and texts, I had no means of knowing what United might be doing for the media, but they usually had a Friday lunchtime session. I explained that I'd had a very busy week, but wanted to make sure that we gave due acknowledgement of United's potentially historic match next day. I asked if there'd been a good turn-out from the media. "Naebody came," was his disconsolate response.'

Roddy was astonished that, on the eve of United's most significant match in its 74-year history, there was no radio or TV presence on that Friday morning, so he saw his chance, once he'd concluded his interview with Mclean. 'Look, I made the effort to come and see you, so when you win the league will you come up to the stand and do a bit for *Sports Report*?'

McLean's lugubrious response was hardly encouraging, 'We'll see.'

Next day, with both Aberdeen and Celtic still in contention for the title, United won the derby 2–1 and history was made. So, would the notoriously prickly Jim McLean help out Roddy Forsyth?

'Wee Jim was as good as his word. After the initial celebrations, he strode from the United dugout, along the track and up to the broadcast positions. He walked past both BBC Scotland's radio and TV teams, and other stations, who were beseeching him to come and talk to them. So we got the first reaction from the manager, who had just secured himself a place in the pantheon of Scottish football legends.'

Two years later, Roddy became a valuable member of our team, when he was appointed BBC Radio Sport's reporter in Scotland, delivering any number of exclusives and offering pithy observations on Scottish football.

But perhaps his most satisfying accolade came from Bobby Robson. Roddy was interviewing the England manager for a TV documentary and, after the inevitable small talk and the call to 'run VT,' Roddy was just about to ask his second question when Robson's face lit up. He'd obviously been preoccupied with something and had solved it. With a broad smile, he said triumphantly, 'I know who you are, now. You're the lad who does the Jock football!' There are worse ways to describe Roddy's splendid career.

1983: Ron Atkinson's devastating put-down

For more than a decade, Ron Atkinson was one of the managerial reliables for *Sports Report*'s various production teams. He had a quick Scouse wit, knew how to give the media what they wanted, while remaining a serious student of the game, with justifiable ambitions. His expansive personality and desire to play open, attractive football made him an ideal choice for Manchester United. 'Big Ron' was his moniker, a reference to his character, rather than any physical prowess.

Usually, Big Ron had the last word in live interviews, delivering the killer riposte with a chuckle and a 'See ya later.' As Jimmy Melia discovered one very hot April afternoon. Melia had, remarkably, steered Brighton to the FA Cup Final, beating Sheffield Wednesday in a tremendous, open match at Highbury. It was a great story. Brighton had been fighting relegation from the top flight ever since Melia took over in December 1982. Yet they kept winning Cup matches, including the first FA Cup home defeat in nine years for Liverpool, for whom Melia played almost 300 times. A Scouser himself, Melia started living the dream after that remarkable win at Anfield. Flights of fancy came easily to him.

Melia was a media darling, the longer that amazing Cup run lasted. He wore white shoes every match – 'my disco shoes' he called them – and, to the envy of some of his players, was now going out with a glamorous model girlfriend, considerably younger.

By 1983, it was almost a given that *Sports Report* would get on air, live, the two successful managers from their semi-finals. Ron Atkinson was, by now, an old hand at this kind of caper and duly presented himself at our interview point at Villa Park. I was producing the outside broadcast that day and, after his Manchester United team had beaten Arsenal, Ron's mood was as sunny as the weather when he rocked up to talk live with the programme presenter, Mike Ingham. After I assured Ron that Jimmy Melia was waiting to talk to him from Highbury, he smiled conspiratorially. Ron appeared in a mischievous, playful mood.

He clapped on the headset, accepted Mike Ingham's congratulations, and listened intently to Jimmy Melia's excited ramblings from Highbury. Usually, such semi-final chats were as cagey as the matches, with both managers intent on giving no hostages to fortune, nor offering grandiose forecasts for Wembley that would end up biting them on the backside. Not this day. As Melia warmed to his task, predicting great times ahead for Brighton, promising United the hardest game of their season, Atkinson winked at me.

It just happened to be Eurovision Song Contest day. Atkinson was always into popular music, favouring the classic singers like Frank Sinatra, but he knew all about the exploits of Abba, Bucks Fizz, Lulu and Johnny Logan, accompanied by Terry Wogan's acerbic commentary.

I wasn't aware where Ron's puckish mood was taking him during that live chat with Jimmy Melia until he heard Brighton's manager burbling on about winning the trophy and taking his boys to greater glories abroad. 'We want to get into Europe,' he trilled. That was the opening for Big Ron. 'Write a song then, Jim,' and as he handed me back the microphone, strode off, shoulders shaking and cackling loudly. Having verbally outflanked Jimmy Melia, Atkinson did the same on the pitch at Wembley, winning 4–0 in a replay.

1995: Juninho signs for Middlesbrough

When Boro fans heard that in October 1995, they assumed it was a spoof. One of Brazil's brightest young stars coming to Teesside from São Paulo? Brazil's player of the year? Why would he join us? Those sceptical supporters needed confirmation as the rumours swirled around. It came from *Sports Report*.

It looked like being a quiet Saturday for the *Sports Report* team. There were no Premier League games, due to international matches, but none of those were Saturday afternoon kick-offs, so there was little live football action. Time for some rugby union, horse racing and studio discussions, but editor Andy Gillies had spotted something on the AFP wires. Something about Brazil's new young dazzler being lured by Middlesbrough. Surely Juninho, precociously talented at the age of 22, had more lucrative, attractive offers if he was planning to leave his hometown club? But Gillies was intrigued – it would be a hell of a story if he could stand it up.

Gillies contacted BBC Radio Tees for guidance, gleaning that manager, Bryan Robson, and chief executive, Keith Lamb, were rumoured to be in São Paulo. Time to bash the phones; this was too good to dismiss, even if it appeared highly unlikely.

At this stage, with the Premier League just three seasons old, the flow of money into the English game was beginning to attract talented overseas players. Many big names were being bandied about in the football gossip columns, but the likely destinations were clubs in London, Manchester and Merseyside – not Middlesbrough.

Gillies and his team got closer and closer, until… 'We called every hotel we could find in São Paulo. Then we got lucky. We were put through to Bryan Robson's room and he answered straight away. He was distinctly unimpressed at being flushed out and slammed the phone down. He knew we were on to something. We knew that Keith Lamb was kindly disposed to *Sports Report*, so if we couldn't get confirmation from the manager, the chief executive would do fine.'

So Gillies rang Lamb's room. He answered. 'How on earth did you find us?' He was impressed by Gillies' persistence and agreed to record an interview with Ian Payne, in which he confirmed that Boro was set to sign a top Brazilian for just £4.75 million. 'If you've spent all this time trying to find us, I can't say no comment.' Would that all football chief executives were so gracious…

The interview was given pride of place an hour later on *Sports Report* and the Boro fans were thrilled. Juninho became a folk hero on Teesside, relating naturally to the fans, playing football in the street with schoolkids and bewitching with his sumptuous skills. He was nicknamed 'TLF', as in 'The Little Fellah', and is lauded as one of the club's greatest players.

2004: Matthew Hoggard's hat-trick, live on air

Some Saturdays, the big story just lands in your lap and all you must do then is make the most of it. On other days, the production team has to work a little harder. Then it helps if you know the nuances of a particular sport, enabling the programme to judge when it's time to plug into the live action.

The third Test match at Bridgetown, Barbados, was a perfect example of that. England tours to the Caribbean are in the perfect time zone for *Sports Report* – five hours behind Greenwich Mean Time – so that any significant action over an hour can be highlighted in the programme. A hat-trick for England's swing bowler, Matthew Hoggard, definitely came into that category.

Sports Report had just wrapped up a football interview when producer Claire McDonnell and editor Joanne Watson spotted that Hoggard had just dismissed Ramnaresh Sarwan, caught in the gully. McDonnell buzzed Jonathan Agnew at the ground to bring that news, which coincided with a wicket next ball – Shivnarine Chanderpaul, lbw. Agnew covered that dismissal live and handed back to the studio, even though Hoggard was now on a hat-trick. That feat had only been accomplished by just nine England players in 127 years of Test cricket, but it looked as if *Sports Report* would miss out on that possibility, live on air, due to the prevailing broadcast regulations.

BBC Radio didn't have the broadcast rights to that West Indies tour. TalkSPORT was in the driving seat, which meant that 5 Live could only have two minutes every hour live on air. That would normally comprise 30 seconds at the top of the hour, the same again on the half-hour, and the remaining precious 30 seconds dotted around that 60-minute period. So how could *Sports Report* get round that and broadcast the hat-trick ball?

This is where Watson's knowledge of cricket was essential. She'd always been a devotee, covering Yorkshire for Radio Humberside, doing the production for *Test Match Special*'s winter tours from the London end, impressing the most entrenched members of the sports department that a woman could know as much about the game as any man. She knew that it invariably took a few minutes before a potential hat-trick ball was delivered. The batsman on strike would be trying to calm his nerves, delaying the bowler, the fielding captain would be taking an age to get his players in the key areas, and he'd then be having intense discussions with his bowler. Everyone on the field of play would be keyed up and time would appear to be standing still with the crowd in a ferment. No point in going back too early to Bridgetown.

Watson did her calculations. Under the restrictions, she still had around 45 seconds to play with until the end of the programme. She asked her technical operator to put talkSPORT on a speaker in the studio and was delighted that our commercial rivals were concentrating on a football story, rather than Hoggard's possible hat-trick. McDonnell let Agnew know that she would be trying to get to him for the crucial delivery, but be ready to hand back swiftly, whatever transpired. That two minutes regulation mustn't be breached. They had pictures from Barbados in the studio, talkSPORT (still preoccupied with football) on speaker and our cricket correspondent fired up, ready to commentate with excitement and tension, but with one beady eye on his stopwatch.

Presenter Mark Pougatch, another passionate cricket fan, was equally pumped up, judging the moment to cross over to Bridgetown. He summarised the day's football results, trailed what was coming up later in the programme, then handed to Agnew just as Hoggard ran in to bowl to the new batsman, Ryan Hinds.

Hinds edged the perfect outswinger to Andrew Flintoff at second slip and Hoggard had his hat-trick. At 45 for 5, the West Indies were now out of the game, leading by only 43. Thousands of England supporters, packed into the Bridgetown ground, added to the passionate, exuberant atmosphere, and the result was 45 seconds of radio gold on *Sports Report*. Agnew ensured the BBC hadn't exceeded its quota of seconds by handing back swiftly to Pougatch and talkSPORT, luxuriating in the exclusive commentary rights for the tour, caught a cold. The cricket foot soldiers on BBC Radio were mightily chuffed to have pulled that one off.

All radio cricket reporters have experienced that sinking feeling when they've built up the possibility of a hat-trick, only to see the relevant delivery sprayed harmlessly outside the off stump. Then you hand back, apologetically, to the studio, infused with anti-climax. Not this time. The stars aligned perfectly. Cricket dominated the first few minutes of *Sports Report* on a big football day, thanks to a hefty dose of flexibility.

2005: Graeme Souness hangs two Newcastle players out to dry

It was funny, unless you were a Newcastle United supporter. It's bad enough losing 3–0, down to 10 men, but when you have two more of them sent off for fighting each other, it all gets a bit surreal. Then their manager hauls them in front of a live press conference, making them apologise.

It's not as if, as a player, Graeme Souness was a Bobby Charlton or a Trevor Brooking himself. He was no stranger to fights, earth-remover tackles and red cards. But he was furious at Lee Bowyer and Kieron Dyer, as the roof fell in on Newcastle and Aston Villa sauntered off with the spoils and a muffled titter.

It all started when Bowyer confronted Dyer, near the end of the game. Why wasn't he passing the ball to him? Dyer made an uncomplimentary remark about

Bowyer's ability – or lack of it – and Bowyer climbed into him. Players from both sides tried separating the warring duo and Bowyer's torn shirt added to the drama. Both were sent off and they carried on their sparring in the tunnel. Souness allegedly challenged both to a fight with him and at last discretion ruled as they demurred. Their manager was not a character to rile. A superb midfield player in his time, he was also known as a genuine hard man, willing to sort anyone out with his fists.

Back in the *Sports Report* studio, the production faced a dilemma – how do we kick this one on over the next hour? There was little chance of interviews with Bowyer and Dyer. Perhaps a bland statement from them? It would all depend on the furious Souness.

Editor Joanne Watson played a hunch. 'I knew that Souness was such a good talker that he was likely to say something and probably give Bowyer and Dyer a bit of welly. In his interviews, Souness never ducked a question, so I hoped he'd be good value.'

Word came through from St James' Park that there would be a presser, scheduled or around 5.30 p.m. Watson asked her technical operator Steve Bridges how difficult it would be to take the press conference live into *Sports Report*. He thought he could make that happen. But Joanne would be taking a flier that Souness would climb straight into Bowyer/Dyer, rather than talking about a 3–0 home defeat.

Fingers crossed, then. Please, reporters – ask Souness about the fight, first up. As the manager filed into the press conference, everyone was astonished to see both Bowyer and Dyer walking in with him, suited and booted, looking very sheepish. Panic over. They were bound to lead off with the fight.

Souness, flanked by the pugilistic duo, listened implacably as Bowyer kicked off, apologising to all and sundry. Dyer followed suit, missing out nobody, including 'everyone connected with the club.' With contrition in the air, Souness reverted to his combative self, throwing some kerosene on the dying embers. 'I think Lee Bowyer is indefensible. I think he is guilty, as the pictures show, of throwing more than one punch and he has to accept whatever punishment comes his way. But Kieron, we feel, has an argument here. I have seen the incident on television and I have been assured by Kieron that he did not throw any punches.'

Classic Souness. He loved to have the last word when convinced of the justice of his cause and he was courageous enough to air his convictions. With Newcastle fining Bowyer a record six weeks' wages while contesting the three-match ban incurred by Dyer, it was clear that manager and club officials felt Bowyer was the main transgressor.

Some press conferences turn out to be damp squibs, but this one lit up *Sports Report*. I'm certain that today any club would throw a media *cordon sanitaire* around the issue, handing out an anodyne statement, trusting that reporters would soon tire of being knocked back, hoping that 'the brand' would survive a tricky couple of days. Mercifully, Graeme Souness believed in a more open style of communication. For that, I can even forgive him his ruthless tackling as a player.

2017: Benítez and Shearer bond

When you're the manager of a club that's overachieving and many fans still aren't sure of you, then it helps if you can have the club's most legendary living former player alive pitch his tent on your plateau.

Rafael Benítez was content to come on *Sports Report* in September 2017 to reflect on an encouraging return to the Premier League for Newcastle United after relegation on his watch the year before. The fans hadn't yet fully bought into the Spaniard, but with a 2–1 home win over Stoke they were starting to warm towards him. Admittedly, it was the embryonic part of the new season, but Benítez had given strong indications of what it meant to him to be the manager of Newcastle. He was in tune with the Toon Army's passion and determined to keep the club in the top flight.

Benítez never blanked *Sports Report* at any of his clubs and often stayed for a cheery chat afterwards with the reporter/producer, engaging with genuine warmth and fondness for a spot of gossip. This time, he had a pleasant surprise when coming on air to be interviewed down the line by Mark Chapman.

As he clamped on the headset and checked with the producer that the volume levels were satisfactory, Benítez realised that the Geordie accent he was hearing on air was that of one Alan Shearer. Newcastle's most prominent supporter was waxing lyrical about his club's fine start to the season. Chapman had already read out the top six placings, with Newcastle fourth in the table. Shearer told him, 'Read that out again', glorying in the heady delight of Newcastle in Champions' League territory – admittedly after just one month.

Chapman obliged, enjoying Shearer's beaming delight, and then interrupted his eulogy, 'You'd better shut up now, Alan – because we've got Rafa Benítez on the line.' Shearer was now a fan, not a former player...

Shearer: 'Well done, Rafa!'
Chapman: 'Alan's made up, Rafa.'
Benítez: 'So am I!'

Benítez then tried to play down Newcastle's fine start to the season, trying not to raise expectations, but Shearer the fan would have none of it. Mark Chapman loved the exchange, admitting, 'It was pure fluke. We had Shearer in from the *Match of the Day* office, reflecting on the day's results and what to look out for on that night's programme, when a voice in my ear said, "We've got Rafa Benítez waiting on the line." I knew straight away it would work and they chatted away happily, without any nudging from me. Pure instinct. Rafa was great with Alan, he knew all about his status on Tyneside and seemed genuinely chuffed at Alan's support.'

Simon Foat, the producer that day, admitted it wasn't predetermined. 'It just happened to be Alan Shearer that day and Newcastle just happened to be fourth. The planets aligned and Rafa turned up just at the right time. It made for three minutes of brilliant radio. It's not always as seamless as that!'

2018: Keeping up with the Jones'

A live interview when the principal character is being particularly combustible really tests the mettle of the *Sports Report* broadcaster. In February 2018, at Twickenham, the wheel of fortune spun the way of Chris Jones, our rugby union reporter at the time.

Chris had enjoyed a lively relationship with Eddie Jones, the England coach, always a challenge due to his contrary ways and fondness for manipulating the media. There was no doubting the Australian's stature as a coach, nor his sharp antennae about what would play well over the airwaves or in print, and it was Chris' task to give him enough leeway without being railroaded.

Eddie Jones sometimes appeared to think that media appreciation of his methods and his players should be modelled on that of North Korea, but usually it was just knockabout fun, harmless enough. Jones would get his message across and his inquisitors would withdraw, bloodied but still standing.

On this occasion, Eddie Jones gave a good impression of the younger sibling who always got the tap end at bath time and never forgot the slight. He was in a strop, spoiling for a contretemps – and Chris Jones was on the receiving end.

It was Chris' good fortune that Jones usually came early to the *Sports Report* interview position in the bowels of Twickenham, but unlucky that Jones was fired up, so soon after England's 12–6 win over Wales. The source of his ire was scepticism among some of the pundits and correspondents about the continued selection of the experienced full-back, Mike Brown. The feeling in some circles was that Brown, in his 66th Test, was a reliable yet limited player, and that England needed more flair and dynamism in that position. We would soon learn what Eddie Jones thought about that collective view.

Chris Jones had no idea that the bomb was ticking as he warmed up the coach, live on air, with some routine questions about the Welsh opposition, their steadfast defence and the difficulty of turning the players round in just six days since the last international, blah blah blah. Then Chris brought up the good performance of Mike Brown. The mood of the interview abruptly changed…

Eddie Jones: 'You guys all tell me he can't play Test rugby, now you're telling me he's good.'

Chris Jones: 'I don't think that's quite fair.'

EJ: 'You guys are unbelievable – fair dinkum – you guys are unbelievable. You're always criticising him, now he has a good game, you're all on the bandwagon.'

CJ: 'I don't think you can treat the whole media as one.'

EJ: 'I think we can and I'm sick of it, mate. You guys are better selectors than we are – that's what you think you are… and now he plays a good game and you're all on the bandwagon.'

CJ: 'I think most people would agree that Mike Brown was excellent today.'

EJ: 'He's been excellent for 23 Tests for us, so I don't know what was different today.'

CJ: 'Thanks for your time, Eddie.'

EJ: 'Thank you.'

Mark Chapman picked up off the back of that in the Twickenham commentary box and said simply, 'Blimey.' It wasn't the usual anodyne exchange that has increasingly hallmarked sporting interviews and Chapman's single word recognised that. He sought the views of ex-players turned pundits alongside him about Eddie Jones' hostility and Matt Dawson gave a pithy reaction.

'All coaches have their favourites. I think Chris Jones did well to stay in the ring. I was worried for Jonesy for a minute, thought the physio might have to come into the ring and give him a hug. Well played, sir!'

Seconded. Eddie Jones had tried to create a siege mentality in media briefings all week and was continuing in the same vein after the match. Chris' interview went viral immediately after it went out live, his text messages exploded into overdrive and the press dined out on those explosive quotes.

Chris Jones certainly earned his stripes that day. He stuck up for his profession, without getting involved in a slanging match, leaving the listeners to make up their own minds about Eddie Jones' opinions. And it all ended amicably. Three days later, Chris received a phone call, asking him to have coffee with Eddie at the team hotel, where a pipe of peace was happily passed around.

Fair dinkum, as Eddie Jones would say.

2019: FA Cup tie abandoned due to racial abuse

Raw emotion and anger can make powerful radio, especially when it involves sport, supposedly a soothing release from so many of life's tensions.

When a football match has to be abandoned because some fans are racially abusing opposition players, it's time to clear the decks on a live sports show and shine a light on such disgraceful antics. *Sports Report* did just that in October 2019, after Haringey of the Isthmian League Premier Division conceded their fourth qualifying round tie against Yeovil Town. Haringey's manager, Tom Loizou, said, 'If we get punished and thrown out, I don't care. The abuse my players got was disgusting.' To be fair to Yeovil's players, they said to their opponents, "'If you're walking off, we're walking off with you."'

The news resonated throughout football that weekend. Aston Villa's England defender, Tyrone Mings, is of mixed race and had experience of such incidents while learning his trade in non-League football. When the Haringey news broke, Mings tweeted, 'Well done for taking a stance, sometimes it can get brushed off in lower leagues.'

Racial abuse was the week's main football story before Haringey played Yeovil. Four days earlier, in Bulgaria, England's Euro 20 qualifier had been halted twice after Bulgarian fans were warned about Nazi salutes and monkey chanting. Cue any amount of pious handwringing and sonorous sentiments, with little offered in the way of proactive deeds. Now it was clearly seeping down to the grassroots of football.

Mark Chapman had spotted the story on social media during 5 Live Sport's second-half commentary and immediately recognised its significance. He alerted the production team, adding the salient information that he knew the Haringey manager and that might help get him on air. 'The season before, Haringey had enjoyed a good FA Cup run and I'd presented the early draws on TV, live from some non-League grounds – twice at Haringey. They can be bedlam, but one of its beauties is that you get to meet some lovely non-League people. I don't just show-and-go at these events, I spend a bit of time with nice folk. Tom Loizou seemed a genuine bloke, with a good heart, and I just hoped he'd trust me and the programme to come on, with plenty of time to tackle the issue.'

The production team managed to track down Tom, while Chapman was anchoring the first part of *Sports Report* and he didn't need much persuading to come on air. The interview proved searingly honest and heartfelt.

'As we were lining up to take a penalty, my goalkeeper was spat at and a bottle thrown at him. My number six got called names and to see the look on the kid's face... the FA Cup's not worth that much to us – we're never going to win it. I got these boys out of local Sunday leagues and to be subjected to that, 10 or 15 feet away... They've never had that experience, so I took them off the pitch.'

Chapman, 'What have Yeovil said to you?'

Loizou, 'Their manager and players were different class. They tried their best to calm their supporters down. I don't want Yeovil Town to be punished. I've got no answers. My players had been looking forward so much to this game.'

Chapman, 'Do you despair?'

Loizou, 'I see and hear it all the time. My side is a multi-racial side, because of where we come from... people aren't interested in us... we keep our heads down and carry on. I feel helpless all the time. My goalkeeper is a churchgoer, training to be a pastor, he's the politest person I've ever come across. It's such a shock to him. There must have been 300 behind his goal, so much abuse coming from there.

'I haven't heard one abusive song at this ground in the past two years and we've got up to 500 supporters. We just don't treat people like that. There's only one race – the human race. I just don't understand people anymore.'

The interview lasted 12 minutes, very long by *Sports Report*'s compressed standards. Several items were jettisoned because this was a breaking news story, duly picked up by other media outlets. Chapman gives full credit to his production team. 'They were the ones doing the chasing, trying to find the manager. I just got on with the rest of the programme. Phone bashing is absolutely vital on *Sports Report*.'

True enough. It was one of those raw interviews that keep you in your car or standing silently in your kitchen. Subsequent events sadly suggest that it won't be the last of its type to be heard on the programme. Racial abuse will continue to circle around the drain. Hopefully, such interviews will be much scarcer in the future than those encompassing joy, relief, surprise – the very essence of sport, with its infinite capacity to engage those who listen to *Sports Report*. But the programme won't shy away from the realities, no matter how unpalatable.

It was such a different age, when Stanley Matthews saved the day for *Sports Report*, up in Blackpool Tower. Seventy years separate the impromptu efforts of a group of smokers and the emotional effects of racial abuse on a football manager, bewildered by the hostility towards his players for just the colour of their skin. Simpler times back in the Matthews era. It's up to the sports fan to discern if they were happier times. *Sports Report* has tried to reflect the changing mores, respecting the right of the listener to judge. It adapts to changes in society, while remembering we're only talking here about sport.

2022 – Shane Warne's sudden death.

When the news of Shane Warne's untimely death broke one Friday afternoon in March, the *Sports Report* team knew something different was needed to mark the passing of such a towering figure in sport. Warne transcended the confines of cricket through the force of his vivid personality, apart from his remarkable playing career.

The programme's editor Graham McMillan realised that, over the next 24 hours, hordes of Warne's playing contemporaries would be wheeled out across the media to lionise his great cricketing gifts. *Sports Report* needed to celebrate him in the round as a personality. Not just the greatest wrist-spinner of all time.

Jim Maxwell was the perfect choice. The veteran commentator from ABC Radio in Australia had covered almost all of Warne's international appearances and, with his appreciation of cricket history and rounded awareness of Warne's personal foibles, Maxwell got his personal tribute note perfect. It was no hagiography, but a statement of how extraordinary Warne was…

Maxwell said Warne was 'one of the greatest sportsmen of all time. With a career of theatrical deception Warne emptied bars when he bowled… Warne's larrikin after-hours image masked a generous spirit. He was always thinking about how he could contribute – an autograph, a selfie, unsolicited advice to a lad, giving time to a charitable cause and forever relishing the poker game or the golf course, when he wasn't caring for his family and friends'.

The presenter Mark Chapman wisely restricted himself to 'Jim Maxwell. Thanks for listening' after Maxwell's graceful tribute. No need to say anything more.

9

AT THE SHARP END

'But at my back I always hear time's wingèd chariot hurrying near' – Andrew Marvell, poet, satirist and Member of Parliament could almost have had a certain radio programme of the future in mind when he penned that couplet 350 years earlier. For if there's one defining sentence that binds the various contributors to *Sports Report*, out in the field, it has to be, 'Bloody hell, is it that time already?'

The plangent tones of 'Out of the Blue' may stir a sense of cosy familiarity among many listeners that all is right with the world at 5.00 p.m. on a Saturday afternoon, but to the programme's foot soldiers it's a terrifying call to arms. Time is running out. You're on your own for the next hour. You have your check list, so get on with it.

You have to don a coat of many colours, particularly if you're at a football ground, and especially if it's a Premier League game, when coverage from all sections of the media reaches saturation point, and players and managers can't move a couple of yards from a microphone, camera or notebook. There's no time to dwell on earlier decades, when post-match coverage seemed so leisurely, with matches ending at around 4.40 to 4.45 p.m., competition from other media outlets was minimal and managers were happy to stand around, chewing the cud before going live into *Sports Report*, and then enjoying some off-the-record gossip afterwards. Today, the Premier League has lucrative broadcasting contracts with almost every country in the world and when the TV broadcaster calls the tune, the club has to indulge them. As a result, almost every square foot in dressing-room areas seems to be commandeered by the Panzer regiments of television, with radio indulging in desperate hand-to-hand combat for precious space, hoping for a modicum of quiet amid the babble, so that a short, live interview might possibly be conducted into *Sports Report*.

Going live into *Sports Report* requires a thick skin, a pugilistic strain, some semblance of diplomacy, a rat-like cunning, orienteering capability, the flexibility to launch straight into an interview when your quarry suddenly materialises, and a decent relationship with someone in newspapers to find out if you've missed anything from any press conference that takes place over the next hour. Finally, you need the knack of writing a considered report at speed and delivering it in a semi-literate manner at one minute's notice – sometimes with the nominated manager standing balefully in front of you, listening intently to your opinion on the game, before being interviewed by you. That can lead to some testing encounters...

First, you have to get from your position in the press or commentary box to the designated interview point in the dressing-room area. That's where the orienteering skills come in handy. It's amazing how some doors that remained reassuringly open pre-match, when you did your recce to check out the terrain, are now resolutely locked, resistant to any knocking. The helpful security official who happily exchanged banter with you at 1.30 p.m. ('Yeh, I'll be here after the match, I'll recognise your face') has unaccountably been replaced by an implacable foe, for whom the term 'jobsworth' is deemed to be an honour. The club officials whose mobile numbers you have in your system are not answering, understandably occupied elsewhere, feeding the voracious broadcasting beasts.

This is where a knowledge of the stadium's innards is vital. At Wolves, we used to have to pass through the crowded hospitality area to get back out into the stand below the press box, then negotiate the playing area before diving into the tunnel, which wasn't lit – useful in the crepuscular gloom of a winter's afternoon, when you're trying to look your interviewee in the eye. Now, the intrepid reporter has to join the Wolves fans as they wind their way down three flights of stairs, before you can dive off to the right, after fielding a stack of advice about how you should describe the match. The same applies at Norwich City, where the journey from press box to interview point can take up to 15 minutes. At Stoke City, you have to rely on a friendly local radio reporter to guide you through the labyrinthine corridors, squaring things with security. At the London Stadium, West Ham's newish home, there are four stairs to negotiate, alongside the public, and it usually takes 10 minutes to get through to the business area. Those hoping to have the time to construct an elegant, epigrammatic narrative of the match are invariably disabused of the notion when they first battle against the tide of humanity. It's best to write the report in your head, committing it to memory as you wade through, then just hope you can deliver it with a modicum of authority.

Conor McNamara, who has battled the system down below for 20 years on BBC Radio's behalf, has a whimsical view on a situation that can become very fraught. 'You have to get to know the back passages around the stadia. It's the whole Boy Scout orienteering thing. Sometimes you have to go out into the street and back in again elsewhere. Don't take that staircase, it's too busy! We're like Deliveroo people. You have to get down there, set up your equipment and be ready as fast as possible. If you miss your slot, then you can't rely on the press officer to come back later with the person you want to interview. Getting a calm piece on air, live, then conducting a coherent interview, amid all the commotion from other media outlets, is very challenging.'

Once you've reached base camp, there's no time for a breather. Does your equipment work? It's in a box and the idea is that you plug it into a socket on a wall, dial a number and – *mirabile dictu* – it connects you to the *Sports Report* studio. Sometimes, for no good reason, it just doesn't work, even though it did a few minutes earlier, up in the commentary area. No time to work out why. Record your interview, tell the studio you're going back to the commentary position, from where you'll deliver your deathless prose and send back your interview. The technical fault will just have to be followed up next week. Recording interviews on a mini-disc always troubled Conor McNamara. 'That infernal machine gave me most grief. I used to get so paranoid that it wouldn't work that I'd use two mini-discs for a three-minute interview! I'd dread playing it back and getting nothing.'

Juliette Ferrington has hacked her way through the maze at all the major clubs in the North of England for more than 20 years with a great deal of charm, understated tenacity and good humour. 'Sometimes it's so chaotic that you just have to wing it. The equipment is always a worry, because you're on your own. I've had the batteries in my machine pack up on me, without any notice – they just die sometimes. Now and then I forget to switch on my lip mic and the producer has to shout down the line to get it sorted when I'm on live. I can arrive, out of breath from rushing down to the tunnel, and I'll be bending down, trying to dial into the studio and suddenly look up to find Jürgen Klopp or Pep Guardiola standing over me, waiting to be interviewed by me. Best thing to do is smile, have a laugh and hope they don't mind. It's often a beautiful mess.'

Amid all the tumult around the various dressing rooms immediately after a match, it can be taxing actually to get a message to a key figure. It's advisable to talk to the relevant press officer before kick-off, discussing interviewee options. I usually favoured interviewing a player, because they can be surprisingly informative and aren't always in as much demand as a high-profile manager, who will probably be bored and talked out by the time he gets to you. However, the press officer sometimes forgets your conversation and hurried, agreed decision about the preferred interviewee and he or she is last seen disappearing with the manager, en route to yet another TV interview. The next time you see that press officer, apologies are proffered to you with a sheepish grin, just before *Sports Report* goes off air.

Some press officers are excellent, proactive, attuned to our programme and will do all they can, given the multifarious demands from elsewhere. Others are insignificant wisps, in thrall to their manager, nodding along sagely while he delivers his truisms and evasions, as if they had agreed the line to take in advance. It's best not to lock horns in such situations. There is no time to spare, your producer back in the studio is getting twitchy and a row would be counter-productive. You swallow hard and try another tack.

If you're lucky, the players file past you, having showered and had treatment, en route to friends and family. Sometimes they stop and agree to talk, others cock a deaf air and slope off. The best response from a player for a quick word came in 1978 from the then Manchester United captain, Martin Buchan – 'Yes, velocity.' Martin was a well-educated man and knew what he was doing. He didn't like the journalist who asked brusquely for a quick chat and had no qualms with being dismissive. It would be remiss not to laugh at such a stylish response, even if you failed in your quest.

The experienced, wily reporter calls in favours once *Sports Report* starts. There is little time left for niceties. Bobby Robson, a natural communicator, often used to sigh dramatically, look to the heavens and say wearily, 'OK,' before talking expansively and winningly. Two answers from the great man were usually enough. He had grown up as a player, then manager, with *Sports Report* and no one can ever recall him turning us down. Niall Quinn, another engaging guest on many occasions, obliged just 20 minutes after his Manchester City side had slunk off the pitch, having been relegated in 1996. Keith Burkinshaw was always endearingly co-operative during his eight years as Tottenham's manager, never more so than one Saturday at Luton Town. After winning 4–2, Burkinshaw was getting on to the team coach when our reporter Ian Darke rushed up to him with a late request to appear on *Sports Report*. 'Where do you want it done?' he asked Darke, who then led the manager back up to the top of the stand, stuck a pair of headphones on him and Mike Ingham interviewed Burkinshaw down the line. 'I couldn't believe he agreed to do that, 'recalls Darke. 'It was a massive inconvenience to drag him all that way. Can you imagine a current manager doing that?'

Peter Slater once had cause to congratulate himself on doing a favour for a Manchester United executive that eventually landed him an exclusive interview with Eric Cantona after the 1996 FA Cup Final at Wembley. Cantona had scored the only goal of the game to beat Liverpool, but Slater never expected to get anywhere near the enigmatic Frenchman, whose contempt for the English football media had always been obvious. Slater was biding his time near the United dressing room when Ned Kelly, in charge of the players' security, came up to him, checked his name and said, 'Come with me.' Ushered into a room, Slater encountered Eric Cantona. Kelly said, 'You've got five minutes.'

It dawned on Slater that his fairy godfather was Ken Ramsden, then the club's assistant secretary, and part of the Old Trafford furniture for decades. 'Ken was a huge Formula One fan and for many summers I was the Grand Prix reporter. I managed to get Ken tickets into the paddock at Silverstone one year and he never forgot that. So he returned the favour. What I really remember about that Cantona interview was a huge eagle tattoo on his chest. He didn't say anything of consequence, but I was chuffed to get him on tape.'

Peter wasn't quite so lucky at the 1987 Cup Final, when Coventry beat Tottenham. The match had gone to extra time and Peter was desperate to land a live interview from the Coventry camp before *Sports Report* went off air. Radio reporters weren't allowed on the Wembley pitch, so he set up a place at the top of the tunnel, with the engineers patching a line through to the studio, so he could be on air in a trice. Peter spotted the Coventry captain, Brian Kilcline, walking towards him, clutching the trophy. Perfect. Enough time left in the programme. Peter said on air, 'Yes, Brian – you're live on *Sports Report*. What sort of moment is this for you?' Just before the willing Kilcline could answer, a burly steward ambushed the interview, with the heartening message, 'You're not supposed to be here, I've told you before.' The Kilcline interview was duly postponed. The glamour of a Wembley Cup final.

May 1987 wasn't a good month for Peter Slater in his dealings with stewards. He was at Carrow Road when Everton clinched the League championship, beating Norwich City 1–0, and the initial target afterwards was Everton's affable manager, Howard Kendall. Unluckily, Peter was on a gantry on the opposite side of the ground to where the interviews were taking place. He made his way over the pitch to the main tunnel, but found it barred. 'The doors had been shut because the Everton fans were getting a bit rowdy. But the steward wouldn't let me in, he just wasn't for turning. In the end, after it got heated, he just threw me to the ground. It was technically assault, but I had no time to pursue it. I got in after finding a way via the street on the other side of the tunnel entrance. I just had to get to Howard Kendall and after battering my way through all of that, Howard met me with 'So where have you been?' But we got him on *Sports Report*.'

The agile Jonathan Overend landed a superb scoop in October 2000 at Wembley, when Kevin Keegan resigned as England's manager after losing to Germany. The problem was one of geography. The football correspondent, Mike Ingham, was due to interview Keegan, on a small balcony, up a flight of stairs, away from the dressing room. There was no ISDN point in that interview area and Jonathan had to take a chance that the line wouldn't go down once the Keegan interview started, on a radio microphone. And he also had to get the crucial information about the manager's resignation to Ingham before he started the interview, because Mike had already left the commentary point to get to the area where he would encounter Keegan.

'There was a very real chance that Mike would start the interview without realising that Keegan had gone and before I could get up the stairs to him. The studio tipped Mike off about the possibility, I speculated live about that in the dressing-room area, then as Keegan walked towards Mike, with me following him, I said, live on air, that the England manager had something important to say to our football correspondent. I nodded to Mike, he grasped what that meant and began with, "Kevin, I believe you have something important to tell us." It was perfect, giving Keegan a half volley to get started, but thank God Mike was smart enough to realise the significance of my nod to him. On air, we sounded totally on top of the story, with the radio mic line holding up OK, but it was a close-run thing.'

Luck, as Jonathan Overend acknowledges, plays a big part amid the post-match mayhem. Once you've called in a favour, ensured the equipment's working and your target has been harpooned for interview, there are still hurdles to surmount. Getting the studio to come over to you quickly is a major challenge. At the sharp end, you do your best to ensure the easy option of a recorded interview isn't taken, because there is then no guarantee it will be aired later on, before the programme ends. No blame attached to the production team, there are simply not enough bodies or time available to do justice to many recorded interviews.

When you are standing alongside a household name in football, and your producer is asking you to keep him sweet while trying to wrap up the interview that's now on air, some fancy footwork is in order to avoid losing him. His press officer is grandstanding, trying to exert some flimsy authority by asking how much longer the delay will be, the manager picks up on the twitchiness, starts looking around the dressing-room area and you know some other media outlet will be delighted to take him away, never to return. You find yourself going, 'Yadda, yadda, yadda', babbling inconsequential tosh, just to keep him there. You're told by the producer, 'With you in a minute' and you dare not pass on that precise message, so you witter on about the other scores and outline what your first question will be. Anything to keep him there.

Juliette Ferrington has an excellent working relationship with Liverpool's manager, Jürgen Klopp, and she always finds a clever way to keep him from striding off. On Grand National Day in 2021, she kept him interested by telling him the winning jockey was at last a woman and Klopp responded by riffing on the horse he had backed. It made for a highly entertaining entrée to the football part of the interview. Pep Guardiola can be enigmatic and abrupt, but Juliette knows he's a big golf fan and she is always ready with some news on the latest big competition, somewhere in the world. It normally works. She enjoyed a friendly rapport with José Mourinho when he managed Manchester United. The Special One became surly and uncooperative, but Juliette always seemed to jolly him along, saying, 'Oh, it's you!' when it was her turn to interview him. It's an underrated art, keeping a big football beast sweet, and Juliette is excellent at it. 'I always smile, don't make them feel under pressure and try to bring some humour into the interview. I'm just normal and hopefully they don't mind talking to me.'

Some managers are clever enough to see through your filibustering tactics and I suffered at the hands of Brian Clough one afternoon in December 1986. He had agreed to come on *Sports Report* for the first time in five years after I'd told him I was off to Australia the following day, covering the Ashes tour. Clough, a huge cricket fan, expressed envy and agreed to come on the show – 'It'll be an early Christmas present for you, Patrick.'

I'd brought along a close friend, Geoff Cook, then captain and opening batsman for Northants CCC and a former England player. Like Clough, Geoff hailed from Middlesbrough and within a minute of meeting they were locked in reminiscences of growing up on Teesside. Brian had brought in two massive tumblers of whisky, presenting one to me and hanging on to the other one. By the time Brian and Geoff had established their fathers had known each other, my glass was snatched from me and handed over to Geoff with the reassuring rasp from Clough, 'You have this, Geoffrey, it's wasted on that…'

By now, Brian had limbered up, demanding to get on with the interview. I pointed out that even he had to wait for James Alexander Gordon to finish the football results, but we wouldn't be long. After interrupting the Teesside reminiscences, I began the interview with, 'Brian – did you think you'd be in third place in the League as we approach Christmas?' He proceeded to level those deep hazel eyes on me and asked, 'Tell me, Patrick – what were the other scores today then in our division?' Helped by my editor down my headphones, I managed to get them right. First hurdle cleared, but Clough knew about the assist from Broadcasting House. Over the next eight minutes, he tested me out in all areas and, as the sweat coursed down my face, I realised that I'd forgotten to tell him the interview was live. Brian had a habit of lacing his interviews with salty, industrial language, a test of our editing skills. I feared the worst.

I managed to get off lightly, but not before he put me away in classic Clough fashion. Tired of my editor saying, 'Keep going, Pat,' I thanked Clough for his time and, sufficiently emboldened, I said, 'It's the first time we've had you on for five years, Brian.' Those eyes bored into me again, with a withering response, 'Patrick, you come back from Australia a bit more talented than you are today.'

Never assume you've cracked it was the lesson I took from that Clough interview, more than 35 years ago. Managers go through the wringer of tension and frustration every game and it's understandable that they snap sometimes, as they're trying to rationalise what they've just witnessed. Conor McNamara has a shrewd assessment on the psychology of it all. 'At the training ground, managers are the alpha males, in charge of almost everything. When it's match day, they are accountable to the fans and then the media. You can deal with the fans issue, because usually they don't get near the manager, but the media can be a problem if they don't back off or refuse to be browbeaten. Fuses are short just after the final whistle if tricky questions are asked.'

Chris Jones, our rugby union correspondent, knows that feeling. That sport seems to be getting more and more pressurised every year, as the demands of professional status become more acute. The tense post-match atmosphere can feel almost like the Premier League. In autumn 2018, Chris had to interview the Australian coach, Michael Cheika, in a tiny cupboard area at Twickenham and he soon grasped that it could turn testy. Cheika was unhappy about a couple of decisions that went England's way and Chris gently asked Cheika for his thoughts. 'He was around 6ft 5 ins. I'm not that tall and soon there was a physical dimension to the interview. He said, "You can poke me all you want, but you'll get nowhere" and I took the hint. What began with a handshake didn't end with one!'

Sonja McLaughlan, an old hand at post-match international rugby union interviews, sums up the strategy perfectly, 'You've just got to stay in the arm wrestle, without antagonising.'

In football, the intimidation can take various forms. Conor McNamara has had experience of the infamous blue-eyed stare from David Moyes, when managing Everton. 'I was standing with my back to the tunnel, shielding from the biting wind, climbing into Everton, after they'd played badly and lost. I was keeping an eye out for David Moyes, but when I turned around after doing my live report, there he was. He fixed me with a steely look and just walked off. He didn't come back.'

Phil Wye, a football producer for 12 years and veteran of three World Cups, had the same experience with Moyes when he was at Everton. 'A goalless draw with Middlesbrough, a turgid game. My first question was, "Not a classic, David" and he looked at me grimly and walked away. His press officer tried to have a go at me, saying, "Just ask the question," but I can't see what was wrong with my opener. Things can get very tense post-match.'

And physical. Phil experienced the wrath of Alan Pardew, when he had just been appointed manager of Charlton Athletic in 2006. He had recently been sacked by West Ham after taking them to the FA Cup Final six months earlier and no doubt he was still raw about that as he prepared for his first League game at the Valley with Charlton. Pardew had agreed to be interviewed by presenter Arlo White from the studio before the match and all went predictably until near the end, when he was asked about his thoughts now about the West Ham board. Pardew was disconcerted by the question, but dealt with it capably enough. But as soon as he was off air, he turned on Phil Wye, the innocent party as the match producer.

'He shoved my shoulders against a wall and stuck his finger in my chest. He had a real pop at me and said he wouldn't be talking to us after the match. He was raging. I didn't think it was an appropriate question – what manager is going to slag off his former employers when he's had a pay-off after being sacked? – and I had a go at Arlo White after the programme. He stood his ground and we agreed to disagree. But he'd landed me with a professional problem as the

Southern and London producer, dealing with a furious Charlton manager. Our summariser, Mark Bright – who'd played at Crystal Palace with Pardew – managed to smooth it over, convincing Pardew it wasn't my fault. But that's what happens when the presenter in the studio misreads the mood.'

A decade later, I had my own run-in with Pardew, after he had succeeded the sacked Tony Pulis as West Brom's manager. To be fair, knocking out a full-strength Liverpool 3–2 at Anfield in the FA Cup was a great performance and his leadership of the playing staff after Cyrille Regis' tragic death in January 2018 was sensitive, but a spiralling series of defeats and a disintegration of dressing-room discipline convinced many of us on the West Midlands patch that Pardew would not be lingering long at the Hawthorns. A disastrous 4–1 defeat at home by Leicester City set the alarm bells clanging. I interviewed him on *Sports Report* afterwards, asking what he would say to the dismayed fans about such a pallid performance, and he took it badly. As Pardew walked away, he fixed me with what I assumed was a threatening stare. As he lacked the bottle to have it out with me, I let it pass and gladly held the gaze until he was off to the press conference.

I was at the Hawthorns three weeks later for the match against Burnley and beforehand the West Brom press officer, Martin Swain, told me that Pardew would not allow me to interview him post-match, because of my disrespectful attitude to him after the Leicester debacle. I had always enjoyed the company of Martin in the previous 35 years and had no intention of getting tetchy with him. But I wanted to front up to Pardew, to let him know I didn't give a tinker's cuss whether or not I ever interviewed him again. West Brom had enough good professionals in their dressing room who shared my view of their current manager and would happily grant me post-match interviews, if desired.

After West Brom lost 2–1, I duly made my way to the dressing-room area to face Pardew and see what he would have to say, without his press officer conveying any message. At a convenient hiatus, he informed me, from 15 yards away, that my attitude to him had not been respectful enough and that's why he wouldn't be interviewed by me. I pointed out that I didn't want to talk to him anyway and as he continued his diatribe in front of around 10 radio reporters, club reporters and TV floor managers, I interrupted him, playing to the gallery, and said sarcastically, 'Tell you what, Alan – somehow, I'll cope. I think I'll get by.' Basically, I was saying, 'I'll be here at the Hawthorns a while longer than you.' With that, Pardew advanced on me. In response, I did the same to him. He was then ushered away firmly by Martin Swain, but not before fixing me with what he clearly felt was one of his fearsome stares. I would not have initiated any physical rejoinders, but Pardew would not have got away with how he had treated Phil Wye at the Valley. It wasn't quite, 'Hold my beer, mate,' but the antlers on the two rutting stags were being sharpened.

Two days later, Pardew and West Brom parted company. I am not concerned about whether he was sacked or not, but West Brom were bottom of the table after eight successive League defeats and 10 games without a win. Goodwill towards him was in short supply – especially from this quarter.

You can never assume anything about a *Sports Report* interview you're trying to set up at short notice. Everything organisationally may be functioning, but the manager can easily throw you off kilter. Alistair Bruce-Ball had to deal with Jürgen Klopp at his most contrary in February 2020 after Liverpool had lost 3–0 at Watford. Klopp is normally great value in interviews, but this time bridled when Alistair suggested mildly that Liverpool's goalkeeper, Allison, didn't have the best of games. 'He's a lot taller than me and tried to put me on my mettle by throwing the question back at me. He was testing me out, so I just stuck to my opinion, which wasn't exactly controversial.' Perhaps it eventually dawned on Klopp that this, Liverpool's first defeat of the season, had still left them 22 points clear at the top of the table and the Watford result hardly constituted a crisis.

Ian Darke also once experienced a disconcerting reaction from a high-profile manager who would have been expected to be in high spirits after a great result. Lawrie McMenemy's Southampton had beaten Liverpool 4–1 at the Dell in a tremendous performance and Darke understandably assumed that a live chat would be a formality with such a media-friendly manager. Not so. As Ian walked down towards the Southampton dressing room McMenemy shouted, 'No interviews for you today, Mr Darke!' 'Why not, Lawrie?' 'Because you said on the radio that Liverpool played badly and you gave us no credit at all. So nothing for you!' – and as his player, Alan Ball, walked past, he said, 'That goes for you, too, Bally – nothing for the BBC!'

This from a manager whose career had blossomed due to his own prowess, but whose profile had also been raised by frequent appearances on BBC TV as a pundit and *Sports Report*. Darke could only assume that McMenemy thought he'd concentrated too much on Liverpool's frailties that day. 'At least that showed Lawrie listened to us – many dressing rooms had *Sports Report* on in those days.'

By common consent of my BBC contemporaries out in the field, Arsène Wenger was the most consistent of all the big beasts in the managerial jungle. A clever man – Peter Slater recalls him doing three post-match interviews, one after the other, in different languages – he fully understood that a reporter was entitled to ask any questions. I don't recall him ever ducking a question or storming off. He didn't take defeat well, giving an impersonation of someone sucking on a particularly sour lemon sweet, but he'd grit his teeth and be respectful. Wenger had the priceless knack of giving you his full attention in an interview – or at least appearing to do so.

If Wenger struggled to contain his distress at a defeat, Brian Clough and Sir Alex Ferguson were then particularly impressive, showing genuine leadership. They'd stick out their chests, exude defiance and defend their players, no matter how much they'd just excoriated them in the dressing room. Clough would deflect searching questions with humour and distinctive braggadocio, while Ferguson's brooding demeanour as he took in the next question would suggest an eruption was imminent. Commendably, he stayed calm many times in such situations, aware that he was representing a great football club.

It's a matter of sadness among all the *Sports Report* foot soldiers that Sir Alex never established a consistent, mutually respectful understanding with us. A highly intelligent, self-educated man with an elephantine memory for perceived slights, he developed an animus towards the BBC in general, and the TV and radio sports departments in particular. In such a mammoth media organisation, there are bound to be times when a public figure of Ferguson's stature is angered by comments, programmes and reports that paint him in an unflattering picture, especially when he would happily tilt at various windmills himself, entering the fray in socio-political matters, risking public opprobrium. But Sir Alex invariably failed to differentiate between the real transgressors and the innocent ones he'd come up against on match day. He once told a colleague of mine, 'BBC, eh? Still telling lies?' when asked for an interview. Programmes made by the BBC's Talks and Documentaries Unit would sometimes evoke foam-flecked Fergie fury, but they had nothing to do with the football producers and reporters doing their job.

It was a great pity. Ferguson had been very co-operative with the BBC in Scotland, when his Aberdeen side challenged the Glasgow hegemony and, when he came down to Old Trafford in 1986, he clearly grasped what *Sports Report* was all about. I recall one early example, when Peter Jones did his live report and handed over to Mike Ingham in the tunnel, interviewing the new manager live. And when Fergie wanted to do a proper interview, he was outstanding.

Sir Alex just clocked up what he perceived as the BBC's own goals and pulled up the ladder on us for years. Mike Lewis, our head of sport in the early nineties, went up to United's training ground at the Cliff, trying to put our case, and Ferguson was commendably civil and receptive. Mike persuaded him to give *Sports Report* a chance and, soon afterwards, our commentator John Murray was told at Old Trafford that the manager would talk to him. 'I didn't believe Ken Ramsden when he told me that, but [I] followed him and Sir Alex was as good as gold. But that peace didn't last very long!'

Those of us around at the time will always be grateful to Steve Bruce, who understood the media demands on a Manchester United captain, especially when his manager was blanking us with increasing hostility, while ensuring the likes of David Beckham, Ryan Giggs and the Neville brothers would be off-limits as well. Bruce knew the background, but refused to blame those in front of him on match days. He has continued to co-operate willingly throughout his managerial career. None of us can ever recall a time when Steve Bruce turned us down. He even gave Ian Dennis a lift once, as he walked up the road from Craven Cottage after his Hull City team had played Fulham. 'And he had *Sports Report* on in the car. I was impressed by that!'

There was never any worry about protecting Ferguson during one of his rare *Sports Report* interviews. The old bruiser could always look after himself. Yet there are times when you're stuck between Scylla and Charybdis. Do you climb into the manager when criticism is deserved or do you cut him some slack, because he's at least had the decency to front up and do the interview? Only you can decide the narrative; there is simply no time to ask the advice of the studio.

John Southall had the excruciating job of interviewing a coach when he was at his lowest after Doncaster Rovers won a dramatic match against Brentford at the end of the 2012–13 season. Whoever won that game would be promoted to the Championship and the game was meandering along to a draw when Brentford missed a penalty in the 90th minute. The ball ricocheted up the other end and James Coppinger scored for Doncaster in added time. If Brentford had scored from that penalty kick, instead of Marcello Trotta hitting the bar, then they would have been automatically promoted and Doncaster would have been in the play-offs. It couldn't have been more dramatic and *Sports Report* led with John's gripping commentary of the final minute.

John's next task was to find Uwe Rösler, Brentford's manager, and try to get him to talk. 'I've never seen anyone as shell-shocked as Uwe that day. Normally he's a great talker, but he could hardly string a sentence together. I had to coax him to talk, with my arm around his shoulder. I felt so sorry for him. You don't get many moments like that in your broadcasting career. It had been a terrible match, but then suddenly you're centre stage on *Sports Report* and you have to raise your game.'

John's been in the business long enough not to be surprised by anything, but he was taken aback by an encounter with former England manager, Kevin Keegan. Southall, one of football's more courteous characters in the media, rubbed Keegan up the wrong way in 2005, towards the end of his time at Manchester City. By then, Keegan was 54, tired of all the internal politics at the club and far removed from the ebullient character who had endeared himself to many when Newcastle United's manager. Before the match against Middlesbrough, one of his best players, Nicolas Anelka, had told the press, 'City aren't big enough for me', which, on top of a 4–0 defeat by Boro, meant Keegan was far from happy afterwards. Southall, recording the interview because Keegan wouldn't stand around waiting to do it live, asked the key question politely. 'Can I just ask you about Nicolas Anelka?' Keegan stared at Southall, walked away, turned and looked at him from the top of the tunnel, then raced back to shout in his face, 'If you ever ask me a question about that again…' and stalked off. Southall recalls how everyone went quiet in the tunnel. 'No one moved. I suppose it was quite entertaining to the others there. The bloke from Sky said, "I thought he was going to get a stepladder and punch you on the nose." But I hadn't asked him the direct question. I said could I ask him the question about Anelka. If I'd behaved like that, I'd have been reprimanded or sacked. Within a few weeks Keegan was gone. He'd got too emotional by then. I was just in the firing line.'

You have to be ready to walk on eggshells when doing post-match interviews amid the maelstrom. Arsène Wenger and Pep Guardiola won't put the headphones on to talk to the studio presenter, because they just don't trust the process. They want eye-to-eye contact with the interviewer. When he was at Leeds United, Terry Venables told our reporter Dave Woods, 'I'm not putting those headphones on – you saw the game, you do the interview.' Woods remembers a feeling of satisfaction, 'We always feel out there that if you've been at the game, then you're better qualified to do the interview. You understand the nuances of the match more than someone back in the studio.' Amen to that. It's been a running sore throughout my time on the programme. It's been fascinating how many former presenters admitted to me that, although it was great for their ego to interview a big name down the line, it made more editorial sense to trust the reporter on the spot. Not that they'd ever admit it while still occupying the chair!

Mark Chapman, the current presenter, admits the programme relies heavily on contacts developed over the years in securing interviews in haste. 'Without the fantastic network of experienced reporters and producers who are totally on top of their regions, we'd struggle. We don't have the clout of television, but we do have an integrity that's stretched over the decades. We're good at playing a long game, developing a great relationship with press officers in the EFL, who appreciated us getting their clubs on air after 5.30. And although some of the foreign managers and players don't really understand what we're about, I'm finding that a lot of the younger British players coming through are very receptive to us.

'Players like Conor Coady, Trent Alexander-Arnold, Ollie Watkins, Ben Mee, Ben Chilwell, James Maddison, Dominic Calvert-Lewin, Kalvin Phillips, Patrick Bamford and Andy Robertson know what we're about. They're much more media savvy than in previous generations and that helps us build up trust. Media training at the clubs has helped a lot. There's just a snapshot in time after a match when our man or woman is struggling to get us an interview and I believe *Sports Report* is still a recognisable brand.'

We must recognise that we are lucky to get interview points installed in the various tunnels. Clubs aren't bound contractually to provide access so close to sensitive areas such as dressing rooms and we have to tread carefully in case we overplay our hand. *Sports Report* flies by the seat of its pants, relying on our contacts and past prestige to get permission to be close enough to be rejected or accepted in our requests. It can be a very tense situation.

Alastair Yeomans certainly went through the wringer of tension at Manchester City in December, 2009 – but emerged triumphant. An experienced, highly reliable reporter/producer in the North West, Alastair was the designated foot soldier that day, charged with finding out if Mark Hughes had been sacked as City's manager on the day they played Sunderland at home.

Rumours swirled around at lunchtime that Roberto Mancini was set to replace Hughes and after the match, Yeomans had to glean as much as he could from his vantage point in the tunnel. Aware that he was on borrowed time down there, with the security staff on edge, Yeomans had to make do with meagre scraps of information that he fed live into *Sports Report* over six reports. Eventually he could confirm a board meeting was imminent and that Hughes was likely to be sacked.

For his pains, Alastair was eventually ushered outside the Etihad Stadium, before Sports Report ended, to battle against swirling snow, on a bitterly cold Manchester evening. With no ISDN available, he kept broadcasting live on his mobile phone into *Sports Report*, then *606* and his tenacity was finally vindicated at the confirmation of Hughes' departure.

It was dedicated reporting of the highest order, flying solo, relying on his wits and contacts within the club. It was the 52nd game Alastair had covered in a season that was, by then, only four months old.

There's a necessity to be unobtrusive yet prominent down in the tunnel area. You don't want the relevant club official in charge of access to forget you, while not wishing to become a pest by persistently pressing your case. Every Saturday is different, with so much depending on the result. Angst is all around. TV floor managers stalk around self-importantly, muttering into their walkie-talkies, as if the president of the United States was imminent, rather than a footballer. Your studio producer, trying hard to be sympathetic, also wants to know what's happening. Do they run the TV interview with your agreed target or hold on for your own radio one? Any self-respecting reporter will always say the latter, but how do you reassure the producer when all you have is a hunch, based on the fact that he's never let you down before?

It's a scene that fascinated the politician Andy Burnham, when he once worked at Goodison for talkSPORT. Long before he became a cabinet minister, and then mayor of Greater Manchester, Burnham wanted to be a sports reporter and he was thrilled to witness what went on behind the scenes when talkSPORT booked the devoted Evertonian. 'I couldn't believe the electricity, all the tension and excitement. I knew all about the emotional intensity of Westminster, but that day at Goodison I realised reporters have to detach themselves from what's going on and yet remain in the thick of it.'

That's about the size of it, Andy. Alistair Bruce-Ball, now a highly experienced football commentator, considers the job of reporter and interviewer on a Saturday afternoon to be tougher than just commentating on the second half, 'Somehow, you've got to write your match report while looking out for a player or manager – and then think of something to ask them, often live on air, without making a fool of yourself. It's great when a manager turns up just as you're finishing your scripted report and you can get straight into the live interview. All this with the scrape of boots on the floor adding to the atmosphere. I wish it worked as well as that all the time!'

Tony Adamson had a different experience one day when he was sent to cover Nottingham Forest. He was told that Brian Clough would speak to Des Lynam in the *Sports Report* studio afterwards and, sure enough, Cloughie barged in, ready to sparkle. Straight away, he barked at Adamson, 'Young man, where were you at 1.30? Bryon Butler rang me to say you were coming and I had a whisky ready for you!' At least he was being friendly to Tony, but his mood changed as our intrepid reporter read out his account of the match, before handing the microphone and headphones over to Clough. His first sentence was typically trenchant. 'Hello Desmond, I don't know who your reporter was today at the City Ground, but I don't recognise what game he was actually at.' A salutary experience, confirming that Brian Clough invariably got the last word.

In his 30 years on *Sports Report*, Tony Adamson was a byword for chaos, misfortune, cock-ups… call it what you wish. Addo was often sent to non-League grounds on FA Cup afternoons, partly because he was talented enough to weave an amusing tapestry from the most utilitarian threads, but also because he was so adept at turning his own misfortunes into great humour on air.

Things happened to Tony that luckier reporters managed to swerve. In 1977, he was sent to Northwich Victoria for the Cup tie against Watford, recently taken over by Elton John and full of ambition. The producer felt a shock might be possible, so a good reporter was needed. In those days, there were no such fancy accessories like ISDN lines or mobile phones, so Adamson went in search of the telephone that had been allegedly booked by BBC Radio Sport. 'There isn't one,' he was told, 'No one's ordered it. The nearest spare one is in the middle of Manchester – will that do for you?' The resourceful Adamson had to cajole another radio reporter into sharing a phone, while commandeering a seat in the press box, that also hadn't been booked. It would have suited him if there had been no FA Cup shock that day, but Northwich's 3–2 victory meant he was on air a lot and high up the running order for *Sports Report*, on a phone line that was distinctly wonky. 'I sounded like I was broadcasting from North Korea. Cock-ups like that seemed to become a regular event for me.'

And misfortune dogged Tony after games as well. At Southampton, he was late arriving at the Dell for a match against Ipswich and parked his car where he could. 'When I came out afterwards, it had gone – towed away to a police pound.

It cost me a fortune and hours of my time to find it. No help from the BBC in paying the fine!'

Tony could always be relied on to turn in a whimsical report at short notice, whatever travails he had experienced that day, but the discipline and speed necessary to write your piece on the match for *Sports Report* must not be underestimated. Basically, you have to be ready with it at 5.06 p.m., after the headlines and 'Out of the Blue', then the classified results. Invariably you are not needed then, but you try your darndest to be ready to open the batting. I always considered it the most important piece of work I did all week. The tradition of the programme would be uppermost in my mind and the awareness that people all over the world were listening. There'd be the feeling of relief that I'd finally made it to the interview point and that my first interview request had gone in. Time then to concentrate on my report, eschewing too many facts, concentrating on the atmosphere, delineating the key moments. I felt the listener didn't want to hear about the 34th minute, then the 42nd minute, then the 56th minute. 'Just before half-time' or 'early in the second half' was enough. Try to start and end with a telling phrase and hope the rest takes care of itself, all the while looking out for your requested interviewee.

A smidgeon of colour and humour never goes amiss, as Ron Jones discovered when he joined the sports department from Radio Wales. Ron had a melodious Welsh accent and his reports were very easy on the senses. But the editor, Derek Mitchell, told him 'They're OK, Ron, but they don't make the listener sit up. Think in advance of a good line to shoehorn in somewhere.' Ron thought that was sensible advice and came up with a striking first sentence for his next match report, at Anfield, when QPR were the visitors. 'Groucho Marx once said, "When sex is good, it's very good and when it's bad, it's still pretty good." That summed up Liverpool's performance today.' Derek rang him that night, praising his intro, yet by Monday there'd been complaints to the BBC about one of their football reporters banging on about sex before the watershed! But Ron was grateful to his editor, 'Derek made me think and I realised average wasn't good enough.'

Iain Carter can relate to that. Our golf correspondent since 2003, Iain has always venerated the tradition of *Sports Report* and in 2013 he was covering the US Masters when a major story involving Tiger Woods broke on the Saturday. Woods had taken a drop in the wrong place after his ball disappeared into the water. He should have been disqualified under the rules, but the

Masters committee found a loophole and allowed him to carry on. It was a huge story and Carter was to lead *Sports Report* on it, beginning with a 10-second teaser, followed after the headlines with a 90-second report, clarifying a rather abstruse situation.

'I was broadcasting from the back row of the media centre at Augusta, with so many others listening to me as [I] did my live reports and I felt under intense pressure. It was a tight deadline and everything I said would be booming out all over the media centre. I knew it was a big call to lead *Sports Report* ahead of the football and I remember thinking, "I hope I've got this right." I was so tense that my shoulders and neck were rigid as I delivered my reports. I wanted my 10-second hit over that historic music in the headlines to be immaculate. I was pleased with it, but that was because I respected so much the enduring excellence of *Sports Report*.

'I have always wanted my *Sports Report* contributions to be my best of the week – and I've done tennis, rugby union, golf, football and cricket in the programme. And I loved it when Lee Westwood, a huge Nottingham Forest fan, would be playing a tense round in the Ryder Cup, and he'd come over and ask how Forest were getting on. If I said they were leading, he'd nod, play his shot and then come back over to ask who scored! That's the stature of *Sports Report*, right there.'

Our football correspondent John Murray also feels the weight of history on a Saturday, as he battles against time. 'So many games go on way past 10 to 5 these days and, if I'm doing the commentary match, there's a good chance that I'll be leading *Sports Report*, if the story's good enough. I'll sit there, trying to fill in the gaps of my report with the right words. We'll be on to the Scottish results in the classifieds and I'm still not quite there, yet I'm on in about a minute. Sometimes I have to say to myself, "I'm just going to have to busk this" as the presenter hands to me. I'll try my best not to rush it and deliver it properly, but there are times when I've thought, "That wasn't good enough." Even if I'm not working and I hear that signature tune, I'm telling myself I'm running out of time.'

Which brings us back to Andrew Marvell and that relentless ticking time machine. When you've finally clocked off – one final check with your press cronies that you missed nothing vital while scurrying around – you mull over the afternoon as you trudge back to the car. If you value your involvement in such an historic programme, you'll hope you weren't too peevish with the studio; that your written piece hit the right notes; that your first question to that beleaguered manager wasn't too provocative; that it was a good idea to schmooze that new press officer before kick-off. It should take a few hours to get that day's *Sports Report* out of your system. If you care enough about it.

Cornelius Lysaght knows all about the time constraints involved. He made over 900 contributions to *Sports Report* over a 30-year career at the BBC, 20 of them as racing correspondent, and he remains justly proud of the snappy, informative packages he and his producer James Porter would compile every Grand National day. With the race starting at 4.15 p.m. and often around 40 horses involved, it was their job to pull together some relevant interview clips and give the story of the race, letting the listener know what happened to every horse.

'It was billed in the programme as "What happened to your horse" and it took me back to my childhood, when I wanted to know all about the fortunes of each horse. When the stewards handed out the finishing order, that was the most important piece of paper I'd get all year – and we'd set to on the list.

'It was really tight after 5 o'clock. Make sure you write a tight script, get the clips in the right order, capture the atmosphere of National day. We owed the listeners a detailed explanation, while the programme producer was, quite rightly, wondering how much longer we'd be working on it and how long it would be. James and I would cross every finger and toe when that package went out, hoping no glitches had been left in.

'It was an absolute thrill and it worked every time. I loved the idea of people in their cars on the way out of Aintree, finding out what happened to their horse. For me, it was good public service broadcasting.'

Cornelius and the rest of us out in the field were aware that the production team didn't minimise our respective contributions, even if were rushing to the pub as we searched for our car keys. There is never really time for a debrief, as each day on a 24/7 radio network merges into another, but the best producers don't forget how we earn our campaign medals.

Claire McDonnell was an excellent producer of *Sports Report* before moving on in 2006 and I asked her if there'd ever been a perfect edition on her watch. Straight away, she nominated one in May 2005, when *Sports Report* broadcast on a Sunday, the last Premier League fixtures of that season. 'It was an absolute joy, everything worked perfectly.' It wasn't a joy for those interviewed on the programme, as we managed to get live on air the managers of the three Premier

League clubs who'd been relegated that day – Nigel Worthington of Norwich City, Crystal Palace's Iain Dowie and Harry Redknapp of Southampton. And for good measure, the Norwich goalkeeper, Rob Green, and the chairman, Roger Munby. All within the first half-hour of the programme. 'Sad for them, I know but brilliant for us. All the drama you want, plus Bryan Robson, who guided West Brom to that Great Escape that season. I was worried stiff that one of them would turn up at the wrong time and we'd keep someone waiting, but no. Disappointed managers were our priorities and I was so proud that our status got them talking to us.'

Claire always appreciated the engineers and technical wizards in her studio, but she was first to acknowledge the hard work done by the reporters and producers at the sharp end. 'You can have a brilliant presenter and clever technicians, but without you lot delivering the goods, it's a crap programme.' On behalf of the poor bloody infantry, I'll take that.

10

THERE WERE SOME LAUGHS AS WELL

It wasn't all noses to the grindstone in the radio sports department, and the amalgamation with sports news and outside broadcasts in 1972 brought an overdue rapprochement between both warring factions. Angus Mackay had no time for the OBs unit, whom he thought stuck in a time warp that forever bowed in the direction of the BBC's fearsome pioneer in its early days, Lord Reith. Mackay cherished his own sports news empire, working his staff fearsomely hard, with relaxation only coming after 6.00 p.m. on a Saturday night, when all who worked on *Sports Report* adjourned to the BBC Club for a prolonged debrief, under a three-line whip, until at last Mackay summoned his driver to take him home to Teddington.

When Mackay finally retired in 1972, the sports department merged, under the leadership of the inspirational Cliff Morgan and his workaholic deputy, Bob Burrows. They were both imbued with Mackay's driven ethos, but they were relaxed enough to let the staff loosen their stays and enjoy life in the office more. Individualism was encouraged. The office atmosphere became considerably more boisterous.

With the bosses closeted on the fourth floor, the sports room, a floor below, became a haven for practical jokes and jolly japes, and its narrow length was perfect for indoor cricket – bowler lining up against batsman from the regulation 22 yards, fielders standing on desks. Often a reporter or producer, working to stand up a story or book a guest, would have to apologise over the phone for the whooping and hollering, while getting thumped on the head by a stray, edged tennis ball. The women in the department had no qualms either about joining in enthusiastically.

Many in the newsroom, on the same floor, were bemused by the hilarity they overheard in the sports room, but conceded that professional standards hadn't slipped in this new, irreverent atmosphere. Newcomers to the sports department – including myself – would be startled at being introduced to new colleagues by philosophical bosses amid the mayhem of disputed umpiring decisions and mighty blows to the far end of the room. Awareness that these enthusiastic players were also titans of sports broadcasting whenever near a microphone soon banished any reservations about joining in, especially when the protagonists sometimes included the former England captain, Tony Lewis (allegedly researching on a Friday for his Saturday morning show *Sport on Four*) and the former England batsman, Chris Broad (on a brief internship after retirement).

The cricket correspondent, Christopher Martin-Jenkins, a fine batsman in his pomp, captured the high spirits perfectly one day, while captaining the fielding side. As the impromptu game entered its final stages, the controller of Radio 2, David Hatch, walked into the sports room, paying what he hoped would be a morale-boosting visit. As Hatch surveyed a chaotic scene unknown in his experience, the quick-witted CMJ said to him, poker-faced, 'Sir, could you move a little wider at mid-on, please?' To his credit, Hatch caught the mood swiftly and joined in the hoopla.

The sports room in Broadcasting House, with its own office and studio for sports desks, was a haven of independence, envied by other departments elsewhere. Not that it stopped human resources complaining one day to Cliff Morgan about the unconventional behaviour in the sports room. Morgan, no stranger to childish antics in a rugby clubhouse, simply ignored such strictures and let his charges enjoy themselves. Those antics ever got in the way of preparing and broadcasting the day's sports desks or setting up *Sports Report* later in the week. Burrows and Morgan were relaxed at the appropriate times, but never allowed standards to slip on their watch.

Many amusing characters on the staff of BBC Radio Sport contributed to the sheer enjoyment of working on *Sports Report* and the camaraderie engendered over the years undoubtedly helped when the extra yard was called for. Some of them were high-octane showmen, whose large personalities beamed out when they broadcast, others just inspired the troops in the Broadcasting House fun factory by making them laugh and leading by example.

Some of them, sadly, passed on too early. But they are never forgotten whenever ageing graduates from the *Sports Report* Academy gather. Selective anecdotes lose none of their appeal, recounted with affectionate smiles.

The anecdotes about Peter Jones have gathered since his premature death in 1990 and they aptly sum up a great broadcaster who just seemed to breeze through life.

Ecuador 1982. Peter's covering the World Swimming Championships. A sport he knows little about technically, but he has the nous to lean heavily on his co-commentator, the Olympic champion, Anita Lonsbrough. A sample clip from Peter would be '… and Wilkie turns NOW… then later… and Wilkie wins the gold!' with Anita providing all the clever insight in between.

It's a day off from commentating and Peter's met up with an old friend from the sports room, Dick Scales, who's now working for Adidas. Dick suggests driving over to the coastal resort of Salinas. Good suggestion. The fact that they have to cross a mini-desert en route to Salinas seems not to matter a jot.

Halfway across the desert, a tyre blows out. The spare in the boot is a motor cycle tyre. Somehow Scales negotiates the car to the next town, where the only business open is one that specialises in tyres. With small pigs running down the only street and barefoot kids playing in the broiling heat, Scales sets to work. Jones finds a spot in the shade, dons his Panama hat, dabs his brow nonchalantly and proceeds to read *Tales from a Long Room* by Peter Tinniswood. Little fazed Peter Jones. He always seemed to find ways of passing the time agreeably.

Dick Scales could be exasperated by Peter's detachment, but was very fond of him. 'He could talk for five minutes about nothing, a great gift for a live radio broadcaster.' Sometimes the facts just melted away in Peter's reports, because they weren't deemed all that important. John Helm recalls a despatch from Peter after he'd arrived in New Zealand for the Commonwealth Games. 'He talked about "flying through the peach dawn over Afghanistan", which we hadn't. It didn't matter, it sounded great. Jonesy could get away with that.'

Peter Jones was a masterful exponent of the broad-brush technique. Creating atmosphere and passion were his leitmotivs and nobody did it better.

In August 1981, Swansea City played their first game at home in the top flight against Leeds United. Ron Jones was there for Radio Wales and Peter was the obvious choice for commentary on Radio 2. Born and bred locally, a Swansea Grammar School boy, Peter was in his element, recalls Ron. 'The build-up all week had been fantastic for such an historic day. I sat alongside him in the commentary box and he launched into this brilliant, emotional preview. 'I'm standing in the centre circle at the Vetch Field, looking over at the terraces I used to stand on as a boy,' and so on. It was brilliant, but much of it was fiction.

'But when up against it, there was no one better than Jonesy, because he just loved the acting involved in his role as commentator. I worked with him at West Ham once, when the lights went out after 10 seconds of his live summary of the game. He was in complete darkness, but barely paused. He did the rest of the report without missing a beat.'

Peter was, in the words of his co-commentator, George Hamilton 'the unscripted master', but he could tax his producers. 'He was like the Scarlet Pimpernel – always close to the wire,' says Emily McMahon. '"Where the bloody hell's Jonesy?" was often the anguished cry, but when safely installed, he was the archetypal safe pair of hands.' He was the master of the commentary clip, the short piece that would lead *Sports Report*. Something along the lines of 'And Dalglish makes it two nil – with just two minutes left… the goal that seals another title for Liverpool.' Only Alan Green has rivalled Jones for economy of words amid the drama for the goal clip. Peter knew that the archives would be chockful of his commentary clips and he never missed a trick.

Yet Peter kept most colleagues at arms' length, despite his bonhomie. He'd use his voracious reading as a prop to keep himself away from colleagues if he didn't relish the office gossip. On a train journey, he'd say 'I hope you don't mind, but I'm engrossed in this book and I want to finish it before I get there.' Yet his thirst for extending his vocabulary added to his lustre as a broadcaster, so one shouldn't complain.

Liam Nolan was one of the few in the sports room who got close to Peter. They started in the department within a year of each other, (Liam 1964, Peter the following year), both latecomers to the *Sports Report* world, both outsiders, who hadn't followed the traditional path to presenting or commentating via national radio. They recognised a strong strain of intellectual curiosity in each other and would often steal out of Broadcasting House, stroll up to Regent's Park and set the world to rights. 'We'd talk about everything under the sun. Peter was a good listener as I confided in him about the emotional pull of Ireland while wanting to do well at the BBC.'

Peter even allowed himself to get sucked into practical jokes in the sports room, something that would have appeared heretical to those who worked with him in subsequent decades. Liam remembers the day Peter sabotaged his reading of the cricket scoreboard one lunchtime. 'I was going through it when I felt this ice-cold sensation running down my neck. Peter poured a jug of water down my back while I was live on air. I got my own back next day, though – I set fire to his script when he was reading the cricket scores! Childish, I know, but we were that close.'

Peter never used one word when several better ones were available. If ever I'd enquire after his health, I'd always get this fulsome response, 'I'm exceedingly well, dear boy.'

If Peter Jones had the cultured, smooth voice of the Cambridge modern languages graduate, Peter Lorenzo's voice belonged on the terraces at West Ham. A proud Eastender who loved football with a passion, many in the department were amused at his unbridled enthusiasm for the Hammers on air and there were a few patronising smirks when he was finally taken off West Ham games, because he was so obviously biased. He was nicknamed 'Lucky Lorenzo' after once admitting on air, 'I'm so lucky – I'm here watching West Ham playing and they're winning. Call me Lucky!'

But Peter was an old school Fleet Street soccer hack, who knew his way around that murky world with consummate ease. The flowery phrases, elegant match summaries and probing interviews were the province of other talented reporters. Peter spoke in technicolour, relating to the fan with his hamburger, holding his little boy's hand, willing his team to score another. The hallowed objectivity of the BBC that was hardwired into we lifers early on was lost on Lucky Lorenzo, because he joined us in his late forties. He was hired to bring an extra, vivid dimension to our football coverage and for a few memorable years, he did just that.

No one in my experience had better football contacts than Peter Lorenzo and that extended into showbiz people who loved sport. If ever *Sports Report* needed something different for an interview, a call from Peter would inevitably secure the likes of Jimmy Tarbuck or Morecambe and Wise.

One day in the sports room, Mike Ingham and a few other football scholars were going through the Argentine team that lost to England in the 1966 World Cup, courtesy of Geoff Hurst's header. They got stuck on Argentina's centre-forward. Peter solved the problem, picking up the phone and dialling a number. 'Is that you, Alf?' He had written Sir Alf Ramsey's newspaper column for years and knew that England's former manager would know. He did. And Peter didn't have to look up Sir Alf's number.

In 1983, Kenny Dalglish was elected Footballer of the Year and the Football Writers' Association managed to fly in Pelé, as a special surprise, to make the award. Amid the inevitable standing ovation as he made his way to the stage at the Café Royal, Pelé stopped just once. He had spotted Peter Lorenzo at the

BBC Radio table and stopped to embrace him warmly. He remembered Peter from the 1970 World Cup when, at his peak as a formidable tabloid journalist, he had the innate self-confidence and brio to stand out in a profession awash with charismatic characters.

Mike Ingham admired Peter's immense brio. 'Peter didn't really understand the nuts and bolts of radio, but he knew all about getting people on air with his fantastic range of contacts. I remember him getting Bobby Moore into the studio one Saturday. He stayed all afternoon and came to the pub afterwards, because he trusted Peter. People in the business just liked him enormously.'

As assistant editor in the sports room, Peter would fire off all sorts of ideas. 'What about…?' became one of his favourite phrases. He'd tell his producers, 'I want three fresh ideas from you before the end of today,' and bash the phone to show how it was done. When he floated an idea concerning a famous former cricketer, he was told, 'He's dead, Lucky,' only to expostulate, 'Well, no one told me!' After he'd calmed down, he appreciated why everyone was laughing at him.

Peter found it easy to make friends in sport, because he could be trusted and he made them laugh. His son, Matt, who became a distinguished TV and radio sports presenter, remembers how he never really clocked off, even on holiday. 'We'd be driving around in Portugal and he'd say to Mum, 'Oh, let's stop at this wine bar, it looks nice.' We'd walk in and there's Bobby Moore or Martin Peters or Alan Mullery or Don Revie and Dad would go, "Fancy seeing you here," as if Mum didn't know he'd already been on the phone, arranging a get-together. He loved socialising with sports people.'

Peter was so full of life that it was a grievous shock when he died, aged 59, of a heart attack, in 1986. He was on his way home after work and when the medics got him to Charing Cross Hospital, it appeared he had survived, but a second attack a few hours later proved fatal. Matt, on holiday in Portugal, didn't know about his dad until he got home 48 hours later. 'The church was packed, of course. Dad was enormously popular. He once told me that he would help anyone who came to him for professional advice, because older journalists should do that. Contacts are so vital in sports journalism and he proved that, year after year. When Ossie Ardiles moved to Tottenham in 1978, it was a huge story and Dad got an early exclusive with him for BBC Radio. Why? Because Dad and I were in church one Sunday and saw Ossie there. He had come to live locally. Dad spoke Italian, so did Ossie, and next thing I know is that Ossie's having tea in our living room. That was typical of Dad.'

Some colleagues could brighten up the dullest of days. Derek Thompson was certainly in that category, during his stint on the programme throughout the 1970s. 'Sunny' just about covers his personality. Few have conveyed as much warmth and sheer enjoyment as Derek over 50 years reporting on horse racing and equestrianism. At 22, he was the youngest commentator on the Grand National and he's never lost that boyish enthusiasm. He's like a frisky Labrador, tail wagging happily, no day too long.

Known to all as 'Tommo', he has been a ubiquitous presence in the racing world, adding colour and humour to the more detailed contributions of the big hitters. If there was ever a need for a light-hearted report, send for Tommo. He'd happily laugh at himself and drag a smile out of the most curmudgeonly of the racing fraternity.

Tommo freely admits he gets carried away at times, oblivious to his producer's preference for restraint. Jim Rosenthal, a presenter who never forgot his training in hard news, often used to laugh at Tommo's exuberance. 'Tommo was a very good broadcaster on radio – warm, liked a joke – but he did get carried away sometimes, convinced we were all enthralled by horses. He was doing the *Horse of the Year Show* one Christmas on *Sports Report* and we came to him a little late, for the usual, unavoidable reasons on a live sports show. Tommo started his piece with, 'You have just missed the greatest piece of horsemanship I've ever seen,' which threw the producer under the bus. And I seriously doubted if that round of jumping really was so great.'

Tommo's gaucheries meant he was ripe for plucking when the practical jokers racked their brains in the radio sports department. One assignment he was particularly pleased with put him in the firing line. The Duke of Edinburgh's expertise in carriage driving, driving four-in-hand teams, led to him representing Great Britain in the World Championships and he was a regular competitor at the Royal Windsor Horse Show. He developed the rules and was instrumental in getting the three-day event included in the Windsor Show in the late seventies.

All this was too much for Tommo's puppyish enthusiasm. He had to get an interview with Prince Philip – somehow. After weeks of clandestine negotiations, Tommo was summoned to Windsor Castle and secured the exclusive interview. He had been banging on about the prospect in the sports room for weeks and his elation at finally landing the interview was too much for those of a more republican, sceptical persuasion. Tommo seemed oblivious to the downbeat reaction in some quarters, even when he returned to the office in triumph.

'It was a great interview and afterwards Prince Philip said to me, "What are you doing for the next two hours?" I said I was going back to the office to work on editing our interview and he said, "Let's have a drive around Windsor Great Park," and it was incredible. He was enormously skilful and strong, driving the carriage. He was great company. I do remember he swore a lot – but nicely.'

Over the next few days, Tommo continued to dine out on his royal exclusive, as more and more pairs of eyes were rolled to the ceiling in the sports room. No one begrudged him his scoop, but the feeling was that a large dose of restraint was now in order. With the interview due to be aired next Saturday, a plan was hatched. A BBC acquaintance from outside the sports department had a splendidly posh accent and could easily have passed for a Buckingham Palace official. He was detailed to ring up Tommo when he was next in the sports room, so that those in on the jape could enjoy his anticipated discomfiture.

John Helm was in on the joke. 'Tommo was told Buckingham Palace was on the line and his face dropped as he digested the news. "What do you mean the interview has to be postponed?"... pause, listen … "But it can't be, it's billed in *Radio Times*"... pause, listen... "We can't run it, then?"'

It was so rare to see Tommo's natural ebullience punctured, that Helm just had to put him out of his misery soon. 'We were in stitches, but Tommo was so deflated, he took it badly. To listen to him before the call, it had been the highlight of his career. We had to put him out of his misery quickly.'

Tommo had no qualms about door-stepping the most illustrious figures in the racing world. Many knew him anyway – there was barely a day when he wasn't somewhere on a racecourse – so his contacts were enviable. He once boasted, 'Give me a microphone and I'll walk anywhere. I'd walk up to Her Majesty the Queen and say, "Excuse me, Ma'am."' No one doubted that, and one Grand National day, he surpassed himself.

In 1977, Red Rum won the National for the third time. The horse was a major sporting hero at the time, but where was the new angle for *Sports Report*? Tommo's forte was breathless interviews with winning jockeys and/or owners and trainers as they neared the winners' enclosure. This time, Tommo had an idea – why not interview Red Rum instead?

He told the editor Bob Burrows to get Des Lynam to hand over to him and it duly happened. The next minute was surreal. Tommo asked the horse how the race had gone, was he the best Grand National winner in history and how good a jockey was Tommy Stack? In return he got a few neighs, some heavy breathing and a head brushing away the microphone.

Tommo was unrepentant. 'I thought it was one of my better interviews! Red Rum was opening betting shops and switching on the Blackpool Illuminations by this time, so why not try to talk to him? It was just a bit of fun and it didn't take up too much time.'

One weekend Tommo reported for duty on a Sunday afternoon, ready to do the overnight and Monday morning presenting of the sports desks. He spotted a slight figure in the corner, intently watching the Grand Prix on telly. Friendly as ever, he said hello, wondering who he was, but happy to engage in chat about Formula One. After a while, Tommo ventured, 'Don't I know you?' It was George Harrison. 'He had a mate who worked at Broadcasting House, who said he could get him into the sports room to watch the race live. In those days it was recorded and went out in the evening, but George told me he was a huge Formula One fan and wanted to watch the race live. We sat on our own for a couple of hours, chatting away about normal things and he was appreciative. A lovely memory – watching a Grand Prix with a Beatle.'

Ask Derek Thompson about *Sports Report* and he's off on his long run, as hyperbolic as ever. 'It's the greatest sports programme ever. I tune in from all over the world. I must know how my team, Middlesbrough, has got on. People have a go at the BBC for many things these days, but never the 5 o'clock show. It's over 40 years since I was a regular on it, but it remains sacrosanct to me.'

Thompson's zany, breezy approach to horse racing was completely lost on his radio confrère, Peter Bromley – to whom it was a very serious business. Only the very best was good enough for both Bromley and those who worked with him in nearly 50 years as BBC Radio's peerless racing commentator. The hardest of taskmasters, yet the kindest of men, Bromley was contrary, combustible, fearless and utterly professional. But he was also unwittingly hilarious. Bromley's tirades were the stuff of legend and no one was safe when he'd built up a head of vitriolic steam.

'Get me the Director-General on the line!' was his familiar refrain to a succession of phlegmatic racing producers down the years, when he was particularly displeased. Bromley didn't believe in wasting his time with mere minions; if he had an issue, then he'd go right to the top. His contempt for studio-based producers, making decisions that diluted his time on air, was only as profound as the calm professionalism he displayed on mic when the offending programme finally crossed over for his magisterial contributions. We often used to joke that the words 'Come to me now!' should be engraved on Peter's tombstone when he finally passed to the great unsaddling enclosure in the sky. Peter never thought he was given enough time to set up a race for which he had prepared assiduously. Yet he was fiercely loyal to his racing producers at the race course. Only he was allowed to rebuke them and a Bromley bollocking was a collector's item, recalled with shudders. But then the fury would suddenly blow over and he would be charming, receptive and fully supportive against 'those bloody idiots in the studio'. As a former cavalry officer, schooled at Sandhurst, he knew the importance of maintaining morale out in the field. As a result, he was hugely admired and liked by his on-site team as much as he was feared back at base.

'It's good to have people frightened of you,' he once confided in one of his racing producers and Bromley was never frightened about getting on the front foot with anyone who gave him grief. Anyone who nabbed his parking spot at a race meeting or tried to bar him entry was a particular target for the Bromley temper. He once ran over a steward at Royal Ascot who refused to budge, as Peter demanded he move to allow him into his usual parking spot. The unlucky steward escaped with just bruising, but there was an almighty kerfuffle as a result, only resolved by Bromley – for once – playing the diplomatic card, saying that his foot had slipped on the accelerator. He was less diplomatic at Longchamps, covering the Prix de L'Arc de Triomphe, when the French version of a jobsworth barred his entry. He wound down the window and delivered this withering volley, 'If you lot had shown this sort of resistance in 1940, we wouldn't have had to come over here and save you!'

There was always a chance that Bromley would blow a gasket, but the fascination was which target it would be that day. Graeme Reid-Davies, who produced him for four years, says he often stormed into the engineer's room on arrival, demanding that the car in his allotted space be removed, but he surpassed himself in Vesuvian eruptions one day at York. 'He demanded I ring the clerk of the course and I meekly asked why. He thundered, 'There's no bloody paper in the toilets and I've had to use the greyhound page of the *Racing Post*!' Classic Bromley. It was always 'Bromley', perhaps because he was so much older than us and his military bearing led to the use of surnames.'

Bromley was simply a juggernaut who wouldn't be gainsaid. The long-suffering Reid-Davies grasped that when he first went to York races. His reporter was Jeff Stelling, who enjoyed a night in the pub, as did Graeme. Not Bromley. Stelling alerted Graeme on the first night that if they wanted to get to the pub, they needed to head off Bromley, who would want to go the cinema. Bromley was deaf in one ear and only heard what suited him. 'So Jeff walked up to Peter and was about to say, "Come to the pub with us," when he barked, "Let's go to the pictures – *Platoon*'s on!" *Platoon* it was…'

But even Peter Bromley had to yield one day at Broadcasting House. He had come in mid-morning one Saturday, to pre-record a piece for later in the afternoon setting up the day's racing, but he couldn't get into the studio and demanded the day's sports editor, John Taylor, sort it out. Taylor reasonably pointed out that the studio had been booked at short notice for an interview with a rather important sporting personality – one Muhammad Ali. Bromley's hilariously splenetic response is fondly remembered down the years, 'I don't care who's being interviewed, this is my studio and I want it now!' He stomped off to complain to the boss, Bob Burrrows, and got nowhere – one of those rare occasions when a Bromley rage was unproductive.

Everyone who produced Bromley brings up his 'you said' cards. This was an aid to help him avoid repeating himself in commentary. The producer would quickly write down the names of the horses Bromley had called past the post in first, second, third and sometimes fourth, then show them to Bromley as he wrapped up his summary of the race. He was concerned that he'd forget who he'd called as the winner. His encouraging address to a new producer was always, 'If I'm wrong after you show me the "you said" card and I do repeat myself, then I'll live with it. If you're wrong, then I'll shoot you.'

I have no awareness of any other commentator going to such pains to avoid repetition. His attention to detail and preparation were extraordinary. His race cards were works of art. He got a stamp made of a head and body which he would then use and colour them in ahead of races. Eventually he would know all the colours – an incredibly taxing task if you are commentating on a race involving around 30 horses in fading light or a three-quarters of a mile sprint at Goodwood like the Stewards' Cup. Peter would regularly auction off those exquisite race cards for charity and every jockey that won the Grand National in his time would be presented with the card and, duly signed, Bromley would then get them framed and hung.

Peter Bromley was a mass of contradictions. He never forgot a slight or studio mistake, yet he was wonderfully kind to his team at a race. He bought one of the producers a trilby once ('You may know nothing about racing, but at least look the part'), he'd bring a giant Christmas cake to the commentary box every Boxing Day meeting at Kempton, then insist the team came back to his home for tea. When Graeme Reid-Davies married, Peter couldn't be at the wedding, but recorded a delightful message for the happy couple, which touched and surprised all those present. He was the life and soul of the office Christmas party, charming all the ladies, impressing with his effortless dancing skills ('I hope I have you on my dance card').

He astonished Jim Rosenthal once, ringing up to say that he'd just heard there was a media sports day and could he be on the BBC Radio team? Jim, picking his words carefully with such an apparent ogre, pointed out there would be athletics, football and other sports that might tax someone of his maturity. 'There'll be shooting, won't there?' he barked at Jim. 'Put me down for that!' Jim was unaware that Bromley had been close to the UK Pentathlon team for the 1952 Olympics, his shooting and horsemanship being outstanding. So Peter turned up at the media sports day, won the shooting competition by a distance and bellowed at Jim, 'There you are – I thought I might be of some use to you!'

Cornelius Lysaght got to the essence of Bromley the man with this summary, 'He was a classic English gentleman of a certain vintage – he could shoot superbly, ride a horse very well, loved the countryside, danced very well and behaved impeccably to the ladies. And on a personal level, underneath the fearsomely short fuse, he was very, very kind.'

It was a matter of great sadness to the department that Peter only had one year of happy retirement before pancreatic cancer claimed him at the age of 74, in 2003. Someone of his dedication to his craft and remarkable professionalism deserved many more years in the sun. Producer Rob Nothman gave the eulogy at Peter's funeral, ending with this, 'It is said "To know a profession is to own a kingdom." Well Peter reigned unforgettably over racing on the radio for 40 commanding years.'

Rob says he learned so much about life and broadcasting from Peter Bromley. 'It was an honour. He brought a splash of colour to an increasingly grey, monochrome world. Peter was, above all, a genuine character.'

Peter commentated for BBC Radio on 42 Grand Nationals, 202 Classics and over 10,000 races, an unsurpassable body of work, carried out with rare brilliance. He worked with many at race meetings who later carved out great careers in radio sport, but the one who attained the greatest eminence was happy just to jog along in Bromley's slipstream. Ian Robertson, eventually the BBC's rugby correspondent over four decades, swiftly worked out how to keep in with the volatile maestro and enjoyed the craic over the summers, when rugby didn't claim him. 'I basically carried his bags and did a few interviews for six years. It was great fun, although Peter took no prisoners.'

Robbo, as he was always known in the sports department, didn't follow Bromley's example in turbulence. His droll, understated sense of humour was never concealed on air for long and he was shrewd enough to play the system. The best piece of advice he ever got was from our football correspondent, Bryon Butler, not long after joining the department in 1972. 'Bryon said, "Even if you can work the tape recorder or the other equipment, just don't let on, because they'll keep sending an engineer out with you and you won't have to worry about all that technical stuff." For over 40 years I got away with it.'

Robbo maintains the secret of his longevity until his retirement at the age of 73 was 'just living off my wits.' He savoured his good fortune, being recommended by Bill McLaren after co-commentating on some games in Scotland in the early seventies, and never gave the impression that being rugby correspondent fulfilled a lifetime's ambition. He basically fell into it, gave the job his best shot, never opted for the anodyne, always delivered strong opinions when necessary and particularly relished the closing stages of a key international match, when his cultivated Scottish tones would increase urgently amid all the tumult. But the job never consumed him.

He was lucky enough to have management who understood his idiosyncrasies and foibles, allowing him to bumble along in his own style, untouched by any need to modernise his approach. It was a simple game to Robbo, a good enough player to win eight Scotland caps and forge a fine reputation as an imaginative coach, and he excelled at communicating the nuances of a sport that can appear complex to the uninitiated.

Robbo was always a genial presence on air, distinctive and humorous – but he could drive his producers to distraction sometimes. Good time-keeping usually seemed to elude him. 'Where's Robbo?' would be the familiar cri de Coeur. Then he'd simply saunter in, wondering what all the fuss was about. Gordon Turnbull was the rugby producer for a time and he remembers the day at Twickenham when Robbo really taxed, then enthralled him.

'He was due to give us a preview piece and I was told he was on in two minutes' time. No sign of Robbo. He was finally located after chatting to his pals, with time an irrelevance to him. I said to him, "Robbo – what are your out words so the studio can pick up from you?" He produced a blank sheet of paper and wrote "France to win by 10 points." His preview was to last 90 seconds and all he had written down were those six words. By now, I'm in a pool of sweat as I hand him my stopwatch. Robbo never bothered with things like a stopwatch. He talked effortlessly, without a fluff, ending with the out words he'd mentioned. It was a brilliant example of talking with great insight, ending in the allotted time. A great gift – but he did tax your patience at times.'

Ed Marriage, Robbo's producer for 17 years, agrees, but maintains it was worth it. 'He was so easy-going, never minded if we were dropped in favour of a football story or we were cut back. A terrible timekeeper, but brilliant when he opened his gob on air. Robbo had superb contacts in the game and was highly respected. At Twickenham he used to slope off for a time, doing what he called 'wigwams' – slipping into a hospitality tent for a few minutes, talking about the game ahead and making everyone laugh. He'd say, 'I've got a couple of wigwams to do, but won't be long – I'll be back by two o'clock.' That was the tricky bit, because he was never back on time. But the plus side was having someone of his stature in your commentary box.'

And the subject of a teasing pub quiz. Name the stalwart of *Sports Report* who once taught English to a future prime minister? Ian Robertson, no less – and Tony Blair was the pupil at Fettes College, in the early seventies. Robbo spent four years at Fettes, acknowledged to be the Eton of Scotland, and young Blair stood out. 'He was in the Oxbridge class of the sixth form, clearly destined for great things. He liked his guitar and was very able. I didn't see him as a prime minister in the making, though. Mind you, I was just blundering around, wondering what to do with myself.'

Robbo hasn't made a bad fist of it, though. One of the great raconteurs of the sports department, he drops names and encounters with an enviable, low-key whimsy, self-effacing to the last. Nelson Mandela is as good a name as any for starters. Robbo was in South Africa for the BBC in 1993, taking a look at the preparations for the forthcoming World Cup two years later, while assessing how the post-apartheid Republic would embrace what is essentially the white man's game.

Robbo knew that an interview with Nelson Mandela would justify his trip 10 times over, so when he heard that Mandela was at a rugby function in Pretoria, he tried to blag his way in. 'The security goons wouldn't let me in, but when I saw President F.W. de Klerk, I waved at him and he waved back. I was encouraged by that and asked if he could get me in. The BBC name seemed to work and I was in. I saw Mandela, went over to him and dropped in the World Service, because I knew how important it had been for him to listen to it in prison. I asked him for an interview and he hesitated, then looked away. I chanced my arm and told him, "Sir, there's a punishment awaiting me if I don't get this interview." He asked what it was and, cheekily, I said, "The BBC will send me to Robben Island for 27 years." He roared with laughter, thank God, and said, "Come with me, my friend." He led me to a small room, containing two chairs and a small desk – nothing else. I asked him just five questions and he spoke brilliantly for 25 minutes. Every word a pearl.'

Two years later, it's the Rugby World Cup and Robbo's back in South Africa. Emboldened by his earlier success with Mandela two years later, he fetches up at the Vineyard Hotel, near Cape Town. He sees Mandela in the foyer, surrounded by about 10 bodyguards. 'I thought he'd never recognise me, even though our eyes met, and I carried on walking towards the dining-room. He shouted across the foyer "Hey! We met two years ago – now you ignore me!" It went deathly quiet and all his security men were staring threateningly at me. I had to say something, so I opted for humour. I said, "I'm so embarrassed, I was about to speak but couldn't remember your name." He roared with laughter and said, "My friend, you're coming into lunch with me." The most famous man in the world and I'd made him laugh. My lucky day.'

Due to his close friendship with the South African captain Francois Pienaar, Ian was invited to the post-match party after the hosts had won the World Cup. Mandela was there. He waved to Robbo to come over. 'I'm so happy for you, sir,' said Robbo. 'What? Happy that South Africa won the World Cup and not Scotland or England?' Robbo replied, 'Yours is a great story for a start and besides – four years ago, I put a £20 bet on at 20 to 1 for South Africa to win it, so I'm happy, yes!'

For at least one day in Robbo's career, he deserved all the flattery. On 22 November 2003 in Sydney, England beat Australia to win the Rugby Union World Cup for the first time – dramatically, pulsatingly. Ian Robertson was the perfect commentator for the drama at the end, when Jonny Wilkinson's drop goal sealed it. Robbo's commentary was immediately consigned to the archives, marked 'Do not ever destroy,' a clip that will be played whenever great British sporting moments are aired on BBC Radio. We're all word-perfect in the sports department... 'There are 35 seconds to go... This is the one... It's coming back for Jonny Wilkinson. He drops for World Cup glory. It's up, it's over, he's done it! Jonny Wilkinson is England's hero yet again... and there's no time for Australia to come back. England have just won the Rugby World Cup!' He got everything right in those few seconds – suspense, exhilaration, historical context. No wonder John Inverdale slapped him on the back as he passed Robbo a few minutes later, offering the classic British understatement, 'That was definitely not your worst-ever commentary.'

And yet Robbo almost blew it, in his eyes, retrieving the situation just in time. After telling himself, 'It's time for a drop goal,' he was gearing himself up for an effort from Jonny Wilkinson, but hesitated fractionally. 'The ball was on the kicker's right foot and for an instant I thought it was Mike Catt, who was right-footed and had done that for England in his previous position of fly-half. But I sensed it would be Wilkinson, even though he dropped goals with his left foot, always. Our commentary position was at the back of the stand, on the ten-metre line, and I reckon we were about a hundred yards away from the key piece of action. I panicked about the identity of the kicker as the move developed to give him the chance of a drop goal. I smacked my binoculars into the glasses hastily, and I'd already started with naming Wilkinson, so I went for it. I could easily have got that wrong.

'I'll have a large bet that, out of his thousand-plus points for England, Jonny never scored another drop goal with his right foot. It was just instinctive for me. I was lucky and hugely relieved. Just imagine if I'd got that clip wrong. I did around 50 commentaries a year over 47 years for the BBC and I'm only remembered for that one. I certainly didn't prepare for that, but I was duly grateful for years later on the after-dinner circuit!'

Ed Marriage, his producer in Sydney that day, reckons that immortal clip made a rod for Robbo's own back. Four years later, England again made the final and Robbo was nervous on the day of the match. 'People kept saying to him, "Looking forward to another great piece of commentary," and that spooked him. It was the first and only time I saw him nervous. He spent some time in the loo before coming to the commentary box.'

That commentary clip in Sydney did indeed aid Robbo on the after-dinner circuit, but also the Wooden Spoon charity that he founded, as well as raising funds for Alastair Hignell's ongoing treatment, after he was diagnosed with multiple sclerosis. Robbo is a brilliant speaker and compère at fundraisers, and such is his range of contacts and stature that he has helped raise more than £1.8 million in just over 20 years to help Hignell, 'Robbo has been fantastic and inspirational to me. I feel humbled and amazed that he continued raising money, long after I retired from the BBC in 2008, when I just couldn't carry on.'

Robbo was rarely aggravated in his post as rugby correspondent, but his equable disposition was tested once, in 1999. He was reported to the BBC for bias by a listener, after Scotland had clinched the last game of the Five Nations Championship. Scotland had already won an historic victory in Paris and if Wales triumphed at Twickenham, the title would be Scotland's. That duly transpired, as Scott Gibbs crashed over for the vital try near the end, under the posts, leaving the conversion as a formality.

Robbo's commentary stated, with justifiable excitement, that, 'This means that Scotland will be the Five Nations Champions this year and next year, and year after year for ever more' – a reflection on the fact that Italy's introduction in 2000 would mean it would now be the Six Nations Championship. But Robbo's vocal pleasure caused one irate listener to complain officially. It went all the way up to the Director-General after a tribunal investigated, but he was exonerated. 'The DG said I was over-enthusiastic, but absolutely accurate. I gave four accurate statements about an historic moment. It's not as if Scotland won the Five Nations as a matter of course down the years. I'd have been amazed if I hadn't been cleared.'

He notched up another couple of decades after that, still exasperating his producers at times, but mostly delivering pearls of dry humour at the microphone, interspersed with salient insights into the game. Unashamedly a technical Luddite, grateful for Bryon Butler's invaluable advice back in 1972, he remained blissfully unaware of new-fangled things like podcasts, Snapchat and Twitter. I could never envisage Robbo surfing the information highway or twerking on TikTok. 'It's all up there,' he'd say archly, pointing to his temple.

He was 73 when he finished, in 2018, at Twickenham, appropriately enough with England playing Australia – a reprise of his special performance in 2003. Typically, he was amused by all the fuss, but grateful to get out with his marbles still intact. 'I had a great run, didn't make a bollocks of anything and got to tell the bosses when I could go, on my terms. That meant a lot.'

Ian Robertson owes so much in his career to a couple of rugby greats – Bill McLaren, who first worked with him on a part-time basis, and Cliff Morgan, who followed up Bill's hearty recommendation and lured Robertson away from the groves of academe. Spotting young talent was one of Morgan's broadcasting

▲ Angus Mackay in his early days as producer of *Sports Report*. He was the presiding genius for 24 years, from 1948.

▲ Eamonn Andrews. As a hugely popular presenter of the programme for 12 years, he and Mackay were joined at the hip.

▶ The sheet music for 'Out of the Blue', *Sports Report*'s perennial signature tune.

◄ Eamonn Andrews, flanked by journalists Bill Hicks (to his right) and Roy Marler, together with Millwall's manager Charles Hewitt.

▼ John Gibson, studio manager, controlling the programme's technical challenges alongside Jill Reeves, the producer's invaluable assistant.

◄ Angus Mackay thought nothing of sitting alongside Eamonn Andrews as he presented *Sports Report*. Mackay left nothing to chance!

▲ Raymond Glendenning, *Sports Report*'s first presenter, at the 1955 Derby. Splendid moustache, big personality!

5.0
SPORTS REPORT
with
Eamonn Andrews
A comprehensive and up-to-the-minute survey of the day's sport from reporters and observers throughout the country and overseas

5.0 Football and Racing: the day's results read by John Webster and Gerald Sinstadt

5.10 app. Special Reports and news flashes and interviews from the grounds

First Division: Birmingham City *v.* Tottenham Hotspur; Burnley *v.* Chelsea; Everton *v.* Cardiff City; Fulham *v.* Manchester United; Ipswich Town *v.* Aston Villa

Second Division: Leyton Orient *v.* Bury; Plymouth Argyle *v.* Liverpool

Scottish League: Highlights of the day's play and a report on an outstanding match

Association Football: A report on the schoolboys' international match between England and Germany at Wembley

Lawn Tennis: Fred Perry reports from Bournemouth on the British Hard Court Championships

Talking Sport: Leading players, administrators, and journalists join Eamonn Andrews at the microphone to discuss topics of the moment

5.52 app. Classified Football Results
Produced by Angus Mackay

▲ Denis Law, reflecting the glamour of *Sports Report* in Liverpool FC's changing room, about to go on air.

◄ A *Radio Times* billing from the early sixties. Note the rare credit for the producer. Angus Mackay earned it!

▼ Angus Mackay, the inspirational producer of *Sports Report* for 24 years. The most important figure in *Sports Report*'s history, even though he retired in 1972.

Opposite page:
◄ Jim Rosenthal, presenting the programme from the Boat Race, on the Thames.

▼ Des Lynam, the first to present both *Sports Report* then TV's *Grandstand*. In many colleagues' eyes the charismatic Lynam was *Sports Report*'s greatest ever presenter.

This page:
► Peter Jones, brilliant commentator, superb presenter, one of *Sports Report*'s great allrounders. Tragically collapsed while commentating on the 1990 Boat Race, and died the following day. He was just sixty. A huge loss.

▼ Charlotte Green (seated) and her classified results producer Audrey Adams, reflecting the restrictions due to COVID. The key role they played underlined the growing influence of women on *Sports Report*.

▼ Pat's invitation to the dinner marking 40 years of *Sports Report* in November, 1987.

▲ Peter Bromley, an outstanding racing correspondent for so many years – away from a racecourse, but still close to the animal he dearly loved.

▲ Red Rum wins the 1977 Grand National for an historic third time (*left*), while Rachael Blackmore triumphs in the 2021 race, the first woman to do so in Grand National History (*right*). And *Sports Report* was all over both great sporting events.

◄ Rugby Correspondent Ian Robertson bowing out of *Sports Report* after 47 years' service – England v Australia at Twickenham in 2018.

▲ John Inverdale – not only a brilliant *Sports Report* presenter but an excellent host of racing outside broadcasts. Cheltenham Festival, 2010.

▲ Mark Pougatch, the longest-serving *Sports Report* presenter.

▶ Mark Chapman, the current presenter of *Sports Report*.

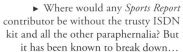

► Where would any *Sports Report* contributor be without the trusty ISDN kit and all the other paraphernalia? But it has been known to break down…

◄ Football correspondent John Murray interviewing Gareth Southgate during the 2020 Euros. Covid restrictions meant interviews required extended microphones.

◄ Pat in full flow for *Sports Report* at Villa Park. The press box empties very quickly after 5 o'clock.

▼ Pat's script for one of his countless appearances on *Sports Report*. Many a hieroglyphics expert would be challenged – but time precludes neatness!

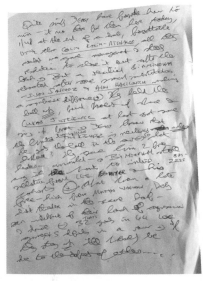

fortes and promising the English schoolmaster that the BBC would double his Fettes salary of £480 a year sealed the deal.

It was typical Morgan. His stature as a great Welsh fly-half was a given, while his sales pitch down the years for the BBC beguiled tougher nuts than young Robbo. Cliff Morgan knew which buttons to press and his influence in the radio sports department was immense as broadcaster, executive and truffler for talent. And raconteur. Few told a tale in the sports room better than Cliff, with just a soupçon of exaggeration and an engaging smile.

Morgan had the full package if you wanted to impress hard-nosed sports broadcasters, with a keen antenna for the phoney. It does help if your boss knows what he or she is talking about, based on practical experience and Cliff had a superb CV. After his glittering playing career ended, he graduated seamlessly into the media, clocking up a tremendous body of work that lasted more than 40 years.

He produced and edited BBC TV's flagship Saturday afternoon programme *Grandstand*, then *Sportsnight With Coleman*, he was one of the original team captains on *A Question of Sport*, became a vital figure in the radio sports department, progressing to head of sport, then fulfilled a similar role in BBC TV Sport. Then, for a decade, he presented Radio 4's *Sport on Four*, essential listening for those interested in the character and personalities of high achievers in sport. Cliff was the perfect, empathetic host, his gentle but insistent probing a model of its type, leading to so many insights that would be denied to a more stentorian interviewer.

Cliff also made innumerable, classy contributions to *Sports Report*, both as a reporter on overseas rugby tours (his apogee the historic Lions tour in 1971 to New Zealand) and elegant essayist, eager to focus on the more positive sports stories. And he will always be remembered for his gloriously lyrical live TV commentary on the Barbarians v All Blacks match at Cardiff in 1973. Drafted in at two hours' notice because Bill McLaren had a throat infection, Cliff was outstanding, revelling in the sort of rugby display in front of a packed, partisan Cardiff crowd that echoed his own career. It was the definitive sports commentary of the age, full of passion, clarity and affection. That day, Cliff spoke for all sports fans, live and unscripted, articulating perfectly what we all felt about that fabulous match. 'What a try! What a man!' he roared, as Gareth Edwards scored that wonderful, multi-passing try early on. No need to say any more, as Cliff knew instinctively.

So when Cliff Morgan wandered into the radio sports room and sat on your desk, you would be well advised to give him your full attention. Ron Jones got an early brickbat from Morgan at the start of his career in Broadcasting House. Ron had just had his first commentary stint at West Ham, with Peter Jones, and was pleased with his efforts. Peter Jones was also warm in his praise. Sitting in the sports room next day, Ron saw the stocky, bow-legged figure of Cliff Morgan walking towards him and he prepared himself for what he hoped would be praise from a man he regarded as an authentic sporting legend.

'Heard your commentary last night, boyo – very good – I got into the car and you were in full flow… My wife said, "Who's this?" and I said, "A young fellow called Jones, he's going to be very good." You caught the light and shade and the rhythm very well.'

Cliff walked away from the desk and Jones started to preen himself. Then he turned and delivered the killer message, 'By the way, I'd love to have known the score. You need to give it every two minutes. Don't keep the listener waiting for four minutes, as you did. No one will ever complain about you giving the score too much.'

Ron thought that was brilliant man-management. 'He knew how to lodge the vital message in your brain, while also praising you. And any broadcaster would listen to Cliff Morgan about the skills needed for broadcasting, because he displayed them every time he sat at a microphone.'

John Helm can testify to Cliff's personal support. When he came back from the Commonwealth Games in New Zealand in 1974, Cliff organised for his wife to come down from Yorkshire to stay in a West End hotel, as a surprise. 'That was fantastic of him. He obviously thought I'd done well at the Games and this was his thank you. He got me on *Sports Report* that night, doing a postscript on the Games and, again, that was clever of him, giving me a confidence boost. He loved regional accents, never cared about me being from Yorkshire, wanted different voices on *Sports Report*. Cliff was a magnificent boss – he'd give you a right bollocking, deservedly, then 10 minutes later, he'd buy you a pint.'

Cliff summed up his love for the BBC one day when he rejected an expenses claim from one of his highly valued editors, John Taylor. 'He called me in and said, "Look, boyo, you've put Tube fares receipts on your expenses. Not good enough. Get me some taxi receipts. You work for the greatest broadcasting organisation in the world, so make sure you don't sell us short with Tube receipts." Can you wonder why we loved Cliff Morgan as our boss?'

He was the natural choice to give the eulogy at the memorial service for his great friend, Peter Jones, in 1990 at All Souls Church, alongside

Broadcasting House. In front of a daunting array of sports legends, Cliff struck just the right irreverent yet affectionate note right from the start. He pointed upwards, imitating Peter's vibrant broadcasting style and began with, 'If Jonesy was here, he'd be saying, "What's going on here now?!"' Then Cliff launched into a wonderful, seamless tribute to Peter, full of rich anecdotes and humane insights. All done without a note. For those who had never heard Cliff Morgan speak on the after-dinner circuit or at charity lunches, it demonstrated just how brilliant he could be at charming an audience of over 500 folk. And it's rumoured he never charged a fee. No wonder he was such a soft touch for so many charities.

Sports Report remained vital to Cliff, even in retirement. He had listened with his father to the first programme, back in January 1948, in their terraced house overlooking the Rhonda Valley in South Wales, and at just 18 he fell in love instantly with the romance and breadth of the show. 'Nothing was outside the range of the programme, for it appealed to all the masses and represented every aspect of contemporary sport which we all yearned for in those days after the war. It had good words and successfully incorporated the surprising line and the classic use of the English idiom. It understood that the spoken word was so different from the written word.'

Few broadcasters on *Sports Report* have matched Cliff's facility with the spoken word. But few have conjured up more laughs among colleagues than Peter Brackley.

Peter wasn't just a highly talented member of the radio sports department, commentating on football and athletics with distinction, presenting *Sports Report* with equal success. His ability as an impressionist and comedian hasn't been matched by anyone else. Time and again, he would lift the spirits on a dull day with a brilliant jape at somebody's expense, but always with harmless intent. Good nature ran through Peter Brackley.

When Jim Rosenthal first spotted Peter in the sports room, he thought, 'Who's this? Wurzel Gummidge? He was so scruffy and seemed so insignificant, shy and ill at ease. Barely uttered a word in those early days. But when he stood up in front of hundreds of people, he was transformed. I remember one turn of his at a PFA dinner – he was sensational, his impressions really hitting the spot. He brought the house down and that was usually a tough audience. I congratulated him afterwards and he said, "Yeah, but the Jack Charlton gag didn't work, did it?" Peter was such a perfectionist.'

171

Peter's new sports-room colleagues never knew how he had moulded himself into this second, lucrative career, alongside his undoubted skills as a broadcaster. But they relished using him to hoodwink others. Peter Lorenzo was often an easy target. Peter, an inveterate namedropper and dedicated seeker after the big interviews with household names, was ripe for teasing.

Emily McMahon remembers the day that Lucky Lorenzo was taken in by someone he thought was Franz Beckenbauer. She took advantage of Lucky being out for lunch, rigged up a studio, then told Lucky he had to interview the great German when he returned. 'Lucky didn't know that Brackers was on a phone in another studio, ready to impersonate Beckenbauer. We also rigged up a speaker in the sports room so that everyone could hear it. They were all in on the spoof.

'The interview went on for about 15 minutes and you just wouldn't have known that it was an impersonation. Lucky came out of the studio in triumph – "That was pure gold!" he shouted – and everyone was desperately trying not to laugh. We were now terrified he'd give the quotes to the papers so Peter went into Lucky's office, spoke just like Beckenbauer and you should've seen Lucky's face. He took it well, though – he had to!'

Peter Lorenzo was on the receiving end again in November 1981 when England faced elimination from the World Cup the following year and all the speculation was about whether they could beat Hungary to make it, against all odds. As duty editor, Lucky was all over the story and told Garry Richardson to get some big names talking about their own comebacks in their particular sport. Garry was deputed to find Jack Nicklaus, the great American golfer.

With Lorenzo out to lunch, Richardson and Brackley recorded a spoof interview, with Peter impersonating Nicklaus. It worked a treat. When Lorenzo returned, he was given the good news. 'You got Nicklaus? Recorded? Good boy – let's have a listen.' Very soon, Nicklaus/Brackley was displaying a depth of knowledge about the England football team that was rather surprising. 'I think they can do it, but Ray Clemence's handling in goal is dodgy and their back four look as if they've never played together.' Lorenzo was amazed, 'How come he knows so much about football? This is gold-plated. Did he say anything else? How did he end the interview?' Richardson obliged by playing the last couple of sentences he'd recorded, 'I'd just like to wish my great friend Lucky Lorenzo a happy birthday, because I know it's coming up shortly. This is coming all the way from San Diego.' After a few seconds, it dawned on Peter that again he had been duped by the master impressionist. Always a good sport, he took it well as the sports room erupted with laughter.

Brackley could also laugh at himself. His hypochondria was legendary. His desk always seemed to be covered with potions and pills, and if you had a spare half-hour, you'd ask Peter how he was. When he left to join ITV in 1982, no one could think of what to buy him as a farewell present. Gill Pulsford was deputed to go to Boots the chemist, where she bought a whole bagful of remedies for a wide range of ailments.

At Mike Ingham's wedding, Peter gave a speech of such brilliance that the guests who weren't from the sports room were astonished at his hilarious contribution. Mike remembers, 'You wouldn't want to follow Peter if you were both speaking at a function. He just came alive, yet he'd be paralysed with nerves before he stood up.'

Garry Richardson witnessed that many times when they worked together on the circuit. 'He'd worry so much. If the tables were 10 feet away, he'd insist they were moved back. If we did a gig at Leeds one night and Liverpool the next, he'd spend all the time in the car, en route to Liverpool, rehearsing and then carry it on in the hotel when we got there. Yet he loved making people laugh. He was such a great comedy writer. I'm convinced he would've been one of the greats in that field if he hadn't gone down the sports broadcasting route.'

Peter merged the two in his uncanny impersonation of Jimmy Greaves for the ITV show *Spitting Image* and his Ray Wilkins impression while working for Channel 4's *Football Italia* was pitch-perfect. Always done with good humour, never malicious, his subjects were flattered to be chosen by Peter.

His popularity in the sports department was so great that many of his former colleagues kept in touch after he followed a successful TV career. Sadly, ill-health continued to dog Peter and he passed away in 2018. Heart failure at the age of 67. Garry Richardson was particularly close to Peter and saw him in hospital the night before he died. When he had phoned Peter to say he'd see him in a few days, he said, 'It'll be too late, Richo, I won't be here.' So he raced to the hospital. 'I held his hand, his eyes were closed and I thanked him for all he'd done for me. I loved him to bits. We couldn't have been closer friends.'

Peter passed away next morning. In the end, his concerns over his health as a young man that had afforded his sports-room colleagues such amusement proved accurate. Not that it bothered Peter at the time, he took the leg-pulling in good part, sometimes playing up to the cliché. Sadly, clichés often provide a deal of truth and Peter just ran out of road, far too early. But 40 years after he left the radio sports room, he's still remembered with great affection.

It's a special boss who can be remembered with the warm glow accorded to someone like Peter Brackley, but Iain Thomas was one of them. Known to all as 'Jimmy', he was the classic hard-drinking Scottish newspaper hack who wound up in the BBC sports department as managing editor in the late 1970s, in the process guiding the careers of many talented broadcasters to greater things, while amusing everyone in the sports room.

Jimmy just didn't realise how much he made his colleagues laugh. He seemed oblivious to the stifled smirks and muffled titters when he went off on one of his tirades, becoming more Scottish and profane with every sentence. Then the tempest would blow over as quickly as it had arrived and he'd reassure the recipient of his rant, 'Don't worry, son, you'll be fine.'

It was Jimmy's unenviable task to draw up the *Sports Report* rota for the staff broadcasters, invariably disappointing someone when they copped for reading the racing or rugby union results in the programme or presenting the 'best of the rest', prospecting for hidden treasures in the lower divisions and having a two to three-minute package ready for around 5.45 p.m. A thankless slog, invariably unappreciated by the broadcasters who would far rather be out, reporting from a rugby or football game. Those of the stature of Ian Robertson, Christopher Martin-Jenkins, Mike Ingham, Ian Darke, John Rawling and Gerald Williams had to bend their shoulders to these mundane wheels at times, and no one rushed to Jimmy Thomas to thank him for being selected.

Jimmy was shrewd enough to nip any protests in the bud when he spotted dismay and disaffection. He'd watch closely as the week's rota was pinned up and, if he thought someone might harbour a grudge, would saunter over to the pouting party. 'Come with me son,' he'd say, leading them over to the window that looked down on Regent Street. 'If ye dinnae like it, there's always Barclays Bank – you could always go and work there, you know.' That usually quelled any rebellious instincts and 'Barclays Bank' became one of the stock quotes from the inmates of the sports room if they were discontented. However, it was uttered with a smile, because they knew that Thomas had them where he wanted.

If Jimmy was particularly annoyed, it would be time for an outing of 'Dearie, dearie me'. That was an early harbinger of a Thomas volley, buttressed by an impressively salty vocabulary. Long before Sir Alex Ferguson became associated with the 'hair-dryer' rollickings, Jimmy's stress levels were connected to the number of 'Dearie, dearie mes' he used. Mike Costello, who admits he owed an enormous amount to Jimmy's guidance and encouragement early in his career, reckons the most he heard were four, but some claim to have heard seven in a row.

Even the royal family was not immune to Jimmy's derision. As a proud Scot, he was no respecter of Establishment figures just for the sake of it and one day the Duchess of Kent was on the receiving end at the annual Sports Writers' Association Christmas lunch. For reasons best known to herself, the duchess had agreed to be guest speaker. It didn't go down well, as she told stories that were too familiar to the assembled gathering of unimpressed hacks. In fact, it was like watching cheese grow fur as yawns were ostentatiously stifled. It was all too much for Jimmy, by now in his cups, unable to stand the tedium much longer. Mike Costello was sat beside him. 'Iain had heard the gags too many times already and so unleashed a barrage of "Dearie, dearie mes" in the direction of the hapless duchess. In a room that was almost totally silent, she was made to feel like we did whenever we handed him a dodgy script.'

Jimmy liked a colourful putdown. After surveying the requests for time off at Christmas, something he always granted grudgingly, he told one member of the sports room, 'If you want to celebrate Christmas, then join the Salvation Army.' He told one softly spoken producer who'd been press-ganged at short notice into reading the rugby results on *Sports Report*, 'What are you doing on air? You're a stoker, not a star!'

Yet the staff loved him. He would accompany them on nights out, consuming eye-watering amounts of alcohol, then treating them to a raucous rendition of 'Flower of Scotland', while draped around a lamppost like Gene Kelly in *Singing in the Rain*. When England played Scotland at rugby or football, all pretence at BBC impartiality was set aside by Jimmy. When some Scots fans broke the crossbars at Wembley in 1977, Jimmy saw it as perfectly acceptable high spirits. As Jim Rosenthal confirms, 'He was transformed when Scotland came up against the Auld Enemy. The classic stereotype. But people wanted to work for Jimmy, he cared about his staff, even when handing out bollockings.'

It was a measure of the staff's affection for Jimmy that he was subjected to a classic jape one day. He had been chuntering for a while about the time his presenters wasted when the Radio 1 presenters like Gloria Hunniford or David Hamilton handed over to the hourly sports desks and he issued a decree that they must now get straight into the details and cut out the social chit-chat. Emily

McMahon, the sports desk producer on the day, decided to wind up Jimmy with a spoof tape, featuring the presenter, Chris Rea. The tape would be relayed into Jimmy's office, where he'd be listening intently, determined the desks would now be snappy and sharp, instead of the waffle that annoyed him so much.

So while Chris was reading the authentic sports news on air from studio 3H, Jimmy was apopletic at what he was hearing from the speaker in his office, at the other end of the sports room. Chris began the spoof by wittering on about what he'd done at the weekend, wishing his Aunty Doris a happy birthday in Brighton, then launching into results from three race meetings, all with the sound of horses' hooves playing in the background. Jimmy looked down the room, into the studio, saw Chris Rea's lips moving, and was convinced this nonsense was going out live on air. He came thundering down the office towards the studio and was hijacked by several rugby tackles just before he burst into the studio to yank Rea off air. 'It worked a treat' recalls Emily, 'and Jimmy saw the funny side of it, but it was a mark of our respect for a great boss that we could play that trick on him.'

Jimmy really cared about his sports-room charges. He would privately advise his staff on anything, even their romantic lives, if asked. When the production assistants went on strike, Jimmy, very much part of senior management, still brought trays of coffee and tea to the picket line.

Mike Costello was given his chance by Jimmy when he became managing editor at BBC World Service Sport. 'I have felt his presence ever since, all through the years, as if he's on my shoulder, chipping away when I make mistakes and dropping a card in the post when it goes well.' Mike did the eulogy at Jimmy's funeral in 2015, paying tribute to his constant encouragement. 'I came from a background very different to that of the people I worked with. I was surrounded by talented operators I regarded as heroes in broadcasting and Iain was so passionate about making me feel I belonged.'

Perhaps Iain recognised in Mike a fellow outsider, someone who would champion the underdog. He managed the difficult feat of being a respected, feared, authoritative and loved boss in a highly pressurised environment, while unaware just how funny he could be. Jimmy presided over a convivial yet highly disciplined office environment, a self-policing one of 'work hard, play hard.'

In the early 1980s, Jimmy held the office together, as the sports room lost to television varied talents such as Bob Burrows, Bryan Tremble, Phil King, John Taylor, Peter Brackley and Jim Rosenthal – a deep pool of broadcasting and production expertise. Jimmy's unselfish leadership, personal touch and light, humorous hand on the tiller, when necessary, helped the department maintain the high standards demanded by Angus Mackay all those years earlier. The new breed maintained the tradition of moaning about Jimmy's rotas, but the Regent's Street branch of Barclays Bank never had any new recruits from Broadcasting House.

It would be fascinating to have observed how these genuine characters would have adapted to life in the sports room when the department moved out of Broadcasting House in the late 1990s. The hostelries and pubs around, first, TV Centre, then Salford wouldn't have appealed as much to those used to long lunches and schmoozing contacts, with half an eye on the clock and approaching deadlines. Now the demands of 24/7 news and sport on 5 Live have consigned those days to affectionate memory. It's more serious now, inevitably, with competition so fierce and the media landscape unrecognisable from 30 years ago. Quite simply, work takes priority now during a shift. No complaints about that from any quarter, but it was fun working with Bromley, Morgan, Jones, Lorenzo et al. They're not forgotten.

11

READING THE CLASSIFIEDS

It's not as easy as it looks, you know. Reading the classified football results in a precise, authoritative yet friendly manner – and finishing on time – is a challenge. One man managed it so deftly over four decades that he became one of the most loved figures in *Sports Report*'s history. Thankfully, the prestigious results readers who have been front of house so early in the programme have been almost a seamless robe. But that part of Sports Report has now ended. From the start of the 2022–23 season, the results section was scrapped.

The deal negotiated by BBC Radio Sport to secure exclusive commentary rights for a Premier League game starting at 5.30 meant difficult choices and tough decisions. When a programme is reduced in time by a half, casualties are inevitable. The feeling is that football fans can now get all the results elsewhere, reflecting the multiplicity of choices and outlets now available, rather than waiting till just after 5pm. With the immortal signature tune and headlines deemed sacrosanct, the presenter would normally cue up the results at 5.02. That could then take up the next five minutes, so the programme would only have around 20–22 minutes for live reports, interviews and comments before handing over to the commentary team to introduce the live 5.30 match.

Something had to give and this time it was a feature indelibly associated with Sports Report's long history. Those of a sentimental disposition will mourn its departure while many others will point to the exigencies demanded of a programme that must move with the times.

For 70 of its 75 years, only three results readers have been consistently in situ. The first to make a major impression was John Webster. Angus Mackay knew how important it was to have an experienced, reliable figure at the helm, exuding a reassuring presence at the start of this adventure. Within a few weeks, Webster had become one of the *Sports Report* regulars. Mackay was too old a hand to leave such appointments to chance. He had heard enough of John Webster reading the news on the Home Service and presenting various music programmes to know that here was an unflappable professional, who would do the producer's bidding uncomplainingly. His brief was to read the football results in 270 seconds, providing a vital buffer to the presenter's opening link, enabling him to pick up afterwards with reports, interviews and comment.

Webster was aware that Mackay wanted 270 seconds, no more no less. That would be fine. He was disciplined, mature and could be relied on to time his contribution to the second. In the modern idiom, John Webster was low maintenance and continued to be so on *Sports Report* for the next 22 years.

Webster was of his time. Measured, calm and free of ego. As a newsreader, he knew the content was paramount, not who was reading it. Mackay could relax and when Webster was, for some reason, unavailable, Robin Boyle filled in. A veteran of British Forces Network, who had lied about his age to ensure he was called up in the war, Boyle proved an outstanding radio presenter, best known for *Friday Night Is Music Night* on Radio 2, until he retired in 1998.

Sports Report undoubtedly had teething problems early on, but at least Mackay had the reading of the results nailed down – so important at a time when millions were filling in pools coupons and reliant on trusted information, soon after full-time.

Eamonn Andrews was hugely impressed by Webster and, when he filled in, Boyle, 'These two have to be seen to be believed. They drift into the studio at 5.29, calmly slip the written results from the hands of some breathless attendant, slide into a chair, give a sly sidelong glance at the clock and bestow a sort of silent benediction to the gabbling, whispering reporters in the four corners of the studio. A half-smile in my direction and I feel they're saying "Relax, I'm ready." And they always are.'

John Webster returned the compliment when he was brought back in 1972 to read the classifieds on Angus Mackay's final programme as producer. On air, he shyly thanked Eamonn for all his kindnesses when they worked together, emphasising what a privilege it had been over the previous 24 years. Always immaculately dressed, with perfect manners, he represented a different age. Bob Burrows, Mackay's lieutenant says he was, 'Very Radio 4 ish' compared to the more relaxed members of the team in the early seventies. One of them, studio producer Bryan Tremble, describes him as, 'An English country gentleman in dress and in his charming manners. He'd turn up exactly on time when required, ask how long he should be reading that day, and he'd go away and read it through. John would deliver on the button, to the exact time, in a perfectly modulated style. John was all that you'd expect from a Home Counties BBC Radio announcer.'

A safe pair of hands doesn't really do justice to John Webster's contribution in those early years of *Sports Report*. The highest accolade that can be given to him is that he never caused a moment's concern to that exacting taskmaster, Angus Mackay.

When John stood down, a number of announcers served an apprenticeship. One of them lasted for a couple of football seasons prior to moving to more glamorous pastures – one Simon Bates. Before he became a high-profile Radio 1 DJ, Simon was on the rota of staff announcers and his lack of knowledge on football didn't preclude him from doing the classifieds. His strong, deep voice was in contrast to John Webster's lighter touch, but he carried off the task perfectly capably. Dick Scales, one of *Sports Report*'s executives, remembers having to coach Bates. 'Simon wasn't a football man, but neither was John Webster. But we had to get the right flow and tempo instilled into Simon. We had to get him reading at the right speed all the way through... Early on, he made the classic error of starting slowly, then having to speed up, but he got there.'

Simon was aware of Mackay's fearsome reputation. 'Des Lynam told me. I did my best to avoid him after seeing him get exercised a few times.' But he acknowledges what a privilege it was for a young broadcaster to appear on *Sports Report*. 'It was unbelievably successful and a model of production values. My primary memory is the drama of the thing. It was quite epic every Saturday. Des on lip mic, the producer guiding him over the telexes that were chattering away, and huge focus and concentration everywhere. Not much noise, no whooping and hollering. Everyone seemed to know exactly what they were doing and exactly what was expected of them.'

When Simon Bates was called to greater things, Bob Burrows and Bryan Tremble wanted to have some permanence and gravitas from the classifieds reader. The results, repeated just before 6.00 p.m., were too vital to be trivialised and they were aghast when Jimmy Kingsbury, standing in one Saturday, began his reading with, 'Eyes down, children, may your felt tips never run dry.' That was considered far too flippant and the new executives could only imagine what the combustible Mackay would make of such a solecism. The situation was compounded by the fact that Kingsbury was Head of Radio Presentation and also organised the rota for the other announcers. How could he be sidelined without causing internecine offence?

Luckily, Kingsbury – a doyen of *The Shipping Forecast* and another alumnus of *Friday Night Is Music Night* – wasn't all that enamoured of sport, so he was happy to let others pick up the *Sports Report* gig. One day, he said to a pleasant young Scot, who seemed inordinately eager to please, 'Do you fancy nipping to read the football results, old chap?' And with that, James Alexander Gordon began a love affair with *Sports Report* that lasted 39 years.

JAG, as everyone in the sports room called him, was perfect for *Sports Report*. His light Scottish tones and lively inflexion with a hint of lurking humour were ideal for a programme that tried to blend authority with entertainment. The dapper, slightly built, chirpy Scot spoke on the radio just as he did away from the studio, always a good idea when you're hoping to be natural. Quite simply, JAG became an institution. Listeners would write offering him bribes to read results that suited their pools coupon. He once had a letter from a jilted husband, imploring him to ask his disaffected wife to return home, on air. Listeners rightly judged him to be friendly and rather good at his job.

James was immediately popular with the troops on Saturday afternoons, because he'd volunteer to get the teas in from the canteen – not a usual gesture from an august announcer. It was also a bit of a physical challenge, because JAG wore a built-up heel and had difficulty walking very far, a legacy from contracting polio that afflicted him from the age of three months. James was adopted and he spent long spells in hospital, remaining in leg supports until he was a teenager, and he also suffered from a speech impediment in his formative years. He had no formal education, because of prolonged spells in hospital, and left school at the age of 14. Some crash courses in various subjects after that helped, but silver spoons and whispered recommendations from influential folk were not a factor in James' professional success.

After working in music publishing for a time, he inveigled his way into the BBC as an announcer in 1972. By 1974, he was *Sports Report*'s established classifieds reader, a role he absolutely loved. 'I just gave the results reading a bit of a lift. I play the cornet and piano, and thought "How can I make this like a song?" So intonation for the two teams was important. After a time, the listeners knew who had won before I got to the second team. The score wasn't as important as home win, away win or draw. The pools remained very important to a lot of folk for a long time.'

As James knew only too well. In 1989, he and a friend won £52,815. 35 on the treble chance pool – the very same results that he read out just after 5.00 p.m. 'I got more and more excited as I read out the results. My friend was a doorman in Broadcasting House reception. We kept it quiet! I still kept doing the pools!' James looked after his close friends with some thoughtful gifts and took his wife, Julia, away for a good holiday, but, like a good Scot, he didn't fritter away his £26,000.

There was a thespian quality to JAG, having learned a thing or two about hyperbole from his time in the music industry, plugging bands and records. His after-dinner routine was peppered with anecdotes from his BBC career, some of which were a tad fanciful, but no one ever cared to dispute them. If he really was caught for speeding one day, en route to reading the results at TV Centre, only to be let off by the traffic officer because he recognised his unique voice, I'd like to believe it were so. James maintained it was. And did he really see a ghost in his Langham Hotel bedroom, opposite Broadcasting House, as he hunkered down to do the early morning newsreader's shift? JAG always insisted he did.

Audrey Adams, his classifieds producer for 30 years, smiles at James' stories. 'He was a bit of a Walter Mitty character, embellishing his tales, but no one minded. James was a great team player, he loved being in the sports room on Saturday afternoons. And very kind and generous. At the end of each football season, he'd take me to lunch at Le Gavroche, because our birthdays were 10 days apart, and always insisted on picking up the tab. The maître d' made a great fuss of James.'

Julia, James' widow, is happy to take his stories at face value. 'He loved a tall tale and I never knew how true they all were. But it's funny how others would corroborate any of his stories long after he'd told me them and I'd be just smiling, wondering just how likely they were. But underneath all the funny anecdotes, James was determined to prove himself after such a tough upbringing. His only education was from books; he was rarely at school.'

James used to tell Julia how grateful he was to Jimmy Kingsbury for asking him to pop over to the *Sports Report* studio. 'It was strange, because he also read the news so many times as a staff announcer, but *Sports Report* established his reputation, where his real charming personality came through. He used to say to me, "I hope they don't retire me – wouldn't it be lovely if I could do this until I die?" And that's more or less what happened.'

Early in 2013, James developed a sore throat. It didn't really clear up, but he didn't go to his doctor until May. He was told there were nodules on his larynx and he needed an operation. By July, he was informed it was throat cancer. The voice of the classifieds wouldn't return.

Richard Burgess, the head of sport, had the distressing task of informing the department that one of the most popular members of the *Sports Report* team would not be back. In a thoughtful email, Richard paid deserved tribute to him and, 'A voice which is, of course, recognised around the globe through the World Service and a voice which exudes authority, clarity and charm. For so many of us, James has been a mainstay in our lives – a reassuring presence every week. A broadcasting legend.'

James added his own, typically modest, postscript. 'It's with great sorrow that I give up the most exciting part of my career, the classified football results. They have been my life. Such fun getting it right. The most important thing: making it exciting for the listener. How I shall miss you all!'

It was a feeling that was deeply reciprocated. James was greatly touched by the subsequent newspaper tributes, letters from listeners and communications from his 5 Live Sport colleagues. Julia says he was amazed at the public warmth. 'He had no idea he was so loved. He said, "Not many get to read their own obituary." It was a great comfort to us in that final year.'

He never did get to read one imaginary result – East Fife 4 Forfar 5. That always eluded him. It would have been a memorable closure for this proud Scot.

Julia has one particularly poignant memory from their last year together. 'We would go to Glyndebourne every year and after he got out of hospital, we went with friends to see *The Marriage of Figaro*. At the end James leapt to his feet shouting, "Bravo! Bravo!" – but there was no sound. He was stunned. For the length of the production, he'd utterly forgotten that he'd lost his voice.'

James died in August 2014, aged 78. He always seemed so much younger, such was his boyish, Tiggerish personality. 'James was very caring,' recalls Julia. 'He'd spent so much time in hospitals, with scars that never really healed after some unsuccessful operations, that he counted his blessings. He never thought he was particularly deserving of anything, with hardly any education at such a key time for a child.'

The poet and dedicated football fan Ian McMillan wrote a special valediction for James' funeral, ending with a touching farewell…

'Here's James Alexander Gordon;
Soothing, gentle, safe, exact.
Giving a hint of Shakespeare to Accrington Stanley,
Raising 1–1 beyond reported fact
To a kind of poetry. James, we salute you:
Your intonations kept our hopes alive.
Now sit in your garden and dream of those teatimes
When East Fife got 4, and Forfar got 5.'

I'm glad that someone who wasn't a sports broadcaster remains so closely associated with *Sports Report*, whose fame will linger long after so many of we reporters and commentators are just fading, yellowing photos on the wall. For James represented a comforting, reliable presence, as loved as the programme by so many. Every Saturday afternoon in the football season was a joy to James and no one can remember a furrowed brow on him.

Richard Burgess will always remember JAG's contribution when he was running the sports department. 'He was as elegant and comfortable as a Queen Anne chair, with his soothing, honeyed tones. James was the easiest person to deal with – he never quibbled about the money we offered him, always smiled at everyone. James was a true gentleman, a real pro, and the fantastic response from the public when he retired, then died, says it all.'

Mike Ingham remembers JAG's wry sense of humour. 'After I'd finished presenting the programme, James would have to stay on to record the classifieds for use on the World Service over the weekend, incorporating Saturday evening or Sunday results. So, painstakingly, he had to cover all possible eventualities by reading 40 or 50 different variations of the possible final score. The producer's editing blade would do the rest. He'd come out of the studio eventually and say to me, "Tranmere 7 Bury 8. I'd liked to have seen that game." He never complained about having to do all those permutations.'

When James was forced to retire, his place was taken at short notice by Kevin Howells, a staff sports reporter, who'd been in the department since 1999. He once stood in for James at 15 minutes' notice, after he'd got stuck in roadworks on the motorway, and acquitted himself very well. With a pleasingly deep voice and clear enunciation, Kevin was a very capable replacement. He harboured ambitions to be the permanent reader. It was not to be. 'It would have been the cherry on the cake for me in my broadcasting career. It would have married my passion for radio with my love of sport. I was very disappointed for a time, but things happen for a reason and I got over it.'

It's interesting that such a seasoned reporter as Kevin – with experience of overseas England cricket tours and countless football matches, a stalwart of our county cricket coverage – should covet such a role. 'But I cherished and honoured doing it, as I still do whenever I stand in now and then. I'd put myself in the position of the typical football fan and I'd see their faces as I was reading the results. I'd get nervous and think, "Why the hell am I doing this?" but then the music kicks in. It's so emotional and evocative. I'd remember sitting at the kitchen table with my Nan, as she checked her pools coupon. That would help me with the pace of reading the results. Don't be sing-song, develop a rhythm. The adrenalin flows and afterwards there's a sense of relief that an important job has been done satisfactorily.'

Happily, Kevin fills in when Charlotte Green is away. Since her appointment in September 2013, Charlotte has walked in illustrious footsteps with great aplomb. For someone who, at the age of six, used to read the football results from the Sunday paper to her beloved father, the role of the first woman to read the classifieds was one she cherished. 'My father loved it when I read to him at the kitchen table. He'd laugh fondly at my efforts. He'd be so proud now if he were still alive. It does sound banal, but it really was a dream come true for a football fan like me.'

Charlotte owes it to television. In January 2013, she left the BBC after 35 years as, first, studio manager, then reading the news and presenting on Radio 4. She was interviewed by *Newsnight* and, after rightly lauding her vocal clarity, successful efforts in stifling giggles at testing moments and authoritative presence at the microphone, she was asked if there were any career ambitions unfulfilled. 'Yes, reading the football results on the radio' was the surprising reply. That comment was stored away by a few radio sport executives and when James Alexander Gordon had to retire the following May, Charlotte was approached for an interview and a read-through.

Richard Burgess and Audrey Adams supervised Charlotte's demo and she sailed through it. 'She was very professional, determined to get it right,' recalls Audrey. 'Her diction was beautifully clear and precise, as you'd expect from such an experienced Radio 4 newsreader. She clearly wanted this and was thrilled to be offered it by Richard.'

Charlotte was taken aback by the media interest before she first read the results on 28 September 2013. She was gratified to receive a charming, supportive email from James Alexander Gordon. Radio 4's *PM* and *Today* programmes did features, as did the *Daily Telegraph* and, on the morning of her *Sports Report* debut, in his *Telegraph* column Des Lynam referenced her 'soft, cultured, honeyed tones' and commented, 'It is an imaginative appointment and I forecast that any doubters will soon be won over.'

Charlotte's preparation was meticulous, which impressed her producer, Audrey Adams. 'She's very modest and unaffected. She marked out the pronunciations, asked about unfamiliar names and never got flustered. She can't stand cameras in the studio and, on the first day, I had to ensure there weren't too many there, taking photos. Charlotte very much considers herself as a radio person and didn't want any distractions. To her great credit, she nailed it on the first day and that put paid to any carping comments.'

It was a blessing that Charlotte doesn't do social media so she wouldn't be fazed by uncharitable comments. 'I'm sure there were some who thought a woman doesn't know what she's talking about with football, but I was spared all that. I was acutely aware of how brilliant James had been and that I was standing on giant's shoulders, but he advised me to make it my own. I didn't often get nervous as a newsreader and presenter, but that first day my heartbeat was racing just a touch! But I made sure I got the obscure names right, so I managed to sail over my own Becher's Brook.'

After almost a decade, nobody seems to notice that a woman was reading the classifieds, which is exactly how Charlotte wanted it. Des Lynam's prediction has proved prescient. She cherished her involvement in a programme that she's always admired. A Tottenham fan (favourite player, Jimmy Greaves), she would listen with her dad, drinking in all the information, her mood affected by Tottenham's result. 'I know how many people there are, listening intently, caught up in the emotion of a particular result. I was the same, alongside my dad. So I try for a measured, clear approach. When you've heard all the drama and clever use of language from the football reporters before I go on air, you realise you have to detach yourself from all the excitement.'

Charlotte's CV on radio has been so varied and extensive, winning awards and golden opinions from countless listeners and critics, that it's surprising a one-hour, weekly programme enchanted her so much. 'Some of my radio colleagues said in 2013, "What on earth do you want to do that for?" but they just don't get the joy and the delight of sport. It's a phenomenal programme.

'I got the most satisfaction and enjoyment from reading the football results than anything that's gone before. There's the historical significance of the programme, and getting to play a small part in its continuing prestige, and my own huge pleasure from following sport all my life. For me, it's a tremendous achievement to appear on *Sports Report*.'

And you just know that if ever she had to read an Inverness Clachnacuddin result, she wouldn't giggle, because she'd have done her pronunciation homework. But will she ever encounter East Fife 4 Forfar 5?

12

DISMANTLING THE BOYS' CLUB

There are a couple of photographs in a book on *Sports Report*, vintage 1954, that speak graphically about a woman's place in the portals of the BBC at that time. On page 14, there's a gathering of the great and the good around a makeshift table, dutifully obeying the photographer's command to say 'cheese'. There are 13 adults, 12 males and one woman. The caption, left to right, gives full name-checks to the men, including Peter O'Sullevan, Joe Davis, Angus Mackay, Max Robertson, Henry Longhurst, Chris Chataway, Freddie Mills and Eamonn Andrews. Seated on the right of the table is – and I quote – 'Miss Reeves'. On page 19, another behind-the-scenes photo and revealing caption. John Gibson, the programme's studio manager, is seen twiddling the nobs and faders, looking intently at the script, alongside 'Miss Reeves'.

So the blokes get the full name-check, but not Jill Reeves. Despite her undoubted importance to *Sports Report*. From 1952 to 1958, Jill Reeves was a vital ingredient in the programme's outside broadcast reach, booking countless commentary lines and contributors, supervising the split-second timing necessary during the actual Saturday transmission, providing vital input in meetings with the producer, advising what was feasible and what was technically impossible. Jill was, after Mackay and Andrews, the key figure on *Sports Report*.

Mackay had no doubts over Jill's value, or that of her predecessor in the formative years of *Sports Report*, but he framed that professional respect in a manner that, 70 years on, seems patronising and sexist. He wrote, 'First, I was joined by Pat Robinson – a tall, graceful 21-year-old from Belfast – and when she left us for the joys of home and motherhood, I was "taken over" by Jill Reeves, a petite, auburn-haired youngster from the town of Doncaster.'

In that book, I didn't encounter many physical descriptions of key figures like Eamonn Andrews, Bill Hicks or John Arlott – but somehow the reader needed to be informed of the appearance of Jill Reeves and Pat Robinson. Perhaps a woman's place was at home, curled up with a knitting pattern from *The People's Friend*, waiting to get hubby's dinner organised? The image of Celia Johnson in *Brief Encounter* still seemed to linger.

Those captions are a vignette of their time, really. Jill Reeves didn't feel unduly patronised in the grey, conformist fifties, preferring to suggest how much she loved the *Sports Report* job, relishing the responsibility. 'It was a very important programme for the BBC. Before, I worked in the talks department and that was so sedate. *Sports Report* was so fast, so exciting, something was always happening. I wouldn't have left when I did, but my father died and I had to help my family out.'

Jill, a remarkably spry lady in her nineties, still occasionally listens to *Sports Report* and, although she returned to the BBC in the 1960s, working in television drama, finally retiring in 1989, she still has a soft spot for the programme and her old boss. 'I never thought of Angus being difficult towards women – when he was in one of his moods, he could be difficult with everyone. He was undoubtedly in charge.'

Jill can attest to doing what the boss instructed. She was a massive fan of speedway, a very popular sport in the UK in the fifties, and one Saturday night she made her *Sports Report* debut, talking about the year in speedway. The regular speedway reporter was suffering from a sore throat and Mackay, ever resourceful in a crisis, told Jill, 'You know all about speedway, you'll have to talk about it.' He commandeered Eamonn Andrews to draw up a few questions and they recorded Jill's observations. 'I'm sure I was pretty awful, but at least it wasn't live. I had a friend who travelled all over with me, going to speedway meetings – we cycled to Cornwall once, calling at all the speedway tracks. So at least I knew what I was talking about, even if I sounded dreadful!'

So Jill Reeves will always be on the board as the first female reporter on the programme, but who was the first woman football reporter? Several started to make their way in the early nineties and now, 30 years on, no one – mercifully – bats an eyelid at the established group who commentate, report and summarise on *Sports Report*. Yet it was more than half a century ago that Mary Raine reported on Chelsea 5 Sunderland 1 at Stamford Bridge in February 1969 – for just one game only.

Mary, an Oxford graduate in politics, philosophy and economics, was already building an impressive BBC career in the newsroom when Vincent Duggleby, also an Oxford graduate, exercised his right as Angus Mackay's assistant, taking advantage of the old boy's holiday to give Mary her chance on a Saturday. She had been encouraged by the football correspondent, Bryon Butler, who always welcomed Mary warmly when she wandered into the sports room to check the football news on the wires.

'Bryon was so kind and supportive, and never once hinted that a woman wouldn't know about football. But I did. My father was a surgeon and he used to cajole his patients to ask me football questions and I always got them right. I became a rabid Sunderland supporter so you can imagine my joy when Vincent asked me to cover them at Stamford Bridge.'

Mary admits to feeling nervous on the day. 'Petrified! There was a feeling in the press box that I was a bit of a freak, a curiosity piece. Michael Carey wrote a snide piece in the *Observer* next day, referring to me as 'a girl', even though I was 30! That was the only unkind thing written about me.'

Her prose, by her own admission, was rather fanciful. One clip from her final report said, 'Well, there were two teams on the field, but only one in the game, for it was Chelsea all the way.' Mary admits she only saw it as a one-off. 'It was deeply embarrassing to listen back to my boarding school/Oxford accent, it just wasn't the right sort of voice for football reporting. But I did it and they can't take that away from me.'

Goal magazine certainly climbed into the bath of hyperbole, running a feature on Mary with the headline, 'Meet the BBC Soccer Shocker,' saying she was 'the girl who silenced a million males.' Vincent Duggleby was asked by the press if she'd be used again and his response was classic BBC diplomacyspeak, 'The reaction has been extremely favourable – we thought she was very good.' Well, Mary didn't think so and knew she wouldn't be back. She did feature the following year on the Radio 4 news bulletin, reporting on the FA Cup Final between Chelsea and Leeds, but they didn't run her final report on the Radio 2 news. 'The chap in charge of that bulletin said "I can't put a woman on air, reporting on football."' Times have changed!

Mary Raine wouldn't dream of calling herself a trailblazer in covering sport, because it was simply a sideline to her. Not so Emily McMahon. She joined the sports department in 1967 at the age of 17 and, over 21 years, worked her way up to become a highly valued member of the production team. One of 10 siblings from a sports-mad family, Emily initially wanted to be a PE teacher, but the broadcasting bug gripped her, once she'd impressed Vincent Duggleby in her interview. 'I was worried about my shorthand and typing, but Vincent decided to quiz me about my football knowledge. He asked me about the Kop and when I asked him how much longer this was going to take, because I had a coach to catch to get me to Old Trafford, that seemed to go down well with him.

'I was just a nervous, overawed kid when I started in the sports room, surrounded by all these great names, but I never remember any sexist treatment towards me. Angus Mackay was like my dad, stern but fair. He never patronised me, it was just an honour. He taught me so much.'

Emily started booking taxis and hotel rooms for broadcasters and producers, working her way through the ranks to producing Des Lynam at world title boxing nights, producing the Sunday sport show, then *Sport on Four*, and being an integral part of the Saturday afternoon production team, trusted to deliver under great pressure. 'I loved working for Bryan Tremble on *Sports Report*. I'd beaver away at the back of the studio, editing goal clips or interviews. Bryan would say "Does that goal clip work?" and if I said "It's ace," he'd trust me. If I got all three clips in our closing sequence, I'd be chuffed.'

For much of the seventies, Emily was leading the way for women in important production roles in the sports department. Administrative jobs were mostly filled by women, but being in charge of sports desks or programmes was deemed to be a male preserve in the main. That started to change from 1979, when two women joined the department, each clocking up more than 30 years' service, with one of them producing *Sports Report* (Gill Pulsford) and the other editing the programme (Joanne Watson). Gill also produced the live outside broadcast of Princess Diana's funeral, and handled the planning and production of the Queen Mother's funeral, and the weddings of Prince Charles and the Duchess of Cornwall and the Duke and Duchess of Cambridge. Joanne was at times boxing and tennis producer, and ended up the sports department's planning editor, responsible for major events like the 2012 London Olympics, royal weddings and funerals, and the Boat Race.

Gill uses an imaginative metaphor to describe the role of women in the department in her early days. 'I reckon women were seen as the ones who kept the cave warm while the men went out hunting and gathering. I went abroad only about 10 times when I worked there and five of them were for Olympics – keeping the cave warm abroad. But I loved it in the studio on a Saturday, when it all came together. It was like bathing in very warm water. I was only 22 when I first worked on *Sports Report*, but I was steeped in it from my childhood.'

Gill was the first production assistant to graduate to producing *Sports Report*. She would work on the panel, telling the reporters and commentators what the producer wanted, getting them ready for their next live contribution, telling them the expected duration, feeding a scoreflash to the producer or presenter. It's a testing, demanding job, needing clarity of mind and diction. She then became a back-up producer, beavering away at the back of the studio, editing tapes at breakneck speed, communicating closely with her programme producer. After 15 years and a stint with the World Service she was ready for the top job in the studio. 'It meant everything to me. One of the few radio programmes that people remember. You knew you were part of something that was important.'

Gill was highly respected and had earned her passage to the producer's chair. 'When I started there, women were expected to get the teas in from the canteen and to type out the broadcasters' expenses. I soon put a stop to that. The blokes soon realised we weren't there to serve them. I remember Jim Rosenthal laughing, saying, 'You've stirred things up there,' but I didn't care. After a few weeks, things were different.' Blatant sexism wasn't something that Gill Pulsford encountered in her early days; it was more the unspoken assumptions that she'd readily challenge.

Joanne was self-confident enough to take any leg-pulling in her stride. The first time she read the racing results proved a rite of passage – not for her, but her male colleagues that evening in the sports room. When she came out of the studio, they were all on the phones, ostensibly dealing with members of the public. The suggestion was that Joanne had caused a ruffle among the dovecotes by reading the results. Jim Rosenthal, a noted, poker-faced practical joker, was heard to say, 'So you don't approve of a woman in the sports news, you say?... I'm sorry you feel so strongly about that... Yes, I will pass that on to the Director-General... That's not a very kind thing to say, sir.' Joanne saw the funny side of the jape and shrugged it off. She saw it as simply a test of a newcomer to the sports room, checking out whether she could take a joke or not. 'We had great camaraderie. Many of us were around the same age with as similar sense of humour.'

It would be 1987 before a woman became the first full-time producer of *Sports Report*, nearly 40 years after it first aired; a blot on the escutcheon that didn't reflect well on the previous management's myopia. Happily, that lamentable state of affairs was reversed, with three female producers in charge of *Sports Report* for most of the next 19 years. They were initially led by the first woman to become head of sport and outside broadcasts, crashing the glass ceiling triumphantly. Not that Patricia Ewing ever strayed into areas of braggadocio. Her expertise lay in hard work, setting an example to her staff. Pat, a former naval officer, had forged an admirable career as a highly efficient administrator in the sports department, the ultimate safe pair of hands. But there was much more to Pat Ewing than appearing to be a calculating machine. Her natural shyness sometimes held her back in dealing privately with some broadcasters, who at times overdosed on ebullience and charm, but she cared deeply about maintaining the department's high standards. Pat was a dedicated listener to the output and when she became our boss, she was clearly on top of her brief.

Mike Lewis worked closely with Pat as the Editor, Sport. 'She was a very strong defender of our department against senior management. Pat had a thing about women commentators, thinking they didn't cut through strongly enough on air, and she was big on our people on air sounding different. She used to say, "I don't want broadcasters who all sound the same." She was never biased against women on air, but just wanted them to sound distinctive.'

It was Pat Ewing who appointed another Patricia to the post of *Sports Report*'s first woman producer. At the time Pat Thornton had been in the sports department for a couple of years, working as motor sport producer, after cutting her teeth in World Service sport. She thought little of operating in what seemed a man's world, especially as Joanne Watson, Gill Pulsford and Emily McMahon had already cleared away some of the outmoded undergrowth. 'It was only when I started to produce *Sports Report* that the press took notice. The London *Evening Standard* did a feature on me and a photo had me sat at the desk, with a fag in my hand. In those days, you could smoke in the studio. But in the office, there was no "Wow! Trailblazer!" stuff.'

Her *Sports Report* presenter, John Inverdale, thoroughly approved of Pat's promotion. 'The first time I met her, I was impressed by Pat's forthright opinions. She'd more than served her time at the World Service and she knew what she was talking about. She also made me laugh – very important for a programme that goes back and forth, with cock-ups always a possibility.'

For Pat, producing *Sports Report* was a career highlight, culminating in the Saturday afternoon show winning the Sports Programme of the Year gong at the 1991 Sony Awards, the radio industry's version of the Oscars. 'It was such a joyful show to work on. I was never scared, because I was surrounded by such talent in the studio and out in the field. You would never have needed to Google anything with our reporters in those days! I will never forget the privilege of producing *Sports Report* and the massive degree of mutual trust we all had in each other.'

If John Inverdale had helped Pat Thornton ease seamlessly into the producer's chair, he was even more influential later in the career of a woman who would produce *Sports Report* for seven years, starting at the age of just 26.

Claire McDonnell started in the sports room as a sports desk secretary on a two-months internship. The English and history graduate was only 21, mad about sport, an avid listener at home from the age of eight and desperate to get a toehold in the radio sports department. She was highly amused at her first interview to be asked whether she knew who CMJ was. She laughed and said, 'Of course I do – Christopher Martin Jenkins. I've been listening to radio sport more than half my life.'

Claire was not too proud to work in the sports finance unit for nine months, then did her training in local radio, breakfast TV and the World Service. But she wanted to work full-time in the sports department. She'd happily ingratiate herself with them on the third floor at Broadcasting House, ostensibly getting some printing done for the finance unit, but clearly happy to talk sport with anyone.

She asked John Inverdale for advice. 'Make yourself indispensable', he said. 'Hang around here, become a familiar face, and when people who can help you turn around, they'll see you there.' And they did. After the full round of producing sports desks and evening programmes, she produced her first *Sports Report*, the youngest to do so.

Away from the rigours of Saturday afternoon, Claire was a very empathetic producer. She would ring reporters during the week, talk through any issues from the previous Saturday and ask opinions about how to approach that reporter's next Saturday assignment. She also held her nerve at key moments. I recall her calmness in May 2001, when I was at Villa Park, covering Coventry's relegation after 34 years in the top flight. The priority was an interview with Gordon Strachan, Coventry's manager. Strachan could be difficult and tetchy, but could also engage and give you all you needed. How would he react this day? Claire was fully across all the possible pitfalls, made more hazardous by the absence of an ISDN line in the tunnel at Villa Park for some strange reason. So I had to grab an interview with Strachan on my mini-disc, get an exact duration and feed it in live to *Sports Report*, ensuring that my producer had the precise 'out' words to the interview, allowing the presenter, Mark Pougatch, to pick up straight away from the London studio.

Strachan complicated the situation by coming out with his young goalkeeper, Chris Kirkland, for a heart-to-heart after a mistake by Kirkland had led to a Villa goal. The manager had promised me he'd be with me shortly, but why should he be bothered about time ebbing away on *Sports Report*? I kept communicating the complications to my producer on the mobile phone and Claire was commendably low key, confirming that a Strachan interview would be absolutely perfect. By now, a large media gathering was around the tunnel entrance and I feared the worst. At 5.50 p.m. Strachan presented himself and I fired off a three-minute interview with him, in which he spoke very impressively.

I then had to leg it from tunnel to press box, up three flights of stairs, talking to Claire en route, agreeing my 'in' words to the Strachan interview. I knew she'd be stressing about the passage of time, but she didn't communicate that to me. Dreading that I'd sound out of breath, I gabbled a few seconds of scene-setting before pressing play and Strachan was now singing on air like a nightingale. Calmness personified, Claire asked me down the line during the clip what the 'out' words were and the exact duration of the interview. 'Perfect!' she said. 'We'll just get off air on time.' We did – with 30 seconds to spare, leaving Pougatch to wrap up a dramatic afternoon at Villa Park.

My first pint in the Villa Park bar soon after didn't really touch the sides. I got all the herograms for delivering Strachan amid the sharp elbows and the imprecations of other media colleagues, but it was my producer back in London who kept a keen eye on the logistics and steadfastly refused to pile extra tension on to me.

No wonder Pougatch paid generous tribute to her towards the end of her last *Sports Report* in January 2006. Claire had decided to seek pastures new and a fresh broadcasting challenge, much to the dismay of all we regulars on the programme, and Pougatch had a plan to acknowledge her distinguished tenure. Claire came on talkback to Mark, saying he had to cue in a recorded football interview and then close the programme. Mark simply shook his head at her through the glass, which threw her completely. Why was her valued and trusted colleague taking no notice of her final instructions?

'Mark then launched into this tribute to me, calling me the Claude Makélélé of *Sports Report*, the engine room of the operation, letting the stars shine. As it was my last programme, the afternoon was weighing very heavily on me anyway and I was in tears by now. It was typical of Mark, so kind. I went straight to the loo, cried my eyes out as I kept getting texts calling me Claude!'

Claire has worked for a few media outlets since then, easily winning respect from new colleagues, but producing the whole Saturday programme remains the highlight. 'It was the happiest time of my professional life, working with such a valued, large team. I loved trying to get all the planes landing on the tarmac, not necessarily at the desired time. No matter how tired I'd feel after four hours of live sport, leading up to five o'clock, the challenge of *Sports Report* always excited and revived me.'

By the start of the millennium it was no longer worthy of mention that women were playing such a vital role in getting *Sports Report* on air. With Pat Ewing heading operations since 1984 and female producers running the programme from 1987, there were highly efficient back-up producers such as Emily McMahon, Claire Ackling and Audrey Adams on hand, with the reassuring, unruffled Heather Fordham acting as liaison between producer and broadcasters as production assistant. No regular contributor to *Sports Report* over those years was at all exercised by the growing number of influential women in the studio.

It was different, though, when assessing the pool of reporters. The paucity of female reporters was a glaring omission, totally unrepresentative of the gender ratio in the UK and insulting to those women listeners who knew as much as their male counterparts about sport. It wasn't something that the press would fulminate about, because the ratio of female to male reporters in that trade was even more disgraceful. The same applied in the House of Commons, so few MPs would dare to try any cheap shots at the BBC in public.

It needed a transfusion of modern thinking at BBC Radio Sport, but it would be tough on those early pioneers at the microphone. Charlotte Nicol was the first female sports reporter in the department in 1990, and it was a testing introduction for her. She'd served a long apprenticeship in local radio – working in the North East, after a university journalism course – and had wanted to be a football reporter from the age of 16. She'd sold matchday programmes outside Leicester City's Filbert Street stadium and she remembers always rushing to the car to hear the start of *Sports Report*.

Her first game as a football reporter for *Sports Report* was in August 1989 at Plough Lane (Wimbledon 0 Arsenal 3) and Charlotte remembers how nervous she was – and not just because it was her debut. 'There'd been a lot of discussion in the office about me being the first woman reporter and should they herald it? They decided not to, thankfully. I was just wanted to arrive on air, with no fuss, and try my best.'

She appeared regularly on Derek Jameson's breakfast show on Radio 2, a high-profile gig for her and, although Jameson was a doughty champion of

Charlotte, enjoying her sports chats, that early exposure did her no favours. Some uncharitable colleagues would wonder aloud if she deserved such a large focus. Learn your trade, keep your head down and get better over the next year was an opinion expressed in some quarters of the sports room. She picked up a nickname – 'TT', as in 'Token Totty'. It hurt. Understandably.

'Some even called me TT to my face. I found it a very male, uncompromising work environment. I was 29 when I joined the department, I wasn't quite ready, but even if I had been the finished product, I still would've found it tough. I had moved from the North East, just got divorced, trying to settle down in London and earn the respect of my colleagues by trying to show what I could do on air.'

Those early days for Charlotte were also challenging at some football grounds. She was once sent to a press conference at Stamford Bridge and the then Chelsea chairman, Ken Bates, asked, 'Are you working here or just serving the drinks?' The interview room down the tunnel at White Hart Lane was barred to Charlotte, the excuse being that she was a woman. 'They were obviously worried that Gazza would come out of Tottenham's dressing room and run naked down the corridor. The issue was raised at a Tottenham board meeting and the owner, Alan Sugar, said, "If she's got to work in the tunnel, then let her." Fair play to him, but why was it allowed to become an issue?

'I remember one discussion in the sports room about the prospect of a woman becoming the football producer. One guy said, "We can't have a female producer, because she won't be able to go into the dressing rooms." I thought, "When were you last in a dressing room?" I lost confidence as a broadcaster because of attitudes like that.'

Eventually Charlotte did become the football producer, in 1994, and her career and personal happiness blossomed. 'That was the epiphany for me. I really felt I'd arrived; completely at home. Mike Ingham, Alan Green, Ian Dennis, John Murray – the commentators – were all great with me, and our summarisers, such as Terry Butcher, Chris Waddle, Mark Lawrenson, Jimmy Armfield and Graham Taylor were fantastic. I never looked back.'

After her appointment, she displayed her all-round abilities handsomely, including a talent for subtle interviewing. She established a rapport easily with players and managers. David Beckham was a personal favourite. 'He was lovely. Always talked to me about his kids and asked after my daughters. We'd show each other our cherished photos. For three tournaments in a row, we were in the team hotel and that helped me establish a great working relationship with the England squad.'

And it paid off in later years. When England was trying to win the right to stage the 2018 World Cup, BBC TV's *Panorama* programme had broadcast a critical assessment of the England bid. The Football Association mandarins were furious and wouldn't let BBC Radio speak to any of the bid's ambassadors at a media briefing in Switzerland. David Beckham was one of those ambassadors and presumably off-limits. Not to Charlotte Nicol. Ian Dennis, reporting on the occasion, was mightily impressed. 'Because of Charlotte's relationship with Beckham, he agreed to slip away and do an interview for us. So there we were, doing a one-on-one in a plush hotel room, all down to Charlotte. He had great respect for her. The same with John Terry and Steven Gerrard. They'd always stop and chat with her. When it came to working with them, she was always fair, but firm. Charlotte was a real trailblazer out on the road.'

But there were always a few obscurantists lurking. Martin Jol for one. When he was Tottenham's manager, he lost a League Cup semi-final second leg to Arsenal, a tough one to swallow, especially as Arsène Wenger had played a few youngsters that night. During the interview with Jol, Charlotte asked, 'Do you think Arsène Wenger will play the kids for the final?' Jol bristled and said only a woman could ask such a question and was she really a journalist? Charlotte stood her ground, saying he shouldn't speak to her like that. Mike Ingham, commentating on the match, heard about the incident and collared the Tottenham press officer, saying, 'That's the stuff of phone-ins.' Martin Jol twice apologised to Charlotte and she was presented with a signed Aaron Lennon shirt – as if that made a difference. 'It was completely uncalled for, but at least his apology made it less of an issue.' That was in 2007 and Mike Ingham later wrote that blazing a trail for women 'would not have been necessary in the first place if an element hadn't still been living in the Dark Ages.'

Charlotte maintains that if BBC Sport hadn't moved to Salford in 2012, she still would be doing what was, for her, the dream job. She'd lost her husband, David Oates – an admired, popular colleague of ours – to a rare heart condition that same year and with two daughters to look after, the move would have been too much. She now works as a TV floor manager at matches, still cajoling reluctant players to the interview area, still totally on top of her job. A great professional. Many younger female reporters and commentators should nod in the direction of Charlotte Nicol, carving an excellent career from the most unpromising of starts on national radio.

'Local radio ought to have done more for women reporters when I was starting out, so that they could arrive at the national station with greater confidence. The pool was hardly large and I wasn't ready. I remember getting on a plane to cover a big match in Glasgow and, apart from the stewardesses, I was the only woman in the media corps!

'Coverage of women's football is now so positive. If you get such coverage, it encourages people to get involved in it. I fought against the boys' club, which women weren't then allowed to join. It's evolved naturally, where you can have that mix. It also applies to non-white reporters. There's now no job in football that you can't do because you're a woman, so I await the first female football manager in the men's game.'

Mike Lewis, then Head of BBC Radio Sport, points out in management's defence that in those days no female sports reporters were coming through from BBC local radio, a traditional breeding ground for talent. 'I'd walk into a room for a local radio gathering and there'd be 40 middle-class white blokes, aged around 35 – and not one woman. At a time when we were expanding, I wanted women on air and when Charlotte applied from local commercial radio, I was delighted. I know Charlotte had a tough time initially, but she turned it around, becoming a very good reporter and a front-rank football producer. But she was a human shield for women reporters early on. There were hardly any on Fleet Street then, either.'

Eleanor Oldroyd can relate to Charlotte Nicol's travails in those unenlightened times. She arrived in the department a year after Charlotte, via local radio then Radio 1, with Bob Shennan, editor of Radio Sport, determined to expand the range of voices. Although encountering less scepticism from her sports-room colleagues, she took some heavy flak from a few listeners. For a time, despite strong support from the key executives, Eleanor felt she was on her own.

'The atmosphere in the sports room when I joined was very laddish and hearty. If a woman from another department came in and a male colleague talked to her, you knew the other blokes were sizing it all up. As soon as she walked out of the room, there'd be a collective shout of 'Shot!' all around the room from the blokes. It wasn't toxic masculinity, but Charlotte and I would just grit our teeth and try blocking it out.'

Eleanor consciously felt that if she made a mistake on air, then she was letting down the sisterhood – 'whereas if it had been a male presenter, it would just be brushed off. But if it was a woman, it would be "What do you expect? Women don't know what they're talking about." I'd get letters, with no address, telling me how useless I was.'

Sensibly, Eleanor would tear up such poisonous dreck from these quarter-wits and would have seen it as sign of weakness if she'd mentioned it to her strong supporters, like Bob Shennan or Mike Lewis. 'It can be a lonely existence when you're in the minority. If social media had been around in those early days, I wouldn't have lasted. The immediate and cruel pile-ons would have been too much. The trolls no longer need to take the time to write and tell you that you're crap. They can just be nameless and faceless. Much easier.

'I bottled a lot of it up. I'd do a match for *Sports Report* and walk from the ground, worried that I'd got it all covered. I'd buy the Sunday papers, concerned that I might have missed something. Impostor syndrome dogged me for a long time. Talking off the top of my head in a relaxed style was totally different from reading sports scripts on *Newsbeat*. I was raw, but they persisted in me.'

After five years in the department, Eleanor became the first woman to present *Sports Report*, in 1995. 'It was a big moment for me and for women in sports journalism – 47 years on. The ultimate flagship programme. Whatever my own misgivings over my development, I was still very proud to do it.'

That debut didn't go smoothly for Eleanor, none of it her fault. She was unlucky enough to encounter the Everton manager, Joe Royle, in one of his more cranky moods, despite triumphing over Liverpool at Anfield. When he came on the line for what Eleanor thought would be a genial encounter, his mood changed when Eleanor, understandably, put it to him that, as a football realist, he wouldn't be getting carried away by one great result. Swallows and summers and all that.

His response was ridiculous. 'Only a woman would ask that question.' I don't think so, Mr Royle. Not getting carried away is often the stock response from a manager at times of euphoria. There was no call to have a go at a female presenter for asking a reasonable, polite question.

Eleanor managed to wrap up the interview soon afterwards, but she was shocked at Royle's disrespect. 'I wasn't going to bowl him a half volley, but I saw nothing wrong with that question. It absolutely threw me off my game, it was like being hit on the helmet while batting and being expected to face the next ball far too quickly. For the next few minutes my head just wasn't there and I limped to the finish.'

She talked to Bob Shennan about the incident. 'He said to bear in mind that emotions run high after a match and that sometimes football managers say some daft things. My main consolation was that Joe Royle looked more stupid than me. My colleagues all said it was a daft thing to say and Giles Smith in the *Telegraph* wrote that Royle was out of order, but it's sad that my debut as *Sports Report* presenter was marred by that interview. It had been one of the most exciting moments of my career, cueing up that signature tune.'

After that, Eleanor became a regular stand-in for Ian Payne on the programme, but after having two children between 2000 and 2001, her work/life pattern had to change, although she continued to rack up a fine career as presenter of various programmes, state occasions and in recent years as a 5 Live cricket reporter. She has worked on seven Olympics, four Winter Olympics, rugby and cricket World Cups, and all the major sporting events at home. In 2014 and 2016 she was named the Sports Journalists Association's Sports Broadcaster of the Year. Joe Royle wasn't contacted for comment.

She can now laugh off the crusty reaction from some of the more reactionary male reporters one day at the Dell, when she had to report while seven months pregnant. 'The old farts weren't happy about me squeezing past them a few times, but they wouldn't know about your bladder problems, while expecting to be sat in a narrow press box for about four hours.' Then there was the dodgy smoked salmon and cheese bagel that had dire consequences for her at the Valley one Saturday afternoon. Every time the studio came to her, she felt she was going to vomit on air. 'The ladies' loos at the Valley were not greatly maintained. Between the final whistle and the start of *Sports Report* I sat in the loo and just threw up. I told the editor I just had to record my piece, otherwise I'd be sick, live on air. I never had a bagel again on a Saturday!'

Eleanor is the first to credit Charlotte Nicol for being the buffer, one year earlier. 'I was protected to a certain extent by her. She took a lot of flak for women sports reporters before I arrived. Thankfully, attitudes have changed dramatically since then. I now feel, after all this time, I've earned the right to get things wrong and not beat myself up about that.'

The legacy and example of Charlotte and Eleanor are highly valued by Clare Balding, who joined the sports department in 1994 as a rookie broadcaster, before forging a stellar career in so many areas of the media. But she was humble enough to take advice from senior colleagues and act on it.

'I was aware of how hard Charlotte had to fight to prove herself. I was in awe of that, because I watched the way she acted and thought, "God, you're so good, you have to work so hard." And rather than put me off, it made me that bit more determined to do the same. She's a no-nonsense person, who taught me discipline and the responsibility of the job.

'Elly was immensely kind to me, very encouraging. One of the things I've learned from her is not just what you broadcast and how, but it's that generosity of spirit and warmth, that willingness to help people who are younger and less experienced than you. Believe me, you never forget it. I will always be grateful to her.'

Sonja McLaughlan has been another of the female frontrunners – the first woman to be rugby producer, then a rugby and athletics reporter. She encountered some tacit sexism when first covering matches at Twickenham. 'I felt uncomfortable in those early days; I seemed to be the only woman not serving teas and coffees. I started wearing suits, not dresses, because I didn't want to stand out. I just wanted to give myself some breathing space, to hunker down and get on with it. Even at a recent Six Nations match at Murrayfield, I was the only media woman in the room. But it's improving.'

'The department is, commendably, trying to be more diverse, but the really important issue is that the ones who are good get the opportunities. *Sports Report* should be for the best broadcasters, not used as a training ground. I'm so proud to be part of that heritage.'

It's a heritage that's a given now on *Sports Report* – stretching from the 20-plus years put in by reporter/producer Juliette Ferrington, to football commentator Vicki Sparks, summariser Karen Carney, reporters Jacqui Oatley, Delyth Lloyd, Maz Farookhi, Emma Saunders and a handful of others. And the superb Charlotte Green reading the classifieds.

Bob Shennan, one of the galvanising influences on women sports broadcasting 30 years ago, is content that great progress has been made. 'It could've gone further and quicker, but so many have become important sports broadcasters. Look how much Clare Balding learned in the radio sport crucible. The increasing prevalence of women sports broadcasters in radio only reflects the ratio of women to men in society. It's about time.'

And no longer do women in the department have to tolerate the comparative anonymity of Jill Reeves when official photos are taken. Time can sometimes march on at an encouraging tempo.

13

MEMORABLE PROGRAMMES 1989–2022

The first 40 years of *Sports Report* had undoubtedly established it as part of the nation's sporting conversation on a Saturday. Angus Mackay's doctrine still resonated, with enough of his disciples still around to pose the question, 'What would Angus do here?' Invariably the right call was made and occasional sightings of Mackay at BBC reunions indicated he was still satisfied with his legacy.

But it became tougher to set the agenda on a Saturday. Competition was far fiercer than in Mackay's pomp. From the late 1980s, television's tentacles extended deep into the entrails of sports broadcasting, as the cheques got larger and TV's demands more impertinent. As Bob Dylan once sang, 'Money doesn't talk, it swears.' Sports administrators willingly swooned as the TV moguls called so many tunes.

It became harder for a one-hour radio programme to maintain its stature in the face of so much wall-to-wall coverage of sport on television. It's a matter of deep pride among *Sports Report* veterans that we have continued to repel boarders with a swash of the buckle and a fair degree of low cunning, laced with a refusal to fade from the competitive crucible. *Sports Report* has continued to flaunt its plumage unashamedly down the decades, reflecting sport's similarity to life – the joys, triumphs, sensations. And the sorrows…

1989: The Hillsborough Disaster

Anyone who worked on *Sports Report* on 15 April 1989 will say it was the worst day of their broadcasting careers. And we were just the emissaries of an awful story that broke in time for us to attempt to convey the unfolding disaster. For those who lost loved ones that sunlit Sheffield day, it remains simply unimaginable.

After two central pens at the Leppings Lane end of Hillsborough were opened to try to cope with overcrowding outside, 97 Liverpool fans died and 766 were injured. It was the worst death toll at any British sporting event.

I was the producer of our outside broadcast at the ground, working alongside match commentators Peter Jones and Alan Green, with Jimmy Armfield as summariser. Driving towards Hillsborough that day, I was perturbed at the amount of roadworks in the area. Aware that the World Snooker Championships were also being staged in the city that weekend, I wondered about traffic congestion. 'This could be a delayed kick-off,' I thought.

With just 15 minutes before kick-off, I nudged Jimmy Armfield and gestured towards the Leppings Lane end. 'Where are all the Liverpool supporters, Jim?' I asked. We both concluded that we'd be amazed if the game kicked off at 3.00 p.m.

Astonishingly, it did and within a few minutes people began dying in front of us, to our left, about 70 yards away. I passed a note to Peter Jones, asking him to hold the fort on air, fully confident that a broadcaster of his quality (sadly, with first-hand experience of the 1985 Heysel Disaster) and sensitivity would be equal to the task. Alan Green and I then rushed down to our usual post-match interview position, near to the dressing rooms, to get a closer picture of events. It looked serious. How serious we soon discovered.

In pure broadcasting terms, we were lucky to be able to broadcast live from our interview position, which was very close to the Liverpool and Nottingham Forest dressing rooms, stationed in a laundry room. In human terms, we were not so fortunate. We were positioned opposite the gymnasium, which was soon transformed into a mortuary. Bodies in black bin liners were being carried into the gym by grim-faced rescue services. Outside, ambulance sirens were wailing. Alan Green and I tried vainly to count the amount of bin liners and, with growing horror, the enormity of the tragedy dawned on us and everyone else in that vicinity. We were basically then on auto-pilot. We kept Peter Jones primed with as much precise information as possible, careful not to speculate. Television colleagues passed on scraps that could be verified. We both knew that Peter Jones would be the safest of hands to broadcast only the facts, while describing vividly what was happening in front of him…

'I see people lying down, people shaking their heads, 200 to 300 on the pitch, I can see people desperately coming over the top of the goalpost. It should've been a showpiece, a classic. At the moment, it is simply mayhem.'

We interviewed as many eyewitnesses and football figures as possible. Hollow-eyed, deathly pale, they gave faltering yet clear accounts of the desperate attempts to save lives. I have never been in an interview area where every voice was hushed. No one jostling for primacy in an interview pecking order, all egos among the broadcasters parked.

Back in the studio at Broadcasting House, television pictures were available of the developing horror, to which Alan Green and I had no access. Producer Pat Thornton and editor Mike Lewis were gleaning extra information and passing it on to Peter Jones. Mike Lewis was being pressurised by a high-ranking BBC executive to confirm higher fatality numbers than we were able to, down in the dressing-room locality. This executive, who had contacts in Fleet Street, said his journalist pals were adamant that the figure was much greater, but Lewis stood firm. 'He kept on to me, shouting out the latest alleged figures, but we were only dealing with facts. I told him, "We've got the best, most experienced commentator in the business there, plus two fantastic news reporters and Jimmy Armfield, to provide sensible insight. We're going with them." I was determined to tell the story in the best BBC traditions. It was ghastly watching those scenes in the studio, but we had to handle it professionally and calmly.'

While we carried on trying to assimilate as many facts as we could at Hillsborough, John Inverdale was discussing the right tone for 5.00 p.m., back in Broadcasting House. 'I said that we couldn't possibly start the programme with 'Out of the Blue' or end it at six o'clock. It would just be totally inappropriate. Something as tragic as this could only have the presenter opening and closing the programme with the facts.' The key figures in the studio agreed with Inverdale and this is how he opened *Sports Report*…

'You're listening to *Sports Report* on National Radio 2… My name's John Inverdale and this is a tragic day for sport.' He then summarised what we knew about fatalities and injuries, and cued into a clip from Peter Jones, graphically describing the early scenes just after 3.00 p.m.

Then Inverdale confirmed the death toll at 74 and gave out an emergency number. Harrowing interviews were then played out, including Dr Glyn Philips, a GP from East Kilbride, Scotland. 'I've seen about eight or 10 dead. One chap was clinically dead and we worked on him for 10 minutes. We asked for a defibrillator but there isn't one on the whole ground, which is appalling for a major event like this. We were given an oxygen cylinder, but it was empty, which is an absolute disgrace.'

A Liverpool fan told Alan Green, 'It was bedlam outside. There were people in the air on top of each other. About six feet from the front, somebody was down on the floor, people were screaming. Arms were up in the air, grasping for life. A young fellah was mottled and going blue. It seemed like forever nothing was being done.'

Peter Jones was next, giving a live despatch that would be enshrined in the annals of great radio broadcasts. First, he drew on his horrifying experience four years earlier at Heysel. 'Two items I just think of sitting here now in the sunshine that still remind me of Heysel – the gymnasium here at Hillsborough is being used as a mortuary for the dead and at this moment stewards, just as they did at the Heysel stadium, have got cartons and little paper bags, and they're gathering up the personal belongings of the spectators, some of whom died, some of whom are now seriously injured in nearby hospitals. And there are red and white scarves of Liverpool, and red and white bobble hats of Liverpool, and red and white rosettes of Liverpool, and nothing else out there on the enclosure where all the deaths occurred. And the sun shines now.'

It was a devastating, raw eyewitness account. Henry Winter, now chief football writer of *The Times*, but then a young reporter, listened to Peter's account at home and was greatly moved. 'He described the enormity of the situation with proper respect. I defy anyone listening to that and not be affected. Using the word "Liverpool" so often was very effective, it was almost percussive. I can't think of a better sporting commentary in terms of a news appraisal, as well as a lyrical description.'

Our sports-room colleague John Rawling listened to Peter's account in his car. 'I was moved to tears. It's the finest piece of written broadcasting in sport that I have ever heard. Peter painted such beautiful pictures and "the sun's shining now" is so evocative. That piece captured the horrors of what he'd seen and the quiet beauty of the situation, two hours after it was all over.'

Incredibly, the Nottingham Forest players were unaware of the depth of the tragedy until they got into the team coach, just as *Sports Report* started. Brian Clough, trying to shield his players, said in the dressing room, 'That's it, we're going home. There's no going back out. Get in the coach as soon as you can.' His son, Nigel, says it was *Sports Report* that told them the horrifying details. 'Someone shouted "Turn it up!" as the radio on the coach was switched on. The card games stopped. We just sat there in horrified silence. No referee or official had told us anything at the ground. We were aware that the noise from the pitch when we came off sounded serious, but we were in the dark. No mobile phones or social media in those days – just the radio. The mood was unbelievably sombre. We soon grasped that a postponed semi-final meant nothing compared to what we were hearing.'

That mood was mirrored in many a car journey home that afternoon, as Peter Jones' words reduced thousands to stunned silence. Andy Burnham, then a student, was travelling back from Villa Park to Merseyside, after seeing his Everton team beat Norwich in the other semi-final. He had spotted a news flash on the Villa Park scoreboard – '5 dead at Hillsborough' – and wondered what was happening. On the way out of Villa Park, he saw Jim Rosenthal outside the ITV truck, crying disconsolately. This was not just a routine hooliganism story. 'I'll never forget that two-hour journey in the car back home. Peter Jones struck just the right compassionate note.'

Listening back to that *Sports Report* broadcast, I'm astonished we got so much on air before 5.30 p.m. Alan Green and I just grabbed what we could down in the dressing-room area, but the production team in Broadcasting House performed wonders in editing so much, so swiftly. In quick succession, we had on air Maurice Roworth, the chairman of Nottingham Forest, Liverpool's manager Kenny Dalglish, the chief executive of the Football Association, Graham Kelly, and Liverpool's chief executive Peter Robinson.

There was even time for a report by Bryon Butler from the other semi-final, then a live interview with the Everton winger who scored the only goal, Pat Nevin. Known for an impressive social conscience, Nevin didn't really want to do the interview with Mike Ingham, but he was commendably mature, 'The news just deadened everything as we started to celebrate. Our result doesn't matter right now. Condolences to all the families and that comes from everyone at Everton.'

After 5.30 p.m., the programme kept coming back to Hillsborough, as well as rounding up the rest of the sports news. Peter Jones rightly called it 'the blackest day in football's history' and then just before 6.00 p.m., after receiving another update on the fatalities, he summarised the tragedy he'd witnessed,

'Of the thousands of Liverpool fans who travelled joyfully to Yorkshire on a sun-filled April Saturday, at least 80 of them will not wake up on another day. Arms and legs flailed desperately in a sea of bodies, it was chaos and mayhem. On the steps behind one of the goals, they left behind their personal belongings – red and white scarves and rosettes and hats of the fans who'll never watch their favourite team again.'

You couldn't follow that and John Inverdale, in the studio didn't dare. 'Our sympathies and condolences – from BBC Sport, a very sad goodnight.' It was right not using the famous signature tune for once. It would have sounded discordant and tactless, and Inverdale, his editor and producer were at one on this. A few seconds of silence and then the continuity announcer picking up to hand to the news was the respectful way to end the coverage.

Inverdale has never forgotten Peter Jones' contribution to that awful day. 'Now and then I do a bit of media training and I play Peter's pieces into *Sports Report* to the young students. I tell them that's the standard they should be aiming for. Peter was remarkable at Hillsborough.'

Mike Lewis, the editor of *Sports Report* that day, has also listened back to the tape of the programme. 'I sat and cried my eyes out. It was incredibly moving. Just thinking about it makes me emotional. Trying to get the tone right was so important. I was extremely proud of everyone associated with the programme that day.'

It was a memorable *Sports Report* for all the wrong reasons and, just a year later, we lost the broadcaster who held the Hillsborough coverage together with such sensitivity, authority and descriptive brilliance.

1990: Peter Jones' last broadcast

As Jon Champion stepped out of Broadcasting House on the evening of 31 March 1990, he should have been reflecting on the highlight thus far of his burgeoning career. At the age of 24, he had presented *Sports Report* for the first time. He knew he was far from the finished product, but John Inverdale was abroad on holiday and the bosses decided to give the talented young Yorkshireman a go, after just four months in the department.

Jon had done his best, but a personal tragedy dogged his performance in the chair. Peter Jones had, in effect, died that afternoon, commentating on the Boat Race. A massive stroke felled this most elegant and distinctive of broadcasters in the BBC Radio boat. And Jon knew that Peter was not going to live. It would be another 36 hours before Peter's death was announced, but everyone working in the sports department that day knew the worst.

That Saturday had begun so encouragingly for Jon. He had bumped into Peter in reception at Broadcasting House and, typically, Peter had offered words of encouragement. 'You'll be fine – just enjoy it.' And off he went to his taxi, bound for the River Thames, as energised as ever when about to commentate on a big occasion. And for this particular Cambridge Blue, the Boat Race was certainly that.

Gill Pulsford, one of the producers working in the makeshift studio by the Thames, shared a taxi with Peter. 'He was just his usual self, full of beans, very chatty.' Peter then met up with his producer on the boat, Caroline Elliott, and they adjourned to a pub for a pre-race snifter and a final briefing. Peter had some exciting news to share with his friend, who had produced him many times over the previous decade. He had been worried about being sidelined from his senior commentator's status, because he had just turned 60. In those days, it was a BBC rule that you came off the staff at 60, then took your chance as a freelance. Peter loved his job so much that he'd been concerned that the new breed of talented, younger commentators would start to take precedence over someone who had commentated at 21 FA Cup Finals, six World Cups and five Olympic Games, and many state occasions. Was he on borrowed time at the BBC?

Mercifully, the BBC hierarchy recognised Peter's incalculable worth and reassured him. He showed Caroline an official letter in the pub. 'The BBC confirmed he was staying on, to do all the same major events that he usually presented. That's all Peter wanted to do. He was so happy that day in the pub. I felt he was still on top of his game – he looked slim and fit, and intellectually very clear. Still sharp. It was very sensible of the BBC to keep Peter on. He was a showman who found particular words and phrases that stuck in listeners' minds.'

When the race started, Peter was his usual informed self. Caroline Elliott knew that, as producer, she could only pass notes to her commentator on the boat, because the microphones had to be live at all times, allowing the other commentator (Dan Topolski) and the expert summariser (Dr Robert Treharne Jones) to interject when appropriate. This means when something goes wrong, the producer is a little more constrained during a Boat Race. And something did go tragically wrong.

Just after Hammersmith Bridge, Peter Jones suddenly stopped talking and froze. He was still upright, but the mic dropped on to his lap. Caroline motioned to Dan Topolski to take over as commentator, while she eased Peter's mic gently up his arm. But it fell down again. As Topolski kept talking about the race, Gill Pulsford in the mobile studio had picked up there was something seriously wrong with Peter. She shouted down the line, 'Addo! You've got to take over!' and Tony

Adamson, positioned further along the Thames, nearer the finishing line, did just that, aided by the TV monitor and his colleague, David Mercer.

The listeners would not have known the gravity of the situation, other than Peter's voice sounding weird and distorted for a few seconds, before his producer's prompt action, but the nightmare continued for Caroline Elliott. 'Peter started crying. He was conscious, but paralysed and couldn't communicate.'

She had to grasp the logistics urgently, as Dan Topolski valiantly kept the race commentary going. An ambulance was vital, but how could it get to the BBC boat, stranded on the Thames? Caroline couldn't talk over Dan on air, so she had to rely on Gill Pulsford to chase up an ambulance from the mobile studio – and they were scarce; with a massive anti-Poll Tax demonstration taking place in central London that day, the various rescue services were fully stretched.

It would take another 12 minutes before the BBC boat could disembark past Mortlake Bridge, at the end of the race. By then, Peter had collapsed. Treharne Jones, a GP, had done his best, but feared the worst. Pulsford had left the mobile studio to meet the ambulance and three doctors who had been spectating started working on Peter. 'I asked if I should go with Peter to the hospital and one of the doctors took me aside, put his hands on my shoulders and said, "He's not going to make it – all you can do is tell his family." As I walked back to the van I saw Tony Adamson and burst into tears. He said, "It can't be – it's Jonesey. No!"'

The production team in Broadcasting House, shattered by hearing Peter collapse on air, aware what their colleagues were experiencing on the Thames, simply had to regroup. There was a programme to get on air at 5.00 p.m., after the second-half commentary. A new young presenter had to be properly briefed about everything else in the sporting world and the producers at Mortlake Bridge simply had to compile a package of highlights from the Boat Race, without a mention of Peter Jones. Hamlet without the Prince...

The phones just rang and rang in the sports room that Sunday, but the tragic news couldn't be confirmed until early Monday morning, due to sensitivity towards all of Peter's family. It fell to the unfortunate Jon Champion to anchor the main sports desk, announcing Peter's death. Two friends of Peter's were on hand to pay tribute. Cliff Morgan, tears streaming down his face, with no script in front of him, said, 'For me, from now on, there will be a minute's silence every Saturday on *Sports Report*. I always felt comfortable when Peter was at the microphone. He made the listeners feel that they were. For 25 years he was the word.' Des Lynam called him 'the best radio broadcaster of his time – erudite and sophisticated.'

It had been a surreal 48 hours for Jon Champion. 'On that Saturday I went from being nervous and excited to empty and shattered. This after those words of reassurance and support from such a great broadcaster in the morning. When I read the opening headlines to *Sports Report*, I was late by a couple of seconds and I had to pull myself together. I was simply distracted. That night I travelled back by train in stunned silence and for two and a half hours just thought of Peter. It was a thunderbolt.'

The usual presenter was totally unaware of the tragedy until he reported in for work on the Monday morning. John Inverdale had been on a skiing holiday, got home late on Sunday night and breezed into the sports room, in good order. 'I asked how Saturday had gone and was told, "Haven't you heard?" I had no idea. The mobile phone industry was in its infancy in those days, so I'd been totally out of contact. I just couldn't believe it.'

Nor could Caroline Elliot and she still wonders if she could have done anything more that Saturday afternoon. 'I dreamed about it for years afterwards. There was a sense of guilt. In those moments when Peter was conscious, could I have somehow got the boat back to the riverbank? There was no equipment on the boat that could have helped. I'd seen a stroke before and knew that the quicker you get medical attention, the better. Eventually I came to terms with being in the wrong place at the wrong time. I lost a friend as well as a valued colleague that day.'

And Stuart Jones lost his father. At the time Stuart was the *Times'* football correspondent and he was friendly with many of us on the football circuit, often joining the *Sports Report* team in the Dover Castle after the programme. Stuart was convinced that Peter never got over Hillsborough, following the earlier horrors of Heysel, 'In that year after Hillsborough, he never slept properly. He wouldn't talk about it, but it hit him very hard.'

The memorial service for Peter a month later at All Souls Church, next door to Broadcasting House, spoke volumes for the respect the sporting world held for Peter Jones. That gathering was a who's who of the British sporting world in 1990 and Peter would have loved it, working the room afterwards, double scotch and water in hand (no ice, please), swapping yarns, gripping arms fondly, knowing exactly when to glide towards the next friend, steely grey hair in place, immaculately tailored as ever, tie knotted precisely. Peter Jones always made life look easy. Until the afternoon of 31 March 1990.

1993: The Grand National abandoned

This had to be filed under 'You couldn't make it up.' The most famous horse race in the world declared a non-starter, even though seven of the horses finished the whole course. All because of two false starts, with the recall flag stuck around the neck of one of the jockeys at the second time of asking. With the recall flag not unfurling, 30 of the 39 riders set off, unaware that the starter was vainly trying to recall them, all topped off by Esha Ness storming home, only to have the cup of victory dashed from the jockey's lips when told the race was, in fact, not a race after all. And the opinion of the bookies, who had to refund around £75 million in bets staked, can only be imagined.

At the 147th time of asking, the Grand National had descended into farce. The organisers had been concerned at possible demonstrations by animal rights activists. That did materialise, a mini-invasion close to the first fence leading to a slight delay, but they should have looked closer to home, rooting out the incompetence that led to the subsequent farce.

It was the perfect story for *Sports Report*. It fell just inside the ideal timescale, yielding high drama in mid-afternoon, giving enough leeway to collect emotional interviews, paving the way for a riveting press conference, broadcast live close to 6.00 p.m. *Sports Report* stayed on air past its scheduled finish to take that presser, benefiting from the new programming flexibility ushered in by the introduction in 1990 of Radio 5. If the programme had still been part of Radio 2, it wouldn't have been able to bring the vital, concluding part of that momentous day.

Once the second recall flag had failed to stop the 30 horses, vain attempts from officials, trainers and even the spectators to halt the race meant the majority of the field pressed on towards the finishing post. No amount of arm-waving and yelling could stop many horses in full flow until they were forcibly halted.

Peter Bromley, calling the race as usual for BBC Radio, said the race was void very early on, even though he and his co-commentators had to carry on describing the action. Cornelius Lysaght, then a comparative newcomer to our racing coverage, hasn't forgotten Bromley's despair. 'Whenever I think of Peter, I can hear him saying despairingly, "It's another false start!" There was a sense of sadness and despondency. Peter loved the Grand National, he knew it was one of the great sports stories in the calendar and he was disconsolate.'

Cornelius was positioned outside the weighing room and could see the angry reaction from trainers, owners and jockeys. Jenny Pitman, a fiery character when roused, was furious that her horse Esha Ness hadn't after all won the National, throwing her wide-brimmed hat on the ground and stamping on it. Her jockey John White turned a deathly pale when he discovered the greatest day of his racing career was a non-event. 'There was a tidal wave of horror and anger,' Cornelius recalls, 'and we had the caricature of the double-barrelled, cigar-chomping steward. It didn't look great at all; it looked as if they didn't have a clue.' Especially as the erring starter Keith Brown said in the immediate aftermath that he was considering disqualifying all but the nine horses that had finished. He was thinking of starting the race again with just those nine runners. By now, everyone associated with the Grand National was either apoplectic or bewildered. It was proving a monumental cock-up.

At such times, a programme needs a tough, hard-nosed reporter who wouldn't be sidelined or ignored and would persist in asking short, relevant questions. Step forward Mark Saggers. He had been full-time in the sports department for about four years, developing his all-round skills. More importantly, he had forged some worthwhile contacts in the racing world and when he hoved into sight, the relevant folk trusted him. On this day, they flocked to him, ready to vent their spleen. Mark hoovered up searingly angry interviews, his technicians got the recorded ones back rapidly into the system and within minutes they were on air. His live interview with John Upson, trainer of the fancied Zeta's Lad, was graphic. Upson spluttered breathlessly, 'It's a f****** disgrace!' and when Saggers reminded him he was live on BBC Radio, he changed tack, 'It's an absolute disgrace.' John Inverdale, stationed elsewhere, also cleaned up, churning out tremendous, raw reactions to the shambles. Inverdale chuckles at Saggers' determination that day, 'He was like a dog with a bone, absolutely going for it like a Rottweiler. Mark just wouldn't let go when he saw incompetence.'

Saggers was already revved up after an attempt at a rollicking from a BBC TV executive, who had summoned him to what he thought would be a straightforward dressing-down for the radio man. It seems that earlier in the meeting, Saggers had grabbed a quick interview ahead of Jonathan Powell, who was doing a similar job for television, and sharp words were exchanged. 'I was told by the TV guy that they always go ahead of radio when there's flash interviews to be done, to which I responded, 'You weren't even ready to do it, while I was.' That's the beauty of radio – you can be in and out because you travel light. They tried to tell me off as if I was a little schoolboy, but I was having none of it. I was only doing my job, which was to do what I could for the listeners.'

He certainly fulfilled that remit this Grand National Day. At the packed press conference, the managing director of Aintree racecourse, Charles Barnett, the chairman, Peter Greenall, and the press officer, Nigel Payne, were put up to try making sense of it all. Saggers, aware that *Sports Report* had the live coverage falling perfectly into its lap, waded in right from the start, firing off short, sharp questions that gave those in the firing line little time to recover. 'How did you let this happen? … Why did you let the race continue when so many had pulled up? … So where do we stand now?' And he wouldn't yield the floor to any other reporters, doggedly pursuing answers. 'It was a massive international story and I thought "I'm going for it," name-checked the BBC and got stuck in. After four questions I got a dig in my ribs, but I wouldn't let anyone else in – and the room was absolutely packed. I knew it was going out everywhere via the medium of *Sports Report* – immediate, live and challenging. I did it for the programme as much as for me. When it was all over, I was told by another journalist, "You went on a bit there," to which I responded, "Well, you got the answers, didn't you?" I never had a problem trying to outdo other news journalists. Having interviewed earlier so many jockeys, owners and trainers, aware of their anger, I had no qualms about climbing in with pointed questions.'

John Inverdale, gleefully listening in to the presser, was full of admiration for Saggers' chutzpah. 'We started *Sports Report* not knowing what was going to happen and we just hoped Mark would get something. Having a very strong journalist, both during all the earlier mayhem and then at the press conference, was so important for us. He was really on the button and meant we cleaned up, getting all that was necessary, hours before the Sunday papers.'

Cornelius Lysaght agrees. 'In those days there weren't any specialist racing channels so, apart from BBC television, we were the companion for millions of people leaving Aintree wondering what was going on. And, unlike TV, we could just keep the story going because we had all the time we needed in *Sports Report*. I'd worked hard at getting racing people more aware of BBC Radio and I was very pleased at that effort paying off. People just queued up to be interviewed by John and Mark. We had a great news story happening at the perfect time for *Sports Report* and we proved we had a sharp news edge, with some fabulous reporting. Having a presenter like John who knew his racing and relished the big events, and a news reporter like Mark who just wouldn't give up, were tremendous assets.'

The judges of that year's Sony Awards agreed. The production team scooped the Live Sport Outside Broadcast gong, while Mark Saggers picked up the Sports Reporter's award.

1993: Brian Clough gets relegated

For someone of Brian Clough's managerial eminence, the very notion of being relegated was unthinkable. But it was entirely typical that the old actor/manager should mark the occasion with a lap of honour, bathing in affection, tears and idolatry. Only Cloughie could get away with a humiliation that morphed into a triumph of sorts, an encomium penned by his own unique hand.

Saturday 1 May 1993 saw the last rites of a magnificent, enthralling career as Clough stared relegation in the face for the first time. All season, his Nottingham Forest team had faced the prospect of going down. They had been pallid and slow far too often, and by early spring the gossip had it that their charismatic manager had not only lost his alchemy, but that his players didn't know what they were doing. An aimless Brian Clough side, drifting towards the rapids, was a concept almost impossible to comprehend, given his remarkable capacity to get players operating above their former level of adequacy.

With two games to go, both matches had to be won if Forest stood any chance of staying up. If so, they'd be facing next season without Clough. He would retire in a week's time, 28 years since he first breezed into a manager's chair, at Hartlepools, and umpteen trophies later.

At last, Cloughie was done and, sadly, he wasn't in good shape. Alcohol had sapped his unique talent, that remarkable knack for squeezing every last drop from a player's body and psyche. Even a man with such a blowtorch of an ego, such enviable self-assurance in his job, needed to get out of a profession that was taking a serious toll on him. Brian needed to stop drinking and managing a football club. And he knew it.

His retirement was blurted out prematurely by his chairman, Fred Reacher, on Monday 26 April, denying Brian the right to announce it on his terms. He forgave Reacher, with whom he had enjoyed a cordial relationship, but not one of the directors, who had alleged to a Sunday paper that the manager was now over-dependent on alcohol. Chris Wootton's revelations weren't news to Forest insiders, but such was the respect for Clough that many fervently wished he could choose a time of his own to make the break and go of his own volition, with some dignity.

With Clough dominating the sports media agenda all week, it was obvious the home match against Sheffield United would be our chosen second-half commentary game and, even from the distance of midweek, it would dominate *Sports Report* – Brian Clough being relegated was a big enough story, never mind the alcohol issue being blown wide open, with rumours that he had been forced out.

I was the producer and reporter at the outside broadcast that day, with Rob Hawthorne commentating. One scenario was obvious as I discussed the day ahead with our production team in Broadcasting House – we needed Cloughie on the show as soon as possible after 5.00 p.m. Relegation or reprieve, it didn't matter. 'We'll leave it with you,' was the gist of the message to me.

Over the years I'd managed to forge a relationship with Brian that had gone from, 'Who the ... are you?' to 'Not this time, but thanks for asking, Patrick' to 'Coom on in, have a glass of summat.' I wasn't the only one on our Midlands patch to do so, and they shared with me a deep feeling of affection and professional regard for someone who was a genuine one-off: funny, with the gift of timing, totally unpredictable, at times absurdly generous, then exasperatingly rude and obnoxious. At all times, though, his own man. Three decades on, we camp followers at Forest from those days still share Clough anecdotes when we see each other. All of us were under pressure to deliver something out of the ordinary that day.

I at least had a good net, securing an interview with Brian the day before. He was relaxed, sober, philosophical and acutely aware that professional embarrassment was a possibility next day. He promised he would talk to me in *Sports Report* after the match. I had never known him to go back on such an undertaking before in our working relationship. I just hoped he would be able to do himself justice on air. For the first time, I felt protective towards him, wishing he could approach some of his amusing verbal pyrotechnics when he was in his pomp.

We started *Sport on 5* with my Clough interview from the day before and the match went the predictable way, with a muscular Sheffield United brushing aside a Forest team bearing no relation to the juggernauts of previous seasons. They went down with a whimper, assuring relegation, and surely now the Trent End would turn against their egotistical manager, who had joked so many times about walking on the River Trent?

Remarkably, the Forest supporters wouldn't leave at the final whistle as their players sloped away, heads bowed. The Sheffield United fans, who had chanted Clough's name in the second half, stayed on to hail someone who had intrigued generations for decades. How long would they all stay on at the City Ground, serenading a failed manager?

By now, I was downstairs in the corridor alongside both sets of dressing rooms, waiting to grab a word with Cloughie. Our interview position, in a small gym between home and away dressing rooms, was a mere 12 paces from the Forest door, ideal for ushering Brian into a quiet room, with just a BBC *Match of the Day* camera crew in there.

Brian appeared, planted a sloppy kiss on my cheek (not proffered by me!), then, listening to the acclamation from outside, said, 'I'd better go out and thank them, and say tar-rar.' With that, sporting his familiar green jersey and white trainers, he strolled down the tunnel, into the bright spring sunshine, ready to receive what he felt he deserved.

Rushing to our interview point, I buzzed up to Rob Hawthorne, alerting him to the prospect of a dramatic gesture from Clough and informing Broadcasting House. They were commendably swift to clear the decks and come back to the City Ground, where Rob anchored a different sort of commentary, describing the emotional scenes, the scarves and hats draped around Clough, the old ladies getting preferential treatment with a kiss from him. He cried, he smiled, he laughed and, typically, he reacted as if it was no more than his due. He was right. The fans were thanking him for 28 fascinating years, not lampooning him for this abject failure at the fag end of a glorious career.

The remarkable lap of honour, leading *Sports Report*, was being capably described by Rob Hawthorne, as I faced a devilish decision downstairs in the corridor. I could tell from Brian's demeanour, face and speech that he was not in the right shape to do an interview. He had to go on 'live', to capture the essence of those astonishing scenes and to try reflecting on what was truly the end of an era, even for many football fans who didn't ever support a Clough team. Brian had been a terrific, engaging guest so many times on *Sports Report* – surely, he should be on again for just one last hurrah?

The studio editor back in Broadcasting House made it clear it was my decision but, to be fair to him, I was the individual on the spot, the one who had to make the decision. Was I going to risk exposing him to a national audience, live on the radio? Barry Davies, who was there for *Match of the Day*, had always enjoyed a friendly, respectful relationship with Brian and he was lucky in that he could record the interview, with the clever technicians back in TV Centre editing out most of Brian's face, relying on his voice, talking over some graphic, emotional scenes. Television could just about get away without exposing Brian, because it wasn't live. We had no such luxury.

While waiting for Brian to detach himself from his adoring faithful outside, Nigel Clough came to my rescue. He handed me a statement from the Clough family, deploring the timing of his father's announced retirement, abhorring that, 'After 40 years we feel disappointed that words like "hounded out" should accompany his retirement.' The mere fact that Brian's wife, Barbara, had given her name to the family's public displeasure was a story in itself, because she had always stayed resolutely out of any public comments. Breaking news stories kept coming that afternoon...

Nigel confirmed to me that he would come on *Sports Report* within a few minutes and that crystallised my thinking. We had enough without Clough Senior, I felt. Even then, I had to prevaricate with him. As he prepared to be interviewed by Barry Davies, he shouted over to me, 'Won't be long, Patrick – one last interview!' In the end, I had to tell him a massive porky – that we had run out of time, that *Sports Report* had unfortunately finished early. He was undoubtedly in the mood to talk, but I ushered him out into the corridor, keeping an eye out for his son. Brian needed protecting from himself. The press, waiting for one last audience with the manager who had toyed with them for decades, would get their quotes, but Brian's pattern of speech and tone wouldn't matter. Nor did it so much for a recorded television interview, but it would have been too noticeable, live on radio, that Brian was playing from memory as an interviewee.

Within a few minutes, Nigel Clough gave me a dignified live interview, reflecting openly on a terrible day for his club, a sad one for his father and his family's anger at how Brian's retirement was handled by the club. We had enough, I reasoned, as we folded up the BBC Radio tent. It's not many days when a reporter gets the option of refusing an interview with Brian Clough. I hoped I had made the right decision. On reflection, I feel I owed that to Brian for his generosity over the years, after I had served a tough early apprenticeship at the Court of King Clough.

A week later, I did get an interview with him, at Ipswich after his last match ended in yet another defeat. I'd taken the precaution of ensuring it would be recorded, played out a quarter of an hour later in *Sports Report*. By then, it wasn't so vital to have him on live. One sentence from him stood out as I thanked him, 'Patrick, thank you, we'll be working together again soon.'

I never knew if that was a threat or a promise. But over the next 11 years, before he died of cancer, Brian granted me many interviews, some of which were vintage, others that were never broadcast, because he wasn't coherent enough. I prefer to remember the countless occasions when he was at his best in front of a microphone. On his day, there was no one in football who could touch him for originality of expression, clarity of delivery and outrageous cheek. He brightened up many a dull day – even when he finally got relegated.

1996: Frankie Dettori's seven in seven

Some Saturdays, the luck falls into the lap of the *Sports Report* producer. All that's needed is to make the right decision swiftly, then leave it to the fates. But you can make your own luck. That's what Joanne Watson did on 28 September 1996, leading to a nimble-footed, dynamic programme that culminated in a sensational sporting achievement by the flat race jockey, Frankie Dettori.

At Ascot that day, Dettori made racing history as the first jockey to ride all seven winners on the card. Although just 25, Dettori had endeared himself already to the racing fraternity, partly through his natural brilliance in the saddle, but also his bubbly personality. After this Ascot day, he was now a household name, all over the front pages with that trademark 'cheeky chappy' smile, while radio and TV simply lapped up his part-Cockney, part-Italian accent. It seemed Dettori had a quip and a grin for everyone, and his trademark leap from the back of each winning horse cemented his popularity with the press photographers.

After winning the first four races, Watson in the Broadcasting House studio had a hunch that this was going to be an historic day at Ascot. She told the engineers not to de-rig all the equipment, just in case. Rob Smith, the on-site producer, warned our racing correspondent, Peter Bromley, that the studio was going to keep an eye on the rest of the card and that his usual early getaway wasn't certain this time. After Dettori coaxed Fatefully past 17 other runners to land the fifth race, everyone at the course was beginning to sense it was on. Nobody in the media was now contemplating an early departure.

At 5.00 p.m. Ian Payne read out the *Sports Report* headlines, including 'Frankie's had five out of five – no, make that six,' as Lochangel cruised home, so the running order was hastily revised, and the programme would take live commentary of the last race, starting at 5.35 p.m.

Luck plays a part in all such situations and we were fortunate that day to have Clare Balding acting as reporter. Clare's father, Ian, was the trainer of Lochangel and with such an entrée, she capitalised on her friendship with Dettori. If he wouldn't talk to the daughter of such an esteemed trainer, it would be very surprising. Clare had already interviewed Dettori twice that afternoon, capitalising on her knowledge of Ascot by loitering alongside the weighing room, getting a message to him via the valet, instead of waiting with the other journalists at the main entrance. A discreet working knowledge of the shortcuts at an outside broadcast can be invaluable.

By now, Peter Bromley was fully on board for the seventh race. He had always maintained that the secret of professional longevity was getting away early from a race meeting to escape the aggravation of heavy traffic. Clare Balding, early into her broadcasting career, just 25 years of age, had implored him, 'Please don't leave, because I can't commentate!' but he was always very protective of her and he knew this could be a huge story. And then there was Peter's cordial but keen rivalry with his TV counterpart, Peter O'Sullevan. Bromley always knew that the public considered O'Sullevan the star racing commentator, because of his television profile, but he never complained about that. He was a brilliant radio commentator and that was enough. 'Peter [Bromley] was never going to do what his rival had done,' says Clare, 'so the clever thing to do was stay. If this story plays out the way that it might, you're the one whose voice is on it for posterity and your great rival has gone home! It does make me smile now, because I worked so closely with both men over the years. I never asked Peter O'Sullevan whether he regretted leaving early, but I'm sure he did.'

Bromley by now had no time to think of rivalries. He had some serious prep ahead in the next few minutes. 'I moved down from our commentary position to our tiny studio on the ground floor. I seized a race card, glued it on to cardboard and rushed back to the top of the stands. There were 18 runners and I did not know any of them. Working overtime, I almost had them all committed to memory before the off.'

Dettori's horse for the final race had been quoted at 12-1 in the morning papers, but by 5.30 p.m. Fujiyama Crest was down to 2-1 favourite. Its trainer, Michael Stoute, had said earlier it couldn't possibly win. Around 20,000 at Ascot hoped the sage of flat racing might be wrong for once.

So did Joanne Watson and her team back in the studio. It was a smart move to play in a package of the earlier action, interspersed with clips from Dettori's interviews with Balding, building up the anticipation for the 5.35 p.m. race. The package ended just in time for Peter Bromley to commentate on the last half mile. Bromley, the master of such an occasion, went through the gears brilliantly in one of his greatest commentaries...

'They're into the last furlong and I don't think you'll hear a word I'm saying, because you'll realise that Fujiyama Crest and Frankie Dettori have the lead, but Northern Fleet is going after him... Fujiyama Crest has won it! Frankie Dettori's seven! That is history made, the crowd are running towards the unsaddling enclosure to greet today's hero – Frankie Dettori!' It's all there. Precise description, without any padding, the sense of history being made and enough pauses to let the crowd excitement wash over the commentary. Vintage Bromley.

Dettori, in the winner's enclosure, matched the crowd's hysterical delight, screaming his pleasure, holding up his fingers to signify SEVEN. He obliged with his obligatory leap from the horse, flapping his hands on the way down, for which many a press photographer was grateful.

Clare Balding finally got hold of him for their third interview of the afternoon. 'Don't touch me, I'm red 'ot! I'm going to do the lottery tonight, I tell ya!' When he heard that his beloved Arsenal had beaten Sunderland earlier, his memorable day was complete.

Clare will never forget the noise generated by the spectators. 'You thought a jockey riding every winner at an important meeting at Ascot just isn't going to happen. And then, suddenly, you're getting carried along on this wave. Honestly, the roar from the grandstand – I get goosebumps just thinking about it. I definitely think that roar transmitted itself through Frankie's hands to Fujiyama Crest and the horse thought, "This is for me." That day felt so magical and the horse was lifted over the line to win a race he had no right to win.'

Peter Bromley called it 'the most memorable raceday of my experience'. The bookies would also see it as memorable for different reasons, with estimated losses as much as £30 million. For those shrewd enough to go for an accumulated bet on all seven, the odds were 25,095-1.

Joanne Watson says it was 'a no-brainer' to focus on Ascot for *Sports Report*, 'not least because it was Frankie Dettori,' but she was clear-sighted enough to grasp the possibilities as early as win number four, while the second-half commentary on Rangers v Celtic was blaring out of the studio loudspeakers, as well as keeping an eye on the Premier League football scores. 'But I got a real buzz out of that, as horse number seven came home. You want such moments on *Sports Report*, live ahead of the other news outlets. It's about the results and the key interviews, but it's also about the key moments. We managed it that day.'

History is written by the winners, so they say. *Sports Report* was justifiably on the podium by 5.45 p.m. that Saturday afternoon.

1997: The IRA postpone the Grand National

Iain Carter was quietly monitoring a host of football scores one Saturday afternoon in April when the phone rang in the sports room. It came from the *Sports Report* studio. 'Get down here now! You've got to present the show in an hour.'

Iain was due to present the 'best of the rest' in *Sports Report*, a three-minute wrap of the most interesting games outside the Premier League. It was often a thankless task, but needed a cool head, succinct scripting and a worthwhile clip from someone involved. After two years in the sports department, following stints at Radio Leicester, then the World Service, Iain was learning his trade, presenting sports desks and now the 'best of the rest'. Not this afternoon. He was to be the voice of a legendary programme – within the hour. Hardly time to get nervous.

The hurried decision by the editor, Joanne Watson, came after a threatened IRA bomb outrage had caused pandemonium at the Grand National meeting. The 5.00 p.m. show was due to come live from Aintree, presented by Ian Payne, with all the usual drama, romantic stories and organised chaos that always made the National a special outside broadcast. But this time Payne was stranded outside Aintree, along with thousands of punters, trying to work out how he could get to a studio at Radio Merseyside to give some sort of update before 6.00 p.m. There was simply no chance of presenting *Sports Report* from anywhere near the course; the logistics were against it.

Carter will never forget when he grasped the significance of it all. 'Our second-half commentary was Nottingham Forest v Southampton and commentator Peter Drury was getting an update from Ian Payne at Aintree. Suddenly Ian said, "We've got to go," because the police were moving him on. Peter said, "OK, Ian – be safe," in a dramatic way. It sounded scary up there and I knew I was going to be taking up the reins after the Forest match, in just over half an hour. It was a mixture of, "I'm never going to get the chance to do this again," and blind fear.'

Ian Payne had kept the afternoon show on air expertly after the mass evacuation. 'I just knew we had to keep broadcasting for as long as possible, out in the road. I had a brilliant engineer with me and backpack equipment that allowed us to work live, on the move, for as long as the batteries lasted.'

Eventually, after an hour, the backpack died a death, and Payne and the rest of the radio team had to clamber on to a train to Radio Merseyside, to provide updates for *Sports Report*. Meanwhile, Carter was getting his head around the task ahead just in time to introduce the headlines. 'Joanne Watson, in Broadcasting House, guided me excellently, talking me through it all. I was so glad when others were speaking in that hour, because it gave me time to draw my breath, compose myself and not think beyond what I should say next. At six o'clock, I came out of the studio, completely dazed. I'd been given a clear awareness of the fantastic production machine that goes into just one hour of broadcasting.'

To the intense pleasure of the racing world and the city of Liverpool, the National was run 48 hours later. Prime minister John Major came up to show solidarity and, in the week of the 1997 General Election, that gesture was appreciated even among the Labour heartlands of Merseyside. Cornelius Lysaght, our racing reporter at Aintree, considers that National was very significant. 'It was the year that Liverpool fell back in love with the Grand National. After 1997, the people dressed up, made a big day out of the National. And for us on Radio 5 Live – the news and sport channel, only three years old – it came together beautifully on both days. A heady cocktail of news and sport.'

It was memorable for Iain Carter as well. His quiet day, compiling a few thoughts on some nondescript football games, was transformed into the crucible of presenting *Sports Report*. No wonder his first words to his producer on leaving the studio were, 'A pint of lager, please! It never happened again but I'm tremendously proud to have presented *Sports Report* – just the once.'

1998: Sheffield Eagles make rugby league history

Many sports fans just don't get rugby league. They still see it as a Northern enclave, redolent of past generations when whippets were kept as pets and exhausted miners cleaned up in tin baths in front of a roaring coal fire. But even rugby union devotees will yield to the historic upset at Wembley Stadium in the 1998 Rugby League Challenge Cup Final. Played since 1897, staged at Wembley since 1929 (only six years after football's first FA Cup Final there), it's a great day out, good-natured, celebratory, with only a light touch needed from the police presence. Rugby league's shop window day always seems to strike the right note of Northern pride in a proper community sport, where the players are never allowed to take themselves too seriously.

But if ever a team had pretensions to grandeur and deserved a place in history it was Wigan Warriors in the 1990s. They won the Challenge Cup eight times in a row, boasting titans such as Andy Farrell, Henry Paul, Gary Connolly, Jason Robinson and Denis Betts. Worthy entrants into the hall of fame.

Sheffield Eagles, Wigan's opponents in the 1998 final, had no such pretensions or history. Formed in 1984, playing in front of small crowds, uncertain about their home stadium season after season, they often seemed to be lurching from crisis to crisis. Unfashionable didn't do them justice. But they kept going.

And they got to Wembley in 1998. And they beat Wigan 17–8, having the lead all match. They had been 14–1 outsiders, astonishing odds in a two-horse race. It was the biggest upset in rugby league's Cup history, scarcely credible unless you watched the game. As sporting upsets go, it was in the upper echelon.

And on a busy day of football, with critical issues being settled near the season's end, *Sports Report* led the programme on Sheffield Eagles' astonishing triumph. *Sport on 5* had already opted for full match commentary, starting at 3.00 p.m., and as the prospect of a huge upset grew, the production team was delighted to focus on such a big story. Dave Woods' commentary on the game's only try – by the Eagles' Rocky Turner – was pulled out for the opening clip in the headlines, followed by the ecstatic scenes at the final whistle, interspersed with strains of 'Out of the Blue'.

For Woods, it was an emotional couple of minutes. A proud supporter of rugby league, fighting its corner against some rugby union sceptics in the sports department, he was also a football commentator. He could not be accused of narrow parochialism. Well aware of football's overarching importance in the brave new world of broadcasting rights, Dave just wanted rugby league to get a fair shout on air when it was deserved. Well, it did on Saturday 2 May 1998.

'Growing up listening to those wonderful commentators in goal clips on the *Sports Report* headlines made a great impression on me. And I was so proud when my clips were part of that music bed from Wembley that day. Proud also for rugby league.'

Dave's match summary led the reports after the classifieds, then he linked into a chat with his summariser, Peter Fox, a Yorkshireman with the ripest of accents, for whom the description 'legend' was inadequate. Peter, an outstanding coach, a fount of humorous anecdotes, an absolute natural in front of a microphone, was the ideal insider to give a perspective on the Eagles' astonishing feat. And he wasn't surprised. He'd told Dave Woods just before kick–off, 'I give them a better chance than the bookies are offering.' David Oates, who then followed Fox with some superb interviews on the pitch, also had a sneaking feeling for Sheffield Eagles. After interviewing their coach, John Kear, on the pitch in the build-up, he came back to the commentary box and said, 'You'll never believe this, but John Kear says they're going to win this – and I know he believes it!'

Kear had based his conviction on a meeting at the team hotel the night before. He went round the room, asking each player what victory over Wigan would mean to them. It became very emotional and Kean was then convinced Wigan would be beaten. In the tunnel, the Eagles players borrowed a motivational tool that worked for Wimbledon when they beat Liverpool against all odds in the 1988 FA Cup Final. They basically got into the Wigan players' faces as they lined up alongside each other. They started to chant, '1998 – it's the year of the Eagles!' while jumping up and down. It's hard to say if Wigan were out-psyched by that, but they never played in their customary imperious fashion.

Dave Woods' abiding memory came near the end of *Sports Report*, when he summed up the day and what it meant for rugby league. He interviewed Paul Broadbent, the prop forward and Eagles captain, and when it was over he watched Broadbent walk over to two emotional supporters and showed them the trophy. 'It was an empty, echoing stadium, an eerie atmosphere. The lid of the cup had disappeared, but there was Paul showing them the trophy and I felt like captioning the scene, 'Look what we've won.' It summed up the close bond between rugby league players and the fans.'

Not that the city of Sheffield made much of a fuss about the Eagles players. The city council had to be cajoled into staging a celebratory dinner for them and when the team bus dumped the players in the city centre, they had to walk to the council house. But nobody took any notice of them; barely an autograph book to be seen. Football remained Sheffield's sporting passion.

The players did get some brass out of their great day, after their chairman, Tim Adams, cleaned up, having put a bet on the Eagles at the start of their cup run. Not that those bonuses led to any imposing farmhouses in the nearby Peak District, but you couldn't put a price on their day in the sun at Wembley.

Dave Woods, still BBC's rugby league correspondent, considers it a career highlight. 'It was a sensational day, on so many levels. The sport of rugby league often doesn't get the exposure it deserves, because so often it's played on a Thursday or Friday night or a Sunday afternoon. But the production team was right behind us that day and we were all very proud of what we delivered. For me, being part of that *Sports Report* opening sequence, with the music, was very special, when you consider the greats who have graced the headlines down the years.'

Gill Pulsford, the programme producer that day, was always a champion of rugby league when it justified greater exposure. 'My thinking was that every sport has its day, when the story is just too good. Football was the bedrock of the programme on so many other Saturdays, but sometimes another sport takes the limelight. We'd go where the story was and there were a couple of weeks left of the football season. Sheffield Eagles beating Wigan was a huge sporting event and a 3 o'clock kick-off was perfect for us.'

2010: A.P. McCoy wins the Grand National at last

As Sir Gordon Richards strove to achieve as a flat race jockey with the Derby, decades earlier, it seemed that A.P. McCoy would never win the world's most famous steeplechase. His credentials were obvious – the record number of winning rides, champion jockey year after year, three finishes in third place in the National. He knew the Aintree course inside out. Even those who knew little about horse racing, just having a flutter on the National, knew that the Irishman was the real McCoy.

By the time he got to the 2010 race, Tony McCoy was beginning to fret about ever landing the prize. He had long been a friend of 5 Live sport, developing a fruitful working relationship with our correspondent, Cornelius Lysaght, and it had become something of a convention that McCoy would appear on the preview show, the night before the race. He and his friend Ruby Walsh would be the special guests in the Cavern for a couple of hours, chatting live about the National, with all funds raised from the audience going to Alder Hey Children's Hospital, but the predictability of the questions from the audience were beginning to pall.

Mark Pougatch, presenting the show, understood when McCoy pulled out in 2010. 'He was very polite and sorry about turning us down. It was now obviously weighing on his mind. Totally understandable.' Cornelius Lysaght agrees. 'At those preview shows, people kept asking him "Are you going to win it tomorrow at last?" and he was an amazing sport about it, very patient and good-humoured. Not only had he been close, but he'd had such really bad luck in the race, yet he could still laugh at missing out in front of the audience. He'd had this fantastic career – surely, he would win it one year?'

Don't Push It was the horse that finally helped him land the prize and the emotion generated around Aintree that day will never be forgotten by those attending, including Pougatch. 'It was a brilliant story and I got rather emotional on air. I remember thinking, "You're working now, get your professional head on." You don't want to be a cheerleader, but you want to reflect the excitement and the crowd's pleasure. A.P. had done so much for racing. It was one of my favourite sporting days.'

For Pougatch, interviewing the articulate, happy Irishman on such a great day for him would be a doddle on *Sports Report*, especially as he had always been so helpful to BBC Radio. But the presenter didn't have to worry about the hard yards ahead in actually getting McCoy to the makeshift *Sports Report* studio. That was the production team's major problem. How do you get to McCoy, amid the frenzy of euphoria generated by thousands of racegoers, first to establish if he'd agree to the live interview in the studio, and then how do you get him through the hordes of backslappers and seekers after selfies?

The mobile shed that served as a studio was around a hundred yards from the weighing room, outside the saddling enclosure. The studio looked down on to the paddock, so there would inevitably be masses of well-wishers looking up through the studio windows as the great man hopefully delivered his thoughts to Pougatch, live on air. It would be a frenetic few minutes and good luck to McCoy, getting away from all that mayhem when the interview was done.

It was obviously going to be a daunting challenge to get to McCoy in the first place. A good measure of physical presence from the nominated producer to wade through the milling throng would be advisable, as hysteria mounted and punters simply bounced off each other, trying to get close to McCoy, his horse and the victorious associates.

Claire Burns hardly fitted that profile – slim, 5ft 2ins – but full of dogged determination, she wouldn't be gainsaid. 'Security was tight, but being small I managed to slip through the crowds. It seemed everyone had wanted A.P. to win this one, whether or not they'd backed another horse. In the parade ring, he was swamped by media, punters, family, owner and trainer; it was crazy. He's tall for a jockey – 5ft 10ins – so I could spot his white cap above the others, and the famous green and gold hoops of the owner, J.P. McManus.

'I managed to get close enough to him to shout, "A.P., congratulations, can you come on *Sports Report* for a few minutes?" If I'm honest, I wasn't expecting him to say yes, with all the chaos and his other commitments. Sometimes his steely look of determination can be intimidating, but not that day. He smiled and said, "Sure, no problem at all," and he started to follow me. It took a while as everyone was cheering him, slapping him on the back, wanting photos and autographs. It was like a rugby scrum and I was this tiny bouncer trying to usher him through quickly. The lovely thing about A.P. is that he'll take the time to speak to everyone and shake hands, but I could hear my editor in my ear-piece, shouting, "We need him in two minutes." Somehow, we got there in time.'

McCoy was typically gracious and self-effacing in the interview, thrilled for Jonjo O'Neill landing his first National as a trainer. 'I'm just relieved it didn't go wrong again and that I don't ever have to have the conversation again about winning the National.' And with that he was off, ducking under a rail, disappearing into a sea of delighted punters – the ultimate professional, the latest to make sporting history.

McCoy says he was never going to pass up the chance of appearing on *Sports Report*, logistics permitting. 'I was lucky to be asked, because it meant I'd succeeded at last. I wish I'd been on more often as a winner! I'd wanted that for years. I'd often listened to the coverage on the radio going home, listening to the winning jockeys, wishing it would be me one day. There are certain things you feel privileged to do and being on *Sports Report* as the winning Grand National jockey was one of them. I'm a sports anorak, an Arsenal fan, and I always listen to it, to get my all-round take on sport. I like its easy access, its immediacy.'

His day at Aintree didn't end ideally, however. An hour after his *Sports Report* interview, McCoy was driving away from Aintree when his proud mother called his mobile phone from Ireland. Forgetting the law, McCoy didn't use hands-free and simply picked up the phone. He was spotted by traffic police and was docked three points. Another policeman in the van asked for a photo with McCoy. He obliged, of course. 'They were quite right to book me, but it was funny as a few passers-by got pictures of me on their camera phones and shouted that they hoped I'd get off with it.'

His abiding memory of that day was one of fulfilment. 'A lot of things happened to me because of the Grand National. Being voted BBC Sports Personality of the Year was fantastic, because that was from the public and I've always tried to push horse racing to a wider audience. That win made me a happier jockey, not necessarily a better one. Even though the Cheltenham Gold

Cup is the pinnacle for a National Hunt jockey, I'd have been hugely disappointed if I hadn't won the Grand National.'

It was also a memorable day for Claire Burns. Not only had she bagged the prize interview for *Sports Report*, but also a plum job. She became A.P. McCoy's manager ('He's one of the nicest people I know'), so he must have been impressed by her that day. If the Aintree production team were into gold stars, she would have romped home like Don't Push It and A.P. McCoy.

2021: Rachael Blackmore makes Grand National history

As usual, our masterly racing commentator John Hunt nailed it, 'No female rider has won the Grand National… Rachael Blackmore is out in front!... One of the great Grand National stories being told on this cold April afternoon… Rachael Blackmore becomes the first female rider to win the Grand National! What an amazing story!'

The only downside to that epic day was the absence of a crowd to see the unassuming Irishwoman make history. Restrictions due to Covid-19 meant there were only a few hundred at Aintree, compared to the usual throng of around 100,000, to witness the most famous horse race in the world. But at least racing had a new hero to admire after a desperate year, with no spectators around to enjoy such a convivial sport.

It's not as if Rachael hadn't given fair warning of her capabilities, irrespective of gender. A few weeks earlier she'd become the first female to win the prize for the Cheltenham Festival's top jockey. And Henry de Bromhead, the trainer of the winning horse, Minella Times, secured first and second, as he did in the Gold Cup. There was pedigree wherever you looked and, in retrospect, the 11–1 odds against Minella Times were very generous.

Sir A.P. McCoy, who knows a thing about the Aintree course, wasn't at all surprised by Blackmore's triumph. 'She's got it all. This sport is so physically and mentally demanding, but she's been able to cope with both.'

But the acceptance that Rachael is an exceptional jockey and this victory was deserved after a tactically flawless ride was bound to be a big story, because Rachael Blackmore is a woman. After 44 years of trying, a woman had finally broken through the barrier, in the 173rd National. Her modest acceptance of her triumph and the caring way she took a bucket of water from her handler immediately on unsaddling to sluice down the sweating Minella Times only endeared her more to both the racing cognoscenti and those who have a small wager only once a year.

By then, the game was afoot for the *Sports Report* production team. The restrictions at Aintree due to the pandemic were a challenge. Numbers of permitted personnel were down, so the regular presenter, Mark Chapman, couldn't attend. Gina Bryce, a full-time TV presenter, stood in and also carried out the interviews. John Hunt and his producer, Rob Nothman, had to stay in the commentary box. Instead of two on-site producers scurrying around, trying to hoover up live interviews, there was only one, Graham McMillan. It was his task to coordinate with the studio editor, while ensuring there'd be live material after the race, as soon as possible. With a 5.15 p.m. start and history made 10 minutes later, Rachael Blackmore was the only show in town for *Sports Report*. Provisional running orders were ripped up and the Aintree group had to deliver.

McMillan had been speaking all week to Aintree officials, establishing what was permissible. It would be impossible to get to any owners, because of the zoning that was in place, 'So we had to focus on getting to the winning jockey and trainer as fast as possible. Normally we have a free rein on Grand National day, but we couldn't complain, due to the exceptional circumstances. So we were stationary, outside the weighing room, after the race. Aintree were very co-operative in advance, but we knew that with the race starting at 5.15 – hopefully on time – it wouldn't be until 5.45 before we got anything live in the winners' area, so it was going to be tight.'

As Minella Times romped home at 5.25 p.m., McMillan left the outside broadcast truck, sprinted a hundred yards to the winners' area and started trying to gather live reaction into *Sports Report*. Obviously, the main quarry was Rachael Blackmore and this is where the forward planning paid off handsomely. Katie Walsh, the only woman jockey to finish in the National's top four (in 2012), is an excellent contact for the racing team, often helping out in live broadcasts. More importantly, she has been an inspiration and friend to Rachael Blackmore. If anyone could usher Rachael urgently to the microphone, it would be Katie. As Gina Byrne started to interview Katie, she spotted the history-maker and after they shared a private moment of triumph, Katie brought her to Byrne. Understandably, she was still trying to take it all in...

'Unbelievable, incredible – that's all you can get out of me now,' she laughed. 'I just travelled and jumped. I wish I could give you a better rundown on what happened.' She was still smart enough to sidestep the inevitable question about her gender, 'I don't feel male or female, I don't even feel human, I feel unbelievable.'

If Rachael was determined to play down that aspect of her wonderful day, her inspiration Katie Walsh went full throttle, through her tears of joy. 'If you can't cry on a day like this… She's an inspiration to male and female jockeys. I'm her number one fan. She has taken some terrible falls and she bounces back up. She really is an animal!'

It was a shrewd move by Graham McMillan to have Andrew Thornton alongside Gina and Katie, acting as a buffer live on air, while waiting for the key interviews. Winning jockey in the Cheltenham Gold Cup, a veteran of 13 Grand Nationals, Andrew is very popular and familiar around the racing circuit, and his presence gave the small *Sports Report* group extra clout. 'This is phenomenal for the sport – she didn't turn pro until she was 26. This will take racing to a different level. She crossed all the boundaries; nothing's been given to her. She earned this; just didn't walk into it.'

There was just time to fit in an important interview with the modest yet thrilled trainer, Henry de Bromhead, 'She's done it the hard way; it's such a tough sport. She just kept winning and all our horses wanted Rachael on board. Just for a few moments, we almost forgot we had no crowd.'

It would have been wonderful to experience the full-throated acclaim of a massive Aintree crowd, relishing the historic nature of the day and appreciating Rachael's undemonstrative maturity. It would have been in the Red Rum/ Aldaniti/A.P. McCoy category of memorable Aintree days, with the Irish punters celebrating as only they can. But, oddly, the lack of spectators helped *Sports Report*, as Graham McMillan confirmed, 'Normally, there's pandemonium after a National, which makes the logistics very challenging for us. Because it was pared back due to the pandemic, it made it easier for us to get access and get around. Rachael only did a quick interview with ITV, still in the saddle, before coming to us so quickly, with Katie's crucial help. And we swapped Rachael with the Racing Channel, after they'd finished with Henry de Bromhead. It just panned out perfectly.'

It was a brilliant production. Within 20 minutes of the winning moment, *Sports Report* was broadcasting terrific interviews live with the winning jockey, her great friend and inspiration, and the happy trainer, plus a relevant contribution from a former male jockey, a veteran of Aintree, who could put

Rachael's achievement into a practical context. That is a remarkable achievement, given the hassles you encounter on a live sports broadcast and the understandable restrictions due to Covid.

But there was one last contribution needed from Aintree. McMillan told John Hunt he had a three-minute window in which to sum up. He had to mention the sad death of The Long Mile, who pulled up with a serious injury at the 23rd fence. The race itself had to be analysed by him and he had to place Rachael Blackmore's achievement in a historical context. 'Sum up what today means,' was the producer's instruction to his commentator.

John was more than equal to the task. He referenced The Long Mile's owner coming to terms with the fatality, as well as owning the winner. 'J.P. McManus loves his horses. He'll be feeling the pain there as well as the joy.' Hunt had called Charlotte Brew in midweek to talk about her experiences in 1977, when she became the first woman to ride in the National. Charlotte was very illuminating and John wasn't going to spare the crusty nihilists. 'A lot of people then in horse racing were actively against female jockeys. People who were high profile in the game, who really should have known better.'

A few days later I asked John to flesh out those remarks. 'There was a real hostility towards Charlotte in some quarters. Julian Wilson, BBC Television's racing correspondent, was vehemently against female jockeys and so was Red Rum's trainer, Ginger McCain. Female jockeys would turn up at a race meeting and have to change behind a tree or in the car.

'It feels like a different world now in many ways, but 1977 wasn't that long ago in other ways. It took me a little by surprise that such a big deal was made of Rachael after she won the National – appearing on *Woman's Hour* and *World at One*. It was extraordinary, but in 10 years' time we won't ever discuss women jockeys because it'll at last be established.'

But John Hunt has a little quibble about his contribution. 'It would have helped if I'd named the horse more often – but from the last fence to the finish it was all about the rider. I don't think my commentary was the slickest I've done, I just trusted my instinct, but you can always do better.'

Pish-tush, John. You're in the archives now, 'til kingdom come, and you deserve it. So does Rachael Blackmore. But just try telling her that.

14

TROUGHS AMONG THE PEAKS

The history of *Sports Report* isn't one of unalloyed triumph, of key players at the BBC all warbling the same ditty harmoniously. Turf wars are inevitable at a vast, monolithic organisation like the BBC. Vested interests have been defended tenaciously, with many a hill on which executives have chosen to die professionally.

When he was prime minister from 1966 to 1970, Harold Wilson presided over a cabinet of all the talents, replete with Oxford dons, other first-class minds from different backgrounds and rampant egos wherever he turned. Every cabinet minister had a powerful view, dissent was rife and a crisis always seemed imminent. Wilson, the master of equivocation, referred to the cabinet atmosphere as one of 'creative tension'.

That just about sums of many of the internal crises *Sports Report* has faced. It hasn't all been celebratory dinners, with awards racked up effortlessly, and the big hitters of the programme tethered willingly to the sports room, inured to blandishments from other broadcasters with enviable budgets.

From this distance, it seems remarkable that *Sports Report* was only allowed half an hour for its first seven years. Sport was a crucial part of post-war British society, with crowds flocking to live events, but there was a sense that it had to be held at bay when it came to broadcasting it in depth. The BBC didn't wish to air the football results on a Saturday night until 6.15 p.m.; there were more pressing matters such as *In Town Tonight, Dick Barton: Special Agent* on a Saturday and during the week *Housewives' Choice, Woman's Hour* and *Workers' Playtime*. On a Sunday, the most popular radio programme, *Two-Way Family Favourites* (a request show, hooking up Cologne with London, uniting those still in the armed forces) pulled in an audience that just couldn't be matched at any other time in the week.

So sport was tolerated, but many BBC executives held their noses when more enlightened broadcasters pushed for expansion. Sport was somehow seen as rather frivolous on the airwaves. The immediate decade after *Sports Report's* introduction was still deferential, conformist and class-conscious. When Len Hutton became the first professional cricketer to captain England in 1952, it created a stir among the more crusty custodians at Lord's. After Hutton retired in 1955, we soon reverted to P.B.H. May, M.C. Cowdrey, E.R. Dexter and M.J.K. Smith as England captains, in charge of Trueman, F.S., Statham, J.B., and Evans, T.G. It wasn't until 1962 that the distinction between amateurs and professionals was abolished, and the amateur's initials no longer appeared before their surnames. The England football team was selected by a committee of timeservers until 1963, when Alf Ramsey took the job on condition that he alone would be picking the team from now on. Just as well that Ramsey won the World Cup three years later, buying him time in the face of hostility from those now denied a seat at the top table.

Such deadening conformity chafed with Angus Mackay. In January 1948 he had launched a highly successful live sports programme at three months' notice, yet never felt totally supported in Broadcasting House. The innovative coverage by television of the Coronation in 1953 meant radio would soon be facing increasing competition. In 1954, when Roger Bannister became the first athlete to run the mile in under four minutes, the enterprising producer of *Sportsview*, Paul Fox, persuaded him to travel down from Oxford to TV Centre that Wednesday night. 'That made it for us in TV sport,' Fox recalls. 'We went for immediacy on that midweek programme, unashamedly borrowing the journalistic principles of *Sports Report*. We didn't really have proper coverage of the Olympics until Rome in 1960, but after that we were developing massively our live coverage of sport.'

When *Grandstand* started its Saturday afternoon TV sports coverage in 1958, *Sports Report* faced another challenge. 'But children's programmes were on television from 5 o'clock,' says Fox. 'We basically only had rugby league and horse racing, with football scores from the studio – no live reports, like *Sports Report* had. We didn't get back on air until 5.45, by which time *Sports Report* was still leading the way, with its live full-time reports and interviews. It took us a long time to catch up.'

Mackay's restless energy and hostility to television meant he would always be competing hard on behalf of *Sports Report*, but he also had to tackle warring elements inside the BBC Radio empire. Radio sport was under the banner of the outside broadcast department, run by traditional, old-school types who did not approve of this abrasive wild card from Scotland. Mackay's programme came under the news division and was entirely separate from the outside broadcast department, run by a martinet called Charles Max-Muller. Mackay and Muller simply didn't get on, which led to a complete lack of goodwill and co-operation between the two departments. The best description of their relationship was a Chinese wall. Vincent Duggleby, who worked for the sports news division from 1963 to 1970, says, 'Angus regarded outside broadcasts as a damned nuisance; he'd have nothing to do with them. He'd sit in his office at the end of the sports room, there'd be three offices next to him, a few of us dotted about – and that was the extent of sports news. There was a constant air of hostility.'

Max-Muller couldn't understand why Mackay kept using his own reporters, mostly drawn from Fleet Street, rather than the safe option of commentators sanctioned by the outside broadcast people. Mackay preferred the unstuffy, iconoclastic Fleet Street operators, who were no respecters of Establishment standards and perfectly happy to indulge in slick, punchy reportage, with a keen eye for a news angle. Totally antithetic to Max-Muller's austere, conformist notion of what sports commentators could or couldn't do.

The two departments lobbed verbal hand grenades at each other throughout the sixties, with Mackay suffering a blow in 1964, when *Sports Report* was taken off the Light Programme and shunted on to the Third Programme, moving from the home of *The Navy Lark* and the Beatles to the rarefied showcase of Béla Bartók and Dmitri Shostakovich. This was entirely due to BBC politics. With Radio Caroline starting up in 1964 and other pirate radio stations growing in popularity, the BBC was concerned that its popular music output was being marginalised in favour of the irreverent, pacy coverage of the brash new stations. So the Light Programme had to move with the zeitgeist and sport was sacrificed.

The Third Programme was seen as a hinterland, a dense tundra to be hacked through by sports fans, compared to the undeniable popularity of the Light Programme. But the Third Programme wavelength was available for sport in the afternoons, which reduced the potential for the clashes that had always existed between sport and the other competing departments contributing to the Light Programme.

Mackay wasn't powerful enough to resist the change – his fiefdom only ran through Saturdays – and although he grumbled enough about *Sports Report* being dumped on to a network he saw as obscure and elitist, he had to keep his head down. He was, after all, only a producer, not an executive skilled in the sinuous ways of bending an influential meeting to his will.

So the Third Programme it was, for the next six years. Audiences dropped slightly, partly due to listeners being unable or unwilling to find the Third Programme on their wireless dials, partly because televised sport was beginning to find its feet. Vincent Duggleby believes sports coverage up to 1966 wasn't radically different to that in the fifties, 'But after the 1966 World Cup, we had an explosion of interest, with various European Cups, Olympic Games, cricket's Sunday League and the introduction of *Match of the Day* on Saturday nights from August 1964. Newspapers started to give sport more scope. *Grandstand* on TV grew in stature and relevance. *Sports Report* had to adapt to a faster-moving landscape.'

It seems amazing from this distance that England's triumph in the 1966 World Cup Final over West Germany wasn't given blanket coverage. *Sports Service*, introduced by John Dunn, started at 12.30 p.m., but the match preview didn't begin until 2.00 p.m., an hour before kick-off. It lasted for five minutes. Then we had a lengthy preview of the Commonwealth Games from Kingston, Jamaica, before settling down to England's first appearance in a World Cup Final. At 6.00 p.m., soon after Geoff Hurst thrashed in England's fourth goal with the ensuing crowd euphoria, the Third Programme switched from Wembley to a classical music concert. The Hungarian Radio Symphony Orchestra playing Kodály's 'Psalmus Hungaricus', to be precise. Within a couple of hours, radio's chief commentator and BBC football correspondent, Brian Moore, was back home in Kent, watching the celebrations on his television. The Third Programme deemed that classical music held sway, even on such an historic evening. 'That's the way it was on that network,' says Duggleby. 'The game was treated no differently from a major European club final, even though England's triumph led the six o'clock news on the Home Service.'

Mackay battled on in the face of bureaucratic indifference to sport, aware that he still presided over a precious institution in the eyes of those who thought the muddied oafs on all those playing fields had something tangible to offer millions of listeners. But he bridled constantly at the internecine disputes. Sheena Harold, his daughter, says they took their toll on him. 'Dad was not happy with all the rows with management. He'd come home depressed sometimes. He was always one to take things to heart.'

Duggleby helped a great deal. As Mackay's eventual deputy, the younger man had the requisite diplomatic skills to avert too many explosive disputes in management meetings. He helped bridge the gap between two intransigent factions, modernising *Sports Report* with editorial and technical innovations. 'I felt we needed to hear more from players and fans, rather than just the tried and tested interviews with big-name managers. I would go out to a London-based match before kick-off, record interviews with the supporters, edit that into a two-minute package for *Sports Report*, which wouldn't sound dated, and it brought more flavour and colour to the programme. I thought we were a little top-heavy with Fleet Street contributors and familiar interviewees, so I tried to get us closer to the action.'

Mackay respected Duggleby's vision and gave him his head, both as his deputy and, for 18 months, as presenter of *Sports Report*. Duggleby also recommended Peter Jones in 1965, and Des Lynam and John Motson in 1969, before moving on in 1970 to a stellar career as a financial broadcaster, but not before playing a crucial role in a testing period for *Sports Report*.

By the time Lynam was finding his feet as *Sports Report*'s classy new presenter, backed up by the energy and passion of Bob Burrows as the driving force behind Mackay's continued editorial control, the programme was back on familiar terrain. The Light Programme had been replaced by Radio 2 in 1967 and, three years later, the sports output was back on radio's most popular station. Cliff Morgan ensured *Sports Report*'s credibility was recognised in the portals of power when he became head of sport and outside broadcasts in 1974. His collegiate, winning style of wooing executives, dropping a genial word in an influential ear over a glass of something appealing, meant sport wouldn't be banished to the gulag of a niche network again.

The next two decades passed serenely enough for *Sports Report*, with its battalion of brilliant broadcasters and excellent production teams. The programme developed a modus operandi that enabled it to stand cheek by jowl alongside television's creeping territorial ambitions. I hesitate to use the term 'golden age', because comparisons can be odious and self-defeating, but in the seventies and eighties *Sports Report* was at ease with itself, building on the most solid of editorial foundations, adapting smoothly to a more flexible coverage of sport.

Then there was a major challenge to *Sports Report* and it came from within the BBC. For around four months in 1993, there was a real concern that the sports department was going to be swallowed up by the leviathan of news, leaving just a rump of sport to be covered by the new network. It took the equivalent of a peasants' revolt to head off the genuine threat, backed up by appreciative listeners in their droves, highly influential figures from the world of sport and anxious Members of Parliament.

In July 1993, Radio 5 had gone from a derided fledgling network three years earlier to the only one of the five national stations on BBC Radio to show growth. When it was launched in September 1990 it was seen as a dumping ground for sport, children's and educational programmes, with no coherent narrative or strategy. But the sports department thrived from the greater flexibility offered by the new station. Coverage extended to 2200 hours a year – three times the amount given to sport on Radio 2 – and after winning a Sony for its 1992 Olympics coverage and for the 1993 Grand National, the audience figures for Radio 5 were outstanding. But with just over four million adults and 500,000 children listening per week, Radio 5 was coming under threat. It seemed bizarre corporate thinking.

The prime mover was the Director-General of the BBC, John Birt. He had long been an advocate of a 24-hour rolling news channel on radio, pointing to the success of the temporary experiment during the 1991 Gulf War, when anyone with military expertise or knowledge seemed to be tramping through Broadcasting House reception to give their verdict on Saddam Hussein and all his works. John Birt was convinced that a permanent rolling news network, 24/7, would transform the radio landscape and, as a former Director of News and Current Affairs at the BBC, there was little doubt that he was determined to push the concept through, once he became Director-General in 1992.

His original target – Radio 4 Long Wave – was eventually rebuffed by a concerted campaign, with figureheads from the arts world like Sir John Gielgud, Emma Thompson, Dame Maggie Smith, Alan Ayckbourn and Tom Conti, while thousands of articulate, middle-class activists bombarded Broadcasting House, aghast that news might trump their beloved Radio 4, disenfranchising 17 per cent of the station's listeners due to an inadequate FM reception in some parts of the country. It was the most powerful licence payers' pressure group ever lined up against the BBC. John Birt withdrew from that battle, bloodied but unbowed. His sights were soon trained elsewhere.

In such circumstances, the BBC is no different from a government when it comes to testing out public opinion. Birt was going to float the idea of Radio 5 being swallowed up by his news empire and it was time to test the water. An article in the London *Evening Standard*, early in July 1993, dropped the bombshell. BBC Radio 5 was being lined up as a sacrifice to accommodate

John Birt's desire to have a rolling news network. He saw it as a necessity, citing the concept's success in France and the United States. It was alarming that, in a recent speech, he had pointedly praised Radios 1, 3 and 4, but not mentioned Radio 5. He seemed determined to close down a highly successful radio station, just to pile on more news coverage, when so many other areas of BBC Radio covered news, almost to saturation point.

With the BBC now losing exclusive rights to other TV sport stations and satellite television, it seemed fatuous to sideline radio sport, with its strategic importance becoming more and more obvious. But Birt wanted a priority news service. Something had to give. The scuttlebutt inside Broadcasting House was that sport would be swallowed up and marginalised by a giant news station. Even *Sports Report* was in danger. Certainly, sport would not be able to provide its usual service on a news-driven channel. The Warrington bomb outrage, organised by the IRA, happened on a Saturday afternoon in February 1993. Once news had started to cover that in a new 24/7 operation, there would be no prospect of sport taking over the output later on. It would have been tasteless and disrespectful. Therein lay the fundamental issue of news v sport. Clashes would be inevitable.

The sports department was dismayed at the prospect. Time to call in countless favours. Members of Parliament were contacted, major sporting figures were alerted. The department clubbed together for funds to pay for the stationery that was needed to mobilise the campaign. Mike Lewis, then the head of sport, was called in by his boss, Liz Forgan, Managing Director of BBC Network Radio, who told him, 'I have no problem in you fighting for your department, Mike – but not one penny of the BBC's money must be spent on your campaign.'

Bob Shennan, then the Editor, Sport, backed up Lewis, so we had the gratifying case of the sports staff being fully supported by their two bosses. Shennan recalls, 'We feared that sport would be wiped out, but the noise that was generated heightened the importance of sport to the BBC.'

Seb Coe, then a Conservative MP, and a great friend of the sports department, went to Broadcasting House to plead their case. 'Mike Lewis and Bob Shennan were bravely working behind enemy lines and they deserved support. I made the point that Radio Sport had global stature and that cut through the age groups. It was a vital service.'

Tom Pendry, the Shadow Minister of Sport, was incensed when he heard the whispers and after bending the ear of Prime Minister John Major, put down an early day motion (EDM) in the Commons, urging the Director-General to abandon plans that might jeopardise coverage of major sports events, as they were vital elements of national culture. It was supported by more than 200 MPs and even Peter Mandelson, hardly a sports guru, supported it, as did the former Olympics sprinter Menzies Campbell, Tessa Jowell, Jeremy Corbyn, Peter Hain, Angela Eagle and, of course, Seb Coe. David Mellor, admittedly Marmite to many listeners to his *606* programme on Saturday nights on Radio 5, but nevertheless a former culture minister, backed Pendry to the hilt, organising Commons support behind the scenes. John Major also gave tacit approval.

Pendry was delighted with the Parliamentary response. 'It put pressure on the culture minister. The idea was to highlight the situation to the culture minister, then get as many MPs as we could to pepper him with questions in the Commons, so that he got fed up. You find the pressure points. Sport is always marginalised in Parliament. So many MPs say it's part of their lives, but not when it comes to power being exercised. That EDM was a very popular campaign and I remain very proud of the wide support we gathered.'

And not just in the Commons. Reporter Charlotte Nicol had an aunt who was a member of the House of Lords and once Charlotte contacted Baroness Nicol of Newnham, Aunty Wendy did the sports department proud. 'Wendy wasn't really a sports fan, but once we told her what was involved, she was very willing to stand up and state our case. When Radio 4 played a clip of Wendy's comments on *Yesterday in Parliament*, it wasn't just sports fans that were starting to take notice of our campaign.'

The fact that the Radio 5 audience had increased by 47 per cent during this stressful period only hardened the resolve of the sports department's refuseniks. Producer Gill Pulsford and presenter John Inverdale schlepped down to the nearest post office with stacks of letters addressed to key figures in sport, trying to enlist opposition to the rumoured putsch by John Birt and his apparatchiks.

Among those pledging their support were world heavyweight boxing champion Lennox Lewis. He couldn't get to London from the United States in time for the key press conference organised by Tom Pendry, but he wrote in warm support, 'I want to convey my complete support for your early day motion, which I have read with interest. I also noted that over 200 MPs from all parties are of a similar mind that Radio 5's coverage of sports events should not be closed as it makes an enormous contribution to the sporting life of our country. I will be punching my weight for you in your fight.'

Gary Lineker, playing out the last days of his career in Japan, committed his total support. He had dipped his toe into broadcasting in 1992 with Radio 5 and had been hugely impressed. As he proceeded through a distinguished presenting career, he never forgot where he first learned his trade. He now reflects on the success of the campaign he heartily backed. 'Sport in the media has grown to such an extent that it's even more pervasive than at any time. Radio 5 committed straight away to backing sport totally and that emphasised the importance of keeping it on air. Sport plays a huge part in the lives of people in this country and should always be given its rightful status by our media.'

Cliff Morgan expostulated with characteristic vigour, 'It is the craziest notion since they stopped producing fly-halves in Wales. The problem with the people who make these decisions is that they do not go to chapel, they do not go to pubs – they sit in meetings and listen to advertising speak.' As a former head of radio sport and outside broadcasts, Morgan could speak with painful authority on the latter experience.

Many other influential figures from the country's sporting bodies wrote to various BBC executives, including representatives of Cheltenham Racecourse, the Jockeys' Association, the Central Council of Physical Recreation, the PGA European Tour, the Premier League, the All England Tennis Club, the Rugby Football League, the British Horseracing Board, the Sports Council and the British Olympic Association.

Terry Wogan, who had enjoyed immensely working with the sports department at previous Olympic Games, was on board and had a quiet word with some well-placed executives. The campaign, backed up by respected Fleet Street columnists such as Frank Keating and Patrick Collins, soon built up an impressive head of steam. In his *Mail on Sunday* column, Collins wrote, 'Radio Five has no powerful interest group to plead its case or defend its existence. Because Radio Five is primarily a sports station… and therefore expendable. The station has become essential listening for the serious sports follower. In terms of breadth and quality, it has no equal in British Broadcasting.' The press conference at the Palace of Westminster, organised by Tom Pendry and attended by the Tottenham manager, Terry Venables, the athlete, Kriss Akabusi, the jockey, Peter Scudamore, and the England rugby union captain, Will Carling, garnered massive newspaper coverage – to the glee of the staff in the sports department. They posted all the relevant press cuttings on a wall outside the sports room ('The wall of shame' in Gill Pulsford's words) and those who worked in the newsroom had to pass it en route to their office. Tee shirts were printed and everyone's sporting contacts were blitzed – all paid for by the members of the sports department. Not a penny of licence payers' money was spent.

Mike Lewis was dragooned into talking about the campaign in front of a packed crowd at Goodwood Races. 'That wall of press cuttings was amusing in a way, because the news people had to put up with some pointed comments about sport's popularity with the listeners, compared to news. It was banter, laced with a bit of an edge. We were gravely concerned that while sport might have a place on the new network, it would be very much as a junior partner and that the editorial emphasis would be driven by news to the detriment of sport.'

And yet… despite the obvious stature of the sports coverage, there still lurked the conviction of the Director-General that a rolling news service was the way forward for national radio. In a speech to the Radio Academy, Birt said, 'There is one service the BBC as yet does not provide: a continuous news service available all day and all night… following the developments in a major breaking story.' As Frank Keating wrote in the *Guardian*, 'Whose finger will be on the button? The sports editor's or the gaffer on news?'

Mike Lewis knew there was little point in a forensic discussion on the respective merits with Birt. 'You couldn't just walk into his office. It was a very unsettling time.'

I have been fortunate to read the private memos back and forth between the sport and news heads and the relevant BBC executives charged with making the final decision in the autumn of 1993, and Lewis' advocacy was impressively brave. I can think of other Radio Sport bosses who would have been more biddable and those in the department at the time haven't forgotten his unceasing efforts. It was one of those heartening occasions in my BBC experience of departmental management and those on the shopfloor working in total harmony.

One memo from Lewis to Liz Forgan, the Managing Director of Network Radio, dated 6 September 1993, was particularly trenchant by the standards of BBC mandarin dialogue. 'As you might imagine, my department is seething about this story – which I guess was leaked by a senior news figure… because it helps to uphold the belief here that in BOM's [Board of Management's] mind… the decision has been taken already. The overwhelming feeling is that no one wants to listen, because our thoughts challenge the theory that there is "an editorial synergy between news and sport".

'Sadly the message is coming through loud and clear that the Senior Management does not want to hear what we have to say, because their minds are made up and that our objections are anyway irrelevant, because sport is very much the junior partner to be dumped whenever the need arises.'

Tom Pendry – now Lord Pendry of Stalybridge – says, 'I and, thankfully, the BBC itself, was hit by a tsunami of letters from the listening public.' He picks out one from Mr Richard Scott of Fishguard in Wales. He believed that, 'Sport on radio is threatened by the fanaticism and determination of a small clique in the BBC,' predicting that, 'Conflicting interests will lead to a news-dominated network with the continuity and spontaneity of sports broadcasts lost for ever.'

Eventually, Birt lost the battle and a remarkable campaign prevailed. On 12 October 1993, the BBC announced that a new radio network called Radio 5 Live would be launched the following April. The news release stated that, 'The new editorial partnership will combine first-class journalism of all kinds with live action sports coverage in a unique 24-hour service. BBC Radio Sport will continue to provide the most comprehensive sports coverage in Britain.' The decision followed an eight-month review, more than 6,000 letters from the public, and public meetings up and down the country. The outcome was radically different from Birt's thinking that had been leaked to the *Standard* a few months earlier.

Pendry, Coe and Campbell had demonstrated how members of Parliament could be a force for the good, when they listened to their constituents and their own instincts. Pendry notes that it ensured that, 'The elitism that all too often prevails did not ride roughshod over ordinary licence-payers who, like me, are passionate about sports.'

Key players in that 1993 campaign now look back on it with pride. Mike Lewis says, 'It was a serious threat to *Sports Report* and the entire department. The EDM in the Commons brought home to the top brass how much we were appreciated by millions of listeners, rather than the chattering classes. The letters we got from listeners and sports executives were incredible. We thought that there was a real threat of just broadcasting the football results at 5.00 p.m. on a Saturday, then back to rolling news – and no *Sports Report*, as we knew it. I'm incredibly proud of what we pulled off. With such a talented group in our department and excellent audience figures, we deserved to be treated with respect. Eventually we were.'

Gill Pulsford remembers feeling anxious when Radio 5 Live started. 'We still didn't trust them. We thought they'd go off live to some political press conference which didn't amount to all that much, rather than stick with the tried and tested sports coverage. But it all worked out fine, partly because many of the news people were also sports fans and respected what we offered. We were no longer part of a dumping ground.

'It was the biggest challenge the sports department has faced. The Premier League had just started and we were delivering big audiences for the live commentaries and the unique bundle of results, interviews and opinion that *Sports Report* provided. But we had to fight tooth and nail to survive.'

And what of John Birt's memories of that period? Sadly, I cannot offer any. Now Lord Birt of Liverpool, he politely declined to contribute to this book. Ah well. The story of the 1993 revolt can still be told without the input of the man who sparked it all off.

Since Sky altered the sports broadcasting landscape around the time Birt's kite failed to fly, *Sports Report* has had to adapt to the shifting terrain. Once all weekend matches kicked off at 3.00 p.m. on a Saturday – meat and drink to the production team, as they juggled with almost too many riches for a programme starting just a few minutes after the final whistle. Now the challenge is to make a wholesome meal from some thin gruel on certain Saturdays, with many high-profile games starting at assorted times over any given weekend.

A major challenge to *Sports Report*'s relevance came in August 2004 when a new TV contract decreed that a Premier League match would start at 5.15 p.m. *Sports Report* was at the mercy of the BBC's rights negotiators. Live commentary was an essential part of our appeal and if 5 Live didn't bid for the 5.15 p.m. games, many would question our commitment to live football. Other radio competitors would happily climb on board and annex exclusive rights to those matches.

So a compromise. Whenever a 5.15 p.m. match appeared on the schedule, *Sports Report* was truncated drastically to accommodate it. The half-time digest of the day's sport, lasting around 12 minutes, and the 10-minute whizz around key results at 5.05 p.m. would have to suffice. It was messy, unsatisfactory and although the selected match was moved to a 5.30 p.m. kick off in August 2008, buying more precious minutes for reports and interviews, there still wasn't enough time to do justice to the day's sports news on a programme that had prided itself on just that for decades. Some valued members of the production team eventually left the sports department as a consequence – missing the buzz of working on such a prestigious live programme. Shoehorning in relevant live interviews between reporters' contributions, staying flexible and speedy, editing tapes at short notice, watching the clock intently, working seamlessly as a team – that sort of professional satisfaction could never be matched by hearing the presenter cueing to live commentary of Aston Villa v Arsenal at 5.14 or 5.29 p.m.

Those who sadly drifted away from the production team appreciated the dilemma forced on our bosses, who had to hold on to exclusive football commentary deals throughout the week, not just Saturdays. The new dawn just didn't appeal so much to those who relished flying by the seat of their pants for a hectic hour between 5 and 6 p.m. Their frustrations were shared by reporters and commentators who, sometimes, just couldn't get on the programme with a good interview or punchy report, due to time constraints.

John Inverdale, listening from a distance, sympathised, 'Those early evening programmes on a Saturday brought collateral damage to *Sports Report*. When I was presenting it you were spoiled for choice. The cartel running the Premier League didn't care about such matters. Just get more money from the broadcasters and 5 Live had to go with that.'

When talkSPORT won the exclusive commentary rights to the Saturday evening games, there was a sigh of relief among many BBC Radio Sport insiders. Not that it could be publicly admitted. There's a macho aspect to bidding for rights and no negotiator wants to lose out to a competitor, who may or may not possess the deeper pockets. But the essential truth is that a Premier League game chipped away at *Sports Report* for six years. Not holed beneath the watermark. The vessel didn't ship too much water. But, at times, it was a rump of a programme.

Charles Runcie, who produced *Sports Report* a few times in his 15 years in the department, calls the 5.15/5.30 p.m. commentaries the nadir for *Sports Report*, 'Truncating *Sports Report* and *606* – our most recognisable sports programmes of the week on 5 Live – to broadcast the whole of Birmingham v Fulham, for example, was depressing. Sensibly, we stopped bidding for the live rights for the 5.30 game.'

In deciding to bid hard for more prestigious matches at other times of the weekend, BBC's negotiators tacitly acknowledged that radio couldn't now have the whole of the live commentary cake. Losing the Saturday evening match was at the time a reasonable price to pay; it certainly won favour among many regulars working on *Sports Report*.

That challenge, at least, could be tackled. Not so with Covid-19. From Saturday 14 March 2020 to Saturday 20 June 2020, *Sports Report* – like the nation – limped along, doing its best to engage with the listeners via a diet of features, live interviews with sporting personalities and anything of sporting interest from around the world. Covid restrictions limited the amount of personnel allowed in the Salford studio, so it was a case of making do and mending. Zoom connections often went down and buffering became the new normal. 'You're still on mute' should have been printed on *Sports Report* T-shirts.

All that was a trivial sideshow compared to the human tragedies played out constantly across the UK, day after day. 'It's only sport' became the familiar mantra every Saturday afternoon, when the line didn't function from a football ground or the ghostly atmosphere at matches from late June onwards sapped the energy from reporters. At least we were alive, working and (comparatively) healthy. Hundreds of thousands weren't so lucky.

It's in that spirit of relief and awareness that I will try to chart how *Sports Report* coped with the pandemic, at a time when we all hoped that sport could help minimise some of the pain experienced throughout the land. Our technical and logistical problems were a mere bagatelle, compared to what millions of others were going through, out in the real world, so what follows is definitely not a whinge, more an attempt at insight.

The first challenge was the revised TV deal, which led to a spread of all Premier League (PL) games across each weekend, from late June onwards. That meant only one PL match kicked off at 3.00 p.m. on a Saturday, so there wouldn't be the usual frantic period in *Sports Report* where story priorities were juggled and live interviews were conducted in the tunnels, where the various ISDN points were located. Because those tunnels were enclosed and always busy, they were out of bounds, so the interviews had to be conducted pitch-side, using a second microphone on a long arm to maintain distance. No longer could the interviewee share the headphones and microphone with the reporter to talk to the presenter in the studio. Too much of a health risk. Match producers had to remember to bring a mic stand extension to allow the socially distanced interview, while the engineer had to bring along a piece of kit called a Media Port, which facilitated the pitch-side interview.

Mark Williams, the programme's editor, says, 'For me, listening back in the studio, the biggest missing ingredient was the supporters. Those opening headlines didn't sound the same without a loud roar as a goal goes in. We couldn't wait for a return to that atmosphere, with supporters listening as they come out of a full stadium, just as I did as a listener all those years ago.'

Getting hold of post-match interviews was much more of a challenge in the pandemic, because interviewers were limited in numbers. BBC National Radio didn't have commentary rights for English Football League (EFL) or Scottish Premiership matches, so we had to rely on Radio Scotland or the BBC local radio stations to send them back to Salford. But that took time, compared to the instant access via our ISDN points in the tunnels, which usually ensures we are not lagging. And the paucity of staff back in the studio due to Covid restrictions only added to the difficulties in getting items actually on air, after 5.30 p.m., when usually there's a glut of available material and producers available to edit.

The production teams and presenters really had to be on their mettle during the pandemic, listening out for the interviews as they came in, ensuring that the best lines were taken out swiftly and broadcast. The usual preference for our own reporters to do the interviews had to be jettisoned, because it often took just too much time. Compromises were everywhere. No point in comparing previous seasons. New wine was being poured into old bottles, temporarily. Not the best vintage, but at least the show kept going.

Mark Chapman, the presenter, was particularly adept at spotting stories on the wires or via social media that could be tickled up to make a good national sports story. He would often say on talkback to the studio, 'Have you seen this?' while linking live to various reporters. One story he spotted made a great listen. Mark had noticed that Ajax in the Dutch League had won THIRTEEN nil. Mark Williams gave one of his producers the task of finding a journalist who had been at that game that afternoon, who could talk in acceptable English. He remembered the World Service using Michiel Jongsma a few weeks earlier and, luckily, Michiel was indeed at that Ajax game. The story stood out, because the journalist spoke so fluently and knowledgeably, and because it went outside the box of UK football that late October day.

Tragically, it took the pandemic to tilt the emphasis on *Sports Report*, which is not a bad thing for a programme of such longevity. It can't be the same old, same old, but it hasn't been a serene, triumphal march to radio's Valhalla. Getting back to the normal mayhem in the 2021-22 season was all the programme's personnel longed for. When you're nudging 75, you can do without too many more crises.

Yet sports broadcasting is an ever-changing landscape and in the summer of 2022, a triumph for BBC Radio Sport's Rights Department constituted another challenge for *Sports Report*.

The programme's duration was halved from August 2022 to accommodate securing exclusive live commentary rights for the Premier League match that kicked off at 5.30 p.m. For the next three years at least, *Sports Report* will therefore end at 5.30. Some of the content that would normally feature in the run-up to the 606 show will have to be held over until half-time, around 6.20 p.m. A major production dilemma will be how much should be repeated from *Sports Report*, an hour earlier, while trying to include fresh, breaking stories – all within a framework of about 12 minutes, before the second half starts. It is much easier to accommodate the afternoon's major sporting events and reaction in a continuous hour than to shoehorn a truncated summary between a 45–50 minute live commentary bridge.

Understandably Radio Sport executives were jubilant to land the commentary rights to the 5.30 p.m. game, seeing off stern competition from talkSPORT. I am told that talkSPORT's head honchos were disappointed to lose the 5.30 rights and, in a highly competitive world, this was a substantial coup for 5 Live. Seven separate football commentary rights for live matches were up for auction and the BBC's successful bid meant that 5 Live will now have exclusive coverage of a Premier League game on Saturdays at 3.00 and 5.30 p.m., as well as the 4.30 kick-off on Sunday afternoon.

So in a hectic weekly schedule of exclusive Premier League commentaries, 5 Live is better placed than in previous seasons for bringing live commentary on the big games. The key figures in our Sports Department are convinced that success will bring in more listeners after 5.30 on a Saturday and that *Sports Report's* current figures for the hour will be surpassed. I'm told that live Premier League commentaries secure the biggest audience figures on our Radio Sport output and at a time when the BBC faces stern examination from many quarters about its continued relevance, increased numbers of listeners is clearly vital.

It would be purblind to be sniffy at any chance of boosting our audience figures on Saturdays, leading into the early evenings, but what does this mean for the health of *Sports Report*?

I don't expect my veneration for such an old companion to be matched by younger colleagues or indeed many listeners. *Sports Report* is not the soundtrack for every sports fan on a Saturday and I have to concede that live commentaries of big games are a pivotal part of the whole 5 Live Sport package.

But for just one hour a week, *Sports Report* has offered something different. Distinctiveness should also be part of radio's appeal. Of course, *Sports Report* has to adapt, as it has done so often down the years, but curtailing it by 50 per cent will test the production team and its reporters/commentators.

Ben Gallop, Head of Radio Sport, is convinced the new football deal will bring *Sports Report* to a wider audience. 'The new Premier League rights deal means Saturdays are going to be even bigger for 5 Live Sport. With live commentaries at 3.00 and 5.30 p.m. that means more listeners for *Sports Report* on a busy day of top-class football. It goes without saying that all our coverage needs to keep adapting, given the pace of change in the world of sport – but it will always be done with a sense of cherishing what made world-class programmes like *Sports Report* so special in the first place'.

I wish I could be as bullish. I recall the frustrations of many of us at the 5.30 p.m. kick-offs more than a decade ago and the relief at losing the exclusive rights after a few years, with *Sports Report* reverting to an hour's duration. But as a BBC lifer, I must bow to greater knowledge and expertise in such matters. In the modern argot, I must suck it up.

* * *

The various challenges posed to *Sports Report* over the years were as nothing compared to the traumas suffered by so many victims who suffered grievously from the attentions of Stuart Hall for so long.

One of *Sports Report's* most distinctive broadcasters ruined countless lives at a time when his contributions to the programme were being lauded for their distinctiveness and good humour. When Hall's appalling crimes were unearthed, they cast the darkest possible shadow over Sports Report.

A comprehensive history of *Sports Report* cannot ignore how such a constant presence on the show concealed his dark, predatory side for so long, without any of his colleagues being aware of his shocking excesses.

Stuart Hall was undoubtedly a character, bursting on to *Sports Report* for decades with his unique mixture of bombast, theatrical delivery and the chutzpah to use all the adjectival excesses he could cram into his reports. He was popular with so many listeners, and tolerated by *Sports Report* production teams, because he sounded different.

In 2014, Hall was revealed as a sex offender, sentenced to three years and 11 days for multiple sexual offences against children. He was released in December

2015, having served half his sentence. Hall had initially pleaded not guilty, but in April 2013 changed his plea to guilty to 14 charges of indecent assault involving 13 girls.

The sports department was shattered by the horrendous revelations. Hall had always been a singular man, playing an uproarious role on air and with radio sport colleagues on the rare occasions he worked with them, but no one in the department could honestly say they knew him. We were aware of his reputation as a major character on the North West media landscape, a dedicated social animal, but his dark secrets were simply that to his sports-room colleagues, who did not share the same BBC building as Hall. He didn't drop into the sports room at Salford, or London in earlier years; his manor was the TV building in Oxford Road, Manchester.

Hall was mainly employed by us on Saturdays. He would turn up at the ground, be wined and dined by the chairman of the host club, then just riff on air for a few hours. As the department came to terms with its collective revulsion, the BBC Sport executive who had to deal with the issue at the sharp end was Richard Burgess, then head of sports news and radio sport. He is now Head of UK News, TV and Radio.

Burgess was as startled as the rest of us by Hall's ghastly activities, 'When I was informed he was going to be arrested, I had to stand him down, because it was obviously going to be a media circus. When he was subsequently arrested, but not named, that created difficulties for us as a news operation and then other media named him. I had a very difficult conversation on the phone with his son, who vehemently denied all the allegations and thought we were just jumping on the bandwagon. It was a horrible call, because it was such a shock for us in radio sport, but I had to take him off air. Then, as soon as he admitted the charges, it was clear the BBC couldn't employ him again. This was done in concert with all the main BBC executives, going right to the top, but I was front line. It was a very challenging time.'

The horrified reaction in the department cannot be overstated. Stuart Hall brought lustre to *Sports Report* in his pomp, but his crimes were appalling and sympathy for his victims was, and remains, deep.

15

RAVE REVIEWS

There's no doubt that, compared to other long-established radio programmes, *Sports Report* has hidden its considerable light under a substantial bushel. Decade after decade, the change of personnel in the production team hasn't altered the prevailing ethos – get on the job with as little fuss as possible, strive to be the very best and let the adrenalin dissipate agreeably in the bar afterwards.

Pumping up the tyres of *Sports Report* isn't part of its DNA, despite its legendary stature, consistent quality and sheer staying power. Other long-running radio programmes accrue greater column inches in newspapers and magazines – whether it's a soap set in the fictional farming community of Ambridge (*The Archers*), semantic jousting between specious politicians and exasperated presenters (*Today*) or celebs revealing what music they'd take to a desert island (*Desert Island Discs*). The fact that all three occupy cherished places in the hearts of Radio 4 listeners may be significant, as they inhabit a domain that is vocal, demanding and sure of its place in the heart of cultural matters.

With *Sports Report*, it's been a case of just buggering on, as Churchill put it in wartime. I don't recall many trails on air just extolling the wares of *Sports Report*. Plugs for live sporting occasions, yes, and for the whole Saturday afternoon sporting experience, but not simply for a weekly sports programme of sustained excellence and technical triumphs against the odds. A programme that's been part of the radio fabric since George VI was on the throne.

But it's only sport. Many of the *bien pensants* who revere radio don't view sport with any degree of affection or respect. It's out on a promontory, to be tolerated, but not embraced. The occasional article in *Radio Times* over the years or a broadsheet writer's day in the *Sports Report* studio are dutifully logged for the reader's consumption. That'll do for another couple of years. Tick!

It's a situation that vexes *Sports Report*'s current presenter, Mark Chapman. 'We don't shout enough about what we do,' he says, 'We should be brasher, embracing competition, making more listeners aware of the immediacy and the thrills involved in the programme.' I agree. The national affection for *Sports Report* was never more obvious than on the day that I announced on Twitter that I had completed the deal to write this book. I wrote that any anecdotes or memories from listeners would be welcomed. The warm response and fondness of tone were hugely reassuring.

So listeners' tributes to *Sports Report* must occupy front and centre. Their loyalty and affection have been vital. Rajesh Patel summed up the unblinking devotion of the true believer, 'The first time my American wife heard me "singing" the signature tune, she thought I'd gone mad. She still doesn't get it. I still go to my snug at 16.55 for *SR* and wait avidly for the Southampton match report.'

That clarion call of 'Out of the Blue' has a particular significance for Kate Fletcher. She's a Manchester United supporter and her husband is a Liverpool fan. Nevertheless… 'We had the theme tune for walking down the aisle at our wedding in 2007. Then we were invited to the 60th anniversary special, recorded at Grimethorpe Colliery, and the band played 'Out of the Blue' live. Amazing… always special.'

Chris Green will always associate *Sports Report* with a desperate Saturday early in 2005 when he was caught up in the awful floods in Carlisle, when the two rivers flooded simultaneously for the first time in 150 years. Three people drowned, 1800 properties were flooded and Chris was stuck in his hotel, opposite Brunton Park. He and the other residents were trapped, able to move around only by using barstools as stepping stones. Chris, an author and communications executive, was writing a book called *Matchday – What Makes Saturday Special?*, featuring many of the inter-connecting people in the football industry. He'd been hoping to travel on to Gretna, to take in a Scottish Cup tie. Well, it certainly proved a special Saturday for Chris.

After being rescued by dinghy from the hotel – taken over the top of the cars and around wrought iron gates, wading chest high in darkness – the soaked and scared hotel residents were taken to a community centre to dry out and get some food. They felt like refugees. Then the mood lifted for Chris. 'Magically the opening bars of *Sports Report* floated across the hall. It's the Central Band of the RAF playing 'Out of the Blue'. I glance at my watch. It is, of course, 5.00 p.m. and I can hear the start of *Sports Report*. Only I can't really hear it and, to be honest, I don't have the nerve to wander over to listen to the scores. It is comforting enough to know that being in Britain at five o'clock on a Saturday evening, regardless of whatever situation you find yourself in, means *Sports*

Report. Living in Worcester and a West Brom supporter, it was always *Sports Report* that took us home down the M5 each Saturday evening.'

For Dave Smart, the music reminds him of his late father. 'We'd spend many weekends walking in the Peak District and I would be desperate to know the football results. We'd get into the car just before 1700: "and this is *Sports Report.*" Cue the music…' Tim Arnold also recalls precious time spent with his dad in the early 1970s, 'squashed next to him in a player's warm car travelling back from his team's game on some windswept field. Cancer took my dad just a few years later, adding to the poignancy.'

Jon Harvey hasn't forgotten driving back to Cornwall in the 1990s after watching Plymouth Argyle. 'Always lost radio signal driving through the tunnel crossing the Tamar Bridge, just as James Alexander Gordon started reading the classified results. Signal restored just in time for Scottish Division 2…' Phil Withall admits 'recreating imagined match highlights on a Subbuteo pitch as the reports came in. I may have been a strange child…' and for Phil Gardener it was, 'The music preceding the results, the definitive soundtrack to Saturday in the car coming back from the game. Should be the national anthem.'

Brian Winter remembers his time at a boarding school for the blind in Liverpool, in the early seventies. '*Sports Report* was always on in the minibus on the way back from our afternoon trips out. If we did not go out, it could be heard echoing around the school from many radios.'

For Gary Hayes, the *Sports Report* signature tune altered the path of his career. A devoted Chelsea fan, he used to listen to the show every Saturday with his father and four brothers, after leaving early from Stamford Bridge to get into their car. Gary, who now runs and produces sports podcasts after working in the communications department at Chelsea for a decade, was about to take a job in the USA as a football writer, covering the MLS. But *Sports Report* intervened.

'I was driving home and the signature tune came on. I said to my wife, "I can't leave, I can't get this in the US." My Dad had passed away by then, but I remembered how much it meant, being in the car with him and my brothers. It was a really special moment, remembering what I valued so much. The music told me not to leave England – and I didn't. And I never miss *Sports Report*.'

I was struck, reading all those hosannas, how important a role parents played in fostering an involvement with *Sports Report* among their children. That shared experience in travel and proximity at the match, then the journey home, listening to the programme, added up to a precious communality. The torch of intimacy was then passed on to the next generation, as *Sports Report* became an integral part of the family fabric.

That was certainly the experience of Daniel Taylor, the football writer of great distinction, with a groaning mantelpiece of awards in the past decade, for breaking so many important stories. But Taylor is at heart an old romantic, particularly when Nottingham Forest is involved. 'I loved being in the car with my dad, going home over Trent Bridge, after the latest masterclass under Brian Clough. Windows steamed up, freezing cold outside, listening to Sports Report's verdict on the match I had just seen. Usually, the reporter got it right'.

The Jesuit religious society has a motto, coined by its founder Ignatius of Loyola, that illuminates the importance of parental guidance in other, later spheres, 'Give me a child until he is seven and I will show you the man.' A lifetime of belief and devotion to a cause, calling or pastime can be indoctrinated successfully when you are young. Millions of listeners to *Sports Report* over eight decades owe it to their parents for introducing them to the programme.

That is uniformly the case with most of the presenters, contributors and production team members, decade after decade. Their fondness for the programme remains undimmed, decades after they left the BBC. Emily McMahon went to TV more than 30 years ago, but '*Sports Report* and working in the sports room was the happiest time of my career. Being in a football crowd, on a rare Saturday off, hearing 'Out of the Blue' as we filed out was always special.'

Sonja McLaughlan has covered many summer Olympics and is now an integral part of the BBC's Six Nations and athletics coverage, but she's adamant she owes almost everything to *Sports Report* in her formative years. 'Those five years I spent in the studio on production were a brilliant training for me. I was in awe of *Sports Report* before, during and after. You don't lose your love for that programme just because you're now doing other things.'

And those making the headlines were no different. Sir Trevor Brooking was a fan of the programme long before he adorned the West Ham and England midfield, then later a popular match summariser. 'Everyone who loved sport listened to it when I was a kid. After playing football with my brother in the back garden, I'd make sure I was inside for the start of *Sports Report*. The reporters were familiar and I trusted them when I became a pro.'

When he was a lad, Graham Gooch, former England cricket captain and devoted fan of West Ham, used to stand on an orange box alongside his dad at Upton Park to get a better view. 'It's always been part of my life, an institution like *Test Match Special*, and I still listen. For me, it adds to my national culture. I identify with *Sports Report* as a patriot, proud to be part of my growing up. In the Essex and England dressing rooms, we always tried to listen in if we were batting or it was raining.'

Matt Dawson, rugby union World Cup winner with England, loves the tension of post-match reactions, live on *Sports Report*. 'I tip my hat to the reporters who have to respond so quickly afterwards, then go and poke the bear, jousting with the players and managers. The passion you hear makes for fabulous radio, when it's live and raw.'

Mark Steel, comedian, author and a Crystal Palace supporter, agrees. 'The live interviews are microcosms of stress, triumph or despair. You can almost taste the emotion, it's so compelling, especially if the interviewee seems in a state of shock. I had a bleak childhood and *Sports Report* comforted me. It doesn't overdo it, like some crazy American channel, shouting at you, as if war is imminent.'

Seb Coe, one of this country's greatest athletes, has been an avid listener since he was a boy. He still has *Sports Report* on an app when working in Monaco as President of the IAAF. A Chelsea supporter for more than 50 years, he would fit his athletics schedule around the programme when running at home. 'In the winters, when I'd run at Crystal Palace or Cosford, I'd cut short my press conferences, so that I could be back in the car in time for the start of the programme. When I broke the indoor 1000 metres world record at Cosford, I managed to get to my car for the headlines and I was the lead story, alongside the famous signature tune. I was even ahead of the football news! Very chuffed.

'I remember the winter of 82/83 when I was injured. I followed Chelsea home and away. We needed to draw at Bolton to avoid relegation to the old Third Division and Clive Walker scored the equaliser in the 88th minute. A dash to my battered old Audi car, five of us euphoric all the way down the M6 and we celebrated in London as if we'd won the European Cup! But *Sports Report* was the soundtrack on the motorway' Coe knows all about the tension and intensity of media scrutiny after the event and he can appreciate both sides of the divide. 'I love it when the interviews are live and you don't quite know what's going to happen next. You feel as if you're actually there.'

Lee Child is an expert in building tension. As the author of the phenomenally successful Jack Reacher books, Child relishes the intensity of the post-match exchanges. An Aston Villa supporter, he used to walk two miles to the ground when young, then tune into *Sports Report* while driving to Manchester, once he started working in television. 'I bought a car radio for a fiver when I got my Mini, so I could listen to *Sports Report* on the M6 North, going back to Manchester. When you hear the scraping of the boots as the players clatter past the interview area and wonder how far the player or manager can be pushed after a bad result, you're wondering where this is going to lead. I love that.

'When we won the title in 1981, the radio kept us in touch with how Ipswich was doing at Middlesbrough when we were at Highbury. In the end, both Villa and Ipswich lost, so we won the championship. Listening to all the celebratory interviews on the radio was fantastic. Not so six years later when we got relegated. I was at a wedding reception at a vineyard in Kent and didn't leave my car until I'd heard all the inquests and sad interviews. When I finally got out of my car, there were many other slammed doors. There must have been a lot of Villa fans at that wedding!'

Another Villa supporter has an enduring love affair with the programme. Mervyn King, in the crosshairs of the banking crisis of 2008 as Governor of the Bank of England, knows about crises and defining moments. As a boy, he would stand on the Witton End with his father, then be glued to the radio on the way home to Wolverhampton. 'That signature tune was the calling card – I've got it on my ringtone for the football season and change it to the *Test Match Special* music for the summer.

'The programme is extraordinarily professional, with reporters sticking to their allotted timeslots, with so little time to spare. Every listener is, in effect, blind and *Sports Report* reaches out brilliantly. It conveys superbly the feeling of a game just finished as you are leaving the ground. Even when I studied at Cambridge it was part of my younger days and now, if I'm not in the car, I still want to hear it.'

For David Blunkett, the former cabinet minister, *Sports Report* was as much an education as the residential school he attended. Blind since birth, living in a poor part of Sheffield, he had to develop a tough self-reliance. 'My transistor radio came with me everywhere and it taught me the importance of good English, phrased with intelligence and care. It was a seminal programme for me. The best reports were masterpieces of micro-English and helped me understand the importance of a good vocabulary.

'As a blind person, the geography of the pitch is vital, so that I can picture where the ball is and if the action is going from left to right, or the other way. The best of those on *Sports Report* do that and add a bit of poetry to their descriptions – all at short notice. It's a great skill and hugely valued by blind people. That's why I still listen to the programme. The games come alive with the best radio reporters.'

Andy Burnham shares David Blunkett's political affiliations, as well as affection for *Sports Report* since childhood. Coming from a family of Evertonians, he'd sit in his grandmother's front room at Aintree, four miles from Goodison, waiting for his elders to come back from the match. 'I was only four or five – too young to go then – and I'd get the eyewitness accounts from them and then listen to *Sports Report* to see if they matched up. It was a Magical Mystery Tour for me, appropriately enough. I don't recall ever listening to a report of a match I was at when I wondered, "Was I at the same game?" It's authentic, engaged and doesn't talk down to the fans.'

That might be due to a simple formula that hasn't altered much since Angus Mackay began his form of benevolent despotism back in 1948. Mackay's fealty was not challenged and the programme's shape owes everything to his vision. Results, reports, interviews, opinions.

Paul Hayward, chief sportswriter at four national newspapers, in the business for more than 40 years, says, 'The papers aren't the reference point on match days anymore. We are so heavily controlled in the work environment by press officers with commercial aims and agents who decide if a player speaks or not. Access is a commodity. You wouldn't know that from listening to *Sports Report*. It rarely leaves a big match without a key interview and I love the drama associated with that, when it's live.

'If there's one hour a week of radio that I want to inhabit, it's *Sports Report*. It has resonance, and significance and excitement. We can all calm down and be informed; it doesn't think of itself as shouty entertainment. Its best reporters are skilled, trained and disciplined, and the presenters through the decades have been uniformly outstanding, juggling so many balls, with the producer in your ear, while managing to talk with fluency and authority.

'That marvellous signature tune connects all phases of my life – from Matt Busby to Marcus Rashford. When I'm in the car with my young son and the music comes on, it tells him to pay attention. Even he is quiet after 5.00 p.m. on a Saturday, because we know we're in for escapism and enjoyment.'

Patrick Barclay is the only football writer to have worked for all four national broadsheets and he believes the programme appeals to the conservative instincts of sports fans. 'So many sports fans want to be comforted by the familiar. It embraced a Golden Age in that first decade – the dawn of the NHS, Mount Everest being conquered, a new young queen, England winning back the Ashes after so long, the four-minute mile, Stanley Matthews at last winning an FA Cup winner's medal – and it helped to give us sense of national identity.'

Mike Costello, BBC Radio's athletics and former boxing correspondent was weaned on the programme. 'I grew up in council flats just off the Old Kent Road and I'd sit on our balcony listening to *Sports Report*. I've worked at the BBC since I was 16 and getting on to the programme for the first time was to me like an athlete getting an Olympics vest. It's that special. If I was doing a big fight later on a Saturday night it was always a privilege to get on the programme, to set the scene and plug our coverage – even if the scheduled two-minute piece was cut down to 30 seconds, because a football manager turned up for a live interview!'

John Nicholson, football writer and author, is an unashamed football romantic, for whom *Sports Report* has bridged the decades. 'It's vital to the national conversation and a coda to Saturday afternoons, a beautiful bridge to a Saturday evening. I was a sensitive, isolated boy and felt comforted by *Sports Report*. I still feel the same way now. I hope it keeps its informal authority and doesn't try to be youthful and downmarket. Other sports programmes are more chaotic – this one has a shape to it, a sense of unity'

Graeme Swann, former England cricketer and Newcastle United fan, loves the simplicity of the programme. '*Sports Report* is part of my life. I'd be in the car with my dad as he drove back from his sports club and we'd stop for fish and chips, then listen to the programme, food on our laps. The signature tune made me feel warm and tingly. My kids love the music and if we're in the car, they know why I take so long to drive home, because I don't want to miss any of the programme. It conjures up memories of cigarettes and pint pots with handles after my dad had played rugby.'

Peter Drury, football commentator and accomplished wordsmith, relished the company of *Sports Report* in a lonely childhood and was glued to the programme on Saturdays 'After my last stint on *Sports Report*, in February 1998, it hit me that I was no longer part of it anymore. I was joining ITV and just couldn't turn down the offer, but I wept on the way back from Leeds v Southampton, all the way as far as Nottingham. I had a profound sense of loss. I have never felt so proud of being part of a great team. My career highlight remains appearing on *Sports Report* for the first time.'

John Motson, one of the foremost football commentators over the last five decades, still has a soft spot for the unit where he spent his formative years. 'I was only in the radio sports department for three years, but was honoured to be a part of it. I was proud to present *Sports Report* a couple of times. It was great to have it on my CV. *Sports Report* was, and remains, the market leader.'

Peter Reid, former footballer and manager was, and remains, a huge fan. '*Sports Report* is a national institution. I'd listen to it in my dad's car and still do, when I leave a game 10 minutes early. You could trust their reporters. They were always constructive.'

Barry Davies, one of the great all-round sporting commentators, finally realised an ambition in his fifties 'I presented *Sports Report* a couple of times in the late eighties and I'd always wanted to say, "This is *Sports Report*." Some of my television colleagues didn't understand how much it meant to me, having worked on the programme years earlier.'

David Pleat, football manager and later a shrewd pundit, grew up with *Sports Report*. 'It was the perfect programme for a sports-mad youngster, delivering lucid, accurate reports from superb wordsmiths. The excitement, the tingling – you couldn't miss it. As a manager, I was always fairly treated by the programme. No bias or hysteria.'

John Murray, the BBC's football correspondent, would hear snippets from the programme via fans' transistor radios while walking back to his dad's car after watching Carlisle. He knows that the challenges are tougher today. 'Access post-match to the key people gets harder and harder, when emotions are running high and there's a massive burst of adrenalin. But we still come up with something our competitors lack.'

Lawrie McMenemy, former football manager and pundit, appreciated what the programme could offer a manager who was under pressure. '*Sports Report* was always very fair, allowing us to talk to millions before the press conference. We could get our point of view across to the nation before the press gave its opinion.'

Dan Walker, former BBC TV presenter, is well aware of the programme's stature. 'It's still an appointment to listen. I'm as excited to listen to it now as when I was a kid. I was thrilled to present it once during the football season. Some of the great broadcasters have adorned *Sports Report*.'

Dion Dublin, ex player, TV presenter and pundit would usually swerve other media outlets after a match, but he'd co-operate with *Sports Report*, because he trusted its values. 'When I was a young player, the older team-mates would encourage me to go on the show, because it was so highly respected. And I listened to it in the car. It's a one-stop shop, ticking all the boxes.'

Jonathan Pearce, BBC TV football commentator, has massive professional respect for it. 'When I first started in the business, *Sports Report* was THE football sound. The benchmark. I trust Mark Chapman as presenter and they have some brilliant reporters with great contacts and local knowledge.'

David Lloyd, former England batsman and coach, still listens when coming back from watching his club, Accrington Stanley. 'Essential listening all my life. Eamonn Andrews' stature helped break the mould for people like me in broadcasting who had distinctive regional accents. Eamonn's quality proved that you didn't have to talk posh to be a decent sports broadcaster.'

Robbie Savage, former player, who co-presents the fans' forum, *606*, directly after the show ends also loved its immediacy. 'I think warmly about *Sports Report*, listening to it in my parents' car as we drove back home from away matches, when I was playing for Crewe, all those years ago.'

That point about parental influence isn't lost on an Irishman – Conor McNamara, gifted football, rugby union and golf commentator, and a regular contributor. 'People in the UK sometimes take *Sports Report* for granted. Growing up in Limerick, we didn't. My dad used to tell me: "This is the 'top gun' – these guys are the best in the world at their jobs." When I joined them 20 years ago, I knew I was with the crème de la crème.'

Clare Balding felt the same way before she ever appeared on the show. 'I think there's always been more to it than just a job. It matters to the people who are listening. You're doing it for other people – not just you.'

Broadcasters such as Clare and Conor have been a valued part of the *Sports Report* landscape in recent decades, but I also wanted a tribute from someone who has followed the programme through all its tweaks and modernisations. As an all-rounder among media performers, Sir Michael Parkinson is in the Mount Rushmore class. Polemical newspaper columnist, reliably brilliant radio and TV presenter across a multitude of platforms, and still a keen observer of our trade in his eighties, Parky was a convert to *Sports Report* at the age of 13, when it was first broadcast. After establishing himself in the front rank of contributors to the programme for several decades, his pugnacious editorials and debating skills in the studio cut through the flim-flam, eschewing consensual platitudes.

Like any self-respecting Yorkshireman, praise from him has to be earned. He is unstinting about *Sports Report*. 'It represented the very best of sports broadcasting and an invitation to take part was an accolade. A call from the producer to take part was regarded by any journalist worth his or her salt as being an indication you were in the best of company. I was a fan, a contributor, and grew up listening to and learning from a programme that was a fascinating mix of vigorous journalism and perceptive insight.'

Parkinson always had something stimulating to say, particularly about those sports administrators who were about as relevant as a regimental goat. His thousand-yard stare at sport's imperfections and hypocrisies inspired my generation of listeners and those who later became colleagues. We all remember a flinty broadside from Parky on *Sports Report*, so the eulogy of the previous paragraph should be cherished.

16

SPORTS REPORT – THE FUTURE

Having basked in the eulogies in the previous chapter, it's high time to take a sharp, forensic look at *Sports Report*'s future. Is it still relevant in this multi-dimensional media age, when consumers have so much choice in what they want to hear or see – and when?

The sports media has never been more competitive. Younger sports fans have social media to hand, with Twitter, Instagram and Facebook providing instant access. That was reflected in the decision to drop the classified football results at the start of the 2022–23 football season, reflecting the reality of a shortened *Sports Report*, and the results being readily available elsewhere. While a parent drives away from a match, listening to *Sports Report* or another station on the car radio, the tech-smart offspring is plugged in somewhere, watching a compilation of goals just after the final whistle.

Why would that savvy youngster wait a few minutes longer for *Sports Report*'s take on the afternoon's action, when the chance to make up your own mind about the quality of a particular goal is there at the punch of a button? But once you've seen the goals in a five-minute glut, where do you go next? Isn't there scope for texture, for developing news stories from the games, for expert opinion from neutrals and then the subjective take from both sides?

A radio programme starting at 5.00 p.m. has been a companion for the modern, multi-tasking football fan. The basic remit for *Sports Report* is no different to how it was mapped out by Angus Mackay in 1948 – news, opinions, insights. A newspaper of the air. Only the duration has changed at times. It's a shared personal experience, a social glue bringing you the drama of the sporting day while you get on with other things. But priorities change. Just because *Sports Report* has now been halved to accommodate a 5.30 kick-off doesn't alter its immediacy. Mark Steel, an enthusiastic debunker of cosy myths, is nevertheless happy to bathe in *Sports Report*'s comforting presence. 'It gets sport about right, with irreverence as well as information. It keeps you company.'

But the programme doesn't settle for a permanently roseate glow. Social media may indeed park some tanks on *Sports Report*'s lawn, but it's mighty handy for the production team to get its message across throughout *Sport on 5* and then after 5.00 p.m.. The 5 Live and BBC Sport Twitter feeds total around 10 million followers and the website constantly unpeels developing news stories on Saturday afternoons. Presenter Mark Chapman is an acknowledged master at pulling out a plum from the over-stacked basket of facts – the ideal choice to drive on the modern approach to sports broadcasting on *Sports Report*.

The competition provided by social media is welcomed by the production team and its influence is readily utilised. All that's needed then is a willingness to rip up the running order and react accordingly to a breaking story. I had personal experience of this editorial flexibility in November 2021 when Middlesbrough's manager, Neil Warnock, revealed he'd been sacked soon after his team had drawn at West Bromwich Albion. Ostensibly my work was done for the day, but I've always hung around at the ground until *Sports Report* has finished, reasoning that other sections of the football media are just as likely as me to come up with a story from their post -match sleuthing. If they do, good luck to them – but it's then incumbent on me to stand up the tale and get it on *Sports Report*.

So it proved at the Hawthorns. As Warnock came out to discharge his post-match duties (always a task he relished), a statement from Middlesbrough dropped on social media that he was finished at the club. That old chestnut about 'parting company' with hints of 'mutual agreement' was trotted out, a situation I doubted. Now Warnock was always a Marmite managerial figure, loved or loathed depending on who you supported, but he didn't duck many questions in his 34 years in League management at 14 different clubs. Having set a new record in midweek of 1602 games as a manager, Warnock was a figure of substance, whatever you thought of him, so this was a story unfolding in front of me.

I was alerted to the statement at 5.17 p.m., plugged back into my ISDN system and proceeded to work out how best we could cover the story. Fortunately, my tireless colleagues on BBC Radio Tees had got to Warnock quickly in the interview area and his thoughts were being recorded back in our Salford studio, as Warnock readily debunked the official line from the club. There was no mutual agreement, he had been sacked. And he was happy to let everyone know that...

'I was told this morning that I'm leaving the club today... They're going in a different direction, they've got somebody to come in... I'm disappointed... I haven't really had much support at the club, bringing players in... I told the players just before we went out that I was leaving after the game and to let me finish on a high.'

One of the more unusual pre-match motivational speeches but it was refreshing to hear a manager refuse to toe the party line, so we were in business. Just 10 minutes after we had heard about the sacking, I was ready to go live on air, linking into the Warnock revelations. The editor decided to delay it for a couple of minutes, running it straight after the news headlines for extra impact, and I asked for more time, so that I could offer some insights into a combustible character whom I'd known for nearly 40 years. I also wanted to suggest that Chris Wilder was firmly in the frame. My request was granted and the live package was aired by 5.35 p.m.

It was satisfying because our TV opposition was by now off the air and Warnock had provided a typically cranky slant on an unusual sacking. I also appreciated the trust invested in me by the programme's editor. Graham McMillan knew I had too much respect for *Sports Report* just to showboat in my comments; that I had some germane thoughts to offer. And I was quietly pleased when Chris Wilder's appointment as Warnock's successor was confirmed that night.

Not too self-satisfied, though. Anyone with any miles on the clock as a football reporter gets things wrong at times. Only a couple of months earlier I had vouchsafed the opinion that Aston Villa, having bought wisely after selling Jack Grealish, would be a good bet to finish in the top six. After 11 league games, they sacked their manager. So only a quiet smile was in order...

The key point, though, is that I was trusted by the production team. That's something that I and my other senior colleagues value. I have never been told what line to take or questions to ask after a match. That just increases the respect we have for the programme. It's precious to us, but we are cut some slack when it comes to how we write our post-match reports.

Irreverence is also embraced – the conviction that it's only sport, not crucial in the overall scheme of things. You are allowed to poke fun. Now and then a sense of the ridiculous can get you out of a tight corner. That was the case in the 2018–19 season when I conducted a live interview at Molineux with Wolves' Mexican striker, Raúl Jiménez. A prolific goalscorer, very popular with the Wolves fans as soon as he arrived at the club, Jiménez was an obvious choice for a chat after he scored the winner one Saturday. I had been assured he could handle the interview in English, but it didn't go terribly well initially. I say this in the knowledge that Jiménez's English was far better than my Spanish, so there was no tension as we conducted a rather halting interview, but I could sense restiveness back in the studio as we faltered.

I simply wanted to engage more with the charming, smiling Jiménez. In desperation, I threw in a wild card, 'That's a rather nice aftershave you've got on, Raúl.' Light bulb moment! Jiménez perked up immediately, launched into an exhaustive explanation of where he had first picked up his aftershave (the United States), name-checking the department store in Birmingham that provided him with regular supplies of it, and we parted genially, swearing undying affection, with me sniffing his neck like the Bisto Kid loving his gravy.

The point of that encounter is that it was welcomed back in the studio, because it was different. We are encouraged to play the fool if necessary, as long as it's entertaining and it gets you somewhere. Not something in plentiful supply when you're flicking around on your tablet, searching for another camera angle for that winning goal at Anfield or the Etihad.

I can't think of many basics that *Sports Report* hasn't covered in terms of breaking news stories in its hour of transmission. The engine may sound as if it's ticking over smoothly enough, but lift the bonnet and you'll find there's a lot going on. The online service and social media operate brilliantly for those not tuning in, but they can't compensate for those moments when the running order is again ripped up and the presenter links live to a developing story, in the wake of a dramatic match or press conference. We also have the back-up provided by our colleagues in BBC TV Sport, in case we can't stand up a rumour or a controversial post-match comment by someone of relevance. I know I speak for all my radio colleagues that the challenge of getting the key interview on air before our producer opts to use the *Match of the Day* clip is something that drives us on. Lose that sense of competitiveness and *Sports Report's* validity would be diluted.

Bob Shennan, now a high-ranking BBC executive, but formerly the football producer then *Sports Report* editor, posits the weekly challenge. 'It's about getting the top interview of the day, in a draughty corridor, ahead of everyone else and 12 hours before the newspapers hit the streets. A live programme like *Sports Report* is a shared experience in the classic radio way. And the production team have to know what to do straight away, when the signature tune has started. Simple really, but you have to keep earning the love and loyalty of the audience.'

However, it's never been harder to retain that connection with the audience. That's why *Sports Report* will always sound different, a decade on. If you trawled through the archives, the programme may have maintained the core values, but its sound and approach differ markedly. It's then a matter of opinion whether the inevitable tinkering is justified.

Whenever any of the former team members of *Sports Report* meet at social gatherings, there's always an impassioned debate about the current health of the programme. Eeyore invariably outnumbers Pangloss, the conclusion being that *Sports Report* isn't a patch on its halcyon age – whenever that was. Normally, that's an opinion reached in sorrow, rather than anger, an awareness that in a less competitive age, *Sports Report* often had the field to itself. The only serious competition came from bosses in the television industry, eager to poach our most talented broadcasters and producers.

If there's one sentiment standing out from my research, it's the affection for the programme from former colleagues. They take no pleasure in stating that *Sports Report* is diminished through seismic changes in media coverage – for example, the lack of intriguing 3.00 p.m. kick-offs in the top flight, due to TV shifting them to other start times over the weekend. Many conclude sadly that *Sports Report* will become marginalised, if not already.

It would be ridiculous to pretend that all is serene amid the frenzied world of Saturday afternoon competition. So, for me, *Sports Report*'s key challenge is to remain distinctive, stimulating, ready to adapt swiftly to events. We must ignore how TV and other radio stations cover the unfolding post-match dramas. If they get the drop on us over a big story, then find out why on Monday and try to learn from it. If we couldn't do anything about it, don't dwell on it. As many a harassed sporting press officer has burbled to me, 'We draw a line under it and move on.'

Even though *Sports Report* has often had other sports as its top story, football must retain its primacy in the show. It would be perverse to compete with the world's most popular sport. Jürgen Klopp captured the essence of football in the affections of so many when he said, 'It's the most important of the least important things in life,' while the game's timeless appeal was vividly captured by the writer Arnold Bennett way back in 1911, when one of his characters said in his novel, *The Card*, 'Why, you silly goose, didn't you know? Football has to do with everything.'

I wouldn't cleave to the dogmas of Messrs Klopp and Bennett, but football coverage should continue to reflect the public appeal that's increased since the explosion of satellite coverage 30 years ago. To do otherwise would be obtuse and highly damaging to the programme. Other sports get in-depth coverage when justified editorially, but football must remain the bulwark.

But what do the major BBC executives think about *Sports Report*'s future? Young Turks enjoying their new, enhanced surroundings at Broadcasting House are often keen to make their mark swiftly, tilting at a windmill that's been part of the BBC fabric for generations. No point in promoting fresh blood unless that gimlet-eyed executive gets the chance to make waves.

So is *Sports Report* in the crosshairs? Not according to those familiar with the prevailing winds of change. As a former controller of Radio 5 Live and Radio 2, as well as the Head of BBC Sport, Bob Shennan has ascended the slippery pole impressively since he joined our sports room as a trainee producer, back in 1987. As the BBC's group Managing Director, he is ideally qualified to assess how *Sports Report* is viewed in the corridors of power. In his opinion, favourably.

'It's true that the *Today* programme would be followed more closely by most of the members of the BBC executive board, but they all respect *Sports Report*, even if they're not devotees like myself. If you've been in business for nearly 75 years, with such a strong pedigree, you're allowed to tick over, even if many board members don't actively champion it. It's a phenomenal achievement to keep going so long, testament to the skills that make *Sports Report* so special.'

That's also the view of the current Head of Radio Sport, Ben Gallop, a BBC staffer since 1998, who has observed closely the various tweaks to the programme. 'It would be ludicrous if younger people saw *Sports Report* in the same way as people in their sixties or seventies, but the way we ramp up social media to promote what a brilliant product it is shows how we have adapted, remained flexible. The present production team is very proud of the programme's lineage, tradition and expertise.'

Gallop sees absolutely no reason why *Sports Report* shouldn't continue to thrive and, among many sound reasons for that, he cites the attitude of those at the top of the BBC. The Director-General, Tim Davie, is renowned as a massive sports enthusiast; a Crystal Palace fan who listens regularly to 5 Live's sports output and is a huge supporter of *Sports Report*.

But the programme must continue to fight its corner gamely, seeing off competitors by sheer weight of numbers. This is where perception in the media can be illusory. Much is made in the newspapers and social media of the success Jeff Stelling pulled off on Sky on Saturday afternoons – linking *Soccer Saturday* nimbly and amusingly, with contributions from former players in the studio and reporters out at matches. Its timing usually stacks up against *Sport on Five*, then *Sports Report*. Stelling is a master at anchoring the programme and it pulled in rave reviews down the years for a show that was basically radio with pictures, with no live action allowed.

It's looser technically than *Sport on 5* and *Sports Report*, and less ambitious in its lack of other sporting alternatives, but highly valued in the media world. Yet how many actually watch it? In the days after Stelling announced his retirement from *Soccer Saturday* in October 2021, social media and newspapers went big on his departure – and no one who worked with Jeff in BBC Sport would begrudge him such recognition. He was named Sports Broadcaster of the Year for four successive years for good reason.

Yet Jeff's valedictory announcement was hardly seismic in terms of audience size. On the two Sky channels featuring *Soccer Saturday* that afternoon, a combined total of 490,000 tuned in. After 5.00 p.m., it was only broadcast on Sky Sports News (the Premier League channel was previewing Tottenham v Manchester United) and it drew an average audience of 170,000. During that same timescale, 5 Live Sport and *Sports Report* had an average total audience of 1.46 million, while all local radio in England totalled 1.389 million in that period and 562,000 at 5.00 p.m., and our commercial rivals talkSPORT had 322,000. I doubt if *Soccer Saturday's* figures will soar, now that Jeff is, after all, staying on.

Since time immemorial, television has always scooped greater coverage than radio in the eyes of the rest of the media. It's deemed glamorous, all-pervasive. Yet *Final Score*, BBC TV's rival to *Soccer Saturday* and 5 Live Sport had an average audience between 4.00 and 5.00 p.m. (when it went off air) of 1.36 million on the day of Stelling's announcement. So the audience on Radio 5 Live between midday and 6.00 p.m. that day trumped our most obvious competitors in this country. Recent audience figures confirm our continued lead over our rivals. From midday-6pm Radio 5 Live trounced talkSPORT (almost 1.75 million to just over 900,000), and edged clear of all BBC local radio stations in England (just over 1.6 million) while between 5-6pm *Sports Report* had more than double talkSPORT's figures.

It's not as if radio is now cowering in the corner, shielding its eyes from the television juggernaut. A total of 89 per cent of the UK population tune into radio each week, while 29 per cent of adults listen via a mobile phone or tablet, ensuring that *Sports Report* can easily be accessed by busy people on the move. With 38 million having access to a digital radio – more than half the UK population – radio has no need to feel intimidated in a crowded market place.

These figures don't breed complacency at *Sports Report* Towers. The executives are well aware that it's vital to the programme that the period between 2.45 p.m. and 5.15 p.m., when no live matches are on TV, is essential to *Sports Report's* wellbeing. No other league in Europe has this sacrosanct time, with the desire paramount to maintain a sustainable football pyramid. The alternative of 10 different kick-off times over the weekend – which was the case during some months of Covid in 2020 – and just one at 3.00 p.m. on Saturdays would be damaging to *Sports Report*, thriving as it does on reaction to that afternoon's key football results.

Sports Report is used to confounding the sceptics. No one but Angus Mackay thought that it would last very long, as he toured the regions in the early winter of 1947, drumming up technical support from the engineers and outside broadcast producers. When the programme expanded to an hour in 1955, it was made quite clear to Mackay that it was on an experimental basis of three months. In 2004, when *Sports Report* was truncated in favour of live Premier League commentaries, starting at 5.15 p.m., then at 5.30 p.m., many felt the jig was up for the programme. Six years later, it returned to a full hour, still in rude health, even if some key production staff left in sadness, because it just didn't feel the same. In 2020, much of the broadcasting landscape was altered for a time, due to Covid, and *Sports Report* had to be nimble on its feet to compensate for the lack of Premier League analysis and reaction.

The historical sweep of *Sports Report* is remarkable. When it first appeared, no black boxer had held a British title under the Boxing Board of Control regulations. You had to be white to qualify. Just a few months earlier that draconian rule was abolished and, later in 1948, Randolph Turpin became the first black British champion. Now we have countless sports performers taking the knee in support of racial equality, after Muhammad Ali previously became the most popular sportsman in the world. Twelve-year-old Lester Piggott won his first race as a jockey at Haydock Park; 73 years later, a woman rode the Grand National winner for the first time. In 1948, the BBC's Board of Governors wouldn't allow any mention of betting, in case the Corporation was accused of encouraging gambling. It would be another 10 years before that dictate was relaxed, after ITV started to cover racing and happily broadcast the odds. Can you imagine broadcasting any race and not featuring the odds?!

Footballers knew their place in 1948, in the days of the maximum wage and trips home from the ground on the bus, sat alongside the supporters. Many hoped to run a pub on retirement, if they'd saved enough money from their career. Today, a young man called Marcus Rashford can take on the government and embarrass it over its policy on free school meals. Stanley Matthews, Footballer of the Year in 1948, was 41 before he received a CBE in 1956. Rashford was just 24, when decorated by the future king, who nattered away happily with him about football at the investiture.

Millions of sports fans have sat in their cars after 5.00 p.m. on a Saturday, determined not to miss a particular report, having rushed back from the ground. That was certainly the experience of Alan Shearer, now a regular contributor to the programme, as he prepares for his stint on Match of the Day that evening. 'That theme tune sticks out – getting in the car in time to hear it, then the results. It was a constant. When I started playing as a pro, it was always a pleasure to come on *Sports Report*, but even when we'd had a bad day, I'd still go on it, because of my respect for the programme and those happy childhood memories, listening to it in my dad's car'. So many have planned their bath-time or household chores around *Sports Report*. It's helped make interminable journeys around gridlocked motorways more palatable. Meanwhile, 'Out of the Blue' continues to strike terror into the hearts of many reporters, who haven't yet written a word, as Hubert Bath's plangent tune rings out at 5.00 p.m. Plus ça change…

Sports Report won't be stamped out. Tumbleweed isn't blowing through its studio; it's not yet a museum piece; it's in robust health. It remains an integral part of people's Saturday afternoons. The clamour for change in broadcasting gets ever more strident, but any executive who decides on a Poundshop *Sports Report*, stripping away its essential ingredients, will be besmirching a much-loved radio institution. Hard-nosed decisions have to be made at times. Dropping the classified football results is the latest in a long line, reflecting the necessity of keeping abreast of modernity. But sometimes it's wiser not to tamper unduly, especially when such a vital programme continues to stride confidently towards its century.

That's the immediate task facing the production team, feeling their way towards a revamped *Sports Report*. Every minute up to 5.30 p.m. will be precious. No time for waffle or persiflage, with tough decisions ahead of the producer on the day. Discipline from the reporters will be more essential than ever. I can visualise Angus Mackay, lurking in the studio, glaring with baleful eye at his stopwatch, deciding which reporters won't be working next Saturday after exceeding their allotted time in the match report.

Ben Gallop – as he should be – is convinced the new commentary deal won't chip away at *Sports Report's* stature. 'It's a remarkable achievement for *Sports Report* still to be thriving after 75 years. I can't wait to hear how the team move it forward in a new weekend schedule on the most popular sports radio network in the UK'.

Many hours were spent in the summer of '22, pondering how the producers and editors could preserve *Sports Report's* authority while dealing with its new time restraints. With such a small, dedicated production team there is precious little time to stop, think and take a sideways step during transmission. But there's never been a more pressing need for the programme to sound different from the rest. It must not be just a warm-up for the 5.30 p.m. kick-off. It needs time to settle down, but it must sound distinctive.

The task is to remain, in the words of Patrick Collins, 'a weekly miracle'.

17

SPORTS REPORT HEADLINES
1948–2022

Sports Report is fundamentally about the past 75 years of sporting history, both domestically and internationally. It has embraced some sports that drifted in and out of fashion down the decades – for example, speedway, motor racing and snooker in the early years – while reflecting the nation's loyalty towards established favourites such as football, both rugby codes, horse racing and cricket.

Authentic stars from outside the UK have always been welcome on the programme – from Joe Louis, Rocky Marciano, Jack Nicklaus, Arnold Palmer, Muhammad Ali and Franz Beckenbauer to Boris Becker and Roger Federer.

If they've been willing to talk to *Sports Report*, they go on air. From Joe Davis to Ronnie O'Sullivan, Matt Busby to Alf Ramsey, Brian Clough to Gareth Southgate, Jackie Kyle to Martin Johnson. The line stretches from Gordon Richards to Frankie Dettori, Fred Perry to Andy Murray, Stirling Moss to Lewis Hamilton, Denis Compton to Ben Stokes.

Amid the following roll call of memorable sporting occasions since 1948, there's just a minority of illustrious performers who haven't graced *Sports Report* at some stage.

1948

- The London Olympics include four gold medals for Dutch sprinter Fanny Blankers-Koen.
- Don Bradman leads Australia's 'Invincibles' to a 4-0 Ashes series win against England.

1949

- Portsmouth win the first of two successive League Championships – they have not won the title again.
- Sam Snead wins the first of his three Masters titles at Augusta.

1950

- England are beaten 1-0 by the United States in a World Cup match in Belo Horizonte.
- Ramadhin and Valentine bowl the West Indies to their first series victory in England.

1951

- Maureen Connolly triumphs at the US Open – the first of nine Grand Slam singles titles by the age of 19.
- Sugar Ray Robinson wins the World Middleweight title against Jake LaMotta.

1952

- Matt Busby's Manchester United are crowned League Champions for the first time in 41 years.
- Emil Zátopek wins the 5000k, 10,000k and Marathon gold medals at the Helsinki Olympics.

1953

- Stanley Matthews inspires Blackpool to a 4–3 FA Cup Final victory over Bolton.
- Ferenc Puskás leads Hungary to a stunning 6–3 win over England at Wembley.
- Sir Gordon Richards wins the Derby for the only time aboard Pinza, beating the Queen's Aureole into second place.

1954

- Roger Bannister becomes the first athlete to run a mile in under four minutes.
- 18-year-old Lester Piggott rides the first of his nine Derby winners on Never Say Die.
- Juan Manuel Fangio wins the F1 World title for a second time.

1955

- Chelsea win the League title for the first time – 50 years after their formation.
- England bowl out New Zealand for 26 to win the Auckland Test by an innings.
- Rocky Marciano stops Britain's Don Cockell in the ninth round to retain his World Heavyweight title.

1956

- Jim Laker takes 19 wickets to win the Old Trafford Test – England retain the Ashes 2–1 against Australia
- The Queen Mother's Devon Loch ridden by Dick Francis stumbles yards from the finish of the Grand National to hand victory to E.S.B.
- Goalkeeper Bert Trautmann breaks his neck but plays on as Manchester City beat Birmingham City 3–1 in the FA Cup Final.

1957

- Great Britain and Ireland win the Ryder Cup for the first time in 24 years.
- England win the Grand Slam after a 16–3 victory over Scotland.

1958

- Eight Manchester United players are killed in the Munich Air Disaster.
- Garry Sobers hits 365 not out – the highest Test innings at the time – for West Indies against Pakistan.
- Mike Hawthorn beats Stirling Moss by one point to take the F1 World title.

1959

- Manager Stan Cullis leads Wolves to their third League Championship in six years.
- 23-year-old Gary Player wins the Open Championship – the first of his nine major titles.

1960

- An 18-year-old boxer called Cassius Clay wins Olympic gold in Rome.
- Real Madrid thrash Eintracht Frankfurt 7–3 to win the European Cup Final in Glasgow.
- The first Test in Brisbane between Australia and West Indies ends in a tie – the first in Test history.

1961

- Tottenham Hotspur become the first team for 64 years to win the League and Cup double.
- Angela Mortimer beats Christine Truman in an all-British singles final at Wimbledon, as Rod Laver wins the first of his four men's titles.

1962

- Brazil win the World Cup for the second time in a row.
- Top scorer Alan Gilzean helps Dundee to the Scottish League title for the first and only time.

1963

- Tottenham become the first British club to win a European trophy, beating Atlético Madrid 5–1 in the Cup Winners' Cup Final.
- Seven Grand Prix victories in a season for Jim Clark as he takes the first of two Formula One World titles.
- The Tour de France is won by Jacques Anquetil for a fourth successive time – his fifth victory in all.

1964

- Mary Rand, Ann Packer and Lynn Davies are among Britain's gold medallists at the Tokyo Olympics.
- Bill Shankly leads Liverpool to the League title – West Ham win the FA Cup.

1965

- The Scottish League Championship is decided on goal average as Kilmarnock take the title for the only time in their history.
- Stanley Matthews plays his final League match at the age of 50 as Stoke beat Fulham 3–1.

1966

- Geoff Hurst's hat-trick propels England to the World Cup – captain Bobby Moore wins the BBC Sports Personality of the Year.
- Billie Jean King wins her first Grand Slam title at Wimbledon.

1967

- Celtic become the first British club to win the European Cup, beating Inter Milan 2–1 in Lisbon.
- Manchester United – under Matt Busby – win the League Championship.
- 100–1 outsider Foinavon takes advantage of a pile-up to win the Grand National.

1968

- Manchester United beat Benfica 4-1 to win the European Cup at Wembley.
- Bob Beamon sets a new World long jump record at the Mexico Olympic Games and 200m runners Tommie Smith and John Carlos give the Black Power salute as they receive their medals.
- Graham Hill takes the F1 World title for the second time.

1969

- Tony Jacklin wins the Open Championship at Royal Lytham.
- Rod Laver completes the tennis Grand Slam – winning all four major titles.

1970

- Brazil retain the Jules Rimet trophy after Pelé inspires them to their third World Cup triumph.
- Boxer Henry Cooper wins the BBC Sports Personality of the Year.

1971

- 66 fans are killed in the Ibrox Stadium disaster.
- Arsenal win the League and Cup double.
- A Grand Slam for Wales and a famous series victory for the British Lions in New Zealand.

1972

- The Munich Olympics marred by the murder of 11 Israeli team members by terrorists.
- Brian Clough's Derby County win the League Championship.
- Jack Nicklaus wins his fourth Masters green jacket and follows up with victory in the US Open two months later.

1973

- England fail to qualify for the World Cup finals for the first time.
- Red Rum overtakes Crisp in the final strides to win the Grand National.

1974

- Muhammad Ali knocks out George Foreman in the 'Rumble in the Jungle' to regain the World Heavyweight title.
- Leeds United win their second League Championship under Don Revie.

- West Germany come from behind to beat the Netherlands 2–1 in the World Cup Final.

1975

- West Indies win the first cricket World Cup after a century from captain Clive Lloyd.
- Arthur Ashe wins the men's singles at Wimbledon – the women's title goes to Billie Jean King for a sixth time.
- Rangers win the Scottish League Championship ending Celtic's run of nine titles in a row.

1976

- John Curry skates to Olympic gold – Britain's first winter medal for 12 years.
- Björn Borg wins Wimbledon – the first of five successive titles.

1977

- Liverpool retain the League title and follow up by winning the European Cup.
- Britain's Virginia Wade beats Betty Stöve in the Wimbledon final.
- Red Rum completes a hat-trick of Grand National victories – Charlotte Brew becomes the first woman to ride in the race.

1978

- Nottingham Forest win the League title, but Liverpool retain the European Cup as Kenny Dalglish scores the winner against Bruges.
- Argentina beat the Netherlands 3-1 in the World Cup Final.
- Muhammad Ali regains the World Heavyweight title at the age of 36, outpointing Leon Spinks.

1979

- Trevor Francis – Britain's first £1 million player – scores the winner as Nottingham Forest lift the European Cup with a 1–0 win over Malmo.

- A century from Viv Richards helps West Indies win the World Cup Final against England.
- Seve Ballesteros wins the first of his three Open Championships and then appears in the first European Ryder Cup team.

1980

- At the Moscow Olympics, boycotted by the United States, Britain's gold medallists include Seb Coe, Steve Ovett, Daley Thompson, Allan Wells and Duncan Goodhew.
- Bill Beaumont leads England to the Grand Slam.

1981

- Ian Botham resigns as captain and then inspires England to a memorable comeback Ashes victory over Australia
- Alan Kennedy scores the winner as Liverpool beat Real Madrid 1–0 in the European Cup Final
- Cancer survivor Bob Champion rides Aldaniti to victory in the Grand National

1982

- For the sixth time in a row an English club wins the European Cup as Aston Villa beat Bayern Munich 1–0.
- Alex 'Hurricane' Higgins wins the World Snooker title for the second time.

1983

- India upset West Indies to win the World Cup.
- Dundee United win their first Scottish League title as Alex Ferguson's Aberdeen lift the European Cup Winners' Cup.
- Lester Piggott wins the Derby for a record ninth time on Teenoso.

1984

- Perfect scores for Torvill and Dean as their 'Bolero' routine wins them Olympic ice dance gold in Sarajevo.

- A seventh League title in nine years for Liverpool who also win the European Cup in a penalty shoot-out against Roma.
- Carl Lewis matches the great Jesse Owens with four gold medals at the LA Olympics.

1985

- English clubs receive a five-year ban from European football after 39 people die in the Heysel Stadium before the European Cup Final between Liverpool and Juventus.
- Fire at Valley Parade claims 56 lives during a match between Bradford City and Lincoln City
- Dennis Taylor pots the final black to beat six-time champion Steve Davis in the World Snooker final.

1986

- Maradona's Hand of God goal knocks out England as Argentina go on to win the World Cup.
- At 46, Jack Nicklaus becomes the oldest winner at Augusta winning his sixth Masters' Green Jacket.
- 20-year-old Mike Tyson becomes the youngest ever world boxing champion stopping Trevor Berbick in the second round to win the WBC Heavyweight title.

1987

- The first Rugby Union World Cup is won by New Zealand, sweeping aside France 29–9 in the final.
- Europe win the Ryder Cup for the first time on American soil.

1988

- Ben Johnson is stripped of the Olympic 100 metres gold medal after failing a drugs test.
- Steffi Graf takes gold in the women's singles to complete the Golden Slam having won all four of the majors earlier in the year.

- 'Crazy Gang' Wimbledon end Liverpool's hopes of a League and Cup double with a 1–0 victory in the FA Cup Final.
- No stopping Celtic as they win the Scottish League and Cup double.

1989

- 96 fans are killed in the Hillsborough disaster during the FA Cup semi-final between Liverpool and Nottingham Forest.
- Michael Thomas scores an injury-time winner as Arsenal beat Liverpool in the final game of the season to pip them to the League title.
- Terry Alderman takes 41 wickets in the series as Australia win the Ashes 4–0.

1990

- In a World Cup semi-final best remembered for Paul Gascoigne's tears and penalty shoot-out misses by Pearce and Waddle, England lose to the eventual winners West Germany.
- Scotland beat England 13–7 to win the Grand Slam.
- Nick Faldo wins the Masters for a second year in a row and goes on to take the Open Championship at St Andrews.

1991

- England lose to Australia in Rugby Union's World Cup Final.
- Mark Hughes scores both goals in Manchester United's 2–1 victory over Barcelona in the European Cup Winners' Cup Final.

1992

- Nigel Mansell becomes F1 World Champion and wins the BBC's Sports Personality of the Year.
- Linford Christie (32) becomes the oldest man to win Olympic gold in the 100 metres – Sally Gunnell takes the 400m hurdles.
- Leeds United are the last winners of the "old" First Division title – the new Premier League begins in August.
- Ally McCoist scores 34 goals in a season as Rangers secure the domestic treble.

1993

- Manchester United win the first Premier League – under Sir Alex Ferguson they go on to win seven of the first nine titles.
- Chaos at Aintree as the Grand National is declared void after a false start.
- Shane Warne bowls Mike Gatting with the 'ball of the century' as Australia retain the Ashes.

1994

- Three-time World Champion Ayrton Senna is killed after crashing in the San Marino Grand Prix.
- Brian Lara hits the highest first-class innings – 501 not out for Warwickshire against Durham.
- Brazil win the World Cup in a penalty shoot-out against Italy.

1995

- South Africa – led by Francois Pienaar – win the Rugby World Cup in Johannesburg.
- John Daly beats Costantino Rocca in a play-off to win the Open Championship.

1996

- Steve Redgrave and Matthew Pinsent win Team GB's only gold medal of the Atlanta Olympics.
- Damon Hill wins F1 World Championship – the first son of a former champion to take the title.
- Nick Faldo overturns a six-shot final-round deficit on Greg Norman to win his third green jacket at the Masters.

1997

- The Grand National is postponed for two days after an IRA bomb threat – Lord Gyllene wins the re-staged race on Monday.

- Tiger Woods wins his first major, taking the Masters by a record-breaking margin of 12 shots.
- 16-year-old Martina Hingis becomes the youngest Wimbledon singles winner for 110 years when she beats Jana Novotná in the final.

1998

- Zinedine Zidane scores twice as France beat Brazil 3-0 in the World Cup Final in Paris.
- Arsenal win the League and Cup double – the first English trophies for manager Arsène Wenger.

1999

- Manchester United complete a treble of Premier League, FA Cup and European Cup when Ole Gunnar Solskjaer scores a stoppage time winner against Bayern Munich.
- Scotland win the last Five Nations Championship – the following year it becomes the Six Nations with the inclusion of Italy.
- Stephen Hendry wins a record seventh World Snooker title beating Mark Williams in the final.

2000

- Tiger Woods becomes the youngest golfer to win all four majors with an eight-shot victory at the Open Championship at St. Andrews.
- Venus Williams wins her first Grand Slam singles title at Wimbledon and follows up with victory at the US Open.

2001

- Glenn McGrath takes 32 wickets in the series as Australia retain the Ashes 4–1.
- Tiger Woods wins his second Masters at Augusta and becomes first man post-war to hold all four major titles at the same time.

2002

- Ronaldo scores twice as Brazil beat Germany 2–0 in the World Cup Final.
- Lennox Lewis retains his WBC World Heavyweight title with an eighth-round knockout of Mike Tyson.
- Serena Williams beats her older sister Venus to win her first Wimbledon singles title.

2003

- Jonny Wilkinson scores a last-minute dropped goal as England win the Rugby World Cup against Australia in extra time.
- Roger Federer wins Wimbledon for the first time.

2004

- Arsenal's 'Invincibles' remain unbeaten on their way to the Premier League title.
- Brian Lara hits the highest score in Test cricket with 400 not out v England in Antigua.
- Europe retain the Ryder Cup with their largest win on American soil.
- Michael Schumacher clinches a seventh F1 World drivers' title.

2005

- Liverpool beat AC Milan 3–2 on penalties in the Champions League final, having come back from 3–0 down to force extra time.
- José Mourinho's Chelsea win the Premier League title.
- England regain the Ashes for the first time in 18 years after a thrilling 2–1 series win.
- Rafa Nadal win the French Open for the first time.

2006

- Wayne Rooney is sent off as England go out on penalties to Portugal in the World Cup quarter-finals – Italy win the final against France on penalties.

- Ian Woosnam captains Europe to a third successive Ryder Cup victory over the United States.

2007

- South Africa beat England 15–6 in Rugby Union's World Cup Final.
- Pádraig Harrington becomes the first Irishman for 60 years to win the Open Championship.

2008

- Usain Bolt sets new world records on his way to 100 and 200m gold at the Beijing Olympics.
- Lewis Hamilton wins his first F1 World title.
- Rafa Nadal ends Roger Federer's five-year reign as Wimbledon Champion with a five-set victory in the final.

2009

- Usain Bolt wins world 100m title in a world record 9.58 seconds.
- Roger Federer beats Andy Roddick 16–14 in the final set to win Wimbledon and a 15th Grand Slam singles title.
- 59-year-old Tom Watson loses a play-off to Stewart Cink in the Open Championship at Turnberry.

2010

- Spain are World Cup winners – Fabio Capello's England lose 4–1 to Germany in the last 16.
- Champion Jockey A.P. McCoy triumphs in the Grand National for the only time on Don't Push It.
- John Isner beats Nicolas Mahut in the first round at Wimbledon – the longest match in tennis history, lasting 11 hours and 5 minutes.

2011

- Manchester United win the Premier League title but again lose to Barcelona in the Champions League final.

- Northern Ireland dominate golf with Rory McIlroy cruising to an eight-shot victory at the US Open and Darren Clarke winning the Open Championship at Royal St. George's.
- Novak Djokovic is Wimbledon Champion for the first time, beating Rafa Nadal in four sets.

2012

- Great Britain take a haul of 29 gold medals at the London Olympics – their best performance for 104 years.
- Andy Murray wins Olympic gold and follows up with his first Grand Slam victory at the US Open.
- Sergio Agüero scores in stoppage time to give Manchester City the Premier League title on goal difference from Manchester United.
- Bradley Wiggins becomes the first British cyclist to win the Tour de France.

2013

- Andy Murray becomes the first British man to win Wimbledon for 77 years.
- Manager Sir Alex Ferguson retires after Manchester United win the Premier League – the last of his record 13 titles.
- British and Irish Lions complete a 2–1 series win against Australia.

2014

- Germany beat Brazil 7–1 in the semi-finals and go on to lift the World Cup beating Argentina 1–0 in the final – England fail to qualify from their group.
- Europe win the Ryder Cup for a third successive time.

2015

- Tyson Fury outpoints Wladimir Klitschko to win the World Heavyweight title.
- Andy Murray inspires Great Britain to win the Davis Cup for the first time in 79 years.

- England lose to a stoppage-time winner in the semi-finals of the Women's World Cup – USA win the trophy beating Japan 5–2 in the final.
- Serena Williams becomes the oldest Grand Slam women's singles champion at the age of 33 beating Garbiñe Muguruza in the Wimbledon final.

2016

- Leicester City defy odds of 5000–1 to win their first Premier League title under manager Claudio Ranieri.
- England complete their first Six Nations Grand Slam for 13 years.
- San Francisco 49ers quarterback Colin Kaepernick kneels in protest during the US National Anthem, objecting to racial injustice and police brutality.

2017

- Six wickets for Anya Shrubsole inspire England to a nine-run victory over India in the Women's World Cup Final.
- British and Irish Lions draw 15–15 with New Zealand in the final test to tie the series 1–1.
- Serena Williams beats sister Venus in the final of the Australian Open – her 23rd Grand Slam singles title.

2018

- England lose to Croatia in the World Cup semi-final – France lift the trophy.
- Europe regain the Ryder Cup – Francesco Molinari wins all five matches after becoming the first Italian to win a major title at the Open Championship two months earlier.

2019

- England win cricket's World Cup for the first time after a thrilling Super Over victory against New Zealand.

- Liverpool beat Spurs 2–0 in the Champions League final, having overturned a three-goal first-leg deficit in their semi-final against Barcelona.
- South Africa win the Rugby World Cup beating England 32–12 in the final.
- Anthony Joshua loses his World Heavyweight titles in a shock defeat to Andy Ruiz Jr.

2020

- Liverpool win their first League title for 30 years.
- Lewis Hamilton clinches his fourth consecutive and record-equalling seventh F1 World title.
- James Anderson becomes the first pace bowler to reach 600 Test wickets.

2021

- Rachael Blackmore becomes the first female jockey to win the Grand National.
- England reach the Euros final, their first major football final for 55 years, but lose on penalties to Italy.
- Britain's Emma Raducanu becomes the first qualifier in the open era to win a tennis Grand Slam, in the USA Open.

2022

- The Lionesses win the European Championships – the first time an England team has won a major football tournament since 1966.
- Rachael Blackmore becomes the first female jockey to win the Cheltenham Gold Cup.
- Shane Warne dies suddenly at the age of 52.

THE LAST WORD

And – definitely finally – a loving tribute from the Bard of Barnsley, Ian McMillan, poet, writer, broadcaster and proud supporter of Barnsley FC. As usual, Ian gets it spot on…

A Shakespearean sonnet for *Sports Report*

The teatime tune that tells us all is well,
Though life flies like a ball that can't be caught.
A ref's loud whistle sounds a tolling bell:
The game has ended: now here's *Sports Report*,
A still point in a madly turning world,
A voice, and then another, fill the air
As constant as the linesman's flag unfurled
Describe the action and we think we're there.
We won, we lost, we played a hard-fought draw,
This programme paints a picture for us all
Until we see the things we never saw:
That try, that save, that free kick past the wall.
So *Sports Report* lifts us to Extra Time:
Here is transcendence, here is the sublime.

ACKNOWLEDGEMENTS

This is always the part I like most about writing a book. I can think 'The end' after completing this collective encomium.

One of the few plusses on a personal level about the horrible pandemic in 2020–2021 was that I could get to people on the phone, via email or Zoom, while we hunkered down, waiting for happier times. If ever there was a time to research a project like this one, it's been over the past couple of years. No one could fob me off with 'I'm too busy – always' when I chased them up…

To be fair, my sources have been almost uniformly gracious and tolerant of my importuning. Some of those I interviewed have had to handle several calls, as I checked new lines that I'd unearthed or wished to clarify aspects I had misunderstood. I have been touched that so many matched my affection for what is, after all, only a radio programme. That convinced me I was on to something when writing about *Sports Report*.

My sincere gratitude for granting me interviews to the following:

Claire Ackling, Audrey Adams, Tony Adamson, Julia Alexander Gordon, Ron Atkinson.

Clare Balding, Patrick Barclay, Simon Bates, Alex Bath, Michael Bath, Lord Blunkett, Sir Geoffrey Boycott, Sir Trevor Brooking, Steve Bruce, Alistair Bruce-Ball, Martin Buchan, Richard Burgess, Claire Burns, Bob Burrows.

Ian Carnaby, Iain Carter, Jon Champion, Mark Chapman, Lee Child, Nigel Clough, Lord Coe, Patrick Collins, Mike Costello.

Sir Kenny Dalglish, Ian Darke, Barry Davies, Matt Dawson, Ian Dennis, Peter Drury, Dion Dublin, Vincent Duggleby.

Caroline Elliott.

Juliette Ferrington, Gary Flintoff, Simon Foat, Roddy Forsyth, Sir Paul Fox.

Andy Gillies, Graham Gooch, Dave Gordon, Charlotte Green.

George Hamilton, Sheena Harold, Rob Hastie, Paul Hayward, John Helm, Eddie Hemmings, Alastair Hignell, Lord Howard, Kevin Howells, John Hunt.

Mike Ingham, John Inverdale.

Phil King, Mervyn King.

Chris Jones, Ron Jones.

Renton Laidlaw, Mark Lawrenson, Jonathan Legard, Mike Lewis, Gary Lineker, David Lloyd, Matt Lorenzo, Des Lynam, Cornelius Lysaght.

Sir A.P. McCoy, Claire McDonnell, Sonja McLaughlan, Emily McMahon, Lawrie McMenemy, Graham McMillan, Conor McNamara.

Ed Marriage, Roger Mosey, Simon Moore, John Motson, John Murray.

Bob Nettles, John Nicholson, Charlotte Nicol, Liam Nolan, Rob Nothman.

Eleanor Oldroyd, Jonathan Overend.

Andrew Parkinson, Sir Michael Parkinson, Alan Parry, Jonathan Pearce, David Pleat, Mark Pougatch, Tony Pulis, Gill Pulsford.

Mary Raine, John Rawling, Harry Redknapp, Simon Reed, Peter Reid, Graham Reid-Davies, Jill Reeves, Gillian Reynolds, Chris Rhys, Sir Tim Rice, Garry Richardson, Ian Robertson, Joe Root, Steve Rosenberg, Jim Rosenthal, Charles Runcie.

Mark Saggers, Robbie Savage, Dick Scales, Phil Shaw, Alan Shearer, Bob Shennan, Peter Slater, Caj Sohal, Mark Steel, Graeme Swann.

Daniel Taylor, John Taylor, Derek Thompson, Pat Thornton, Steve Tongue, Bryan Tremble, Gordon Turnbull.

Dan Walker, Jonathan Wall, Joanne Watson, Mark Williams, Henry Winter, Dave Woods, Phil Wye.

Alastair Yeomans.

Others were very helpful in opening doors for me, providing contact numbers, pointing me in the direction of invaluable research or simply doing their best to help.

Neil Bennett, Jacqui Brock-Doyle, Adrian Chiles, Pat Colbert, Simon Crosse, Matt Davies, Lorna Dickinson, Heather Fordham, Paul Foxall, John Holmes, Chris Hunter, Mat Kendrick, Paul Lewis, Richard Maddock, Heather Martin, Cathy Mellor, Jane Morgan, Danny Reuben, Ian Ridley, Jimmy Smallwood, Martin Swain, Andy Walmsley and Mike Walters.

My thanks to the noted poet and football fan Ian McMillan for permission to quote from the graceful tribute he gave to James Alexander Gordon at his funeral. Ian also contributed a charming poem, honouring *Sports Report*.

Also to Andy Walmsley and Rob Nothman for some invaluable and essential research. Jeff Walden at the BBC's Written Archive Centre was also very helpful, as were Thad Varey and Claire Coatsworth at the 5 Live Audience Research Centre.

Two former colleagues in the sports department who have risen to dizzy heights up the BBC ladder were notably supportive, during a hectic period for the Corporation's executives, dealing with the pandemic's considerate influence on broadcasting matters. Sincere thanks to the BBC's Managing Director, Bob Shennan, and controller of BBC Sounds, Jonathan Wall. Both joined the sports department as bright-eyed producers and eventually became the boss of Radio 5 Live. But despite their continued eminence, they haven't forgotten where they started and they have been invaluable to me during this project.

Matthew Lowing of Bloomsbury Books got behind the idea of this book straight away and has remained a constant source of encouragement and ideas throughout. Cheerful and positive, 'can do' was always Matthew's mantra.

My wife, Maria was always a beacon of common sense and clarity, sensitive to the days when the words just wouldn't flow or I couldn't track down vital interviewees. She knew how important this project was to me, and never wavered in support.

And finally, to my tireless and conscientious readers – Audrey Adams, Stephen Brenkley, Stephen Chalke, Mike Ingham, Mike Lewis, Claire McDonnell, Rob Nothman, Gill Pulsford and the Revd Pete Worth.

They picked up on my various factual errors, poor phraseology and misunderstandings with commendable zeal. They were so committed that I shall willingly share any critical brickbats with them, while ensuring that any literary praise comes solely my way.

I shall be picking up the tab for all of them whenever we're in sight of a menu or wine list, until the centenary of *Sports Report*.

Patrick Murphy, 2022

INDEX